I0824416

POWER LINES

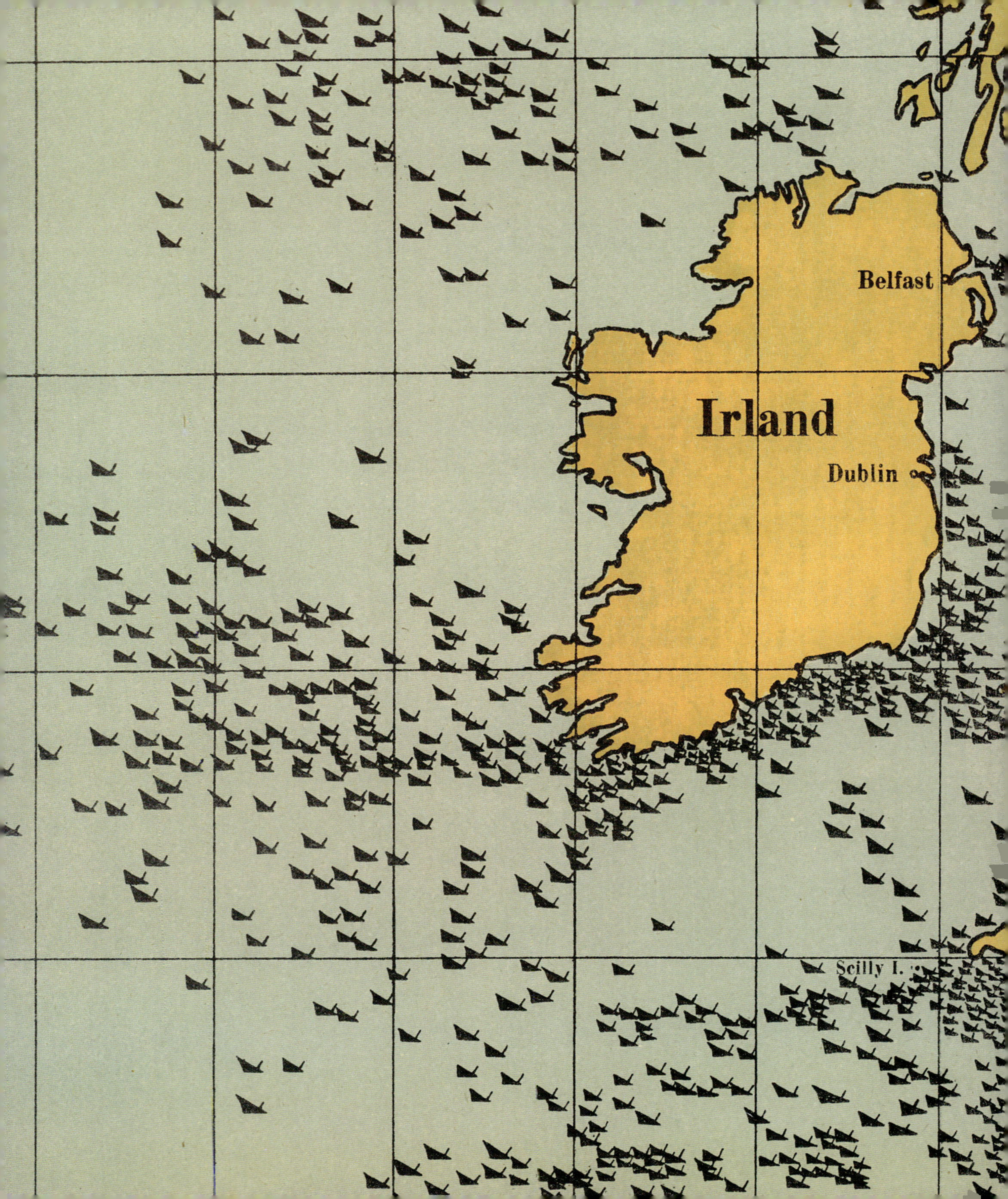
Belfast
Irland
Dublin
Scilly I.

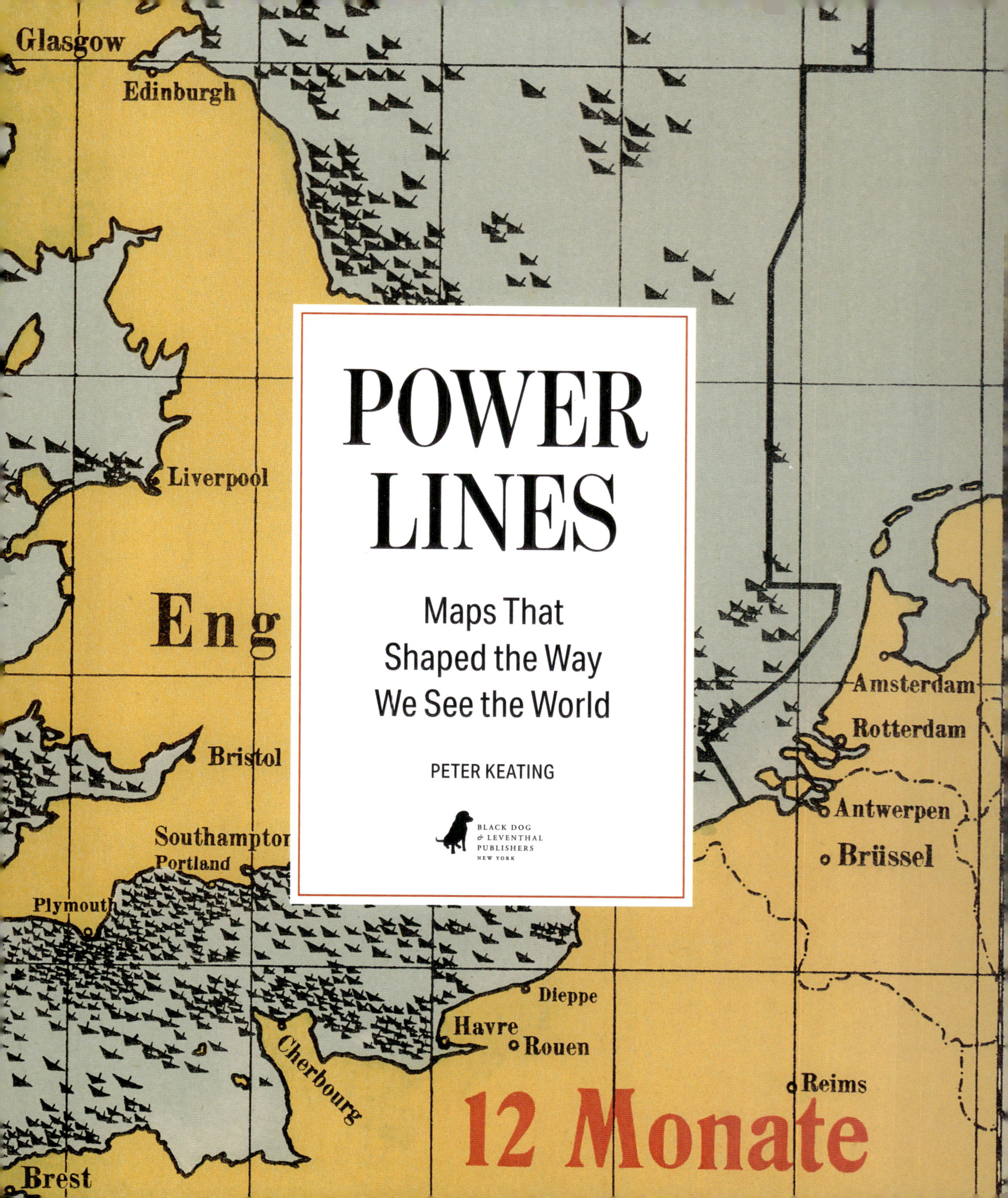
POWER LINES
Maps That Shaped the Way We See the World
PETER KEATING
BLACK DOG & LEVENTHAL PUBLISHERS NEW YORK
Glasgow
Edinburgh
Liverpool
Eng
Bristol
Southampton
Portland
Plymouth
Brest
Cherbourg
Dieppe
Havre
Rouen
Reims
Amsterdam
Rotterdam
Antwerpen
Brüssel
12 Monate

Black Dog & Leventhal Publishers
Hachette Book Group
1290 Avenue of the Americas, New York, NY 10104
www.blackdogandleventhal.com
BlackDogandLeventhal @BDLev

First Edition: May 2026

Published by Black Dog & Leventhal Publishers, an imprint of Hachette Book Group, Inc.
The Black Dog & Leventhal Publishers name and logo are trademarks of Hachette Book Group, Inc.

Black Dog & Leventhal books may be purchased in bulk for business, educational, or promotional use. For more information, please contact your local bookseller or the Hachette Book Group Special Markets Department at Special.Markets@hbgusa.com.

Additional map credits can be found on page 272.

Print book cover and interior design by Katie Benezra

Library of Congress Control Number: 2025025193

ISBNs: 978-1-5796-5877-9 (hardcover); 979-8-8941-4413-9 (ebook)

Printed in Malaysia

PCF

10 9 8 7 6 5 4 3 2 1

For my parents, Frederic (1934–2025) and
Patricia Keating, a lifelong team of teachers
who have inspired a love of learning in everyone
whose lives they have ever touched.

CONTENTS

星星之火
可以燎原
第三世界
团结万岁
种族歧视
自由
1969
亚非人民

INTRODUCTION:
A SINGLE SPARK CAN START A PRAIRIE FIRE

About twenty years ago, my former college roommate brought me a souvenir from a trip to China: a map, which hangs in my office to this day. The thing is garish, and I loved it from the moment I first laid eyes on it. It's big, more than 30 inches tall and 20 inches wide, and striking, with bold, mostly red hues and heavy black brushstrokes on cardboard-colored paper. Its vertical Asia and north-south Africa form one long landmass. Across its midsection, hands—one dark, one lighter—reach in from either side to grasp each other and hold aloft a burning torch. At the poster's bottom, seven figures, all with Asian features and agitated expressions, are pumping their fists.

While the map is dated 1969, I could not read its other, brief blocks of text, which are in Chinese characters. But that hardly seemed to matter. Given the imagery and that date, I could discern the map's basic thrust: Clearly, it was issued as some kind of revolutionary broadside, proclaiming friendship between Asia and Africa at a time when China's political leaders, after splitting with the Soviet Union, were trying to lure recently independent nations around the world into alliances. Whether or not you agree with the map's ideology or approve of its violence, you can *feel* it kicking at Western colonialists and Russian communists.

Of course, not every map carries that kind of charge—or ambition. I have heard Edward Tufte, professor emeritus of multiple subjects at Yale and probably the planet's foremost expert on data visualization, praise the virtues of the maps of the Alps made by the government of Switzerland. These maps are packed with information yet crystal-clear and clutter-free. They are high-resolution and three-dimensional. Their fonts are impeccable. Hikers love these maps, and anyone who creates charts or graphs should admire and study them.

But there's more to life than topography and typography. All maps show us where we are. Some maps also try to tell us what to think—and that's where things get *really* interesting.

PJ Mode, a longtime Washington, DC, lawyer, began acquiring old maps after seeing a Paris exhibit called "Maps and Figures of the Earth" in 1980. Some of the items he found most intriguing were what he called "cartographic curiosities" because they weren't really about geography. "At some point along the way," Mode later wrote, "I realized that there was a

This map, proclaiming "A single spark can start a prairie fire," calls for unity among the peoples of China and Africa. It was produced in 1969, during China's Cultural Revolution, a sustained, often severe crackdown on supposed enemies of the Chinese communist movement.

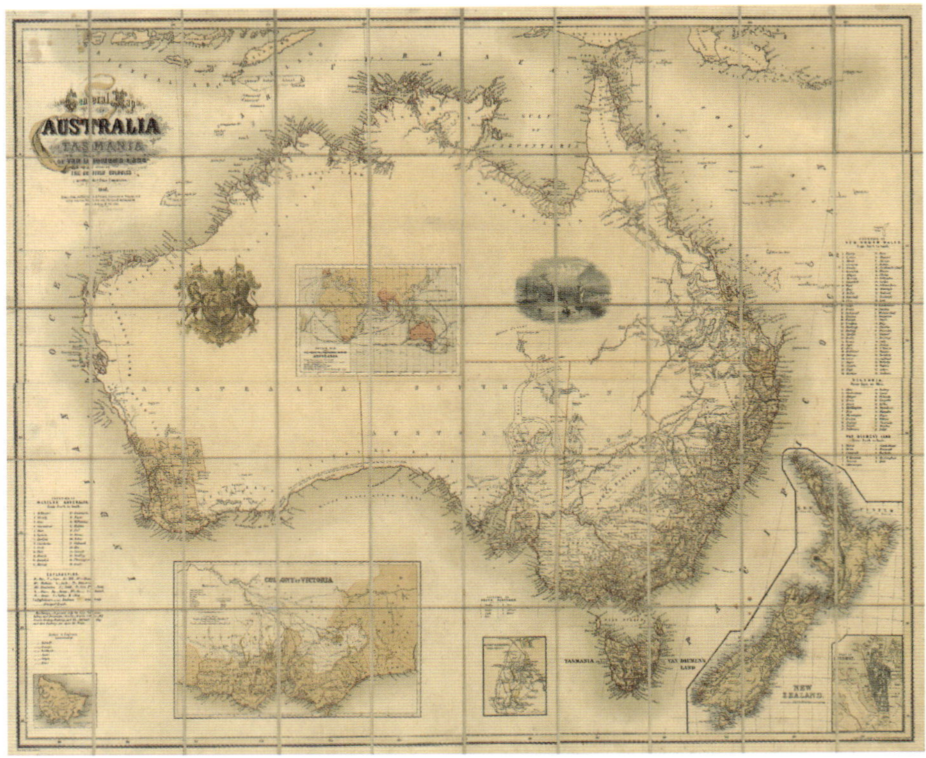

common theme in this group of maps: They were intended primarily to influence opinions or beliefs, to send or reinforce some message, rather than to communicate objective geographic information." Mode was describing, and creating, what's become the world's finest collection of *political maps*, also known as persuasive cartography (or, more pejoratively, cartographic propaganda).[1]

A political map uses elements of text (its language, details, and symbols) and texture (its projection, orientation, scale, and shadings) to deliver a statement. A map can become political because of something as simple as its color. For example, one 1857 map of Australia (above)

Formally titled *General Map of Australia and Tasmania or Van Diemen's Land Shewing the British Colonies as Divided into Counties*, this was one of many "Gold Rush" maps of the continent made in the nineteenth century. It was created by Ernst Georg Ravenstein, a German-English cartographer, in 1857.

---

1 In 2014, Mode donated his trove to Cornell University, his alma mater, and more than 800 of his maps are now available online. His archive, replete with notes reflecting his analysis and research about many of its maps and the connections among them, is both an inspiration and key source for this book.

La Paz de Nixon (*Nixon's Peace*) was published in 1972 by the Organization in Solidarity with the People of Africa, Asia, and Latin America (OSPAAAL), a Cuban anti-imperialist group.

reveals a whole range of wonderful details. Peer closely, and you might notice an inset focusing on the city of Sydney, or a decorative illustration of the docks at Melbourne, or a sketch of the main commercial sea lanes to Australia from around the world. But just a glance shows you one overriding feature: The whole thing is tinted gold! This map reminds readers that the continent was in the midst of a series of gold rushes—and a population explosion—that would last through the second half of the nineteenth century. Its elements, most definitely including its gilded lithography, combine to portray Australia as booming and beckoning.

A good political map communicates both intellectually and viscerally. It exploits the fact that maps are—even in our hyper-cynical times—almost uniquely authoritative. It makes you understand something about its subject's, and often its creator's, place in the world, their outlook and beliefs, goals and intentions. A *great* political map does all this so powerfully that you absorb its meaning before (or even without) processing it as you would a verbal argument. Look at *La Paz de Nixon* (*Nixon's Peace*) (left), produced as the United States was trying to bomb North Vietnam into resuming negotiations between the two countries, and see if you don't agree.

The most dramatic and influential of all maps are political maps. That's my contention, after twenty-five years of writing about politics and history and a lifetime of studying maps. And it's my rationale for gathering this group of outstanding maps that have taught people around the globe how to see the world.

In the pages to come, you'll see maps of explorers' claims and colonial conquests, border disputes that started wars and treaties that ended them, nations established or divided and destroyed, menacing threats real or imagined. In considering what to include, I used a broad definition of "map"—essentially any graphic representation of a terrestrial place or event. Scientists have created amazing maps of the ocean's floor and the moon. Would-be cartographers have given shape to Narnia, Wakanda, and even the Grand Duchy of Fenwick.[2] These were outside the scope of my work. Otherwise, though, everything counted, including many traditional illustrations, but also paintings, stone tablets, even a paper fan. I was similarly inclusive about the word *political*, willing to look at any portrayal of human-defined (as opposed to purely natural) territories or borders. The works here range from ancient cosmography to modern red-and-blue election maps, but I stuck to one important rule: My political maps had to be at least approximately contemporaneous with their subjects. You can find boatloads of maps drawn recently of the Holy Roman Empire or the Confederate States of America. What's truly interesting and instructive is to see such entities through the eyes and minds of the people who defined them while they existed.

From a huge range of possibilities, I culled my final selection by looking for two qualities: historical significance and persuasive power (the latter criteria included a map's visual impact, technical excellence, and strength of conviction). All of these judgments are of course subjective; I cannot claim to have comprehensively rated or ranked these maps. And if you haven't guessed already, by stating that a map combines its features to communicate its messages skillfully, I am not approving of its content, though I often assess it in the analysis that accompanies that map. I don't believe any political entity has ever understood the power of maps, or used them more effectively as propaganda, than the German Nazi Party. Some of its creations come across as shockingly modern even today. (As just one example, one map of Adolf Hitler's speaking engagements in 1933, opposite, looks like a rock concert tour poster.) As in walks of life outside cartography, we need to reckon with the allure of Nazis and other totalitarians. And instead of ignoring or suppressing offensive work, we should ask why some images resonate so strongly with audiences even when they are associated with horrendous ideas.

---

2 Featured in a series of satirical novels by Leonard Wibberley, including *The Mouse That Roared*, which became a classic 1959 movie starring Peter Sellers.

Adolf Hitler became chancellor of Germany in January 1933. Produced later that year, this map marks the sites of Der Führer's subsequent speeches with swastika-emblazoned flags. It was essentially a souvenir for fans.

Political maps are most frequently produced and preserved by countries that win wars and other battles to determine borders and territorial rights. And within those societies, they are typically made by people with the authority to create official or commercial publications. So this is a genre subject to massive selection bias. I have worked to present maps from a variety of regions around the world and eras across time. But writing about political maps is like surveying Nobel Prize winners or astronauts: The field's achievements, reflecting its opportunities, tilt heavily toward modern Europe and the United States, and even more heavily toward men. All I can say is that if you think I have ignored any worthy work, I would be happy to hear from you.[3]

Actually, I can say one thing more: I was wrong about the revolutionary Chinese map. As my investigations for this project were drawing to a close, I figured I really should tie up the loose ends of getting that map translated. I finally got help from two friends, then dug into the meaning of what they found. It turns out that the map declares: "A single spark can start a prairie fire." This is a Chinese saying that Mao Zedong popularized in 1930, at a particularly low point in the communist struggle to ignite revolution in China. Mao meant that even small actions could trigger massive consequences, and specifically that it was worthwhile for his followers to keep seeking

3 And if there is ever a sequel to this group of maps, I will include an image of Gran Colombia, the republic established by Simón Bolívar and his allies after they liberated large swaths of South America from Spanish rule in the early 1800s. Bolívar intended it to be a united Latin American nation, but it lasted just a few years. I learned in depth about its fascinating history—and maps—too late to include here.

support among rural peasants and workers, even if the communists had not yet won mass approval. By 1969, with Mao in firm dictatorial control of the country, Chinese officials repeated the phrase to call for the first steps, no matter how humble, toward anti-colonialism in Africa. One of the map's banners reads: "Long live the unity of the Third World."

But "A single spark can start a prairie fire" has meaning in many contexts. It also turns out that in 1960, a group of young writers started a magazine called *Spark* in central China. It was written by hand and lasted for just two issues, but its expression of dissident dreams was enough to get its creators rounded up and, in some cases, brutally tortured. (One contributor named Lin Zhao used her own blood to keep writing in prison, until she was executed in 1968.) Their stories, and the experiences of rebels who followed in their footsteps, have inspired generations of Chinese artists. In 2023, journalist Ian Johnson published an important book about that lineage. Its title: *Sparks: China's Underground Historians and Their Battle for the Future*.

So when we look at the 1969 "Spark" map, it certainly does carry a message of international solidarity and revolution. But its title and quotation and red colors also remind us of the story of the Chinese people's own struggle for freedom amid a revolution run amok. Political maps often reverberate in ways their own authors can't foresee.

I only came to appreciate the full reach of the "Spark" map once I started to understand its many connections. I hope this book will help you do the same with the maps that follow.

GETVLIA
LIBIA INTER IOR
SINVS
ARABIA FELIX
MARE RVBRV
EQVINOCTIA.
ICHTIOPHAGI ETHIOPES
AGANGINE ET HIOPES
REGNVM ORGVENE
AFFRICA
XILICEIS ETHIOPES
REGNVM NVBIE
ELEPHANTOPHAGI
CALC EI ETHIOPES
TROGLODICA REGIO
NINOTORA REGIO
MARE INDICVM
CINOMIE ERA REGIO
ETHIOPIA INTERIOR
AGIZIMBA REGIO ETHIOPVM
PALVDES NILI
SINVS BARBARICVS
SINVS MAGNVS AFFRICE
REPSII ETHIOPES
MONS LVNE
ANTROPOPHAGI ETIOPES
MARE PRASSO
MARE PRAS
NOTVS
360
10
20
30
40
10
80

PART I

DOMINION

Maps help us find our way around. Even more fundamentally, they let us declare that we exist. The creators of the early maps on the following pages grappled with the questions stemming from that very political act: Where did they live in relation to other peoples? How far did the world they knew extend? And what was its relationship to more distant lands and to the heavens?

Scudo di Achille

The Maps That Took Western Civilization from Myth to Science

The epic poetry and scientific research of ancient Greece inspired maps that still influence us today.

Histories of mapmaking, political or otherwise, often begin with Claudius Ptolemaeus (c. 100–c. 170), known as Ptolemy, a genius of ancient Greece whose research was so extensive and calculations so accurate that his work guided how Europeans and their descendants understood the world for almost 1,500 years.

Fair enough. But almost a millennium before Ptolemy, an epic work of literature provided an image that represented the entire Greek way of life. It is a foundational map of Western civilization. And it comes to us wrapped in a story of doomed heroism, maternal love, and powers so strong they could almost—almost—warp destiny. Toward the end of Book 18 of Homer's *Iliad*, Thetis, the mother of the angry young warrior Achilles, visits Hephaestus, the god of fire and metalworking. The Trojans had taken Achilles's armor from the dead body of his friend Patroclus, and she implored the father of the forges to craft her son a new set:

But thou, in my pity, by my prayer be won:
Grace with immortal arms this short-lived son,
And to the field in martial pomp restore,
To shine with glory, 'til he shines no more!

Artists ranging from the Dutuit Painter, an ancient Athenian who decorated vases, to modern American scribbler Cy Twombly have illustrated the Shield of Achilles (as described by Homer). This engraving by Angelo Monticelli comes from an 1842 edition of *Il costume antico e moderno* (*Ancient and Modern Costume*), a monumental history of clothing by Italian archivist Giulio Ferrario.

Hephaestus has his doubts—"O could I hide him from the Fates," he says, "as well . . . As I shall forge most envied arms." And ultimately, Achilles is killed in battle. But first, Hephaestus crafts a shield in the form of a great map, which Homer describes for more than 120 lines of spectacular poetry. This passage of the *Iliad* has inspired interpretation, verse, and decorative objects for more than 2,700 years, even though no drawing of it accompanied the *Iliad*—and even though there's no conclusive evidence the shield (or Achilles) ever actually existed.

Homer describes Hephaestus using hammer and tongs to form an "immense and solid shield" of silver, brass, tin, and gold in five layers, or nested rings. He placed the earth at its center, with "the unwearied sun" and "the moon completely round," surrounded by the great constellations, such as the Pleiades and the Big Dipper, or Great Bear. (These are often replaced with the signs of the zodiac on later attempts to reproduce the shield, such as the one shown on page 2.) The next ring portrays two cities, one peacefully observing a wedding, the other suffering from the ravages of war. Farther outward, the shield shows a variety of human labor, with scenes of people plowing fields, harvesting grains and grapes, and herding oxen and sheep.

For the outermost rim, Hephaestus rimmed the shield with a metallic depiction of a layer of water, just as an endless river or sea seemed to encircle the world.

> *Thus the broad shield complete the artist crowned*
> *With his last hand, and poured the ocean round:*
> *In living silver seemed the waves to roll,*
> *And beat the buckler's verge, and bound the whole.*

The shield is a literary device, not a literal artifact of history.[1] But through *ekphrasis*, the Greek word for writing a detailed description of a work of art, Homer presented an object that meticulously delineated a representation of the world for a culture that still exerts vast influence on us today.

And here's the key to interpreting the shield, and many very early maps: Their layouts address questions that predate the concerns of modern politics, but are still political. Before mapmakers could get to drawing lines to declare "We are here" and "You are there," they first asked, "Where am I?" Many of the oldest works of cartography are cosmographic maps, which situate people in the world and the world within creation. And as the French scholar Germaine Aujac wrote in *The History of Cartography*, published in 1987, "The shield in Homer's poem . . . was evidently such a map of the universe as conceived by the early Greeks and articulated

---

1 Even if the Shield of Achilles were a real object, it might not be the oldest surviving large-scale map. *The Babylonian Map of the World*, now in the British Museum, is a palm-sized clay tablet that shows Mesopotamia and could date to the ninth century BCE.

by the poet." She called it the "start [of] a history of Greek theoretical cartography."

For centuries following Homer, Greek philosophers and scientists worked to create a new discipline from blending the kinds of traditional understandings depicted on the shield with discoveries emerging from astronomy and exploration. Their names became as legendary as their leaps of insight and deductive accomplishments. To name just a few: Anaximander created the first Greek world map in the sixth century BCE. The great mathematician Pythagoras began teaching around 500 BCE that the earth was spherical. Eratosthenes (c. 276 BCE–c. 195 BCE), who headed the great Library of Alexandria and invented the word *geography* (*geographika*), calculated the circumference of the earth to within 1 percent of its actual size. When Alexander the Great came along, conquering lands from Macedonia to India from 336 BCE to 325 BCE, he sought intelligence about outlying areas. And the work of the philosopher-scientists kept pushing Greek geography and mapmaking toward empirical investigation and practical results.

By the first century, the stage was set for Ptolemy, whose work synthesized and apotheosized almost a thousand years of Greek inquiry. Though best known today as an astronomer,[2] Ptolemy was a multitalented genius, and his *Geōgraphikē hyphēgēsis* (*Guide to Geography*), written around 150, brought together a vast range of material about thousands of places in the world and described how to plot them on a grid. It's the granddaddy of all mapmaking achievement.

This eight-volume opus was rooted in massive research. Ptolemy labored in the Library of Alexandria, which by that time was in steep decline but still a trove of maps, histories, and travelogues, to dig out and cross-reference information about every significant place that the early Roman Empire knew to be inhabited. Ultimately, he catalogued about eight thousand places. Amazingly, he also pinpointed the vast majority of them using coordinates of latitude and longitude. And Ptolemy

---

2 Ptolemy didn't just catalogue more than a thousand stars, and predict eclipses and the movements of the planets. He provided a comprehensive geocentric (or earth-centered) model of the universe. The Ptolemaic system essentially served as the basis for astronomy for nearly 1,500 years, until Nicolaus Copernicus challenged it in the sixteenth century.

further described, in relentless detail, two methods for projecting a sphere, like a globe of the earth, onto a flat surface, like a roll of papyrus.

Ptolemy measured latitude by how long the longest day of the year was at a given place, based on astronomical data he collected. (At 0 degrees, around the equator, where the sun takes its highest path across the sky, maximum daytime is twelve hours, a span that gets longer and longer the farther north or south you go.) When it came to longitude, Ptolemy again relied on a relationship between celestial navigation and time. Following the conventions of ancient Babylonian astronomy and Greek geometry, he divided the earth into 360 degrees. That means the sun moves 15 degrees across the sky in one hour. Which means in turn that if you know that noon (the time when the sun is highest in the sky) happens, say, two hours earlier for you than for me, you are 30 degrees of longitude east of me. This global lattice is still with us today.

For all his brilliance, Ptolemy's calculations were not perfect. He underestimated the overall size of the earth. He relied on astronomical data and witness reports that were sometimes unreliable. His projections, like any attempt to flatten three dimensions into two, were imperfect. If you assemble a world map from the points Ptolemy lists in the *Geography*, you will see southern Africa meeting southern Asia in one big landmass that encircles the Indian Ocean. But, of course, the man was working nearly two thousand years ago, when there was no quick way to find out how high the sun was in the sky 300 miles away, or

This map appears in medieval editions of Claudius Ptolemaeus's *Geōgraphikē hyphēgēsis* (*Guide to Geography*). Dating from the early fourteenth century, it shows the entire world as known to Ptolemy, from the Iberian Peninsula in the upper left, arcing all the way to India on the far right.

even 3 miles away. The *Geography* is a staggering tour de force of applied astronomy, geography, and mathematics—a translation of the physical and political world Ptolemy and his ancestors knew into a form that could be communicated, reproduced, and updated.

It is not, weirdly enough, an actual atlas. The *Geography* describes in painstaking detail *how* to map the world, but apparently didn't come *with* maps. No maps were discovered with its earliest editions, and it's still not clear whether Ptolemy ever created any from all the data he compiled. That might not have been as unusual in his time as it seems in ours. Ptolemy may have seen his work as a grand entry into the annals of Greek scientific discourse, rather than a construction manual. Or he may simply have thought plotting the entire world was sufficient guidance for his readers. The phone book doesn't come with a map, either.

After its publication, Ptolemy's masterpiece disappeared for more than a thousand years. The decline and collapse of the Roman Empire in the fifth century plunged its remains into what historians used to call the Dark Ages, a medieval time where many Greek and Roman achievements in science and the arts, including the *Geography*, were lost to the West. Over this long stretch, intellectual inquiry in fields ranging from history to mathematics to geography thrived instead in Byzantium (the descendant of the Eastern Roman Empire) and Arab states. And it was a Byzantine scholar named Maximus Planudes (1260–1330) who revived the *Geography*.

Working from a monastery in Chora (now the Kariye Mosque in Istanbul, Turkey), Planudes collected, translated, and preserved numerous ancient texts.[3] In 1295, he hunted down a manuscript of the *Geography*, and either drew or commissioned a set of companion maps. He admired the results, remarking in a poem that he had never seen anything so skillful, colorful, and elegant as the way Ptolemy brought the world into view. Andronicus II, the Byzantine emperor, was impressed too, and copies of the *Geography* began to spread. Today, there aren't any existing Greek manuscripts from before the thirteenth century, and several of the oldest editions with maps date to Planudes's work. The version shown on pages 6–7 is one of the very earliest, from about 1300, possibly owned and maybe even produced by Planudes, and now at the Vatican Library.

---

3 He saved at least one manuscript from being chewed up by rats.

The *Geography* reached Italy around 1400 and was first translated to Latin in 1406. Soon afterward, everything converged to make Ptolemy, some 1,250 years after his death, a dominant force in Western cartography and beyond, in various areas of culture where science was firing imagination. The Renaissance brought renewed interest in classical art and history. The printing press powered the wide dissemination of secular texts. European explorers began decamping for other continents and needed guidance. And there was the *Geography*: a brilliant work of antiquity with beautiful maps, ready to fill inquiring minds with knowledge that Europeans had ignored for centuries. By the end of the 1400s, seven editions were in print, with more than thirty more to come in the following century. Ptolemy became such a powerful brand that atlases continued to use his maps, uncorrected, for decades after voyagers showed where they were inaccurate.

Ptolemy's most famous quote is deeply spiritual: "When I trace at my pleasure the windings to and fro of the heavenly bodies, I no longer touch earth with my feet: I stand in the presence of Zeus himself and take my fill of ambrosia." But with the *Geography*, Ptolemy left a legacy of earthly knowledge rooted in exploration and discovery, liberated from the gods, setting up Westerners to try again, like Achilles, to forge their own fates. To find their destinies among other peoples—and to create histories that would be told through more explicitly political maps.

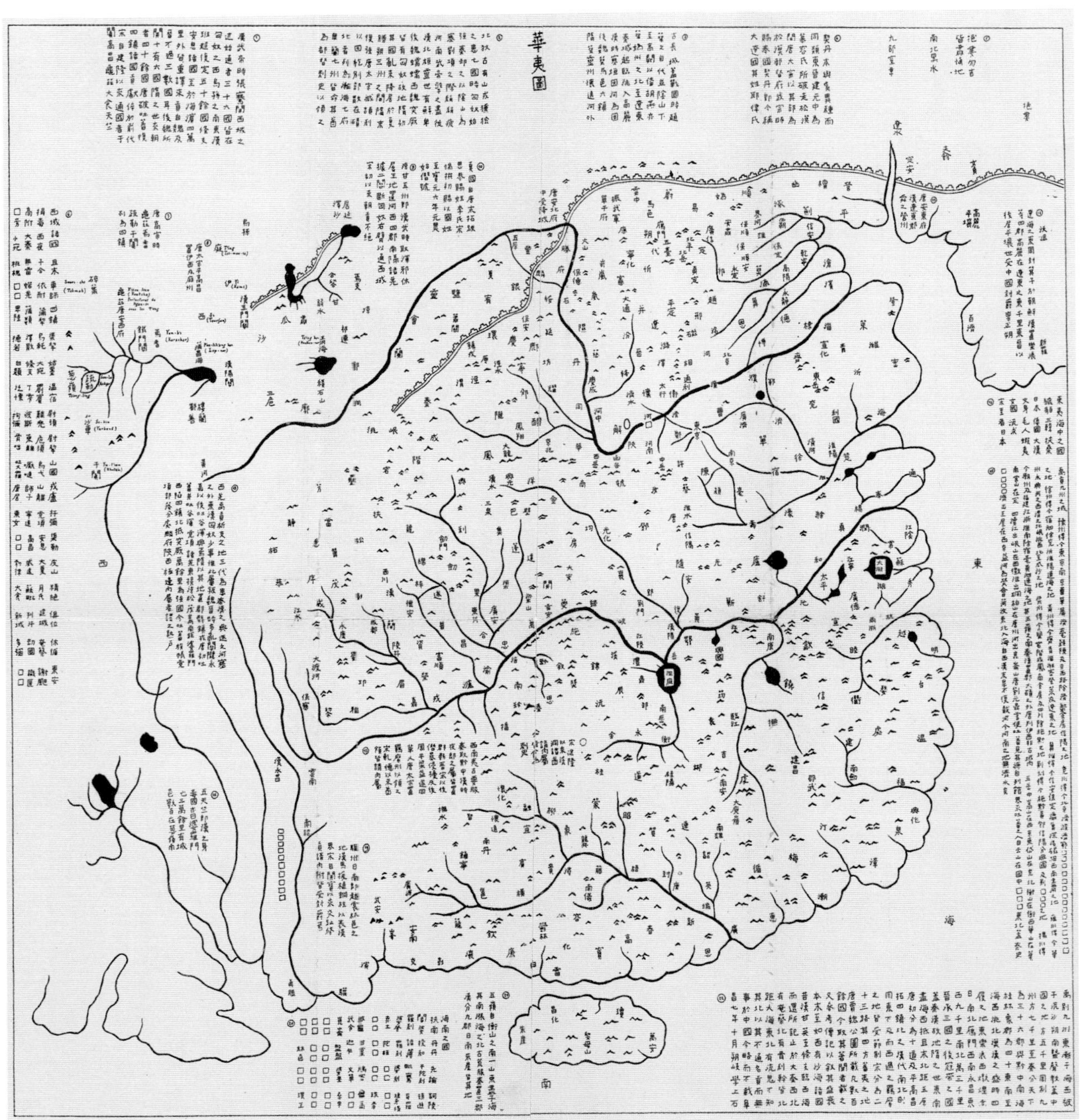
華東圖
東
海
西
南

The Map of China and the Barbarians

Almost nine hundred years ago, the *Huayi Tu* defined which lands and people were inside and outside the Empire of China.

The *Huayi Tu* is China's oldest surviving political map, showing areas as within or outside China during the Song dynasty (960–1279). Entitled "The map of Chinese and non-Chinese territories" (sometimes translated as ". . . Chinese and barbarian countries"), it's an outstanding example of Chinese cartographic traditions, which developed independent of the West for nearly two thousand years.

The making of large-scale maps in China began at least as early as the era known as the Warring States period (475–221 BCE). Early Chinese maps were often pictorial and heavy on text, and performed several functions: They displayed distant territories, delineated areas under the emperor's control, and sometimes showed connections between heaven (usually spherical) and earth (typically flat). Over many centuries, they also incorporated scientific and technological advances made in China. Indeed, of the "Four Great Inventions" from ancient times that are prized in Chinese culture, three massively influenced mapmaking: the compass, papermaking, and printing. (The fourth was gunpowder, which surely changed how maps looked, too, but less directly.) And as China grew, particularly during the Han dynasty (206 BCE–220 CE), so did the administrative and political importance of maps.

Pei Xiu, a minister of works in the third century who is sometimes called the father of Chinese cartography, described six principles for mapmaking: proportional measure, or mapping distances to scale; standard or regulated view, meaning preserving the positions of places relative to one another; road measurement, or determining distances from points along particular routes; measuring altitudes; measuring angles to gauge diagonal distances; and measuring curves.

The *Huayi Tu* (Map of Chinese and non-Chinese territories) was carved by an unknown artist into a stele, or commemorative stone slab, in 1136 China. This stone rubbing dates from c. 1903.

Applying these in combination allowed Pei and generations of Chinese cartographers who followed to create highly accurate maps. "Even if there are great obstacles in the shape of high mountains or vast lakes, huge distances or strange places . . . everything can be taken into account and determined," Pei wrote almost two millennia ago. Apply the principles correctly, and "the curved and straight and the far and near can conceal nothing of their form."

In the late eighth century, Jia Dan, a military officer and cartographer who served in various imperial posts during the Tang dynasty (618–907), undertook a massive effort to compile comprehensive geographic and political information about China and its neighbors. This was an era of expanding trade, and Jia interviewed Chinese travelers as well as outside visitors to bring data about routes, hazards, borders, and foreign ways of life into his project. In 801, he presented his work to the Chinese emperor Dezong. Jia bestowed a book of forty volumes, which described in detail places as far away as torch-lit lighthouses in the Persian Gulf, and a map of Asia called *Hainei Huayi Tu*, or "Map of Chinese and non-Chinese territories between the seas."

Jia Dan's map was huge—about 33 feet high and 30 feet wide—painted on silk, and extremely detailed. It displayed hundreds of places, in black ink for ancient settings and red for then-contemporary locales. Sadly, it is lost to the ages. But it inspired the *Huayi Tu* map shown here.

The *Huayi Tu* is a 31-inch by 32-inch map carved into a three-foot-high stele, or commemorative stone slab.[1] We don't know who the artist was, but the map's annotations make a couple of facts clear: It was made in 1136, and it adapts names for and information about well-known locations from Jia Dan's earlier map.

This map stretches from Heilongjiang, the Manchurian province that contains China's northernmost point, to Hainan Island in the south, and from the Pamir plateau, western highlands that are now part of Tajikistan, to the Pacific Ocean in the east. The *Huayi Tu* names some five hundred administrative districts, and accurately depicts a dozen rivers, ten mountains, major lakes, and, most visibly, the Great Wall of China, which runs along much of the empire's northern border. It pays considerably more attention to the interior of China than its shorelines, which are somewhat out of shape. And in the text blocks around its margins, it offers brief descriptions of nearby lands, including India and Korea.

Another incredibly impressive map is engraved on the reverse side of the *Huayi Tu* stone marker: the *Yu Ji Tu* (Map of the tracks of Yu the

---

1 Famous steles around the world include the Code of Hammurabi, the Rosetta Stone, and the Staff of Oranmiyan.

Great). Its title refers to Yu, a legendary figure in ancient Chinese history who folklore says established the first dynasty in China around 2100 BCE. We don't know who contributed the geographic information for the *Yu Ji Tu* or carved it, but it is almost exactly as old as the *Huayi Tu* and uses a striking gridded scale to accurately convey China's coastline and inland network of rivers.

These maps were set in stone so that people fortunate enough to see them in person, such as state officials and scholars, could create rubbings from them, and they did so for hundreds of years. Of the few tracings that are still intact, most were made by Westerners visiting China around the turn of the twentieth century. The version shown on page 10 is from the Library of Congress, which estimates it's a French redrawing from a rubbing made in 1903.

The tablet containing the *Huayi Tu* and *Yu Ji Tu* is now at a museum called the Forest of Stone Steles in the Chinese city of Xi'an. Three thousand carved stones occupy seven exhibition halls there, on a site that was a Confucian temple more than nine hundred years ago. So the remarkable story of these maps continues: Each nearly a millennium old, they survive as vertical monuments, etched into flip sides of the same rock, recognizably similar but still carrying forth very different conceptions of the society that produced them.

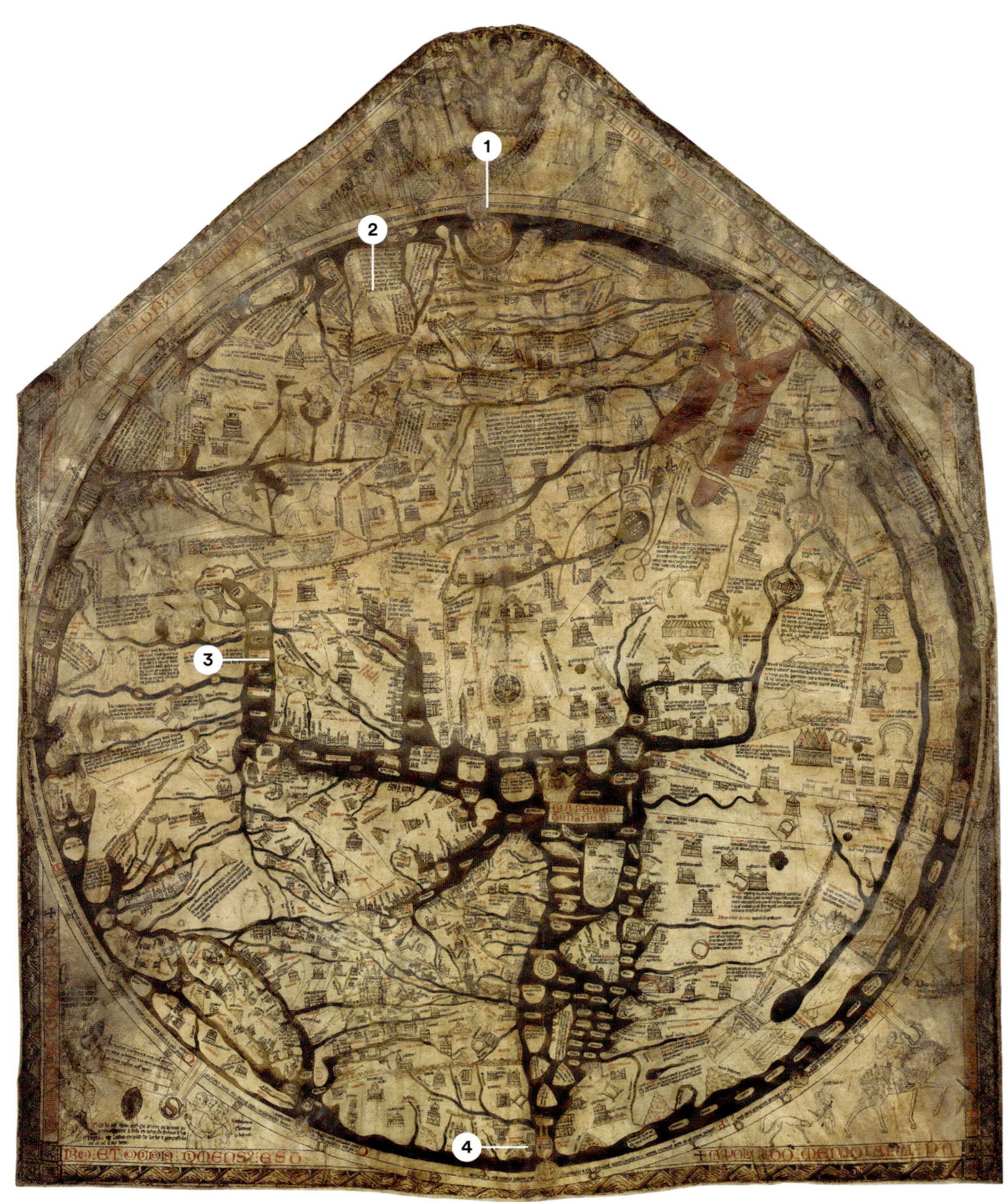
1
2
3
4

The Maps That Centered Christianity for a Millennium

From early T-O maps to the remarkable and mysterious Hereford *mappa mundi*, these maps sublimated actual geographical knowledge to the tenets of the medieval Christian faith.

Not to be overly grandiose, but in Western civilization, the evolution of modern political maps—and many other forms of cultural expression—was part of one broad struggle: reconciling received, largely biblical, sources of wisdom with truths derived from exploration and science. Ptolemy died around 170; the Roman emperor Constantine granted citizens freedom of worship in 313 and later converted to Christianity. With that, an oppressed cult became the imperial establishment, and its creeds became the dogma of the state and the academy, not just the church. Geography—which isn't fully based in either mathematics or language, and never fit neatly into the classical categories of liberal arts—fell out of favor for a long, long time. Its hard-earned discoveries and creative achievements, including scientific maps, disappeared from common conversation as well as from Latin education throughout the Middle Ages. (The actual word *geography* didn't even surface in English until the late fifteenth century.)

Medieval Christian cartographers didn't stop making maps of the world, but they superimposed their beliefs on their work. Historian Daniel Boorstin, Librarian of Congress from 1975 to 1987, put it rather harshly but accurately: "Christian faith and dogma suppressed the useful image of the world that had been so slowly, so painfully, and so scrupulously drawn by ancient geographers. We no longer find Ptolemy's careful outlines of shores, rivers, and mountains, handily overlaid by a grid constructed on the best-known astronomical data. Instead, simple diagrams authoritatively declare the true shape of the world, though they are only pious caricatures."

Known as the Hereford *mappa mundi* (map of the world), this map was made c. 1300 in England. It's a narrative of medieval Christian belief and virtually an almanac of mythological lore.

The most common model for Christian *mappae mundi*, or maps of the world, is so simple that you can easily create one yourself with paper and pencil. Just draw the world as a circle (an *O*), then inscribe it with the letter *T*, reaching across from the circle's left edge to its right at the widest point, and down from its center to its bottom. That's it! You can then visualize the top half of the map as Asia, the bottom left as Europe, and the bottom right as Africa. The line dividing Europe and Africa is the Mediterranean Sea; the line separating Africa and Asia is the Nile River. Right in the middle of the map, where the stroke and crossbar of the *T* meet, is Jerusalem, which, according to the Book of Ezekiel, God placed "in the midst of the nations." And with the *O* and *T*, you have the *orbis terrarum*, Latin for "whole world."

Roman historians used this "T-O" design for maps as early as the first century BCE. And around the world and across the centuries, cartographers from many cultures have decided to put the lands sacred to them—the places they and their ancestors lived, or coveted, or believed were home to their gods—at the heart of their maps. But Christianity and T-O maps made a particularly strong fit: The *T* came to stand for the cross on which Jesus was crucified, and the maps' three sections represented the Holy Trinity of the Father, Son, and Holy Spirit.

T-O maps had a powerful and lasting appeal. And as they spread, they picked up yet another layer of meaning. Christian scholars interpreted them as showing how the world was divided among Noah's sons after the biblical flood (something mentioned but not described explicitly in the Book of Genesis). Shem's descendants were supposed to have settled in Asia, Ham's in Africa, and Japheth's in Europe.[1]

Archbishop (and later Saint) Isidore of Seville (c. 560–636), who assembled a vast encyclopedia of the Latin language called *Etymologiae* (*Etymologies*), included T-O maps in his manuscripts. His works helped spread widely the idea that these maps conveyed Christian belief; and they circulated for centuries. Eventually, the many editions of Isidoran manuscripts included more than six hundred maps. And in 1472, more than eight hundred years after Isidore's death, a printer in Augsburg, Germany, included a T-O map as an illustration in an edition of the *Etymologiae* (opposite). It was barely 2 inches square, but this was the first map ever printed in a book. And its elements are simple and clear: the three continents of Europe, Asia, and Africa, the three sons of Noah, the

---

1 With Asia typically at the top of T-O maps, they were also oriented to the east, which is why "Orient" became a synonym for "East."

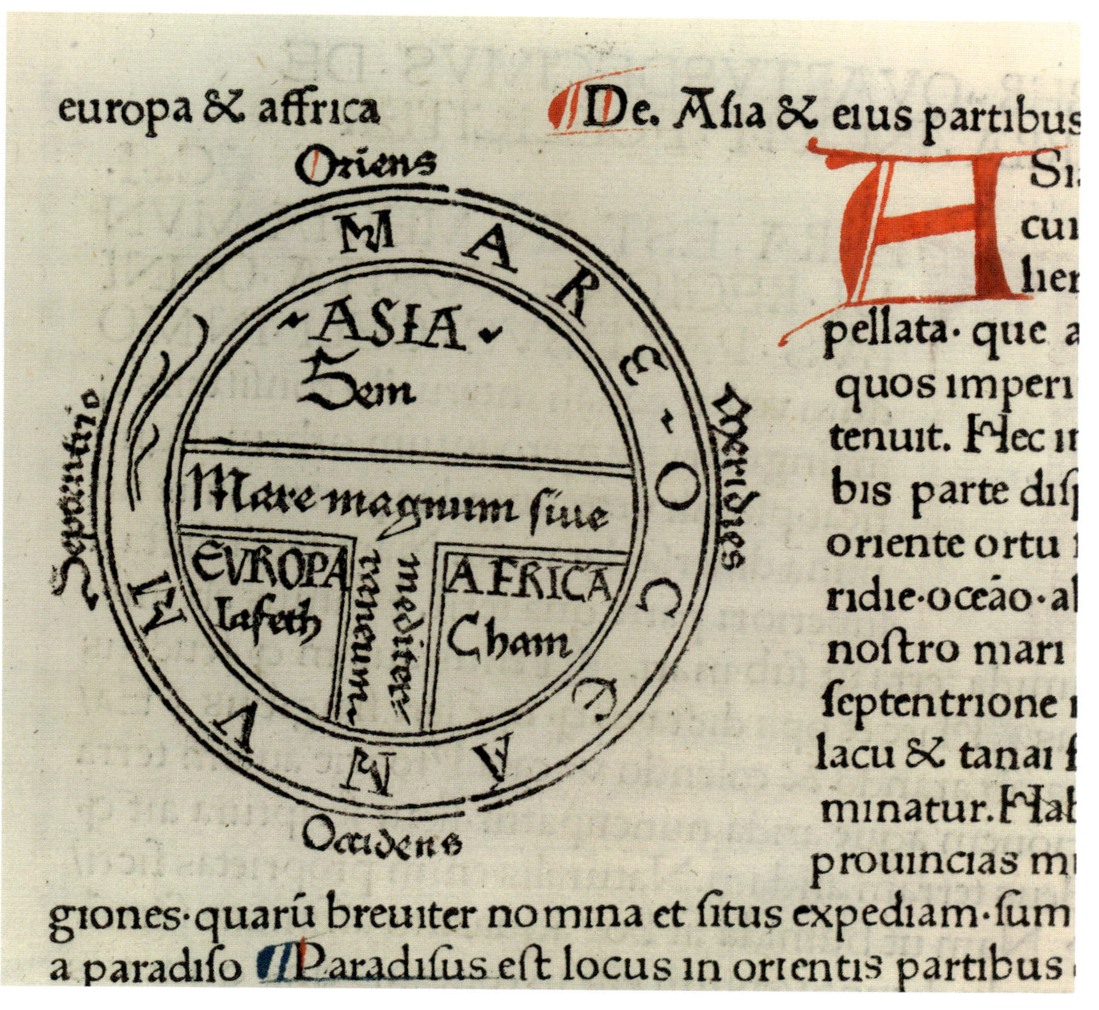

The first map printed in a book, this classic T-O map was published in 1472 as part of *Etymologiae*, a much older work by Archbishop Isidore of Seville.

four cardinal directions, topped by *Oriens*, or East, and the *T* formed by *mediterraneum* ("Mediterranean") and *Mare magnum fine* ("the [river] at the end of the great sea").

Over time, maps adapted the T-O schematic for uses that went far beyond simple tripartite diagrams. In 1095, Pope Urban II declared that "Jerusalem . . . situated in the middle of the world, is now held captive," and called upon European Christians to rescue the Holy Land from Islam. The First Crusade was successful and led to the establishment of the Kingdom of Jerusalem, after which cartographers started making maps of the conquered city—most of them circular and oriented to the east. About a dozen Crusader maps still exist today, including one that was part of a twelfth-century account of the First Crusade by a chronicler known as Robert the Monk (shown opposite). Milka Levy-Rubin, who is now curator emerita of the Humanities collection at the National Library of Israel, rediscovered this map in 1991 at a cartography conference in, of all places, Uppsala, Sweden, where the local university held a copy of Robert the Monk's manuscript. She calls it "the most exquisite and beautiful exemplar of the round maps of Jerusalem."

The colorful Uppsala map is loaded with spiritually significant images, labeled at a moment where many important sites in Jerusalem were under Christian control. The map is obviously not to scale, but does locate most places of worship and monuments in their proper quarters of the city. The Temple of the Lord, which is what the Crusaders called the Dome of the Rock, is most prominent, in the upper center of the map and topped by a cross. To its right on the Temple Mount is what is now the al-Aqsa Mosque, which the Crusaders named the Temple of Solomon. To its left is the Church of St. Anne, which the Crusaders built in the 1130s and stands today as a Catholic church. Even without being able to read much Latin, you can see additional highlights outside the wall encircling the city, such as the Mount of Olives and Garden of Gethsemane to the northeast (at the top left) and the road to Bethlehem (at the bottom).

In the Uppsala map, as art historian Kristin B. Aavitsland has written, "the holy city . . . becomes a visual metonym for the entire world."[2] And by using the familiar and all-encompassing T-O format, this map makes Jerusalem, which the Latin Bible called the *umbilicus terrae*, or "navel of the world," stand for the *orbis terrarum*, the whole of God's domain on earth.

Across the centuries when European cartographers valued religious adherence over geographic science, they also broadened the scope of their maps by incorporating notable places and artistic beings from biblical sources as well as other traditions into the T-O construct. The oldest and grandest surviving example is the Hereford *mappa mundi* (page 14), which dates to about 1300 and is still displayed at the Anglican cathedral in Hereford, England. (The cathedral maintains an impressive website for exploring the map in detail at themappamundi.co.uk.)

---

2 A metonym is a figure of speech that uses a closely related concept to refer to a thing or idea, like writing about "Washington" instead of "the US," or saying "I give you my heart" when you mean "I love you."

The Uppsala Crusader map of Jerusalem, which dates to the twelfth century, was rediscovered in 1991.

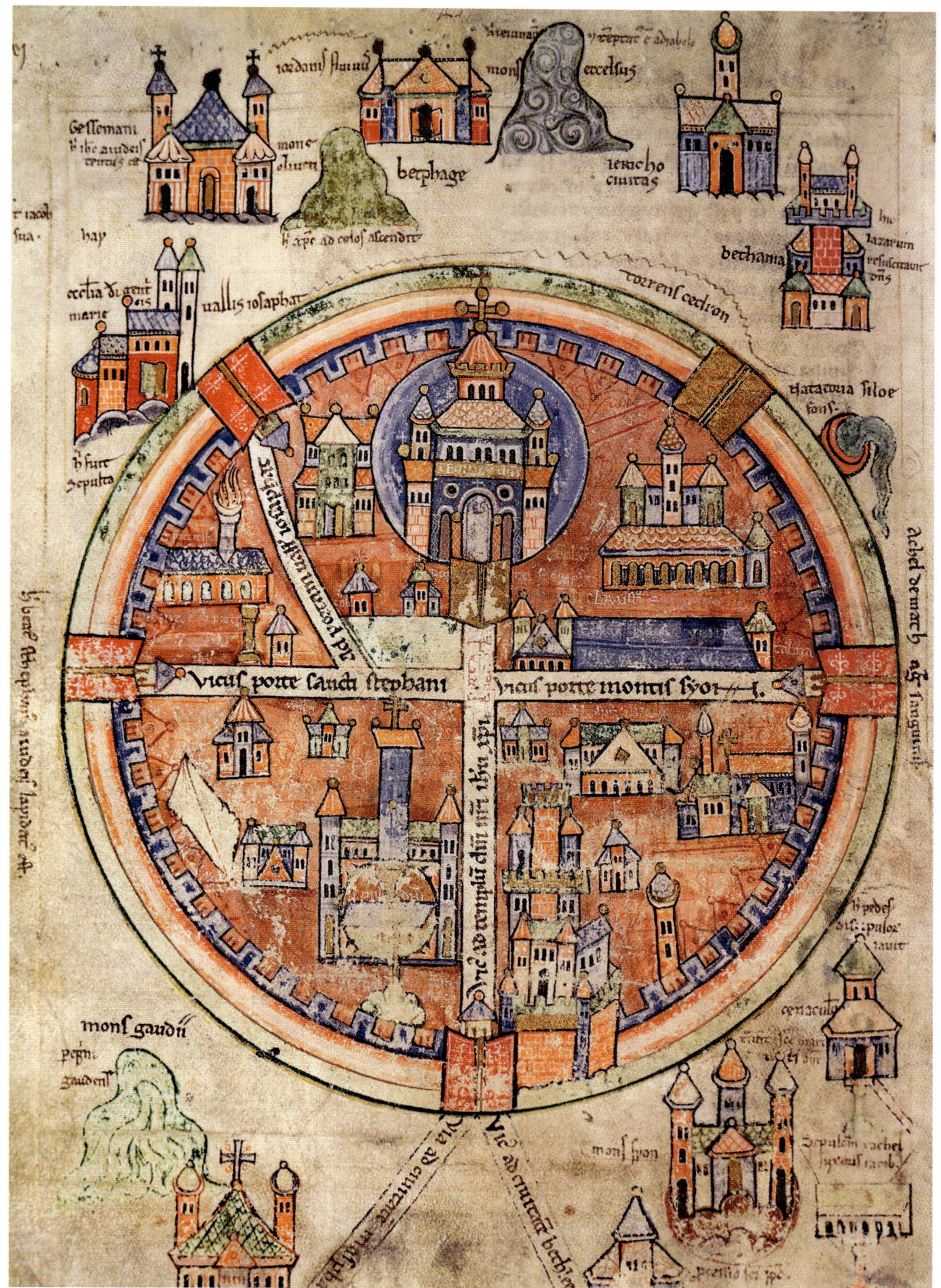

iordanis fluvius
mons excelsus
betphage
iericho civitas
Gessemani
mons oliveti
bethania
uallis iosaphat
torrens cedron
Vicus porte sancti stephani
Vicus porte montis syon
mons gaudii
mons syon

The Hereford map is big—62 inches by 52 inches—and inscribed in black, red, and gold ink on one sheet of vellum (chemically cured animal skin) in the shape of a pentagon. We don't know who designed or drew it, but its many inscriptions seem to be in one set of handwriting. We also don't know why it was made in or came to Hereford, though it was originally the center of a triptych whose other parts no longer exist, and may have been erected for visitors to the shrine of Saint Thomas de Cantelupe, who is buried at Hereford Cathedral. These mysteries only add to the power of the map, which can be overwhelming at first glance—and long afterward.

At its core, the Hereford *mappa mundi* is a T-O map. Most of it is within a large circle with Jerusalem at its bull's-eye, oriented to the east and divided into three geographically distorted continents. But it's also a massive compendium of political territories, Christian eschatology, and medieval myths. The Hereford map names 420 cities and towns, from Rome ("head of the world, holds the bridle of the spherical earth") to Hereford itself (one small structure at the bottom left, and very faint, possibly made so by locals touching the map).

The map depicts a wide range of biblical stories, classical legends, and wondrous beasts. Sadly, some of its accounts are stained by the antisemitism endemic in the medieval Church. As just one example, in its image of the tablets of the Ten Commandments, Moses has horns.

The Hereford map also depicts a series of classical legends and a range of wondrous beasts, including an elephant so strong it can carry a wooden platform for troops and a unicorn. And, especially in areas farthest from Jerusalem, it presents exotic races of humanoids. For instance, a "blemmye," whose eyes, nose, and mouth are on his chest, stands with a spear in Africa. "This is a map of religious faith, with a symbolic center and monstrous margins," Jerry Brotton, professor of Renaissance studies at Queen Mary University of London, wrote in his 2012 book, *A History of the World in Twelve Maps*.

Within this dizzying array of Christian images infused with seemingly every influence that might have entered medieval imaginations, many journeys are possible. Looking at this world, you might trace the paths that pilgrims trod from faraway places to Jerusalem, or the Israelites took when they left Egypt, crossed the Red Sea (whose red ink is parted on this map) and found the Promised Land. Inexorably, though, your eyes are drawn upward, to the map's triangular tip, where Christ sits, outside the world, resurrected from death and triumphant over earthly laws. On

1 2

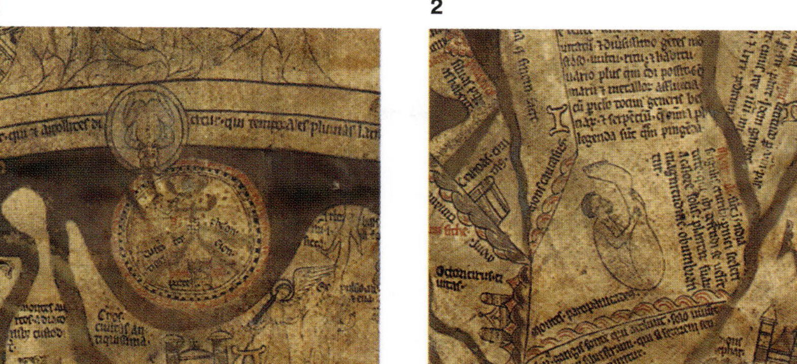

3

4

1 The Hereford *mappa mundi* situates more than a dozen biblical events, placing the Garden of Eden on its own at the top of the circle, set off from the farthest reaches of Asia by water, fire, and a wall.

2 The map depicts examples of fantastically strange peoples, such as a "sciapod," who has one giant foot and uses it to shield himself from the sun in India.

3 A lynx urinates a precious gem, in accordance with ancient legends.

4 The map locates the Pillars of Hercules at the Strait of Gibraltar (pictured), the Labyrinth of the Minotaur in Crete, and the Golden Fleece, pursued by Jason and the Argonauts, near the Black Sea.

one side, saved souls rise from their graves to enter Heaven. On the other, the damned head to Hell. From below, the Virgin Mary asks her son to "Have mercy . . . on all those who have served me, since you made me the way to salvation."

Thus the Hereford *mappa mundi* is the headiest of all T-O attempts to portray the whole world not just in one space, but at one time. It shows the *orbis terrarum* as God had created it, as Christians traversed its brew of Greek, Roman, Judaic, and distant cultures, and as it will ultimately end.

2

3

1

1

AMERICA
Montefregoso
Abbatia omni
Sanctorum

2

CLAVDII PT
ANDRIIN

3

ERICI VESPV

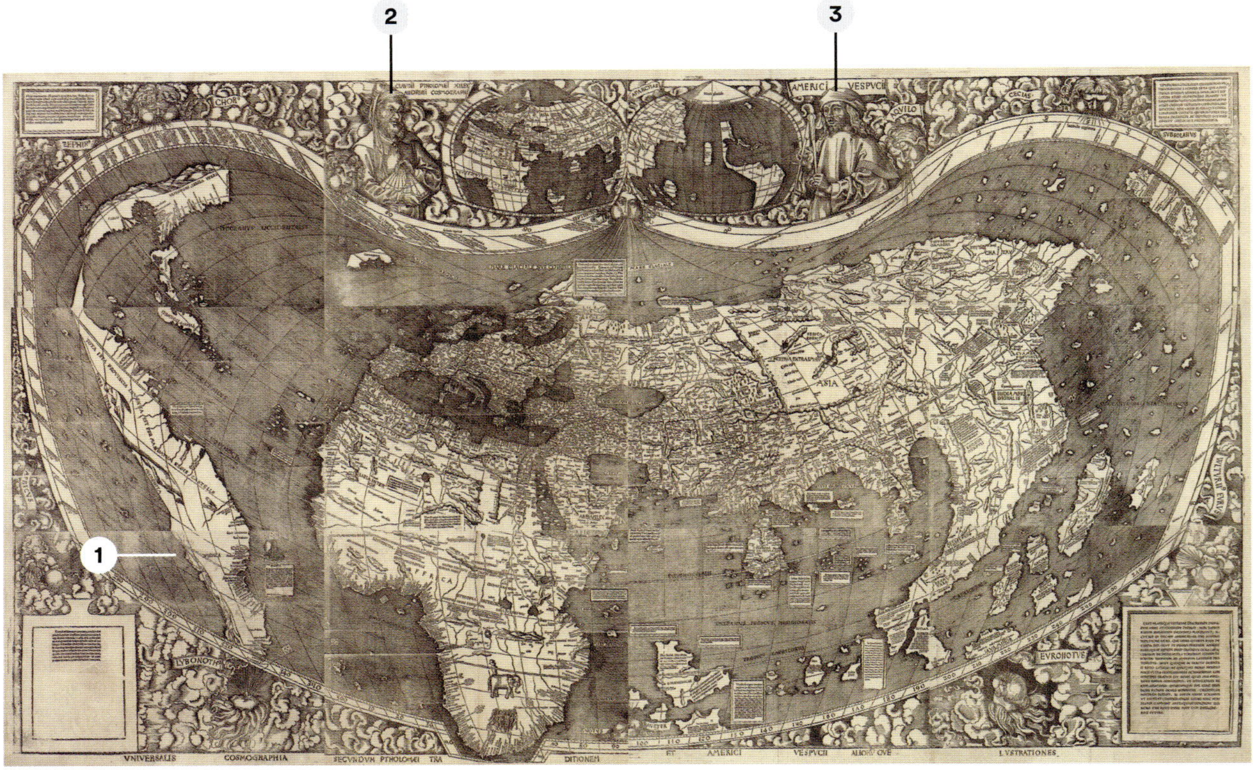

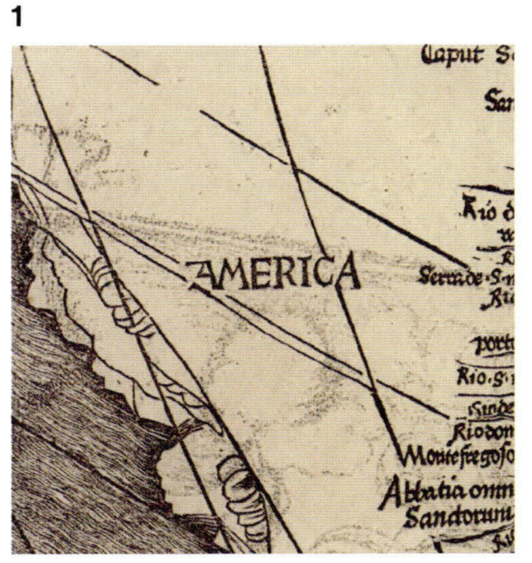

The Map That Became America's Birth Certificate

Universalis Cosmographia, the first European map to claim the Western Hemisphere, held an entirely "new" continent.

Like great athletes or Taylor Swift albums, historical maps are sometimes ranked by experts and buffs who want to share their analysis and stir up popular discussion. Here's one that makes plenty of all-time top-ten lists: *Universalis Cosmographia*, better known by the name of its chief illustrator, Martin Waldseemüller. Whatever the criteria—its historical significance, level of detail, artistic beauty, physical journey of the historical artifact, even its sheer size—the Waldseemüller map qualifies as exceptional.

Around the turn of the sixteenth century, Waldseemüller, who was born in a town that's now called Schallstadt in western Germany, joined a group of humanist scholars in Saint Dié-des-Vosges, a hamlet in the Duchy of Lorraine, which today is in northeast France. Calling itself the "Gymnasium Vosagense," this association planned to create an updated world map. News about the first westward voyages commissioned by Spain and Portugal was just starting to spread across Europe, and the geographers were particularly electrified by the stories of Amerigo Vespucci. For example, Matthias Ringmann, a member of the Gymnasium, read and reprinted the published version of a letter Vespucci had sent to his patron Lorenzo de Medici. Said Vespucci:

> [O]n the seventh day of August, 1501 . . . we anchored off the shores of those parts. . . . We knew that land to be a continent and not an island both because it stretches forth in the form of a very long and unbending coast, and because it is replete with infinite inhabitants. For in it we found innumerable tribes and peoples and species of all manner of wild beasts. . . . And these we may rightly call a new world. Because our ancestors had no knowledge of them, and it will be a matter wholly new to all those who hear about them. . . . [T]his transcends the view held by the ancients.

The *Universalis Cosmographia* (*Universal Cosmography*) by Martin Waldseemüller, published in the Holy Roman Empire (in a region that's now in France) in 1507

1 Though distorted and very thin, this is the first depiction of the Americas bearing their modern name.

It portrays 2 Ptolemy and 3 Amerigo Vespucci, paying homage to the two men that inspired the work.

Beginning in 1506, Waldseemüller and Ringmann brought together classical works such as Ptolemy's *Geography* (see pages 6–7) with reports from the latest explorations like Vespucci's into one comprehensive map. A new world indeed! The following year, Waldseemüller issued the *Universalis Cosmographia*, which was both incredibly detailed and massive: twelve sheets, printed from woodcuts, spanning the earth and measuring about 4 feet by 8 feet when placed together.

The map was accompanied by an introductory booklet, which both men seem to have contributed to but was probably mostly written by Ringmann. Deep in that document, after entire chapters devoted to local climates and to defining axes, poles, and parallels on spheres, the authors state: "[T]he earth is now known to be divided into four parts. . . . [T]he fourth . . . is found to be surrounded on all sides by the ocean." And that's what the Waldseemüller map shows. It shows the Americas looking like an impossibly long barrier reef. But six years before Vasco Núñez de Balboa stood on a high point in Panama and saw the Pacific Ocean, it was the first map to assert that what we now see as the New World comprised a continent unto itself, not an eastern adjunct of Asian lands.

The introduction also says: "I see no reason why anyone should justly object to calling . . . that land of Amerigo, or America, after . . . its discoverer, a man of great ability." And on the map, in the middle of what we would now call Argentina, Waldseemüller inscribed the name "America"—the first map ever to bestow that name.

These were bold moves indeed. As Erin Allen, a writer-editor for the US Library of Congress, wrote in 2016, "The map reflected a huge leap forward in knowledge, recognizing the newly found American landmass and forever changing mankind's understanding and perception of the world itself." The Waldseemüller map was also, at a more basic level, both fascinating and entertaining. It amalgamated a wide range of sources spanning hundreds of years of accumulated knowledge into one huge trove of cities and seas, mountains and ocean routes, and annotated its findings with dozens of insets, all surrounded by illustrations of winds blowing through the clouds surrounding a full globe. And it was a hit: The map reportedly sold out its initial run of one thousand prints, and sketches and copies soon spread across Europe. (Indeed, in *The Fourth Part of the World*, his outstanding book on the Waldseemüller map, author Toby Lester argues that when it reached Poland, the map even influenced the great astronomer Nicolaus Copernicus, who around 1510 was formulating his theory that the earth revolves around the sun.)

As Europeans kept bringing home further information about their explorations, the Waldseemüller map's western contours grew outdated fairly quickly, and it seemed that no copies survived by the end of the 1500s. After Ringmann died in 1511, Waldseemüller himself seemed to hedge on the map's biggest conclusions; in his later work, he did not show a new continent fully separated from Asia or use the name "America." Vespucci died in 1512, and has remained something of a mystery ever since. Historians still aren't sure whether he actually wrote the letters attributed to him, or even how many voyages he took. But when it comes to the nomenclature honoring Vespucci, as Lester has put it: "The name America, such a natural poetic counterpart to Asia, Africa, and Europa, had filled a vacuum, and there was no going back." In 1538, the great mapmaker Gerardus Mercator branded the two great landforms of the New World as "North America" and "South America" on the first world map he published, and the names stuck for good.

But that's not quite the end of the story. As it turns out, back around 1515, a German globe maker named Johannes Schöner took the individual sheets of his copy of the Waldseemüller map along with other maps important to him and bound them in a portfolio. That collection wound up in a library storage room at Wolfegg Castle in Baden-Württemberg, a state in what is now southwestern Germany. And in 1901—nearly *four hundred years* later—Josef Fischer, a Jesuit priest researching the history of transatlantic exploration, came across the portfolio quite by accident. It was inscribed: "Posterity, Schöner gives this to you as an offering."

In 2003, after decades of entreaties and negotiations, the Library of Congress announced it would buy the map from Prince Johannes Waldburg-Wolfegg (who had a royal title without any real authority, but whose family still owned the castle where it was discovered) for $10 million, with a mix of public and private funds. Library preservationists and engineers from the National Institute of Standards and Technology designed a 2,200-pound case made of aluminum and glass, and filled with argon, an inert noble gas, to hold the map. And in 2007, the year of its five-hundredth anniversary, the only surviving copy of the Waldseemüller map was lifted by a crane into a second-floor window of the Library's Thomas Jefferson Building, where it is now on permanent display.

IIII Die gantze Welt in einem Kleberblat/Welches ist der Stadt Hannouer meines lieben V

SEPTENTRIO

Engeland

Dennemarck

Schwe-
den

Franckreich

Saxen

Hispanien

Deudschland

Lothringen

Behemen

Reussen

Meiland

Polen

EVROPA

Vngern

Moschaw

Türcken

Welschland

Griechen-
land

Roma 382.

ARMENIA

Niniue 171.

MESOPO
TAMIA

AS

SIRIA

Haran 110.

CHALDEA

Antiochia 70.

Babylon

Damascus 40.

Vr 156.

ARABIA

Saba 312.

IERVSALEM

Das Rote Meer.

Das grosse Mittelmeer:
der Welt.

Alexandria 72.

Egypten

Cyrene 204.

LYBIA

Merve 24.

Morenland

AFRICA

Köngreich
Melinde.

CAPVT BO-
NÆ SPEI

AMERICA
Die Newe
Welt.

MERIDIES.

The Map of the World in a Cloverleaf

When cartographers had to admit the world was bigger than they had imagined, the Bünting map turned to pure symbolism.

For more than a thousand years, most *mappae mundi*, or medieval European maps of the world, shared a common template: The T-O scheme (see page 15) centralized Jerusalem, surrounded it with the three continents of Africa, Asia, and Europe, and displayed religious as well as geographic knowledge. Gradually, however, voyagers and merchants amassed new details about faraway lands. And encounters with the Americas—an entirely "New World"—forced Western monarchs and mapmakers alike to reckon with new perspectives. How would it ever be possible again for their cartography to show the world with the Holy Land at its heart?

Nearly ninety years after Columbus reached the Caribbean, a German theologian named Heinrich Bünting offered an elegant answer: He went fully figurative. In 1581, Bünting published *Itinerarium Sacrae Scripturae* (*A Travel Book to Holy Scripture*), detailing the journeys of Jesus and his apostles and various prophets and patriarchs from the Old and New Testaments, and describing the coins and measures they used and the distances they traveled. The book proved very popular and was translated and reprinted in more than sixty editions. It contained a series of conventional maps of biblical locations, but also three much more fantastic larger-scale woodcut illustrations: of Europe as a virgin queen, Asia as a Pegasus, and *The Entire World in a Cloverleaf.*

The Bünting *Cloverleaf* acknowledges there are really more than three continents; it nods to America in its lower left corner. (It also shows England as an island and a bit of Scandinavia to the north.) But it still

The Entire World in a Cloverleaf (featured in theologian Heinrich Bünting's *Itinerarium Sacrae Scripturae*, or *A Travel Book to Holy Scripture*, published in Germany in 1581) shows Africa, Asia, and Europe as the three primary continents, placing them as a trefoil with Jerusalem at its core.

foregrounds Africa, Asia, and Europe, placing them in the pattern of a shamrock, with Jerusalem at their center. The map contains small skyline sketches of historical centers of great culture, such as Alexandria and Rome. But its shapes and scales are almost entirely imaginary. Bünting's hometown of Hanover had a cloverleaf on its coat of arms; the three continents probably stand for that as well as the Christian Trinity. The fact that they're obviously unreal simply draws more attention to the map's central theme: These are still the most important parts of the earth—and they meet at a centrally important spot. In an age of European exploration and "discovery," the *Cloverleaf* was a vivid reminder that a map doesn't have to be literally accurate to put across important information, or a visceral message. Later cartographers extended that lesson in modern times, opening whole new approaches in mapmaking, particularly in political art and propaganda.

"Bünting did know that the world does not look like a cloverleaf," writes Jim Siebold, owner of Cartographic Images, an extensive archive of old maps. "But he wanted to go beyond the positivist knowledge of our globe's surface, to the one of symbols. . . . The New World appears uncertainly in a corner. The lands of the Bible remained as central to Protestant Germany as they had been to the Europe of the Crusades."

Today, there's a tile mosaic of the *Cloverleaf* map, created by the artist Arman Darian, in Safra Square in Jerusalem. If anything, the ceramic, rendered in vivid colors and thicker lines, honors symbolism over geography even more than Bünting's original. And puts the map itself in public view at the crossroads it portrays.

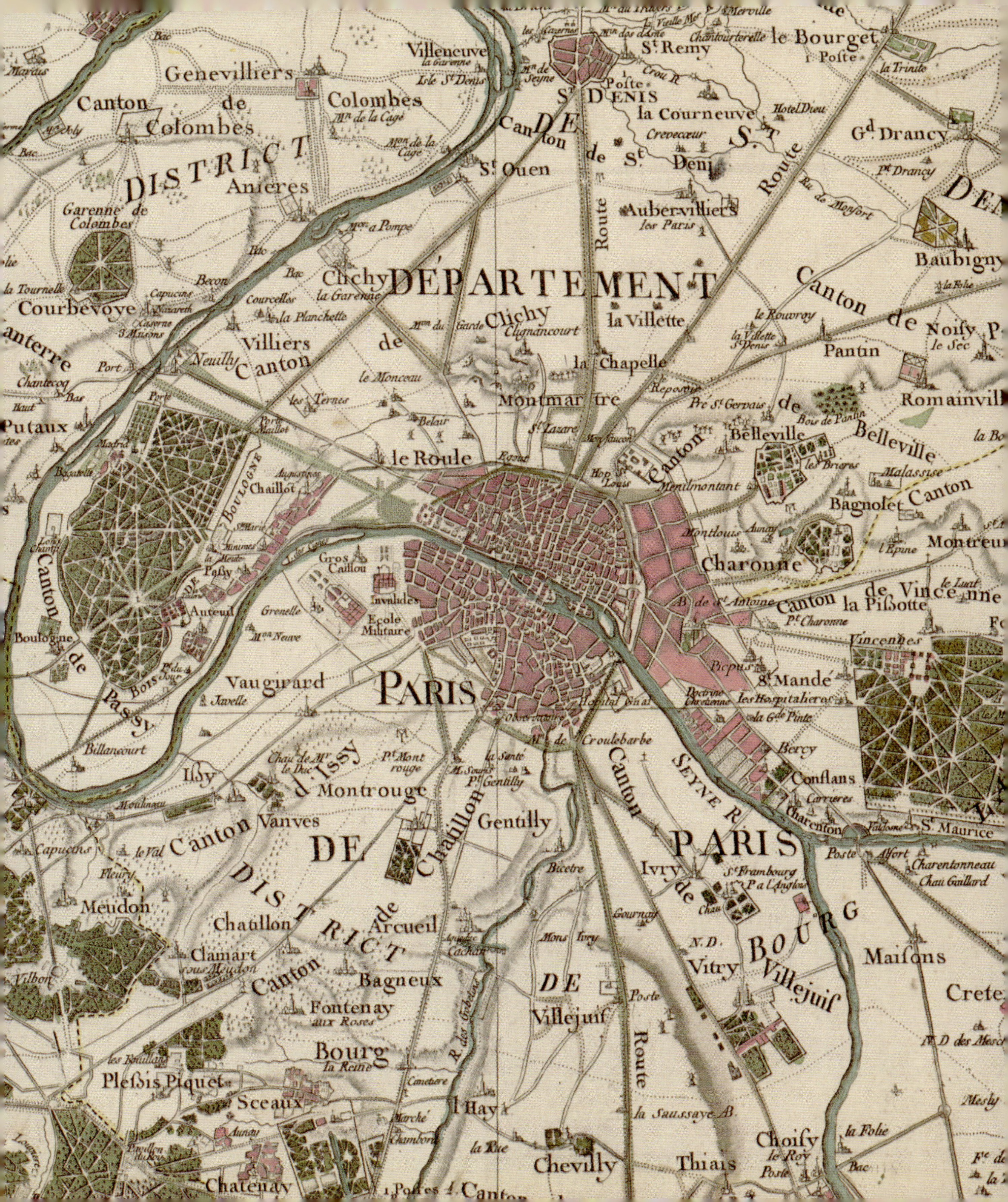

Genevilliers
Villeneuve
la Garenne
Isle St. Denis
St. Remy
le Bourget
Canton de Colombes
Colombes
St. DENIS
la Courneuve
Gd. Drancy
DISTRICT
Anieres
Canton de St. Denis
St. Ouen
Aubervilliers
Route
Garenne de Colombes
Baubigny
Clichy la Garenne
DÉPARTEMENT
Courbevoye
la Planchette
Clichy
Clignancourt
la Villette
Canton de Noisy
Villiers
Neuilly
Canton de
Pantin
Putaux
le Monceau
la Chapelle
les Ternes
Montmartre
Romainville
le Roule
Belleville
Chaillot
Canton
Menilmontant
Canton de Belleville
Bagnolet
Canton
BOULOGNE
Passy
Gros Caillou
Invalides
Charonne
Montreuil
Canton de Boulogne
Auteuil
Grenelle
Ecole Militaire
Canton de Vincennes
la Pissotte
Vincennes
Boulogne
Vaugirard
PARIS
Picpus
St. Mandé
Canton de Passy
Javelle
Bercy
Billancourt
Issy
Montrouge
Gentilly
Conflans
Canton d'Issy
Canton Vanves
Charenton
St. Maurice
DE
Chatillon
PARIS
Meudon
DISTRICT
Ivry
Canton de Bourg
Chatillon
Arcueil
Clamart sous Meudon
Cachan
Vitry
BOURG
Maisons
Canton
Bagneux
DE
Villejuif
Fontenay aux Roses
Route
Bourg la Reine
Plessis Piquet
Sceaux
l'Hay
Chevilly
Thiais
Choisy le Roy
Chatenay

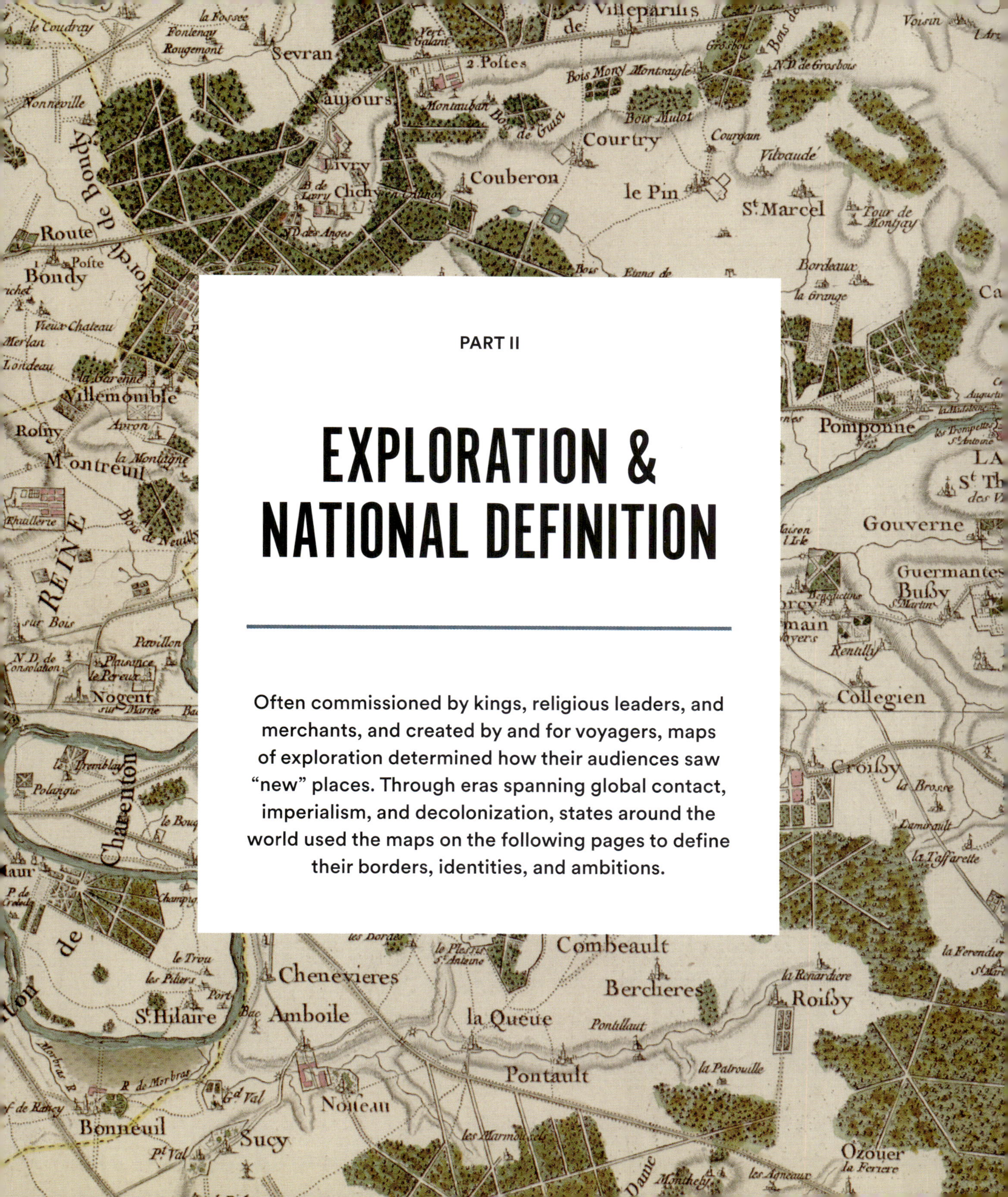

PART II

EXPLORATION & NATIONAL DEFINITION

Often commissioned by kings, religious leaders, and merchants, and created by and for voyagers, maps of exploration determined how their audiences saw “new” places. Through eras spanning global contact, imperialism, and decolonization, states around the world used the maps on the following pages to define their borders, identities, and ambitions.

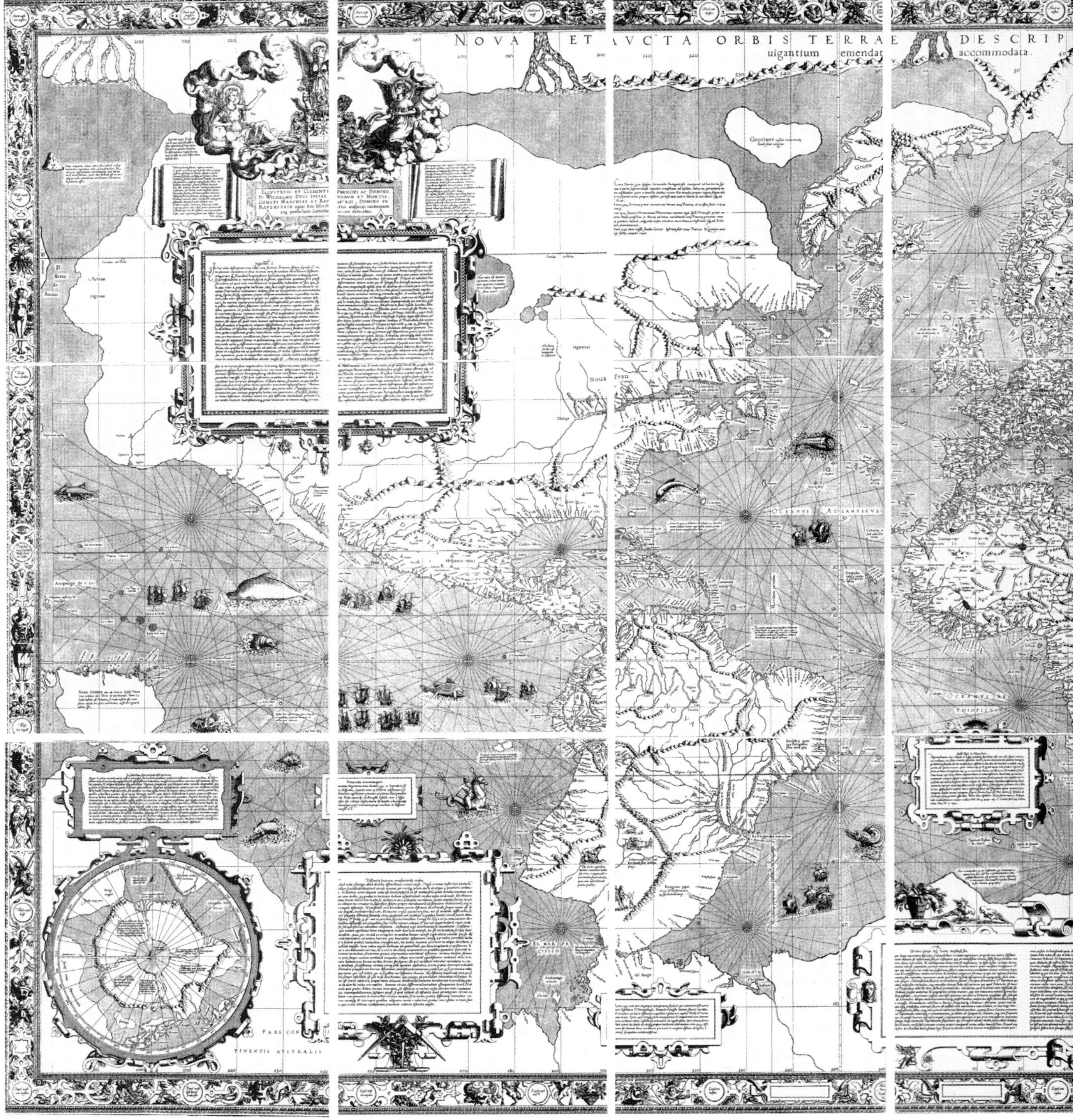
NOVA ET AVCTA ORBIS TERRAE DESCRIP
uigantium emendat
accommodata.
OCEANVS ATLANTICVS
PARS CON
TINENTIS AVSTRALIS

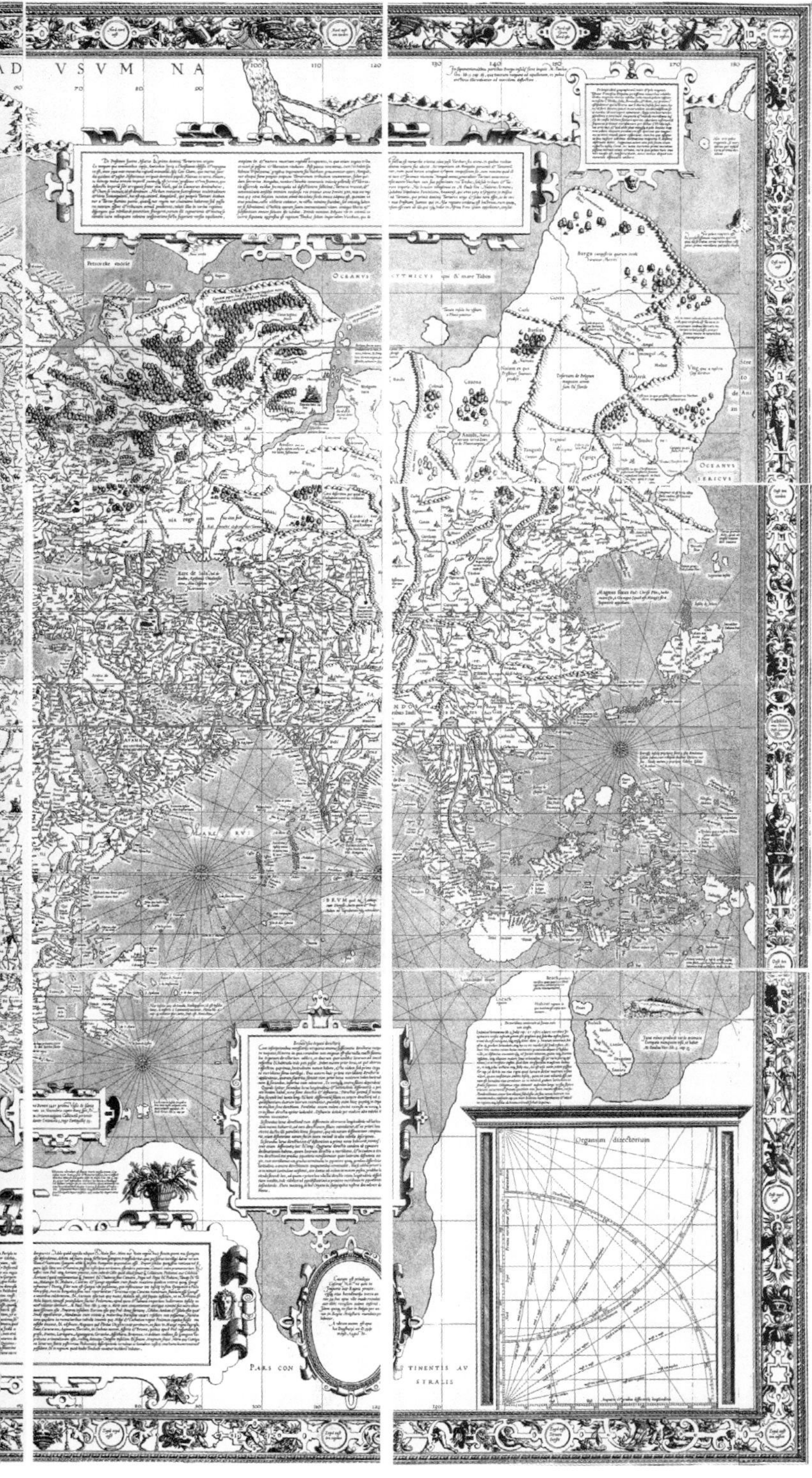

The Map That Became the Industry Standard

Gerardus Mercator set out to improve navigation maps. He ended up permanently changing how we see the world.

Nova et Aucta Orbis Terrae Descriptio ad Usum Navigantium Emendate Accommodata (New and More Complete Representation of the Terrestrial Globe Properly Adapted for Use in Navigation) was created by Gerardus Mercator in 1569 in Germany. Today, we can recognize many of its borders as distorted. But it offered a groundbreaking solution to the problem of representing the spherical earth in two dimensions.

OF ALL MAPS, political or otherwise, the one that least needs any introduction is the Mercator projection. Designed more than 450 years ago to improve navigation at sea, it spread far and wide for centuries, ultimately reaching homes and offices, classrooms and war rooms. It's likely that more people around the world have gained their knowledge about the size, shape, and location of the world's continents and oceans from Mercator maps than any other kind of illustration.

Which, seen from the vantage point of today, is a double-edged achievement.

Gerardus Mercator was born Gerard De Kremer in 1512 in Flanders, a region of Europe that now constitutes the northern part of Belgium. As a young adult, he studied geography, astronomy, and mathematics, and proved to be a gifted calligrapher and engraver. Taking the trade name Mercator, he made scientific instruments and created globes that were considered among the world's best for decades. His research and travels aroused suspicions that he was a Lutheran reformer or religious skeptic; he was arrested in 1544 and imprisoned in a Flemish castle. But Catholic authorities couldn't find written evidence of any heresy, and released him after seven months. He had to spend years rebuilding his way of life, first making instruments, then globes, then maps.

Mercator had diverse talents, and was deeply interested in cosmography, which in those days involved studying and mapping the earth and the heavens to try to understand the entire universe. Little in his background suggested, however, that he would revolutionize mapmaking forever. Yet in 1569, he produced a 48-inch by 80-inch world map in eighteen sheets (pages 32–33) that offered an extraordinarily consequential answer to cartography's most important question: How do you represent the curved earth on a flat surface?

Think about how hard it is to flatten an orange peel. You can squash it, deform it, rip it, but there's no perfect way to translate its three dimensions into two. In fact, it's a geometrical truth that by trying to do just that, all maps distort shapes, distances, and directions. To see how important that became in Mercator's time, when Westerners were just beginning to travel the vast distances between continents, consider what it means to try to plot a course from, say, Portugal to Brazil on a globe. Suppose you sail due southwest, and you cross every line of longitude at exactly the same angle. As crazy as it might seem today to anyone who's spent a lifetime looking at flat maps, because of the curvature of the earth, you will actually travel in a spiral, which is called a "rhumb line" or loxodrome. Navigators looking at globes five hundred years ago needed a way to see and understand that on a page. But how?

Mercator's answer was to stretch the distances between lines of latitude, making the gaps wider and wider the farther they got from the equator, until rhumb lines became straight lines. His map was based on what you'd get from projecting the globe onto a cylinder. Imagine covering the earth in ink, placing it inside a gigantic roll of holiday wrapping paper, and then unrolling the tube. The resulting image of the inked earth would preserve local angles and bearings across large-scale distances. On a Mercator map, you can simply draw a line to the southwest, or in any direction, with a ruler, and that will be the actual direction you travel. (You can see hundreds of straight-edged rhumb lines drawn by Mercator crisscrossing his original map.)

Of course, that fidelity comes at a cost: Because the intervals between latitudes get bigger and bigger as they approach the North and South Poles, and lines of longitude can't converge the way they do on a globe, Mercator maps distort areas, sometimes severely. That's why they either show the Arctic Circle and Antarctica as huge landmasses or cut off most of the polar regions. At latitudes of 90 degrees, the distance between parallels would actually reach infinity.

Mercator recognized the quid pro quo he was accepting: "The shapes of regions are necessarily very seriously stretched," he wrote on this map. But he called it a "New and More Complete Representation of the Terrestrial Globe Properly Adapted for Use in Navigation." He intended it to be useful for sea travel, and could not foresee just how far his creation's influence would outgrow its original purpose.

Mercator explained what he had done, but not how—and we still don't know what methods he used to widen the spaces between his parallels. (It's fairly amazing that he figured out how to create his projection at all, because he wasn't able to use trigonometry tables, logarithms, or calculus—none had been developed yet!) But researchers and mapmakers eventually figured out how to replicate and build on his work. And decade after decade, from the seventeenth century well into the twentieth, Mercator maps proved unstoppably popular as a catalyst for exploration, travel, commerce, and research. Scientists who studied the trade winds, the Gulf Stream, and the magnetic poles incorporated their findings into Mercator maps. Atlases and weather maps adopted the Mercator projection, and then so did textbooks, everyday wall maps, and eventually newspapers, movies, and television broadcasts. Peter Jennings, who anchored ABC's *World News Tonight* from 1983 to 2005, sat on a set where the glass wall between him and the newsroom was etched with a Mercator map.

Along the way, the Mercator map—the original version of which showed no cities, countries, or borders—*became* a political map, because over time, nations and their peoples defined themselves by it. And in exaggerating the sizes of northern Europe, North America, and Russia while downscaling intertropical Africa, India, and most of South America, the Mercator projection advanced the idea that colonial powers were bigger, stronger, and more important than the places they occupied. "No projection has been as abused in the pursuit of size distortion," Mark Monmonier, a professor of geography at Syracuse University, wrote about Mercator in his 1991 book *How to Lie with Maps*.

Particular versions of Mercator maps fit the self-image of various countries. For example, projections centered on 0 degree longitude placed Great Britain near the top and in the middle of the world (because the prime meridian runs through Greenwich, England), and sometimes split Australia into two chunks, putting a possession of the British Empire on both the eastern and western edges of their maps.

In 1932, the US Department of State followed suit by creating a classic map of its Foreign Service posts (right) that put the United States front and center. Here, the US appears as a diplomatic power whose reach extends across both the Atlantic and Pacific Oceans. Various insets detail areas of special concern to Americans, such as the Caribbean and the Atlantic coast of Europe. The equator runs along a line well below the middle of this map, and Alaska (actual size: 665,000 square miles) looks nearly as big as Brazil (3.3 million square miles). It's a grand instance of a nation using a map to showcase its own place in the world.

But the State Department map also carries the seeds of dissatisfaction with the Mercator projection. Probably the most famous criticism of Mercator maps is that they make Greenland and Africa seem roughly equal in size, when in fact Africa is fourteen times as large. Conveniently enough, the 1932 map covers up Greenland almost entirely, with a box showing a close-up of the St. Lawrence Seaway. And this would be the last time the State Department used a Mercator projection in this series of maps.

By the 1940s, the globalization of communications, travel, and war required and triggered world maps that presented different perspectives

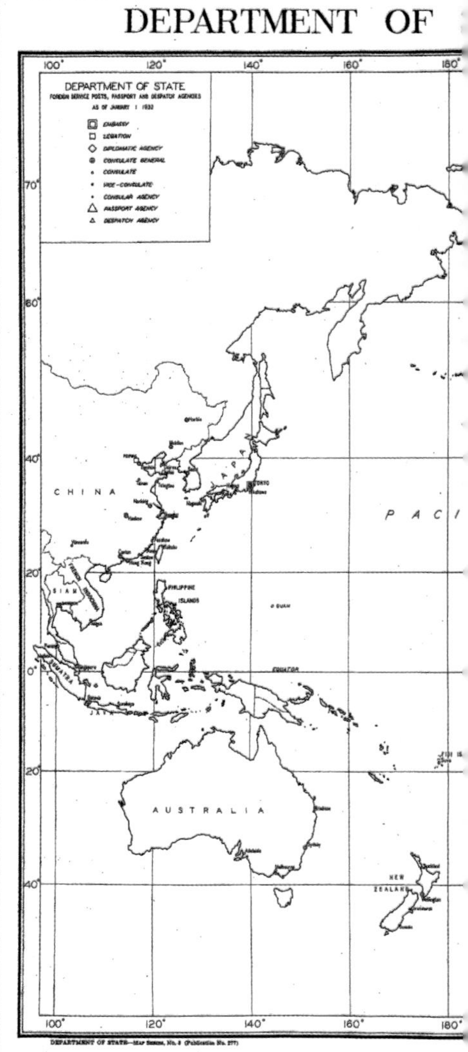

The *Department of State: Foreign Service Posts, Passport, and Despatches Agencies*, produced by the US Department of State in 1932, employs a classic (and cropped) Mercator projection that emphasizes the importance of territories in the northern half of the globe.

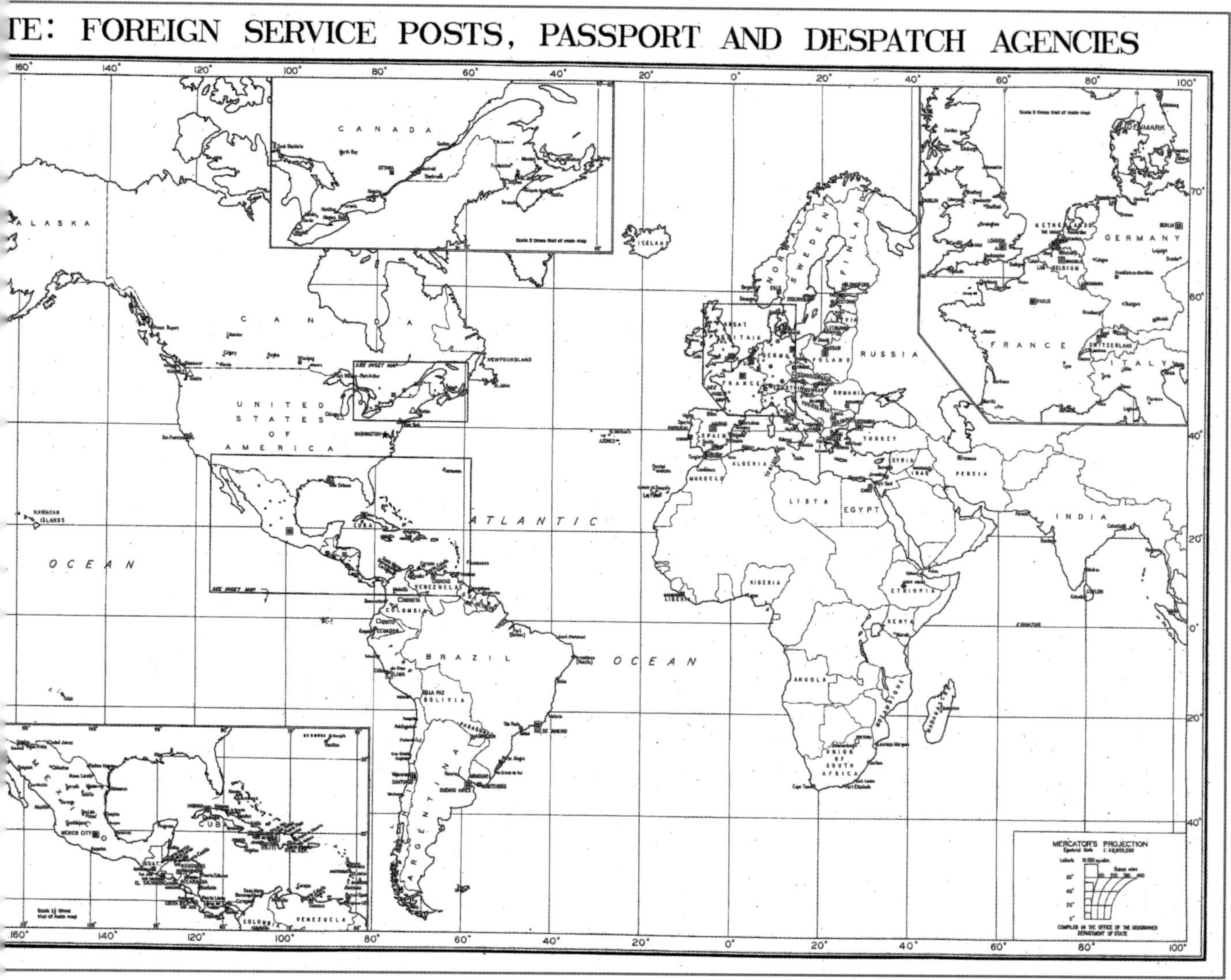

and represented the areas of countries more accurately than the Mercator projection. Even today, however, most online mapping and navigation applications use Mercator, because it shows directions, distances, and intersections correctly for local travel. And the shapes and sizes that most of us carry around in our heads as being "correct" for countries around the world come from, let's admit it, old Mercator maps.

EVROPE
Par N. Sanson le fils
Geographe du Roy
A Paris chez l'Autheur avec
Priuilege pour 20 ans
OCEAN SEPTENTRIO
OCEAN OCCIDENTAL
MER MEDITERRANEE
ALLEMAGNE
FRANCE
ESPAGNE
POLOGNE
TVRQVIE
NORWEGE
SVEDE
DANEMARC
ANGLETERRE
IRLANDE
ESCOSSE
AFRIQVE
BARBARIE
GOLFE DE VENISE

The Map That First Traced States

After the Thirty Years' War, maps showed and sustained national borders, including many that are still familiar.

This is the kind of thing that can be easy to miss but blindingly obvious in retrospect: Old political maps had no interior borders! At least not the kind of clearly drawn boundaries among countries that we see all the time today. Five hundred years ago, a map could have been dotted with duchies or limned with travel routes taken by voyaging explorers. But they wouldn't have looked like maps from the Napoleonic era, say, or the twentieth century, with well-defined outlines marking places from Brazil to Denmark to Egypt.

There's a clear moment of transition from BCE to CE in the history of political maps, and Year Zero is 1648. That's when two treaties concluded the Thirty Years' War, essentially creating the modern nation-state and inaugurating a period known as the Peace of Westphalia. Rather abruptly afterward, maps started to look like *L'Evrope*, or "Europe," drawn by the great French cartographer Nicolas Sanson.

The Thirty Years' War began as a fight between Catholics and Protestants in Germany, but eventually engulfed nearly all of Europe's major powers, and led to at least 4 million deaths from combat as well as calamities like plague and starvation. By the time it was over, there was another casualty, too: the idea that the continent would remain united and Catholic, subject to religious rule by the pope and political dominance by the Holy Roman Empire, which at its peak stretched from what is now France to the Baltic Sea in the northeast and Slovenia to the southeast. Instead, the member states of the Empire and the nations around it agreed to recognize the sovereignty of the others. And with that, independent kingdoms of men—nations—came to Europe.

L'Evrope (Europe) led off French cartographer Nicolas Sanson's first world atlas, which was published from 1648 to 1657. It features few decorative elements—except for outlines circumscribing every nation in color.

One simple way to think about this very complicated period is that before the Peace of Westphalia, legitimate political authority in Europe came from two sources. One was projectable power: If you lived close enough to a noble for their army to reach you, he could tax or conscript you. The other was identity: You could also be subject to the dictates of the faith or customs shared by most people wherever you lived. As a result, states often had poorly defined and even overlapping borders. After the Westphalia treaties, authority came from territory instead. Strong boundaries were both the price and achievement of peace.

For example, from 1568 to 1646—before Westphalia—just 60 percent of political maps even showed dotted lines between states, and only 25 percent included two-color borders, such as a yellow line for France and green for the Netherlands on opposite sides of the French-Dutch border, according to research by Steve Pickering, a political scientist who's now at the University of Amsterdam. But from 1650 to 1700, after the peace, all the political maps Pickering studied included national borders, and 78 percent showed them in two colors. A handful even started shading nations in different solid colors for the first time. "These new Westphalian states are represented with bright colors and clearly marked boundaries," Pickering wrote in 2013.

Nicolas Sanson led the way for this new breed of maps. Born in Abbeville, France, in 1600, he began crafting beautiful cartography as a teenager, and served as "Geographer to the King" for both Louis XIII, who ruled France from 1610 to 1643, and Louis XIV, whose reign lasted from 1643 until 1715, nearly five decades after Sanson's death in 1667. With Pierre-Jean Mariette, an engraver and publisher, Sanson produced a whopping three hundred maps during his career. As a result, Sanson is often called the father of French cartography.

L'Evrope was the first part of Sanson's first world atlas, which also included volumes on Asia, Africa, and the Americas, and which he published from 1648 to 1657. Sanson emphasized scientific observation and geographical accuracy over the literally baroque adornments and decorations that had become popular in Dutch mapmaking. His atlas delineates very detailed coastlines and shows small pictorial mountains in addition to cities and rivers. It offers almost no other embellishments, however, but for its standout feature—hand-drawn colored borders around every nation-state. This is a map for a new age.

Of course, the Peace of Westphalia was destined to be a template for international relations, not a permanent change in reality. For one thing,

European nations have found ways to violate its spirit many times since 1648, both by fighting enormously destructive wars among themselves and by colonizing other nations through conquest. For another, it's still an open question whether anyone can rightly or successfully ask, say, Catalans, or French Canadians or Tibetans for loyalty to national borders over their cultural affiliations without first granting them the chance for self-determination. But the treaties of Westphalia *did* establish boundaries that are still familiar today for England, France, the Netherlands, Poland, Turkey, Spain, Sweden, and the territories that would eventually become Germany and Russia. Political maps first illustrated those borders distinctively nearly four hundred years ago. And afterward, they would bolster the sovereignty of the nations they portrayed.

The Old Masters' Greatest Map

Johannes Vermeer often featured maps or globes in his paintings, including one of his most impressive works.

Mapmaking isn't typically considered one of the fine arts. But it's drawn the attention of some of the world's most notable painters and illustrators—none more intensely than the great Old Master Johannes Vermeer. The art critic Théophile Thoré-Bürger, who rediscovered and popularized Vermeer's work nearly two centuries after the Dutchman died in 1675, said the artist had a "mania for maps." Indeed, of the thirty-four paintings recognized today as Vermeer's work, nine—nearly a quarter of them—portray maps or maplike objects like globes.

Vermeer painted during a golden age of national identity, commerce, and art for what we now call the Netherlands. After a war that lasted most of the eighty-year stretch from 1568 to 1648, the Dutch Republic gained independence from Spain. Dutch explorers were world leaders in establishing trade routes around the globe, generating huge wealth at home. Even citizens beyond the richest nobles were able to enjoy decorative art—including wall maps, which became popular enough that publishers offered to customize their ornamental elements for buyers.

De Schilderkunst, or *The Art of Painting*, is a masterpiece Vermeer probably painted around 1668. It depicts an artist, seated at an easel in his studio, and his subject, a young woman dressed in blue, holding a book and a trumpet. A detailed and decorated map of the Netherlands hangs on the wall behind her.[1] The map is oriented to mirror how Dutch citizens would look out at the sea, with the west at the top.

On one level, *The Art of Painting* is what critics call a "genre work," or depiction of everyday life, because maps hung on many Dutch walls of that era. On another, it's a tour de force demonstration of the power of painting: From the folds in the studio curtains to the shadows on the model's face and body to the cracks on the wall to the pattern of the floor

De Schilderkunst (*The Art of Painting*), created by Dutch painter Johannes Vermeer, c. 1668, contains the biggest and most intricate map he ever put on canvas.

1 Vermeer based his map on one originally drawn about thirty years earlier by a cartographer named Claes Jansz. Visscher.

tile, Vermeer creates astounding sensations of illumination and depth everywhere. It's also a peek inside the artist's studio, showing his creative influences. And the items on the table near the woman, including a sculpted mask and open book, might represent the arts and education.

Two things make the wall hanging in *The Art of Painting* a political map. One is how it divides the seven northern provinces that became the Dutch Republic (to the right of the map's most prominent fold) from the areas that remained under Spanish dominion after 1648 (to the left). If Vermeer was showing us his inspirations, an independent Dutch Republic was among them.

The other is that nearly three hundred years later, Adolf Hitler loved this painting. Perhaps in his own demented way, the German dictator also approved of the northern Netherlands breaking away from the Habsburgs, who ruled Spain. Hitler could simply have admired its composition; he always fancied himself an artist. Maybe he just enjoyed the fact that by 1940, he had the pick of whatever art he wanted from almost any place in Europe. In the case of *The Art of Painting*, he bought it from an Austrian count named Jaromir Czernin, and planned to showcase it at the Führermuseum Hitler was planning to build as an art-themed monument to himself. Instead, by the winter of 1943–44, the Nazis had to stash the canvas in salt-mine tunnels they used to protect their loot from Allied bombing attacks.

In the spring of 1945, the US Army reached the mines, and its Monuments, Fine Arts, and Archives (MFAA) section unit liberated an enormous stash of art.[2] After the war, Andrew Ritchie, an art historian and gallery director who served as the head of MFAA for Austria, personally carried *The Art of Painting* back to Vienna by train. He later said that to ensure its safety, he locked himself in a sleeping compartment "with the picture and a splendid picnic of pheasant and Burgundy supplied by a French colleague." The Czernin family was already claiming ownership of the painting, but Austrian courts since then have consistently rejected their claims, finding no evidence that Count Jaromir was coerced into dealing with Hitler. *The Art of Painting* became and remains part of the permanent collection of the Kunsthistorisches Museum (Museum of Art History) in Vienna, Austria.

2 This outfit was known as the Monuments Men, and were later the subject of a 2009 book with the same name written by Robert M. Edsel and Bret Witter, and a 2014 movie directed by and starring George Clooney.

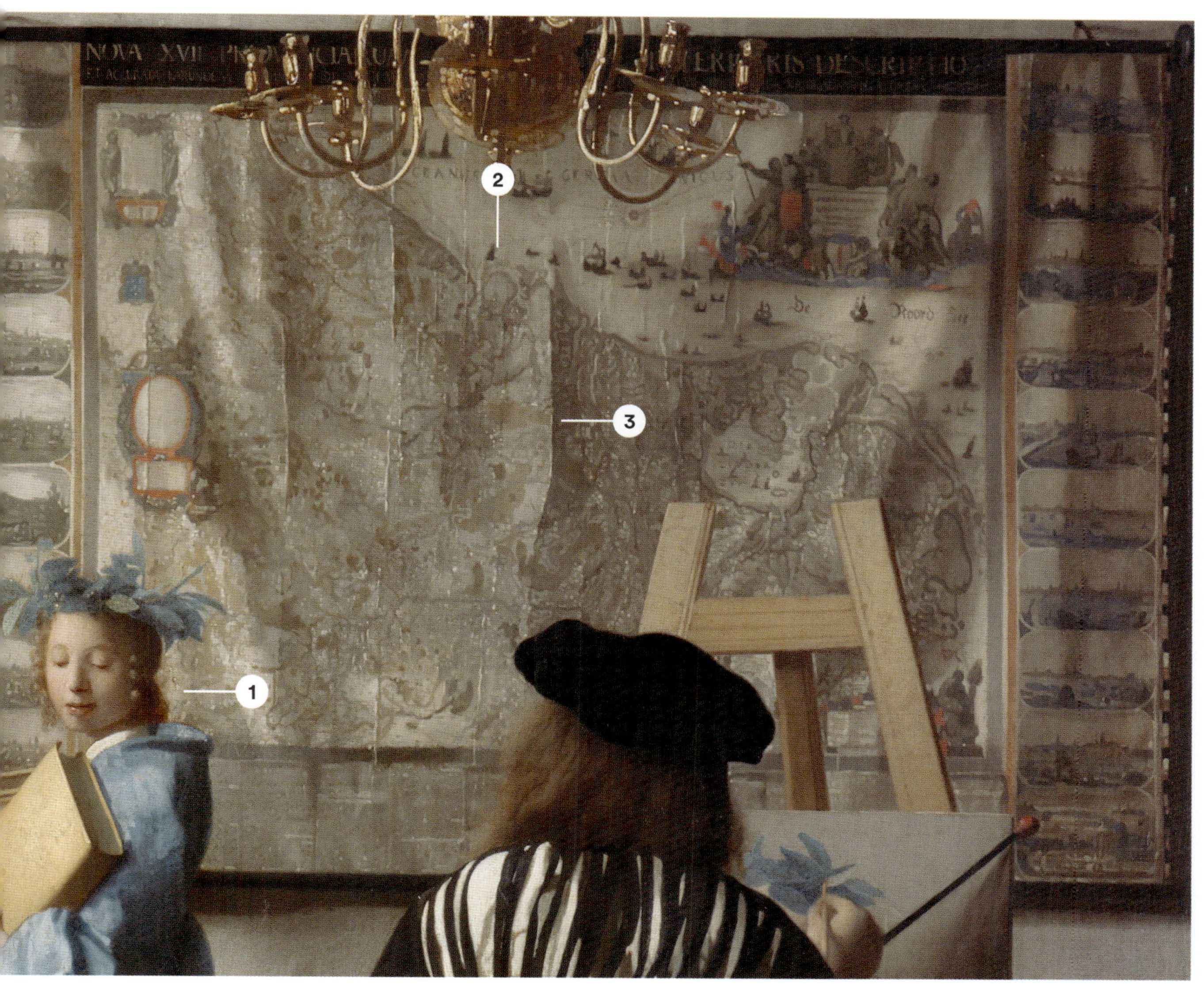

1 Historians have speculated that the woman in Vermeer's painting could be Clio, the Greek muse of history.

2 Our modern eyes may not recognize Holland as the subject of the map, but that's because West is at the top of the map.

3 A crease separates the northern provinces that became the Dutch Republic (to the crease's right) from the areas that remained under Spanish control after the Eighty Years' War (to its left), suggesting that Vermeer may have been interested in an independent Dutch Republic.

CARTE DE FRANCE LEVEE PAR ORDRE DU ROY PREMIERE FEUILL
NORD
OUEST
SUD
PONTOISE
MEULAN
Argenteuil
PARIS
DEPARTEMENT
DISTRICT
DE PARIS
BOURG
FOREST DE St GERMAIN
SEYNE R.
Rambouillet
Echelle de dix Mille Toises.

The Family Map That Built a Nation

Four generations of Cassinis mapped France through times of exploration, innovation, and revolution.

The *Carte de France* (Map of France) was produced and published by César-François Cassini and Jean Dominique Cassini from 1756 to 1815. This sheet, showing Paris and its surroundings, is just one of 182. When fully assembled, they created a France-shaped array measuring 39 feet by 38 feet.

THE *CARTE DE FRANCE* (Map of France), or *Carte de Cassini* (Cassini map), is the first comprehensive map of a nation based on modern surveying methods. It's remarkable for a variety of reasons: As originally published, it occupied 182 sheets. It's amazingly accurate, even by today's standards. And it took decades to complete, largely through the work of multiple generations of one family—the Cassinis.

Gian Domenico Cassini (1625–1712) was born in Italy, became a renowned astronomer, moved to Paris in 1669 at the invitation of King Louis XIV of France, and became the first of four Cassinis to oversee the Paris Observatory.[1] He was also a pioneer in measuring longitude, conducting crucial work for making useful maps that was carried on by his son Jacques (1677–1756), also called Cassini II. Jacques and his son César-François Cassini de Thury, or Cassini III, who was born in 1714, advanced the development of triangulation as a cartographic technique and produced a highly accurate map of France, essentially in outline, by 1744 (shown opposite).

King Louis XV, who had a keen interest in the sciences, then asked César-François to make one at a larger scale, so big that it would involve resurveying the entire country. Royal financing for that project dried up because of the Seven Years' War with England. But César-François was able to put together private funding from fifty supporters, including the king and local officials whose provinces weren't mapped yet.

The Cassinis' technique of triangulation extended the trigonometry that US students now learn in high school: If you know the length of one side of a triangle and can measure the angles made at each of its endpoints, you can figure out all its sides and angles. By gauging baselines and angles, the Cassini surveyors calculated distances to faraway points. They built a web of triangles covering the entirety of France. And then they filled in their maps with information from surveys around the country, adding an extraordinary level of detail in symbols coded by Cassini III.

Exploration was often hazardous duty. Well into the eighteenth century, much of what is now France didn't yet consider itself part of a

---

1 Gian Domenico Cassini discovered four satellites of Saturn and the gap in its rings, which is now named the "Cassini Division" after him. A 1997 space probe to that planet also bore his name.

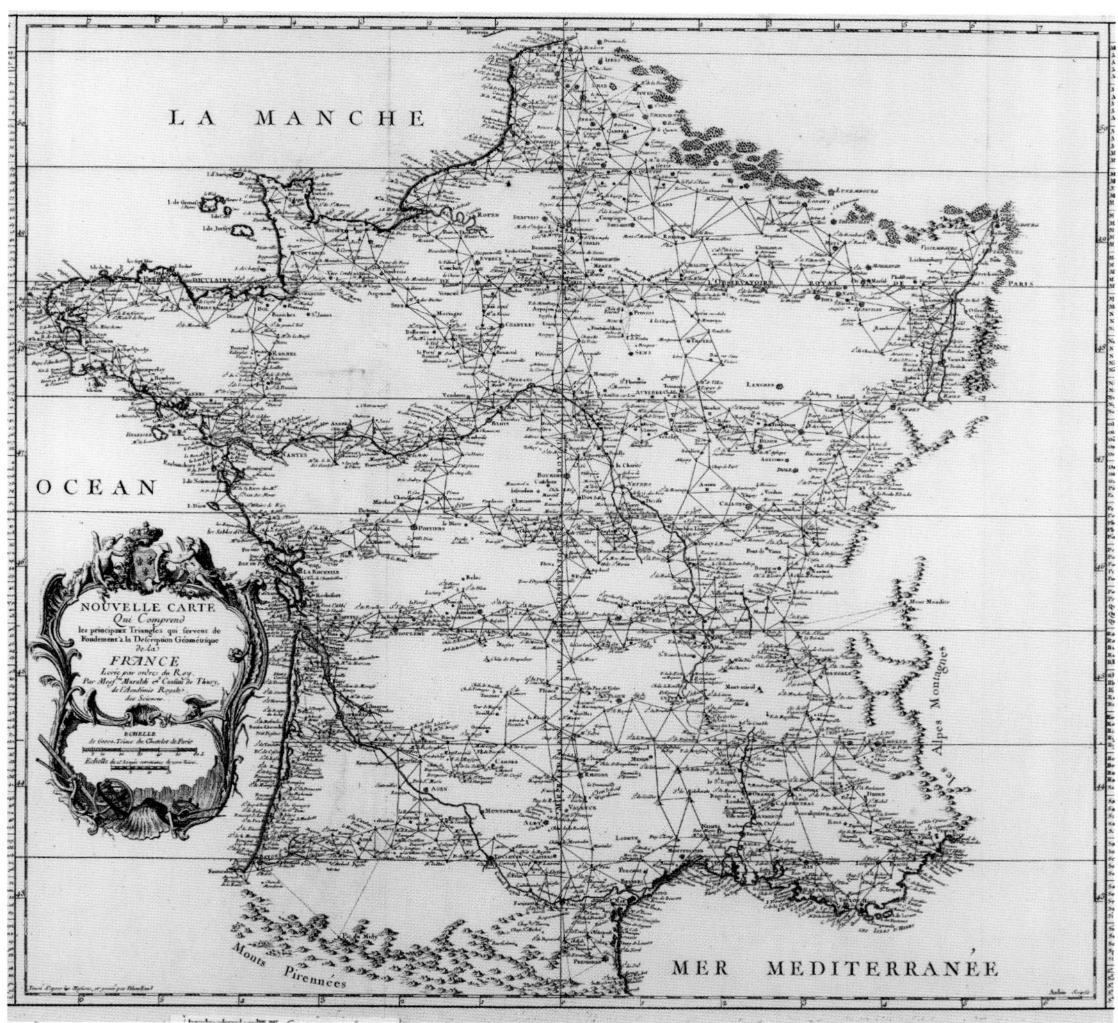

The *Nouvelle carte qui comprend les principaux triangles qui servent de fondement a la description geometrique de la France* (New map that includes the main triangles that serve as the basis for the geometric description of France) was created by Jacques Cassini and César-François Cassini and Jean Dominique Maraldi in 1744.

single country or culture. Outside Paris, there were many places where residents hardly spoke French, conducted business purely locally, stayed within their gates during the day, and pulled up their walls at night. When unfamiliar faces from the capital showed up to collect scientific data with weird contraptions, provincials didn't always respond with open arms. Early in the Cassinis' project, villagers in the southern community of Les Estables put their town on the map, so to speak, by hacking one of the triangulators to death.

César-François lived until 1784, by which time most of the big map's pieces were published. Sheet 1, depicting Paris and the surrounding area, is shown on pages 46–47. His son Jean-Dominique Cassini (born in 1748 and known as Cassini IV) then took over the massive project, which meant that he was racing to complete the Cassini chef d'oeuvre when the Bastille was stormed in 1789. The new National Assembly redivided the country into local districts called departments. Revolutionaries abolished the French monarchy in 1792 and executed King Louis XVI as a traitor soon afterward. And in September 1793, the National Convention, successor to the Assembly, seized Jean Dominique's research and printing materials. His maps, books, engraving plates, and tables were all carried off and declared public possessions, meaning that they became property of the state.

"Can a painter be divested of his canvas before having given it his final touches?" Jean Dominique asked plaintively. "Where is the poet whose tragedy has been wrested from him before he has completed the final scene?"

Jean Dominique was arrested as an ally of the aristocracy in February 1794, and the Convention guillotined one of his cousins in June. He managed to survive. But dismayed by the destructiveness of the Revolution, and by new standards it tried to impose on science, he essentially went into retirement. He lived long enough to see his family's work inspire similar efforts in other places; the United Kingdom conducted a "Principal Triangulation of Great Britain" that lasted from 1791 to 1853. He was decorated by Napoleon, who rose to power after the Revolution and launched a mapmaking campaign of his own.

The Cassinis' efforts bolstered the concept of France as a nation-state, bringing together its towns and topography, its landmarks and local routes, within one vast but precisely defined border. In a weird way, even the confiscation of their work contributed to state-building: It marked the first time a national government seized control of a private mapping project. And the French War Depot engraved and published the final sheets of the map. A one-page version of the final result, drawn by English cartographer William Faden in 1806, is shown opposite. (The original is far too huge to display in its entirety.)

When Jean Dominique published his memoirs, he made his case for the *Carte de Cassini* as a great French work, while regretting his loss in the copyright war that had engulfed him. "One would think I had the right to hope that as long as I would live, I would keep the sacred ownership rights over the Map of France," he wrote.

"Such vain reckonings of men!"

A Correct Map of France according to the New Divisions into Metropolitan Circles, Departments & Districts, drawn by English cartographer William Faden in 1806, is a one-page version of the final result of the decades-long Cassini family project.

MAP of
FRANCE
New Divisions
into
Metropolitan Circles
DEPARTMENTS & DISTRICTS;
from a Reduced Copy of
MONS.R CASSINI'S LARGE MAP.
from the latest Surveys.
London
BRISTOL CHANNEL
ENGLISH CHANNEL
BAY OF BISCAY
MEDITERRANEAN SEA
CORSICA

1
2
3
A NEW MAP OF HUDSONS BAY AND LABRADOR
HUDSONS BAY
LABRADOR OR NEW BRITAIN
NEW FRANCE
LAKE SUPERIOR
LAKE HURON
LAKE MICHIGAN
LAKE ERIE
LAKE ONTARIO OR CATARAKUI
EASTERN SIOUX
SIOUX OR NADOUESSIANS
WESTERN SIOUX
OUTAGAMIS
MASCOUTENS
MESSESAGUES
COUNTRY OF THE PADOUCAS
PANIS
Extensive Meadows full of Buffaloes
OSAGES
VIRGINIA
NORTH CAROLINA
SOUTH CAROLINA
CHICASAWS
CHERAKEES
CREEK INDIANS
GEORGIA
AKANSAS
LOUISIANA
COUNTRY OF THE CENIS
COUNTRY OF THE APALACHES
FLORIDA
GULF OF MEXICO
PENSYLVANIA

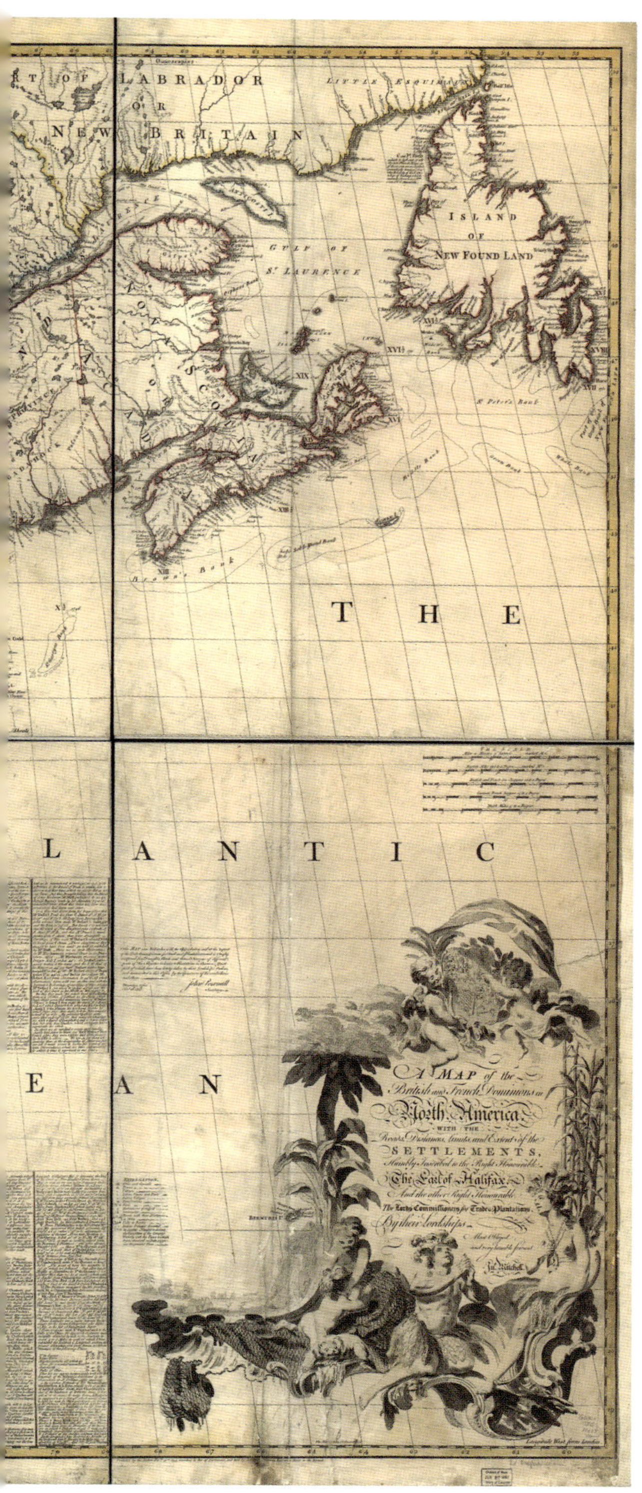

The "Most Important Map in American History"

John Mitchell's map defined the borders of the early United States—more than once.

In 1934, Lawrence Martin, the longtime head of the Geography and Map Division of the Library of Congress, called *A Map of the British and French Dominions in North America* "the most important map in American history." For good reason: It fixed the borders of the United States at multiple crucial times in the nation's development.

John Mitchell took a long, arduous route to creating this map, which commonly bears his name. He had no formal training as a cartographer. Born to a tobacco-farming family in Virginia in 1711, he studied medicine in Scotland, then returned to the Tidewater region in 1732 and experimented in a variety of fields. (Among other pursuits, he conducted autopsies and developed fertilizers.) But by 1746, Mitchell and his wife wearied of the Chesapeake Bay illnesses brought by Atlantic travelers and swamp mosquitoes and set sail for England. Their ship was ransacked by French pirates, so they landed in London with hardly anything in their pockets. Within two years, however, the enterprising Mitchell was elected to the Royal Society, a prestigious fellowship of notable scientists.

Mitchell's membership in the Royal Society and work as a botanist put him in touch with some of the most powerful men in England. As Matthew Edney, professor of geography at the University of Southern Maine, put it to

When *A Map of the British and French Dominions in North America*, created by John Mitchell, was published in 1755, it contained far more detail than any previous map of North America.

National Geographic in 2016: "He's hobnobbing with aristocrats who were really into gardening. And he comes into contact with a lot of politicians who were also demon gardeners."

One of them was George Montagu Dunk, Second Earl of Halifax, a nobleman and key player in English politics.[1] In 1748, Lord Halifax became president of the Board of Trade, which oversaw British possessions overseas. At a time when the British and French were competing ferociously for territory, fish, and fur in North America, he wanted a complete map of the English colonies, and he commissioned Mitchell for the job of preparing one.

Mitchell's first attempt, which he completed in 1750, wasn't satisfactory. But he gained the best resources any mapmaker could hope for, or at least the best available to anyone working more than 3,000 miles away from his subject: Halifax gave him access to the Board of Trade's official documents, and the Board ordered British officials in the colonies to send Mitchell their best maps. And in his follow-up, Mitchell did not disappoint. He synthesized the Crown's surveys, charts, and treaties into one astonishingly impressive new map, which he made in eight sheets. First printed in 1755, a year after war exploded between England and France, the full Mitchell map measured 4.5 feet by 6.5 feet, and contained an amazing wealth of geographic and political data.

Mitchell's map pressed British claims through dozens of inscriptions, while treating the French as interlopers anywhere outside Quebec. "The English have Factories and Settlements in all the Towns of the Creek Indians of any note," Mitchell wrote in one note about an area in western Georgia. "Except Albamas, which was usurped by the French in 1715 but established by the English twenty-eight years before."

It also drew no limits on British authority except borders that were already explicitly accepted by England. The Mitchell map lengthens the western borders of the colonies horizontally, all the way to its left-hand edge. Along those lines, he wrote: "Bounds of Virginia and New-England by Charters, May 23, 1609 and Nov. 3, 1620, extending from Sea to Sea, out of which our other colonies were granted." As far as readers could tell, they stretched all the way to the Pacific Ocean.

---

1 George Montagu Dunk was the Second Earl of Halifax; Halifax, the capital of Nova Scotia, was named after him.

1 Mitchell paid attention to the presence of Native Americans on his map. In its westernmost reaches, for example, he noted the "Country of the Padoucas," an Indigenous people of the southern Great Plains (for whom the city of Paducah, Kentucky, was named).

2 The map's incredible level of detail extends to showing more than a dozen of Lake Michigan's eastern tributaries.

3 Mitchell also listed latitudes and longitudes for locales all along the eastern seaboard of North America.

1

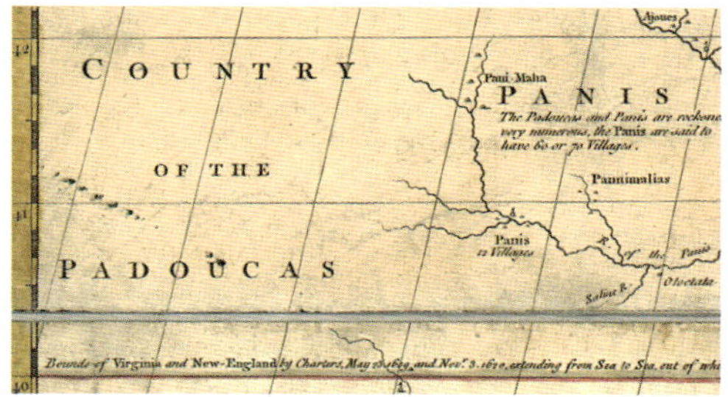

2

3

The Seven Years' War[2] raged until 1763, and when France lost, it was forced to give up its North American lands to England and Spain. Mitchell died in 1768, knowing that his greatest accomplishment had secured for Britain a maximal definition of borders for its American colonies.

Seven years after that, though, the American Revolution ignited at Lexington and Concord. By 1782, it was England who came to the bargaining table as losers. And when negotiators from both sides met in Paris that year, they used an authority they all recognized to come to terms over borders: the Mitchell map. "I am perfectly clear in the Remembrance that the map we used in tracing the boundary was brought to the Treaty by the Commissioners of England, and that it was the same that was published by Mitchell above twenty years before," Benjamin Franklin wrote in 1790, just before he died, to then-Secretary of State Thomas Jefferson. That now worked in favor of the Americans, who won title to land that ranged north to Canada, south to Florida, and pushed west all the way to the Mississippi River—an area far greater than the colonial regions where most of the revolution was actually fought.

A mapmaker who had gone to great lengths to expand British prerogative as far as he could was ultimately instrumental in giving away this same territory. It was, as Edney has stated, "an irony of empire."

---

2 In North America, this conflict has often been called the French and Indian War.

HAVERHILL
AMESBURY
SALSBURY
METHUEN
BRADFORD
N.PORT
NEWBURY
ANDOVER
ROXFORD
ROWLEY
MIDDLETON
TOPSFIELD
IPSWICH
LYNNFIELD
HAMILTON
WENHAM
DANVERS
BEVERLY
MANCHESTER
CLOCESTER
SALEM
LYNN
MARBLE HEAD
CHELSEA

The Most Political of Political Maps

The "Gerry-mander," an ominous creature that sounded the alarm on an even more ominous political tool.

In any representative democracy, legislative constituencies need to have a roughly equal number of citizens for all votes to carry the same weight. Districts in the United States House of Representatives, for example, have an average population of about 760,000. Of course, the number of people in any single district will change over time, sometimes radically, as people move in and out. To correct for this, the US Constitution mandates a census every ten years. After each count, House districts are reapportioned among the states. And then each one "redistricts," or redraws its internal boundaries for state legislative seats as well as congressional districts.

The potential for shenanigans in this process became clear early in the life of the American republic, as political parties began to emerge. If one set of politicians controlled the levers for redistricting, why couldn't they set up voting precincts that would make it hard or even impossible for their opponents to win elections? Well, they could. So they did.

In 1811, for example, tensions were running hot in Massachusetts between Federalists (the political descendants of John Adams and Alexander Hamilton, who supported a strong national government) and Democratic-Republicans (allies of Thomas Jefferson and James Madison, who believed in less centralization and tended to back France over Great Britain in foreign-policy disputes). As the US moved toward conflict with England (which would erupt into the War of 1812), Federalist leaders howled in protest—and Massachusetts's Democratic-Republican Governor Elbridge Gerry not only fired Federalist officeholders, he charged some Federalist-aligned newspapers with libel. Around the same time, Democratic-Republican legislators reworked the map for the Massachusetts State Senate. And instead of following tradition and using county lines as borders, they herded areas heavy with Federalist voters into a minimal chunk of territory in the interior of Essex County (surrounded by one particularly contorted district) and Governor Gerry signed the plan into law. James Austin, who authored a biography of Gerry, wrote that the governor did so very reluctantly. (Then again, Austin was Gerry's son-in-law. Others were less charitable.)

In *The Gerry-Mander*, published in 1812, illustrator Elkanah Tisdale sketched a reworked map of the Massachusetts State Senate district as a hunched beast with a reptilian head and sharp claws, then added wings for a dragon-like effect.

At a dinner of Federalist supporters afterward, an illustrator named Elkanah Tisdale sketched the new district as a curved, clawed reptile. Guests remarked that the creature resembled a salamander. "Gerry-mander," pitched Richard Alsop, a translator and satirist in attendance. The name stuck—and Gerry's legacy was sealed.[1]

Several newspapers published *The Gerry-Mander* (page 57) as a satirical cartoon in March 1812. The *Boston Gazette* called the district "a horrid monster," and dramatically quoted the Gospel of Matthew: "O generation of vipers! Who hath warned you of the wrath to come?" But the map worked. In the statewide vote that year, the Federalists defeated Gerry in his bid for reelection and gained more than one hundred seats in the 649-member State House of Representatives. But in the freshly gerrymandered State Senate, the Democratic-Republicans won eight new seats, giving them a 29–11 majority.

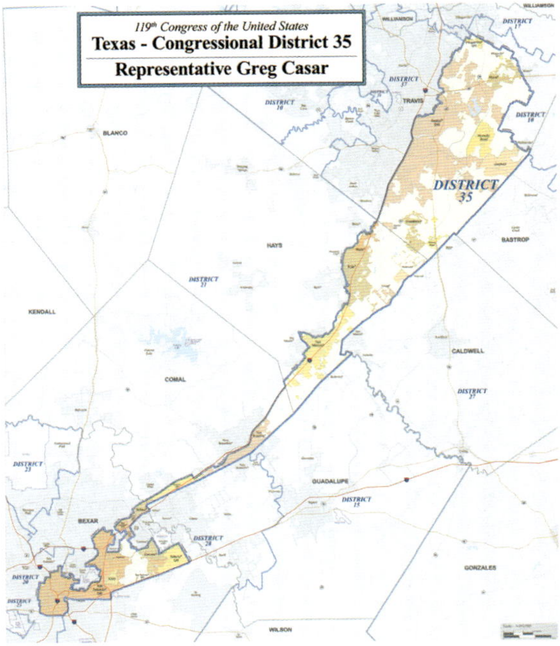

This map, published by the US Census Bureau in 2025, shows modern gerrymandering at its most absurd and precise: Texas's 35th Congressional District in the 119th Congress.

Though gerrymandering spread after Massachusetts showed its potential, for many years there were at least a few checks on just how bad it could get. In most states, neither major political party could be sure of permanent political advantage, so Democrats and Republicans both had to worry that if either party acted in some truly extreme manner, their opponents would someday seek revenge. Further, drawing political districts was never a perfectly precise art; redistricting always left some room for unintentional outcomes. And as late as 1995, the Supreme Court ruled that racial gerrymandering—drawing boundaries to limit the influence of minority groups—was unconstitutional.[2]

But all of those constraints began to collapse around 2010. After Barack Obama's election in 2008, Republican strategists focused on flipping control of closely divided state legislatures. They mounted a national effort—called the Redistricting Majority Project, or REDMAP—to seize control of the line-drawing efforts that would follow

1 Gerry's name, though ever after linked with the word *gerrymander*, was actually pronounced with a hard G, like *Gary*.

the national census two years later. Once these decision-makers were in place, they used new software to craft borders for maximum partisan advantage with surgical precision. Pundits have compared the resulting contours of US congressional districts to amoebas, starfish, the shape of a praying mantis, and an outline of Goofy kicking Donald Duck, among many other unnatural images. And these designs stayed under the control of state and local lawmakers: In 2019, the US Supreme Court (in a 5–4 decision) ruled that questions about partisan gerrymandering involve political issues that federal courts can't decide.

Consider the amazingly sliver-shaped map of Texas's 35th Congressional District (opposite). It includes parts of two cities that aren't particularly close to each other. It runs through five counties, sometimes in swaths hardly wider than Interstate 35. Its shape makes no sense—unless you understand it as an attempt to shepherd Democratic voters in heavily Latino San Antonio and college-town Austin into one and only one district. Its contours were struck down twice by federal judges, but allowed to stand by the Supreme Court. Even this bizarre splinter, however, allowed too much blue onto the map for Republican legislators in Texas: In 2025, they passed a redistricting plan explicitly designed to gain their party up to five more congressional seats, in part by reshaping the 35th.

Of course, both sides try to gerrymander. But Republicans have had a serious first-mover advantage. By 2019, six states were governed by "minority rule"—where the party controlling a majority of seats in the state legislature earned only a minority of votes in the most recent election—according to a report by the University of Southern California. All six were large states with lines recently redrawn to help Republicans.

For now, the last word on gerrymandering rests with strategist Karl Rove. In 2010, he wrote an op-ed entitled: "The GOP Targets State Legislatures: He who controls redistricting can control Congress."

---

2 There are reasons why gerrymandering has proven to be particularly persistent in the United States, compared with other democracies. When lines do need to be redrawn, the US entrusts that job to partisan politicians, rather than independent commissions (as happens in Canada and the United Kingdom) or groups where all major parties are represented (as in New Zealand). And beyond keeping districts contiguous, there are hardly any constraints on how American political artists can redraw boundaries—most aren't legally required to hew to previous lines.

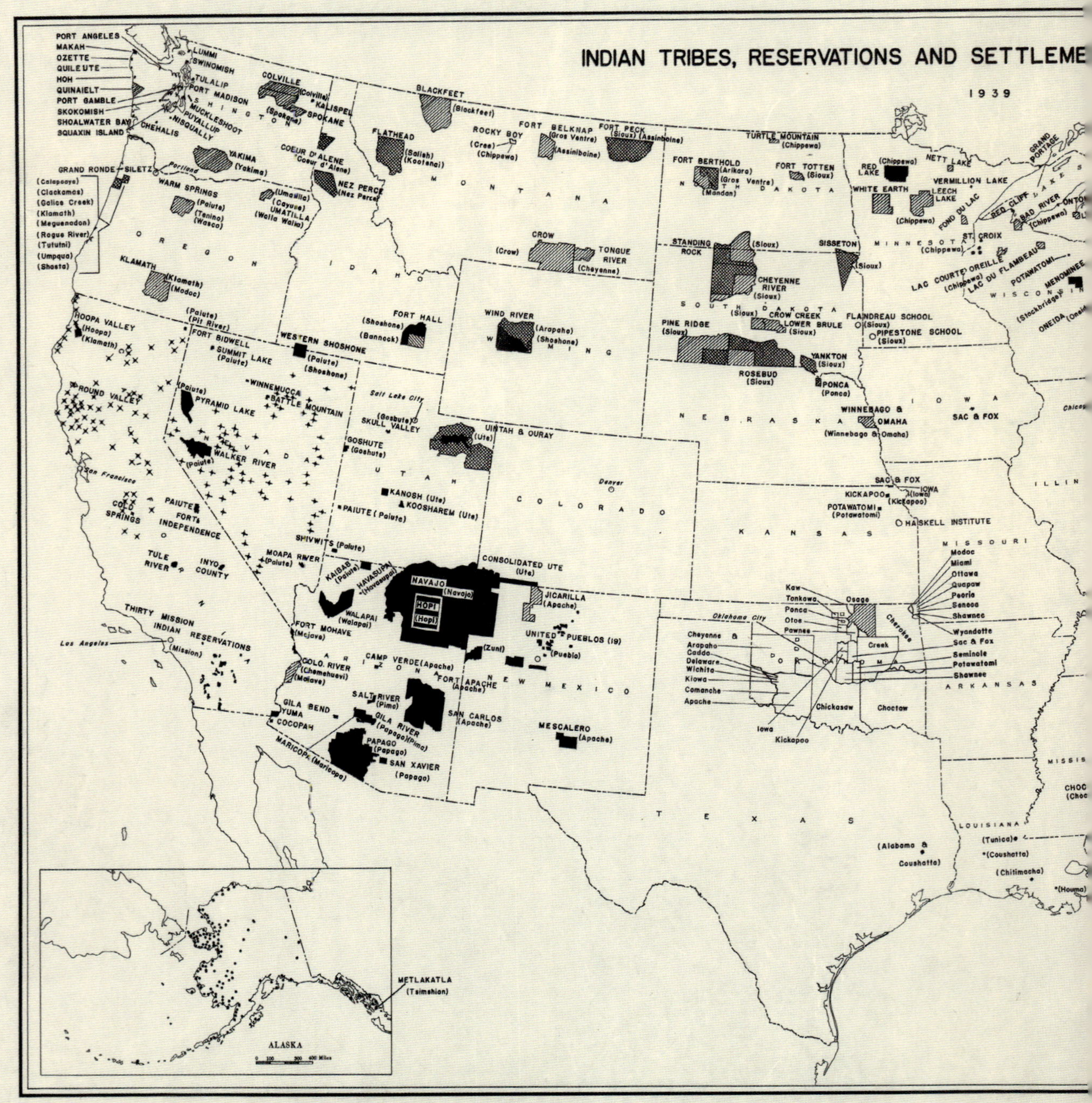
INDIAN TRIBES, RESERVATIONS AND SETTLEME
1939
ALASKA
METLAKATLA
(Tsimshian)

The Map of American Displacement

Official US sources did not preserve many maps made by Indigenous Americans, but they did create this record of their resettlement.

Indian Tribes, Reservations, and Settlements in the United States, produced in 1939 by Sam Attahvich, a Comanche mapmaker for the US Department of the Interior.

PLENTY OF CONTEMPORARY maps will show you where Indigenous peoples of North America used to dwell. But very few maps drawn by Native Americans at the time they lived across the continent survive today, and hardly any are political maps. At the risk of overgeneralizing severely—because hundreds of nations with diverse customs have inhabited regions stretching for millions of square miles for thousands of years—this is for two basic reasons.

One is that while many Indigenous cultures ascribed importance to natural and political boundaries, most didn't record them in ways designed to be permanent. Indigenous mapping traditions include many examples of maps written into the ground itself—sketched in earth or etched in ice, with piles, channels, and stones added for detail. These maps are useful for conveying information from one group to another, but they ultimately wash away like drawings on a beach. Many Indigenous Americans also drew maps on animal skins, which lasted somewhat longer. But consider this astonishing fact: Of the more than 1.5 million single-sheet maps the US Library of Congress Geography and Map Division has in its collection, *zero* are original Native American maps from before European contact with the Americas.

Further, Indigenous maps, including some that provided key assistance to European, Canadian, and American explorers, generally focused on showing the time it took to get from one place to another, rather than striving to represent natural features to scale. Lines "often looked alike, but could indicate rivers, game trails or war routes," according to a 2009 Illinois State Museum exhibit. "Distances were relative . . . the format was a narrative of travel in the area." Broadly speaking, Indigenous American maps were concerned with social rather than geographic reality.

But one outstanding map *about* Indigenous Americans showed in real time what settler colonialism ultimately did in North America: *Indian Tribes, Reservations, and Settlements in the United States*, published in 1939 by the Office (later Bureau) of Indian Affairs, a division of US Department of the Interior. What's really striking is that this map was researched and illustrated by Comanche mapmaker Sam Attahvich.

Attahvich's map distinguishes among reservations, colonies in Nevada, and rancherias in California, but these were all parcels of land reserved for "American Indians" as tribal homelands—though typically exempt from US state laws, these tracts of land were actually owned and administered by the federal government, not Indigenous nations themselves. The map's labeling is careful and clear, its detail is exhaustive, and it leaves one overwhelming impression: The people who used to have the run of the continent are now sequestered in various dots and blots scattered across the country.

Simply by existing, the Attahvich map was a snapshot of dispossession. The United States government had begun negotiating peace treaties with Indigenous groups before the Revolutionary War even ended, ultimately striking more than 370 deals with tribes from 1778 to 1871. But all too often, when American settlers overran agreed-on boundaries, the US then nullified those agreements or forced new tribal concessions. As just one example, the Indian Removal Act of 1830 and subsequent threats by President Andrew Jackson forced almost fifty thousand Indigenous Americans off 25 million acres of (mostly southern) land to "Indian Territory" west of the Mississippi. Attahvich produced his map during a relatively benign time in federal-Native relations, when New Deal initiatives recognized local Indigenous governments and invested in economic development on reservations. But the pendulum swung again in the 1950s, when the federal government terminated its recognition of more than one hundred nations, leading Indigenous groups to lose about 2.5 million more acres of land, and encouraged Indigenous Americans to move to cities and assimilate.

The Attahvich map was first published in May 1939 as part of *Indians at Work*, a mimeographed magazine printed by the Office of Indian Affairs to highlight the efforts of the "Indian Division" of the Civilian Conservation Corps, a federal program that put Americans to work during the Great Depression. In a note called "Where Are the Indians Now?" Floyd LaRouche, director of information for the Office, noted that "schools, clubs, members of Congress, newspapers and magazines" had all asked about the location of tribes. And he lauded Attahvich for his "patience and persistence" in putting that information together and "painstaking map drawing skill." We know essentially nothing else about Attahvich—except that his Comanche identity was important enough to him for him to attach it to his name on this map.

1

LAS
MALVINAS
SON
ARGENTINAS
ARGENTINA
• LIBRE •

2

LANZAMIENTO DE COHETES
EN LA ANTARTIDA
SECRETARIA DE AERONAUTICA
27 50 PESOS
REPUBLICA
ARGENTINA
a. EXPOSICION

3

REPUBLICA ARGENTINA
20c.
LEY 18.188
5º ANIVERSARIO OPERACION 90º POLO SUR
CASA DE MONEDA
1970

4

200
ANIVERSARIO
Primer izamiento de la
bandera nacional en
las Islas Malvinas
MALVINAS
ARGENTINAS
$90
REPUBLICA ARGENTINA
2020
200 ANIVERSARIO
Primer izamiento de la bandera nacional en las Islas Malvinas

The Political Maps That Get Stuck to Envelopes

Propaganda maps can fit in your hand and travel the world as postage stamps.

Argentina has shown how a country can effectively and repeatedly mix cartography, postage, and propaganda.

1 In 1930, it issued a stamp calling the Falklands by their Spanish name (las Malvinas) and vividly asserting, by text and image, that the islands were part of Argentina.

2 Argentina also claims a wedge of territory in Antarctica, including the peninsula it calls Tierra San Martín. A stamp issued in 1966 highlighted its supposed slice of the southernmost continent along with a successful rocket launch—peak points of nationalist pride.

3 In 1965, an Argentine expedition planted its flag at the South Pole. And five years later, this stamp celebrated the anniversary of that trip while using the flagpole to trace the arc of Argentina's Antarctic claims.

4 A 2020 stamp is more subtle, but only a little. It shows a satellite photo of the Falklands—but was issued as part of a sheet that celebrates the two hundredth anniversary of the first Argentine flag flying over the islands.

Billions of people regularly use the smallest form of political maps: stamps.

Even before airmail, countries realized they had to cooperate on basic postal rules so their citizens could send and receive international mail. That's led to a long tradition of nations accepting postage from one another, no matter what incoming stamps might say. In 1966, the president of the Royal Geographical Society said this: "Most governments are now alive to the . . . propaganda value of postage stamps. Since stamps or their equivalent must be used in prepayment of the carriage of mails by any country which is a member of the Universal Postal Union—virtually every country in the world—it costs the issuing country practically nothing to convert this into a worldwide advertising system."[1]

Stamps convey sovereignty. Colonial states typically print stamps for their provinces. Newly independent countries often start issuing postage as soon as they are born. And when a nation ceases to exist, its stamps, often sent into exile unintentionally, live on as symbols of the old country. North Ingria, an area near Finland, was an independent state for under two years, from 1919 to 1920. But you can still find its stamps on eBay.

Other stamps do even more: They proclaim a nation's right to disputed territory. Though the maps they carry may be tiny, sometimes that actually works in their favor, because a little canvas needs a visceral image to make its point. Todd Pierce, a data visualization expert and self-described "cartographic philatelist," has written that maps on stamps carry two kinds of political messages. One is, "This area exists." The other is, "'This area is claimed,' either by locals or by a distant government."

Either way, their meaning is clear: "Don't mess with this area."

1 That man's name was—seriously—Sir Dudley Stamp.

KAESONG
NEUTRAL ZONE (HAN ESTUARY)
KANGHWADO
KORYO-SAN
HYOLGU-SAN
PYORIP-SAN
YONGGAK-SAN
CHESOK-SAN
CH'ONMA-SAN
KUKSA-BONG
P'anmunjom
126°30'
37°45'
SAL-SOM
TONGGO

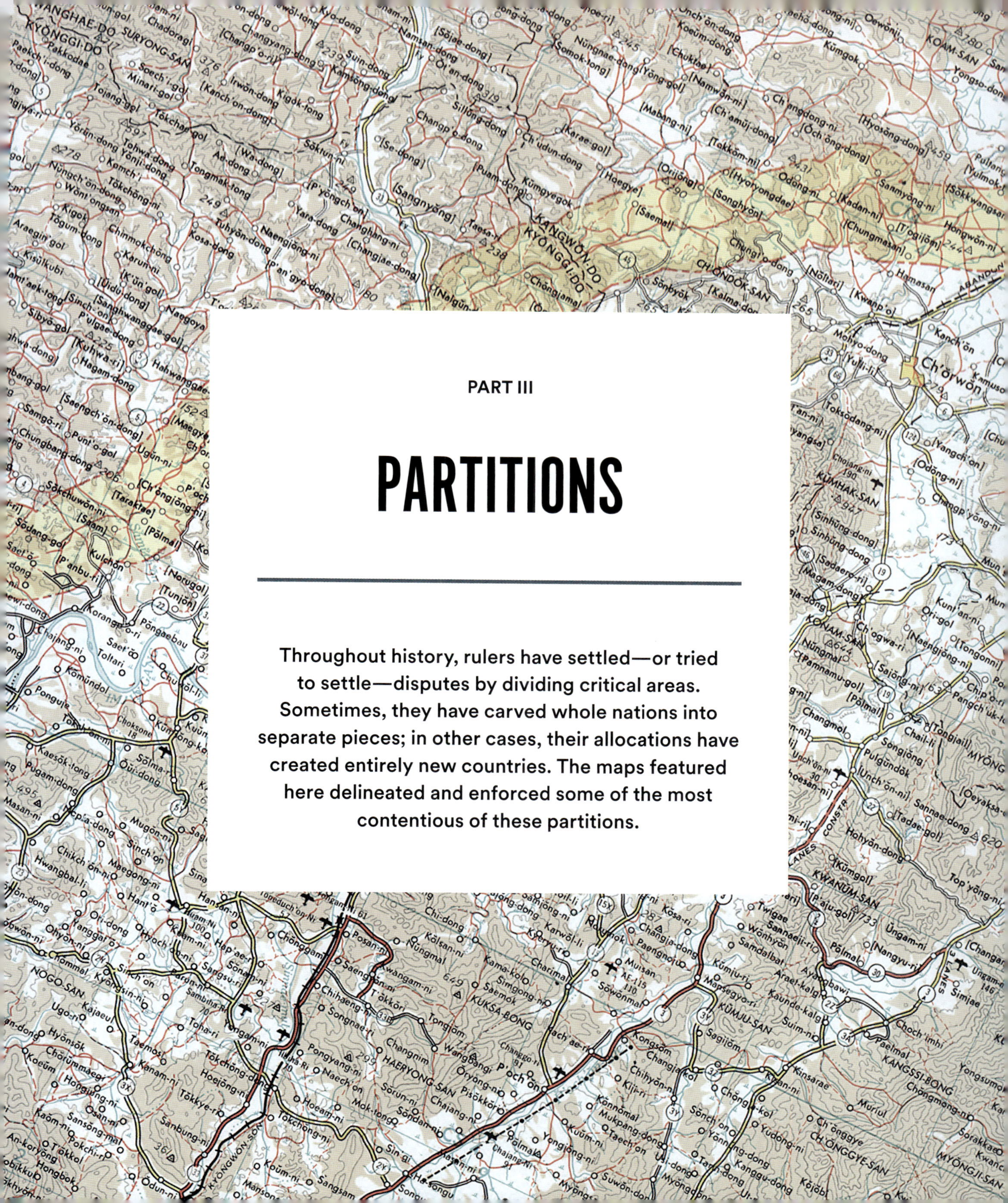

PART III

PARTITIONS

Throughout history, rulers have settled—or tried to settle—disputes by dividing critical areas. Sometimes, they have carved whole nations into separate pieces; in other cases, their allocations have created entirely new countries. The maps featured here delineated and enforced some of the most contentious of these partitions.

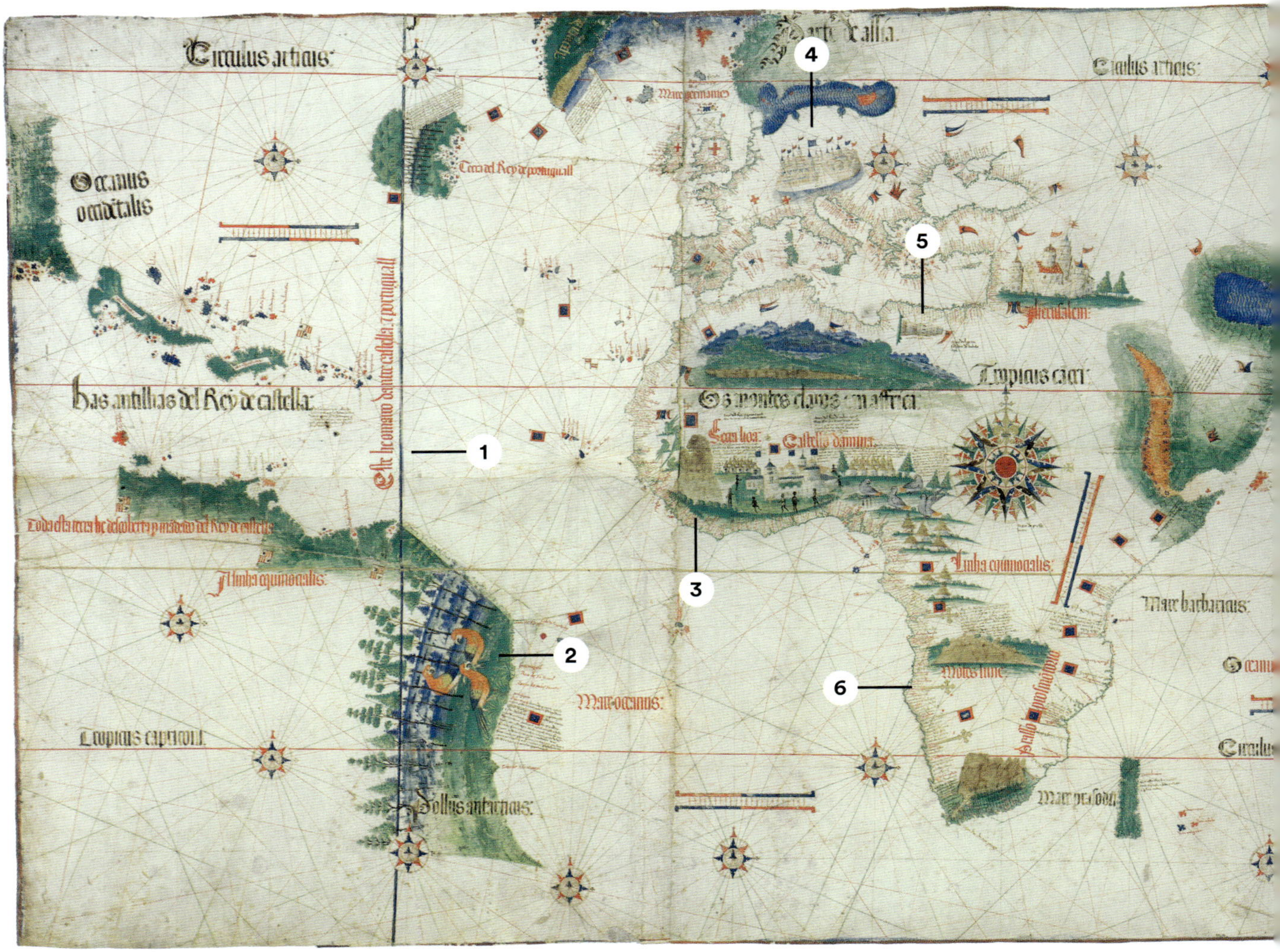

1

2

The Map That Divided the World

The Cantino planisphere shows with great flair how European powers were moving from exploration to conquest at the turn of the sixteenth century.

3

The Cantino planisphere was commissioned by Alberto Cantino and published in 1502 in Portugal.

1 This bold vertical blue line apportioned the entire non-European world: According to the 1494 Treaty of Tordesillas, all lands to the west of the meridian that weren't already Christianized belonged to Spain, while areas to the east went to Portugal.

The map is spangled with fanciful illustrations, such as 2 colorful birds in eastern South America and 3 a mountain in the shape of a lion in western Africa.

4

5

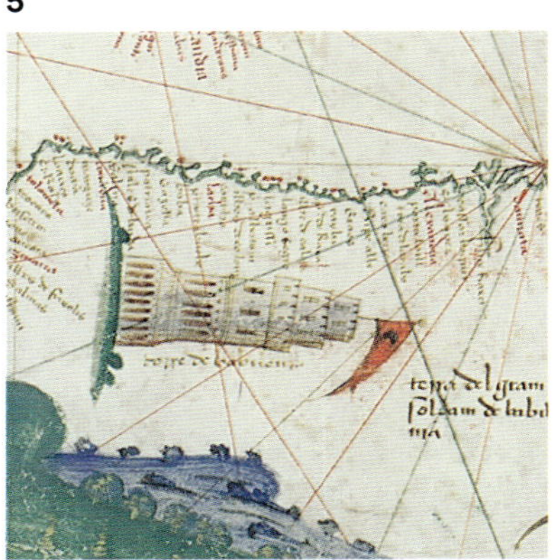

6

THE MODERN HISTORY of political maps begins in the late fifteenth century, at the start of what we now call the Age of Exploration. European voyagers, searching for India and Southeast Asia, extended and compiled geographic information about faraway lands, both to guide future trips and to claim the territories where they planted their flags. This spurred furious competition among the countries sponsoring the expeditions and triggered revolutionary changes in seafaring, surveying, and mapmaking.

When Christopher Columbus, who led the first European expedition to reach the West Indies, tried to return to Spain, he didn't get back there on his first try. Instead, he landed in the Azores, a group of islands controlled by Portugal, and then a storm forced him to dock in Lisbon in March 1493. King John II of Portugal promptly told Columbus he had been trespassing in Portuguese territory, and put the word out that a fleet would head west to take possession of any lands newly discovered by Columbus. In response, King Ferdinand II and Queen Isabella I of Spain asked for intervention from Pope Alexander VI—who just so happened to be a Spaniard (and a member of the notoriously libertine Borgia family, with a brood of mistresses and children). Alexander issued a series of papal bulls, or edicts, that came down so heavily in favor of Spain that King John II objected, and not even the Spanish monarchs believed the rulings would stick. So in June 1494, negotiators from the two countries, meeting in the small Spanish town of Tordesillas, struck a revised deal: All non-Christian lands outside Europe that were encountered for the first time would be split along a line of longitude running north to south about 1,200 miles west of the Cape Verde Islands, off the western coast of Africa. Just like that, they divided the entire Western Hemisphere.

4 Venice, the commercial capital of Europe, and Jerusalem, the spiritual capital of the West, are depicted as great cities flying many flags.

5 The Lighthouse of Alexandria lies on its side, symbolizing its destruction by earthquakes hundreds of years earlier.

6 These *padrões*, or stone markers, were built and left behind by Portuguese explorers in West Africa.

Meanwhile, European explorers were sailing south as well as west. Vasco da Gama of Portugal, for instance, took a route around the Cape of Good Hope in South Africa, landed in what is now Mozambique and Kenya, reached India, and returned to Lisbon in 1499. As a result of his success, it suddenly seemed that Portugal would get direct access to all sorts of treasures—fabrics, gold, jewels, spices, wood—and break the monopoly that Italian merchants had held on trading with the East since the days of Marco Polo, more than two hundred years earlier. All the new trade helped turn Lisbon into an international frontier town at the turn of the sixteenth century—a crossroads for both business and espionage.

In public, Alberto Cantino represented the Italian Duke of Ferrara in Lisbon, attending meetings and negotiating business deals. Privately, he spied for the Duke too. In December 1501, he paid a mapmaker twelve gold ducats to bring together all the latest information Portugal had about coastlines, islands, seas, and trading routes onto one map. The identity of that cartographer remained secret, and historians still aren't sure in what capacity (or even if) he worked for the Portuguese crown. But in the year it took to illustrate the map that has come down through the ages bearing Cantino's name, he created a beautiful depiction of a world where civilizations were about to collide.

Painted by hand from a palette of rich reds, blues, greens, and gold, the Cantino planisphere stretches over six pieces of parchment to form a 40-by-86-inch Renaissance portrait of the world. Naturally, the regions most familiar to southern Europeans are drawn most accurately, with increasing distortion toward the edges of the map. But the entire map is chockablock with decorative elements.[1] Some of the map's adornments, such as its illustrations of great cities, have traditional or commercial significance. But many of the flourishes have little or nothing to do with seafaring or trade routes: Three bright parrots sit in the Amazon, while a large lion marks the mountains of Sierra Leone. The Red Sea is colored red. The Cantino map was drawn in utmost secrecy, but it was created by an artist bursting for an audience.

The blue Treaty of Tordesillas meridian is the most prominent vertical line in the map, indicating just how important the deal was between Spain

---

1 Historians say many were contributed by Flemish miniaturists, artists who were working in Lisbon at the time.

and Portugal. But it's impossible to tell whether it's simply unfamiliarity that warps the lands of the Western Hemisphere on the Cantino map, or something more. Brazil looks like it's turned counterclockwise, while Newfoundland, recently discovered and shown as an island, seems twisted in the opposite direction. It's almost as though someone was trying to maximize the area occupied by both places on the eastern (Portuguese) side of the Tordesillas line! The original Portuguese sources of the data for this map may have believed this rendering to be accurate. Or one of them, or the mapmaker, may have shifted lines for political purposes. After more than five hundred years, bias is visible, but its motives are not.

Late in 1502, Cantino smuggled the planisphere from Lisbon to Genoa, where it was copied by Nicolo di Caverio, one of that city's top mapmakers. The original document reached Cantino's employer, the Duke of Ferrara, while other versions spread Portugal's trading secrets across Italy and influenced maps created throughout Europe for decades afterward.[2]

The Treaty of Tordesillas worked well enough at keeping Spain and Portugal from going to war. But the treaty's two most important effects were mostly unintentional. For one thing, North and South America both turned out to be much bigger than the early European explorers realized. So the Tordesillas line didn't slice the territory the treaty addressed into anything like two even pieces. It granted to Portugal the Atlantic coast of Brazil (where Portuguese is still spoken to this day) and ended up allowing Spain to claim a huge mass of land beyond the line, including the west coast of South America and what is now Florida, Texas, and California.

Further, the Tordesillas treaty didn't apply to territories already conquered by Christian nations. For instance, Columbus had claimed the Antilles Islands for Spain, so they remained under Spanish control even though they fell on the Portuguese side of the pact's line of demarcation. This brought to the Americas the "Doctrine of Discovery"—the idea that a European power had the right to rule any land its explorers

---

2 Centuries later, in 1859, the ducal palace of Modena was vandalized during the Risorgimento, or uprising that led to the unification of Italy, and the Cantino planisphere vanished. Incredibly enough, Giuseppe Boni, the local library director, later came across the map and recovered it at a butcher shop, where it was being used as a window screen. It is now located at the Biblioteca Estense Universitaria in Modena.

reached before other Christians. Other nations, including England and France, were happy to adopt this dogma even if they didn't agree with how Spain and Portugal had divvied up the hemisphere. And for more than two centuries afterward, European powers raced to colonize North and South America, recognizing no authority but their own, waging war on Indigenous civilizations rather than each other. From subjugation to extermination, the consequences for Native peoples were devastating.

Many Americans have no idea that this Doctrine of Discovery, enshrined at Tordesillas, later became a foundation of property law in the United States. The Supreme Court ruled in 1823 that when it came to settling America, finders were keepers, and Natives had no sovereignty.[3] And it has continued to uphold the idea that Indigenous people cannot fully control the land they occupy. In 2005, Justice Ruth Bader Ginsburg wrote: "Under the 'doctrine of discovery,' . . . fee title to the lands occupied by Indians when the colonists arrived became invested in the . . . discovering European nation and later the original states and the United States."[4]

That's half a world and more than half a millennium away from Alberto Cantino, his audacious spy mission, and the anonymous but superb work of art he commissioned. But it all goes to show one of its most important lessons: Sometimes a political map's greatest impact is on the people it renders invisible.

---

3 In *Johnson v. McIntosh*, Chief Justice John Marshall Harlan wrote: "Discovery gave title to the government by whose subjects, or by whose authority, it was made . . . The rights of the original inhabitants . . . were necessarily diminished . . . The history of America from its discovery to the present day proves, we think, the universal recognition of these principles."

4 Ginsburg's majority opinion in *City of Sherrill v. Oneida Indian Nation of New York* held that even after the Oneida Nation bought back some of their original territory, they still had to pay taxes on that land.

The Map for Carving Up a Continent

At Berlin in 1884, Western leaders used a giant map to set the terms of their "Scramble for Africa."

It was the most audacious use ever of a political map.

In November 1884, envoys from fourteen of the world's most powerful countries gathered in Berlin to meet at the palace of Otto von Bismarck, founder and chancellor of the German Empire. And over the following three months, they talked and bargained, mostly in a large stateroom where a 16-foot-tall map of Africa hung on one wall. The image of their deliberations shown here was drawn by Adalbert von Rössler, a German artist, for *Allgemeine Illustrirte Zeitung*, or "Illustrated news," a weekly magazine. (Bismarck is seated on the right side of the table, the large figure with a balding head and walrus mustache.)

Africa was at that time home to about 140 million people, or nearly 10 percent of the globe's population. None of them were at the Berlin Conference. Indeed, hardly any of the men in attendance had ever set foot there. Nevertheless, by the end of the following February, the participants laid the groundwork for dividing up that entire continent among themselves and the nations they represented.

Europeans began establishing coastal colonies in west Africa more than four centuries before the Berlin Conference, and launched the Atlantic slave trade around 1526. Arab forces, including slave traders, had pushed into northern Africa long before that, during the Middle Ages. Mediterranean Europe and Africa had crosspollinated back in the days of the Roman Empire. But the Industrial Revolution triggered a different kind of interest in—and aggressiveness toward—intertropical Africa. To get at resources like copper, ivory, rubber, and palm oil, European empires expanded their conquests into the continent's hinterlands.

An image from the 1884 Berlin Conference, drawn by Adalbert von Rössler, a German artist, for *Allgemeine Illustrirte Zeitung*, or "Illustrated news," a weekly magazine.

Portugal, which already had southern colonies in Angola and Mozambique for more than two hundred years, looked to move inward. Britain eyed a huge stretch of territory running from Egypt—where English investors had provided key financing for the Suez Canal in the 1860s—all the way to South Africa, where it had annexed territory in 1806. France, which had occupied the city of Algiers in 1830, already considered Algeria part of its own country, and aimed to expand its influence around the rest of North Africa. Germany's Bismarck didn't care much about Africa itself, but wanted to thwart the English and French. And nobody could outdo the avarice of King Leopold II of Belgium. Leopold, a cousin of Britain's Queen Victoria, badly wanted colonies of his own, and in 1879, he set up the International Association of the Congo, a private company, to explore central Africa and keep as much of it as possible under his own dominion.

By the mid-1880s, temperatures were rising to multiple flashpoints around the continent. The rivals agreed to meet and, if possible, hash out their differences.

The Berlin Conference has a reputation for being the place where the leaders of Europe ended up literally drawing property lines across the map of Africa, but that's not quite what happened. Rather, they set rules for the grand game they saw themselves playing. They agreed to make the Congo and Niger Rivers (the second- and third-biggest in Africa, after the Nile) free for ship traffic, and to establish the Congo Basin—a huge area in equatorial Africa, which Europeans were only beginning to penetrate—as a free trade zone. They further agreed to notify one another upon taking control of new lands on African coasts. The conference essentially codified the rush to seize and exploit new territories, which became known as the Scramble for Africa. And as European spheres of interest took more definite shape, it was later, mostly bilateral, agreements that set many of their borders. For example, in 1886, England and Germany divided a vast chunk of land into British East Africa (now Kenya and Uganda) and German East Africa (now Tanzania, Rwanda, and Burundi), relegating the Sultan of Zanzibar, its former ruler, to a 10-mile-wide strip on the Indian Ocean.

But the giant map of Africa that literally loomed over the Berlin ballroom provided the context for the negotiations at the conference and afterward. It's as though the continent were a giant pizza and the imperial powers, after many years of gnawing around the crust, all wanted deeper bites—and got them. Within a generation after the Berlin Conference,

General Map of Africa, part of a collection of treaties and maps published by the national archives of the United Kingdom, shows via color-coded borders that by 1909 the proportion of Africa under European rule had risen to 90 percent.

GENERAL MAP OF AFRICA
SHEWING APPROXIMATELY
THE TERRITORIAL BOUNDARIES AND SPHERES OF INFLUENCE OF THE DIFFERENT EUROPEAN AND OTHER STATES ON THE AFRICAN CONTINENT, 1909.
NORTH ATLANTIC OCEAN
MEDITERRANEAN SEA
CASPIAN SEA
PERSIA
MOROCCO
ALGERIA
TRIPOLI
LIBYAN DESERT
EGYPT
FRENCH WEST AFRICA
BELGIAN CONGO
GERMAN EAST AFRICA
NORTH WESTERN RHODESIA
SOUTHERN RHODESIA
CAPE COLONY
SOUTH ATLANTIC OCEAN
INDIAN OCEAN
REFERENCE TO COLOURING
BRITISH, Possessions and Protectorates
FRENCH
ITALIAN
GERMAN
PORTUGUESE
SPANISH
INDEPENDENT STATES
BELGIAN CONGO
RAILWAYS open
constructing or projected
THE FIGURES REFER TO THE BOUNDARY TREATIES AND OTHER DOCUMENTS CONTAINED IN THE BODY OF THE WORK.
The Boundaries shown on this Map are approximately correct, but should not be consulted as regards detail.

Europeans controlled almost the entire continent of Africa, as shown on *General Map of Africa* (previous page), published in 1909.

The Berlin Conference participants signed a document binding them to "watch over the preservation of the native tribes . . . care for the improvement of the conditions of their moral and material well-being . . . and help in suppressing slavery, and especially the slave trade." They might have written these words just to win approval from antislavery and anti-imperialist advocates, but even if the phrases were well intentioned, they were soon overrun by realities on the ground.

As just one example, Leopold II, king of Belgium and a self-proclaimed humanitarian, worked assiduously to convince the other conference signatories to recognize his holding company as sovereign over an enormous area in the Congo Basin.[1] In 1885, after the conference, he renamed that territory the "Congo Free State." And he then set about using forced labor to extract as much ivory, rubber, and wood from it as he could, as quickly as possible. Troops from Leopold's private armies specialized in storming native villages, holding women hostage and ordering men to cut or tap trees. His forces often starved their captives, worked laborers to death, and shot anyone who protested. Most notoriously, to keep track of how many bullets they used, they chopped off and collected the heads and hands of rebels.

Leopold's excesses and unpopularity[2] eventually forced him to transfer control of Congo Free State to the Belgian Parliament in 1908. But by then, something like 5 million Congolese had died under his tyranny.

"The partitioning of Africa . . . with the Berlin Conference of 1884, brought colonial imperialism to flower," the historian W. E. B. Du Bois wrote in 1943. "In the nineteenth century the African trade in men changed to a trade in raw materials. . . . [T]henceforth the political domination which ensured monopoly of raw materials to the various contending empires was predicated on the exploitation of African labor inside the continent."

---

1 The Belgian claim was essentially the expanse that today makes up the Democratic Republic of the Congo, known as Zaire from 1971 to 1997.

2 Among other things, Leopold had what *Encyclopedia Britannica* calls a "well-known penchant for teenaged girls."

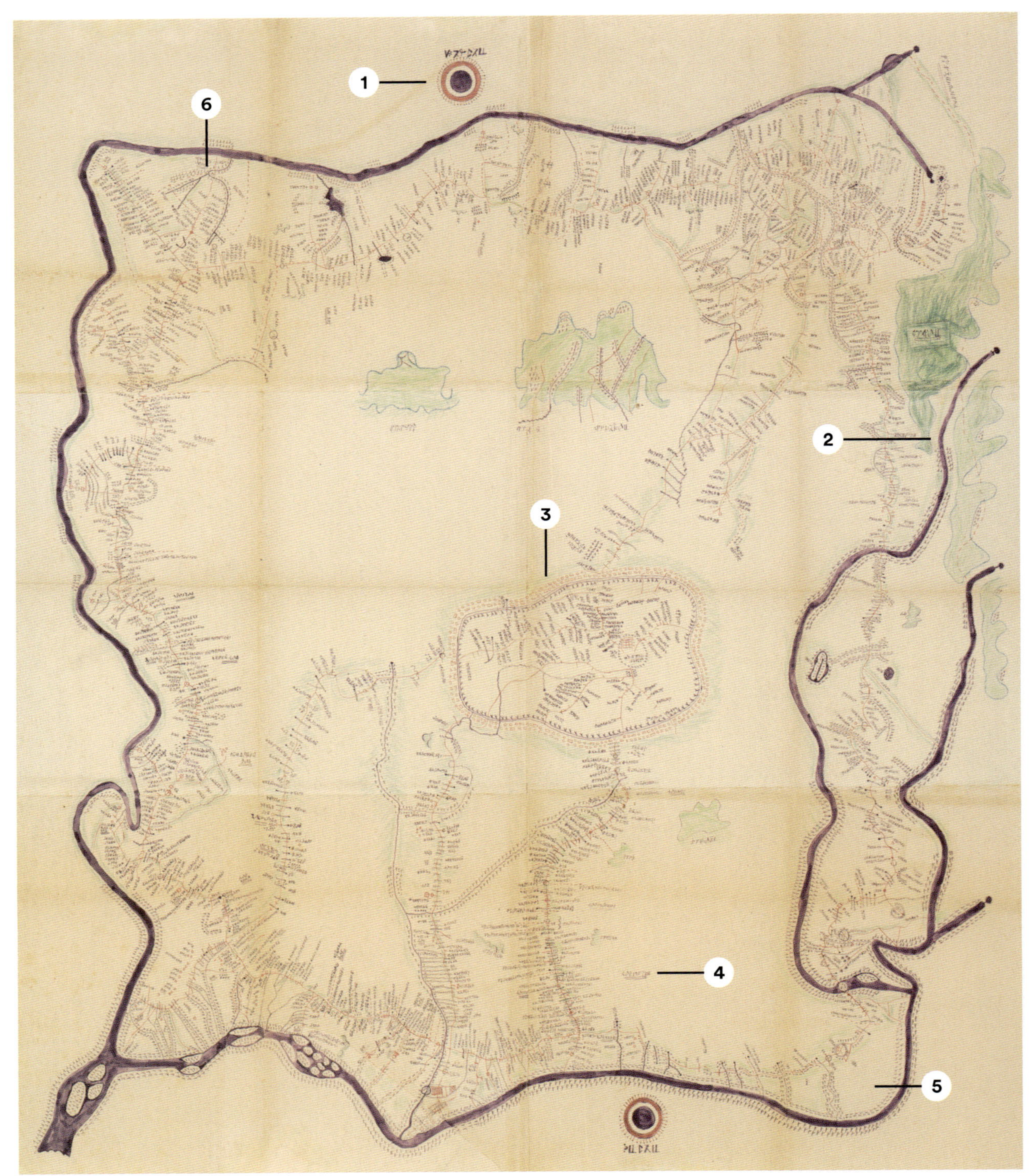
1
6
2
3
4
5

A Map for Africans by Africans

Ibrahim Njoya of Bamum used a language he invented and surveys he led to create a map of his kingdom.

Among the multitude of societies that spanned intertropical Africa in the millennia before Europeans colonized the continent, very few produced documents that most of us would recognize today as political maps. That says more about our modern imaginations than their ambitions or skills. There is, of course, no one "African" style in any art. But eastern, southern, and western African cultures often developed cartography to meet the needs of shifting agriculture, where people cultivate plots for a short time, then move to different land. This practice puts a premium on communicating distances and other information quickly and personally, rather than recording and archiving permanent borders. And it led to very different traditions than those that arose in Europe or East Asia. Thomas Bassett, professor of geography at the University of Illinois, listed some of them in *The History of Cartography* in 1998: "mnemonic maps [memorization], body art (scarification, tattoos), the layout of villages, and the design and orientation of buildings."

"Even if we employ the most general definition of a map as a 'graphic representation of the geographical setting,'" Bassett wrote, "we are bound to exclude the bulk of what may justifiably be called mapmaking in the African context."

One astounding exception comes from the early-twentieth-century work of King Ibrahim Njoya, ruler of Bamum, a grasslands domain in what is now the northwestern part of Cameroon. Njoya descended from a royal line that stretched back to 1394, and became the seventeenth *mfon*, or dynastic ruler of Bamum, in 1886, just as Germany was using military force to cement its claims to the region it called Kamerun. He was a brilliant thinker who invented his people's first written language: Inspired by a dream, Njoya created a phonetic script around 1895, and he and his court developed it into an eighty-character alphabet, called "A-ka-u-ku" for its first four symbols.

Njoya was also a practical man who found ways to work with the Germans who occupied his land. He accepted German missionaries and permitted the teaching of German in local schools. In 1908, he even sent

Lewa ngu (*The Book of the Country*), written by King Ibrahim Njoya and published c. 1920, is the oldest known full-scale map of Bamum, which is now part of Cameroon. Njoya used striking colors, symbols, and borders—and a language he invented himself—to illustrate his country.

his own throne to Berlin as a gift for Kaiser Wilhelm II, the emperor of Germany. But he worked at the same time to preserve and assert his own culture—and his own sovereignty. Njoya used the language he created in compiling a book describing the history and customs of the Bamum. And he set out to map his kingdom.

Starting in April 1912, Njoya led a party of sixty from village to village around Bamum. Crews cleared bush along the way, and at each stop, surveyors noted distances traveled, geographic formations, and local boundaries. This initial expedition made thirty stops in fifty-two days before heavy rains ended their trek. The First World War—during which British, French, and Belgian troops invaded German Kamerun—put their work on hold. But Njoya's topographers surveyed the capital of Foumban in 1918 and the rest of the kingdom in 1920.

The finished product was called *Lewa ngu*, or *The Book of the Country*. It's an impressive achievement. Njoya's map is the first known comprehensive survey of Bamum. And it's one of the very few large-scale maps that survives today of any place in Africa made by Africans before the era of decolonization. The map shows many geographical features in Bamum, exaggerates the size of the kingdom, and highlights Foumba. It's the work of a leader who appreciated the power that maps can wield, shaped to maximize his realm and emphasize its unity and his authority.

But Germany's loss in World War I made Njoya's task of balancing the interests of Bamum against Europeans harder, then impossible. After 1918, Cameroon fell under control of France, which stripped Bamum of its partial autonomy, banned Njoya's alphabet, and closed the schools he had established. Njoya stayed in Foumban until 1931, when he was deported to French Cameroon. He died there in exile two years later.

Njoya had hundreds of wives and children. In 2021, Mouhammad-Nabil Mforifoum Mbombo Njoya, one of his descendants, became the twentieth *mfon* of Bamum.[1] Two years later, the sultan king visited the Humboldt Forum museum in Berlin. He found and sat on the throne that once belonged to his great-grandfather. His role today is ceremonial, but the moment got more than 1.3 million views on TikTok.

---

1 The young *mfon* was a graduate of St. John's University in Queens, New York, where he majored in networking and telecommunications.

1

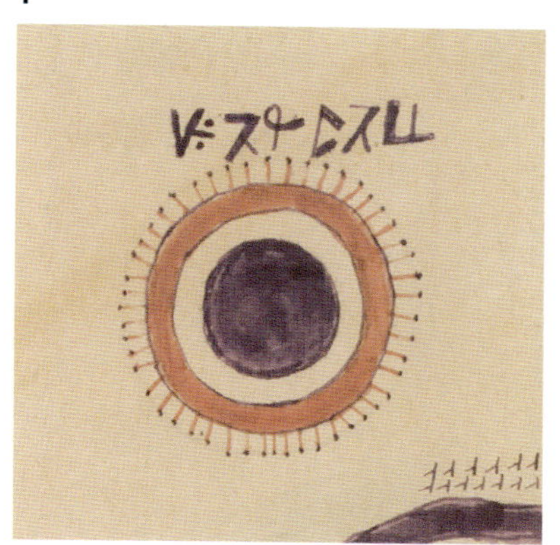

2

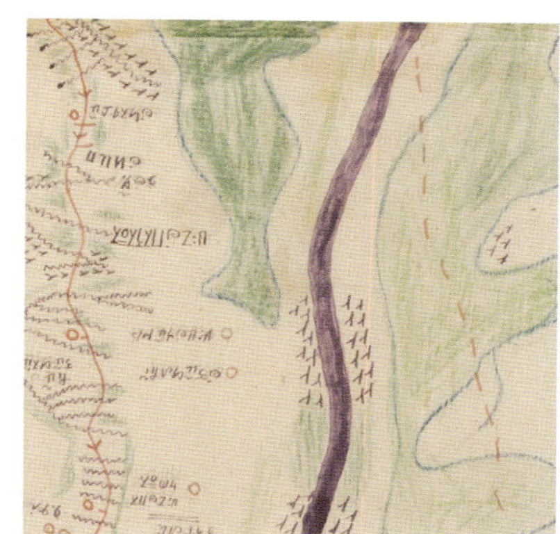

3

4

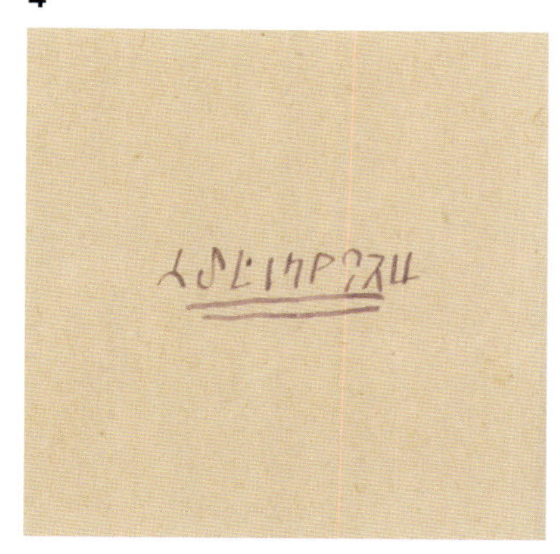

5

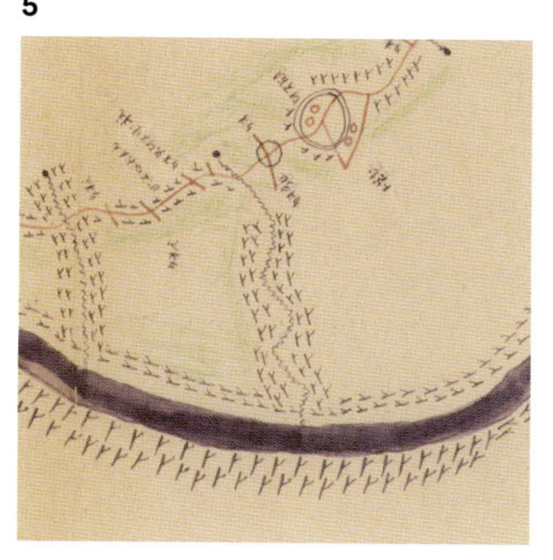

6

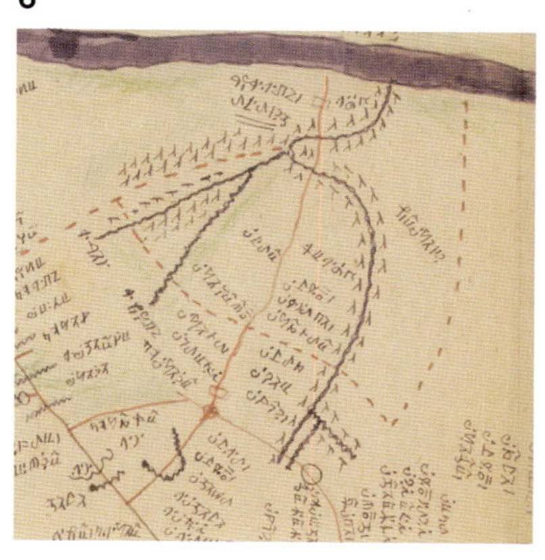

1 *Lewa ngu* (*The Book of the Country*) is oriented toward the west, with a setting sun on top and a rising sun at the bottom.

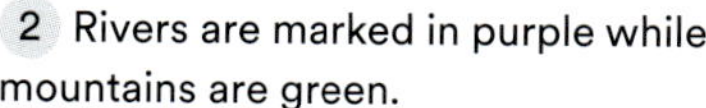

2 Rivers are marked in purple while mountains are green.

3 The walls around the capital of Foumban, and the royal palace within, are depicted in red.

4 The map's annotations are written in Njoya's Bamum alphabet.

5 and 6 The rivers forming the natural borders of Bamum, which was actually shaped more like a triangle than a rectangle, are arranged very symmetrically, making the kingdom seem bigger and geographically unified.

MAP OF EASTERN TURKEY IN ASIA, SYRIA AND WESTERN PERSIA
398
1
2
3
4
A
B

The Map That Triggered a Century of Hate (and Counting)

The map of the Sykes-Picot Agreement helped ensure that the protocol would become notorious as a blueprint for colonialism in the Middle East.

Map of Eastern Turkey in Asia, Syria, and Western Persia is a graphic representation of the 1916 Sykes-Picot deal. The map was originally produced by the Royal Geographical Society and then marked up by the deal's principal negotiators: François-Georges-Picot and Mark Sykes.

1 The agreement assigned the area in blue to France.

2 The United Kingdom was to get the regions in red.

3 In between, France would have "indirect influence" over the area marked *A*, and British over the stretch labeled *B*.

4 The area around Jerusalem would be put under international control, apart from the city of Haifa, which would give the UK a Mediterranean port.

Many political maps are influential because of the ideas or events they portray, but for some, power runs in the opposite direction. It's largely because of this famous map, for example, that so many people consider the Sykes-Picot Agreement such an important historical phenomenon.

From November 1915 to January 1916, as World War I raged, diplomats Mark Sykes, from England, and François Georges-Picot, from France, negotiated a treaty for dividing up the Ottoman (or Turkish) Empire, which was fighting on the side of Germany. France was to get an area stretching around the eastern side of the Mediterranean Sea, including southeastern Turkey, Syria, and Lebanon, and, farther inland, Kurdish areas. (This is the blue region on the map.) To the United Kingdom, the protocol gave a large chunk of what is now Iraq, extending from Baghdad to the Persian Gulf port of Basra, plus a bit of territory around the city of Haifa (now in Israel), to ensure the British also had access to the Mediterranean. (This is the red area.) Between these zones, the sectors would fall under the "indirect influence" of the French (the area marked *A*) or the British (*B*). A fifth region, shown in yellow, reserved the area around Jerusalem for international control.

The deal remained secret until the fall of 1917, when Bolsheviks overthrew Czar Nicholas II in Russia and discovered the agreement. Having no allegiance to England or France, the Communists made the Sykes-Picot plan public. At the end of November 1917, the *Manchester Guardian* printed it too.

But the British government had already promised Hussein ibn Ali, the sharif of Mecca, that it would support Arab independence against the Turks. Indeed, that offer helped trigger the Great Arab Revolt in 1916, which hastened the end of the Ottoman Empire. When Arab nationalists saw that England intended instead to carve up the region to its own benefit, they weren't just outraged at Sykes-Picot's colonial presumptions, they felt utterly betrayed.

And that's the way the deal between England and France has come down through history. Sober analysts and terrorist fanatics alike see Sykes-Picot as the root cause of many of the difficulties still plaguing the Levant. In 2014, al-Hayat Media Center, a media branch of the Islamic State, posted a video celebrating the destruction of part of the border between Syria and Iraq, and called it "The End of Sykes-Picot." Two years later, as the centennial of the deal approached, English-language newspaper stories and academic conferences popped up with titles like "Broken Borders, Broken States: One Hundred Years After Sykes-Picot."

Understand this, however: Sykes-Picot, signed in 1916, didn't actually set any borders that exist today, and was just one in a long line of overlapping, often contradictory arrangements of political power in the region. Representatives from England, France, and Russia met in Constantinople in March 1915 to divide up the Ottoman Empire, and again in London in April of that year to convince Italy to join the Allies. In November 1917, Britain issued the Balfour Declaration, supporting the "establishment in Palestine of a national home for the Jewish people." A series of conferences and treaties after World War I tried to settle the area's boundaries, and created Turkey and "mandates," or territories provisionally under the administration of England or France, for Iraq and Syria. Lebanon was a mountain range, not a state, on the Sykes-Picot map, then a French mandate in the 1920s, a battleground during World War II, occupied by Syria from 1976 to 2005, occupied by Israel from 1985 to 2000, and home to at least half a dozen border-rattling armed conflicts in the past twenty years.

So why has "Sykes-Picot" become shorthand for the origin story of the modern Middle East? Well, as Spike Lee never said to Michael Jordan, "It's gotta be the map!"

The McMahon-Hussein correspondence, in which England stated it would support Arab independence, didn't have illustrations attached. Nor did the Balfour Declaration, nor did most of the other foundational documents of the region's politics. But the Sykes-Picot deal came with a map of bright colors and big letters, signed (in its lower right corner) by its principal negotiators.

With its smooth, straight lines, that map really put across the breathtakingly blithe attitudes of its authors. At one point during the treaty negotiations, Sykes used a finger to trace a path on a map, and told H. H. Asquith, the British prime minister: "I should like to draw a line from the *E* in Acre [which is a city on the Mediterranean Sea] to the last *K* in Kirkuk [a city in Iraq's mountainous northeastern frontier]." And Sykes very nearly got his wish!

Wrapped up in a collapsing empire, territorial pretensions, secrecy, treachery, and leaks, all about a place that has again and again hosted clashes of the world's civilizations, the Sykes-Picot map is one of the most dramatic in history. It also shows how political maps can be both the symbol and instrument of carelessly cruel colonialism.

In 2016, one hundred years after Sykes-Picot, John Oliver appeared on Comedy Central's *The Daily Show* to discuss the origins of Middle East tensions. Wearing a mustache and pith helmet, he announced: "There's nothing the Arab respects more than a strong, steady white hand drawing arbitrary lines 'twixt their ridiculous tribal allegiances." He added, "To call me racist would be to imply that I cared enough to hate them, or was interested enough to learn things about them to dislike."

His character was called Sir Archibald Mapsalot III.

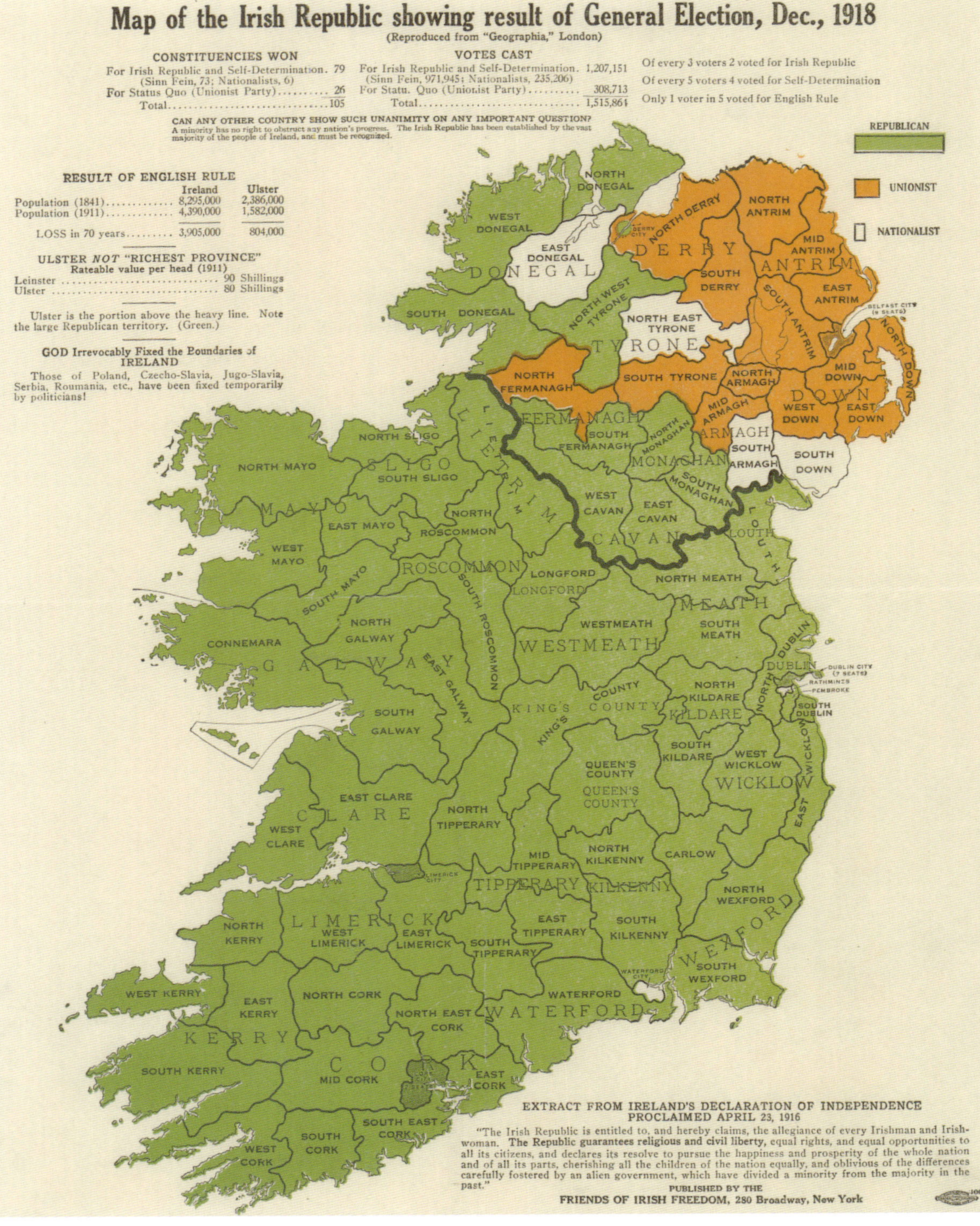
Map of the Irish Republic showing result of General Election, Dec., 1918
(Reproduced from "Geographia," London)
CONSTITUENCIES WON
For Irish Republic and Self-Determination. 79
(Sinn Fein, 73; Nationalists, 6)
For Status Quo (Unionist Party).......... 26
Total.......................................105
VOTES CAST
For Irish Republic and Self-Determination. 1,207,151
(Sinn Fein, 971,945; Nationalists, 235,206)
For Statu. Quo (Unionist Party).......... 308,713
Total.............................. 1,515,864
Of every 3 voters 2 voted for Irish Republic
Of every 5 voters 4 voted for Self-Determination
Only 1 voter in 5 voted for English Rule
CAN ANY OTHER COUNTRY SHOW SUCH UNANIMITY ON ANY IMPORTANT QUESTION?
A minority has no right to obstruct any nation's progress. The Irish Republic has been established by the vast majority of the people of Ireland, and must be recognized.
REPUBLICAN
UNIONIST
NATIONALIST
RESULT OF ENGLISH RULE
Ireland Ulster
Population (1841)............ 8,295,000 2,386,000
Population (1911)............ 4,390,000 1,582,000
LOSS in 70 years......... 3,905,000 804,000
ULSTER NOT "RICHEST PROVINCE"
Rateable value per head (1911)
Leinster .... 90 Shillings
Ulster .... 80 Shillings
Ulster is the portion above the heavy line. Note the large Republican territory. (Green.)
GOD Irrevocably Fixed the Boundaries of IRELAND
Those of Poland, Czecho-Slavia, Jugo-Slavia, Serbia, Roumania, etc., have been fixed temporarily by politicians!
NORTH DONEGAL
WEST DONEGAL
EAST DONEGAL
DONEGAL
SOUTH DONEGAL
DERRY CITY
NORTH DERRY
DERRY
SOUTH DERRY
NORTH ANTRIM
MID ANTRIM
ANTRIM
EAST ANTRIM
SOUTH ANTRIM
BELFAST CITY (9 SEATS)
NORTH DOWN
MID DOWN
DOWN
WEST DOWN
EAST DOWN
SOUTH DOWN
NORTH WEST TYRONE
NORTH EAST TYRONE
TYRONE
SOUTH TYRONE
NORTH FERMANAGH
FERMANAGH
SOUTH FERMANAGH
NORTH ARMAGH
MID ARMAGH
ARMAGH
SOUTH ARMAGH
NORTH MONAGHAN
MONAGHAN
SOUTH MONAGHAN
WEST CAVAN
EAST CAVAN
CAVAN
LOUTH
LEITRIM
NORTH SLIGO
SLIGO
SOUTH SLIGO
NORTH MAYO
MAYO
EAST MAYO
WEST MAYO
SOUTH MAYO
NORTH ROSCOMMON
ROSCOMMON
SOUTH ROSCOMMON
LONGFORD
NORTH MEATH
MEATH
SOUTH MEATH
WESTMEATH
CONNEMARA
NORTH GALWAY
GALWAY
EAST GALWAY
SOUTH GALWAY
NORTH DUBLIN
DUBLIN
DUBLIN CITY (7 SEATS)
RATHMINES
PEMBROKE
SOUTH DUBLIN
KING'S COUNTY
NORTH KILDARE
KILDARE
SOUTH KILDARE
WEST WICKLOW
WICKLOW
EAST WICKLOW
QUEEN'S COUNTY
EAST CLARE
CLARE
WEST CLARE
NORTH TIPPERARY
MID TIPPERARY
TIPPERARY
EAST TIPPERARY
SOUTH TIPPERARY
NORTH KILKENNY
KILKENNY
SOUTH KILKENNY
CARLOW
NORTH WEXFORD
WEXFORD
SOUTH WEXFORD
LIMERICK CITY
LIMERICK
WEST LIMERICK
EAST LIMERICK
NORTH KERRY
WEST KERRY
EAST KERRY
KERRY
SOUTH KERRY
WATERFORD CITY
WATERFORD
NORTH CORK
NORTH EAST CORK
CORK
MID CORK
EAST CORK
SOUTH EAST CORK
SOUTH CORK
WEST CORK
EXTRACT FROM IRELAND'S DECLARATION OF INDEPENDENCE PROCLAIMED APRIL 23, 1916
"The Irish Republic is entitled to, and hereby claims, the allegiance of every Irishman and Irishwoman. The Republic guarantees religious and civil liberty, equal rights, and equal opportunities to all its citizens, and declares its resolve to pursue the happiness and prosperity of the whole nation and of all its parts, cherishing all the children of the nation equally, and oblivious of the differences carefully fostered by an alien government, which have divided a minority from the majority in the past."
PUBLISHED BY THE
FRIENDS OF IRISH FREEDOM, 280 Broadway, New York

The Map That Split One into Twenty-Six and Six

The 1918 election map of Ireland shows a country on the brink of breaking away from Great Britain—and breaking apart.

Few countries have as conflict-riven a history as Ireland, an island nation that's been targeted by settlers, if not invaders, since Europeans first learned to sail. Very few illustrations encapsulate as many years of political turmoil as this map. Produced by an American group that supported an Irish republic, it details the results of the pivotal general election of 1918 in the United Kingdom. It captures the moment when politics, religion, and culture converged to make an independent Ireland inevitable though not stably peaceful.

But this map's story stretches back to 1169, when Anglo-Norman troops landed in Wexford, beginning more than eight hundred years of attempts—often strenuous but only partially successful—by English nobles to control their Irish neighbors.

The English crown drove Irish chieftains out of power. It suppressed local religious traditions. It beat back a full-scale Irish revolt during the Nine Years' War (circa 1593–1603). And in the early 1600s, it opened Ireland to a scheme called "plantation," where England took Irish land and gave it to incomers from Great Britain. The biggest seizures and handouts took place from about 1610 to about 1630 in Ulster, the northernmost of Ireland's four traditional provinces. The British government implanted thousands of English and Scottish settlers there, permanently tilting the map, language, and religion of Ulster toward English and Anglicanism.

The Plantation of Ulster is an early example of an underappreciated fact about colonialism: It literally breeds its own supporters. By the time Algeria won its independence from France in 1962, it was home to more than 1 million *pieds-noirs* ("black-feet," a term used at the time), people of European heritage born in Algeria. White descendants of British migrants comprised about 8 percent of the population of Rhodesia before it became Zimbabwe in 1980. The number of Israeli settlers in the West Bank is now greater than 500,000. There are obviously vast differences among

The *Map of the Irish Republic, Showing Result of the General Election, Dec., 1918*, created by the US-based Friends of Irish Freedom and published in 1918, shows that voting cleaved almost perfectly along regional and religious lines.

these groups. But all of them, and Ulster, had (or has) a deep sense of entitlement to their homes and land, developed over multiple generations; strong opposition to reversing the colonial patterns that led to their way of life; and political power disproportionate to their numbers. The longer a colonial map endures, the more entrenched its provincial beneficiaries and therefore its boundaries become. (Its colonists, rather than Indigenous populations, might even lead revolutions, as happened in the Americas.)

In the case of Ireland, nationalism intensified most strongly in the south, outside Ulster, through further disenfranchisement of Catholics, failed rebellions, and disasters such as the Great Famine of 1845–52. As British politics gradually became more democratic, Parliament considered three bills between 1886 and 1914 for establishing self-government for Ireland within the United Kingdom, but never implemented this idea of home rule, and tensions stayed at a boil. In the Easter Rising of April 1916, a group of Irish rebels took over a series of key buildings in Dublin and declared the existence of an Irish republic. In less than a week of fighting in the streets of the capital, Britain crushed the uprising—and then executed its leaders, sent its participants to internment camps and jails, and put Ireland under martial law. All of this—plus an ill-fated attempt by Prime Minister David Lloyd George to extend the British military draft to Ireland—forced local political parties to take explicit stands on the question of Irish independence.

The UK election of 1918 took place just a month after the end of the Great War, and in Ireland, the results showed regional and religious animosities reaching a point of no return. The Irish Parliamentary Party, which had supported Home Rule, collapsed, winning only the areas shown in white on this map. Sinn Féin ("We Ourselves" in Gaelic) which called for the creation of a separate Irish republic, dominated instead, winning 73 of 105 seats (shown in green) and electing 47 members who were in prison at the time of the vote. The Unionists, who favored keeping British rule, won 23, all in northern Ireland. (These are the orange regions, with the heavy line showing the border between Ulster and the rest of Ireland.)

Afterward, the members of Sinn Féin refused to take part in Parliament. They created a new legislature called the Dáil Éireann (Assembly of Ireland) and declared independence. Another two years of carnage followed, which this time the British could not fully suppress. Instead, war-weary officials pitched the idea of splitting Ireland into two pieces.

Partition combined two related concepts that were in the political air at the end of World War I. One was self-determination. With the Austro-Hungarian, German, Ottoman, and Russian Empires all in ruins, idealists (like US President Woodrow Wilson) promulgated the idea that peoples had the right to rule themselves, and Western realists (like Lloyd George) wanted to cut their losses and preserve as much of their spheres of interest as they could. The other concept was remapping—the notion that leaders could make the world safer and better by redrawing borders, sometimes creating original entities and eliminating whole countries. *Fifteen* new nations appeared on maps as a result of the negotiations that followed the end of the war. This election map shows how Irish Republicans wanted self-determination but weren't interested in another experiment in political cartography. "GOD Irrevocably Fixed the Boundaries of IRELAND," it proclaims. "Those of Poland, Czecho-Slovakia, Jugo-Slavia, Serbia, Roumania, etc., have been fixed temporarily by politicians!"

But in 1921, Irish negotiators agreed to a deal they thought was the best they were going to be able to get from Great Britain. It created the Irish Free State as a self-governing dominion (like Canada or Australia at the time) from twenty-six southern counties, and Northern Ireland, which would remain part of the UK, from six northern counties. The six did not make up all of Ulster, but included two (Fermanagh and Tyrone) that voted for nationalist parties in 1918. Essentially, the British kept as large a chunk of the north as would contain a majority of Protestant residents.

The Dáil approved this agreement, but the pact bitterly divided the nationalists, and after the War of Independence, Ireland plunged into bloody civil war for another year. The pro-treaty forces prevailed, but Michael Collins, who negotiated the agreement and led the Irish army, was killed by an anti-treaty assassin. And for decades afterward—Ireland became fully independent in 1949—Northern Ireland was plagued by ambushes, political murders, and sectarian violence among republican and loyalist paramilitary groups and forces of the United Kingdom. It wasn't until the Good Friday Agreement of 1998 that all sides agreed to lay down their arms and affirmed the right of the people of Northern Ireland to "identify themselves and be accepted as Irish or British, or both." Northern Ireland will remain part of the UK unless a majority of people in both North and South consent to reunification. It took eight decades of rebellion, civil war, guerrilla battles, hunger strikes, and intense negotiations, plus the end of the Cold War and the rise of freer trade, for the colors on this map to fade just enough to allow even that much.

Imperial Gazetteer Atlas of India
PREVA
AFGHANISTAN
KABUL
Herat
Kandahar
KASHMIR AND JAMMU
SRINAGAR
Chitral
PESHAWAR
NORTH-WEST FRONTIER PROV.
Rawalpindi
PUNJAB
Lahore
Amritsar
Simla
Multan
BALUCHISTAN AGENCY
QUETTA
Kalat
TIBET
LHASA
NEPAL
KATMANDU
Sikkim
BHUTAN
DELHI
Agra
UNITED PROVINCES
LUCKNOW
ALLAHABAD
Benares
RAJPUTANA AGENCY
Jodhpur
Bikaner
GWALIOR
CENTRAL INDIA AGENCY
INDORE
Bhopal
Jubbulpore
BIHAR
PATNA
Chota Nagpur
BENGAL
CALCUTTA
Dacca
ORISSA
Cuttack
Puri
Sind
Karachi
Hyderabad
BOMBAY
Cutch
Kathiawar
Gujarat
Ahmadabad
Baroda
Surat
Poona
CENTRAL PROVINCES
NAGPUR
Berar
HYDERABAD
Secunderabad
Bastar
Vizagapatam
MADRAS
Goa
Bellary
MYSORE
Bangalore
Mangalore
Calicut
Pondicherry (Fr.)
Karikal (Fr.)
Negapatam
Trichinopoly
Madura
Cochin
Trivandrum
C. Comorin
Palk Str.
Gulf of Mannar
CEYLON
Trincomalee
Laccadive Islands
ARABIAN SEA
BAY OF BENGAL
Tropic of Cancer
Longitude East 88 of Greenwich
NOTE TO COLOURING
HINDUS
SIKHS
MUHAMMADANS
BUDDHISTS
CHRISTIANS
ANIMISTS
The Edinburgh Geographical Institute

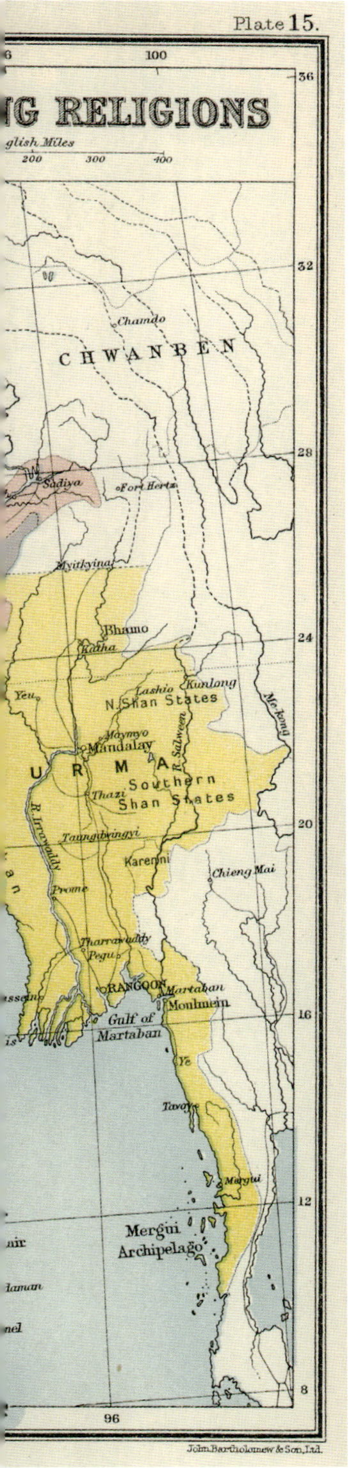

The Map That Killed a Million People

Maps dividing colonial India by religion foretold its bloody partition.

The British spent more than three hundred years trying to control India. England first exerted its influence through a corporation called the East India Company, which had a monopoly on trade in South Asia in the seventeenth and eighteenth centuries and was so powerful that it maintained its own armies. In 1858, the Crown decided to govern India directly, and its rule lasted for almost another century. Over this stretch, the British developed some understanding of the Indian subcontinent's longstanding religious divisions, as shown in this map, published in the 1909 edition of the *Imperial Gazetteer of India*. But when the British got out of India in 1947, they did so in a matter of months by hacking it up according to their guesstimates of religious borders.

Immediately—in fact, *before* immediately, because Britain announced the independence of Hindu-majority India and Muslim-majority Pakistan even before revealing their actual boundaries—residents desperately started scrambling to get on the "right" side of the new borders. And along the way, they began butchering each other. The event that became known simply as "Partition" unleashed migrations and sectarian conflict that turned savage beyond belief. Wanton rage—murders, sexual brutality, arson—seemed to break out everywhere near the new India-Pakistan borders. Ultimately, the Partition of India displaced 15 million people and led to more than 1 million deaths and 75,000 rapes.

Even those numbers understate its impact. As the writer Parul Sehgal asked in 2022, "What do 'figures, only figures' convey of the full horror and absurdity of 1947? Of a border that cut through forests, families, and shrines, that saw wild animals apportioned between the two countries and historical

Prevailing Religions: General, in the *Imperial Gazetteer of India*, published by Oxford University Press in 1909, shows the sorts of oversimplified borders that set the stage for the devastating partition of the country in 1947. (Present-day Myanmar, shown on this map as Burma, became a colony separate from India in 1937.)

artifacts snapped in half?" While the division of Ireland (see page 89), say, was genuinely traumatic and may be more familiar to Americans of European descent, the Partition of India was orders of magnitude more destructive, and affects both South Asian families and geopolitics to this day.

Like the French, Dutch, and Belgians, the British hung on to their most prized colonial possession far beyond the point when they could have made a more graceful and peaceful exit. By the 1920s, a group of English-educated and politically effective nationalists were pushing for independence, including Mohandas Gandhi and Jawaharlal Nehru of the Indian National Congress and Mohammed Ali Jinnah, head of the All-India Muslim League—none of whom supported Partition at that point. But even as the British grew increasingly overtaxed, London did all it could to crush the independence movement, especially during World War II under Winston Churchill, a fierce advocate of British Empire.[1] Agitation between Hindus and Muslims began rising to the level of lethal riots.

After the war—in which Indian forces helped beat back the Japanese invasion of Burma—and with Churchill out of office, Prime Minister Clement Attlee announced that British governance of India would come to an end. Just how quickly, however, came as a shock. In March 1947, Louis Mountbatten, the final British viceroy, arrived in India, and soon decided to conclude negotiations among the various parties by splitting India between its two largest faiths.

By that time, Jinnah was calling for a Muslim state and partition must have seemed expedient if not inevitable to the British. But India had existed for hundreds of years as a place where many religions—and an even greater number of languages and traditions—intermingled. Henceforth, because of the shape that Partition took, the division between Hinduism and Islam would define the subcontinent. Historian Alex von Tunzelmann put it this way in her 2007 book, *Indian Summer*: "[T]he British started to define 'communities' based on religious identity and attach political representation to them, [and] many Indians stopped accepting the diversity of their own thought and began to ask themselves in which of the boxes they belonged."

---

1 Informed in 1942 that the Indian National Congress would continue campaigns of civil disobedience during the war, Churchill replied, "I hate Indians. They are a beastly people with a beastly religion."

There's an important lesson here: Any political map of partition depicts more than a new set of borders. It describes a new, *self-reinforcing* reality of where territories are, will be, and should be because of the rules that led to those boundaries. In this case, it was Hindus here, Muslims over there, with everyone and everything else subordinate. And more than seventy-five years later, Pakistan is a haven for Islamic extremism, Hindu nationalism is stronger than ever in India, and both nations have nuclear weapons.

In June 1947, Mountbatten declared his countrymen would be out of India by August 15 of that year. He entrusted the job of drawing the new map of the subcontinent to a judge named Cyril Radcliffe. Radcliffe was truly a creature of the British establishment—a viscount, wartime director of the Ministry of Information, and Knight Commander of the Order of the British Empire. But he had never been east of Paris.

Familiar with nothing about India and pressed for time, Radcliffe drew all kinds of divisive but arbitrary lines, chopping through the provinces of Punjab in the west and Bengal in the east. His boundaries adhered so strongly to religious separatism that they created a Muslim state in two parts, called West Pakistan and East Pakistan, that were separated by more than 1,000 miles (essentially the areas shown in green on this map). They also left more than 120 regions, called enclaves, belonging to India but encircled by East Pakistan and more than 90 Pakistani enclaves in India. Jinnah called the new territories "maimed, mutilated, and moth-eaten." (After a civil war in 1971, East Pakistan became Bangladesh. India and Bangladesh did not resolve the status of the enclaves until 2015.)

During and after Partition, British administrators failed to consult with local leaders, anticipate predictable violence, or intervene to stop the mass slaughters. None of that was Radcliffe's fault, but neither does any of it excuse his horrible mapmaking. In 1966, the poet W. H. Auden wrote about Radcliffe in "Partition," which never became famous, but serves as a fitting commentary on the cartographic portion of this sad saga:

> . . . in seven weeks it was done, the frontiers decided,
> A continent for better or worse divided.
>
> The next day he sailed for England, where he could quickly forget
> The case, as a good lawyer must. Return he would not,
> Afraid, as he told his Club, that he might get shot.

The Map of the Scariest Place on Earth

Korea has been dangerously partitioned since 1953.

The Demilitarized Zone (DMZ) between North and South Korea is "the scariest place on earth," according to former US President Bill Clinton. It's a largely East-West strip of territory, 151 miles long and 2.5 miles wide, that extends across the Korean Peninsula, established by armistice in 1953, when large-scale fighting stopped in the Korean War. No peace treaty ever formally concluded that conflict; troops on each side simply pulled back 1.2 miles and have essentially been staring at each other on high alert ever since. And over the past seven decades, the DMZ has become the world's most heavily militarized border. More than 1.6 million Korean and US troops are stationed just to its north and south. Barbed wire, watchtowers,

BELOW: *Korea: Demilitarized Zone: 1969*, produced by the CIA, makes clear that while the DMZ is now devoid of nearly all human activity, it's teeming with the ghosts of old towns, roads, and railways.

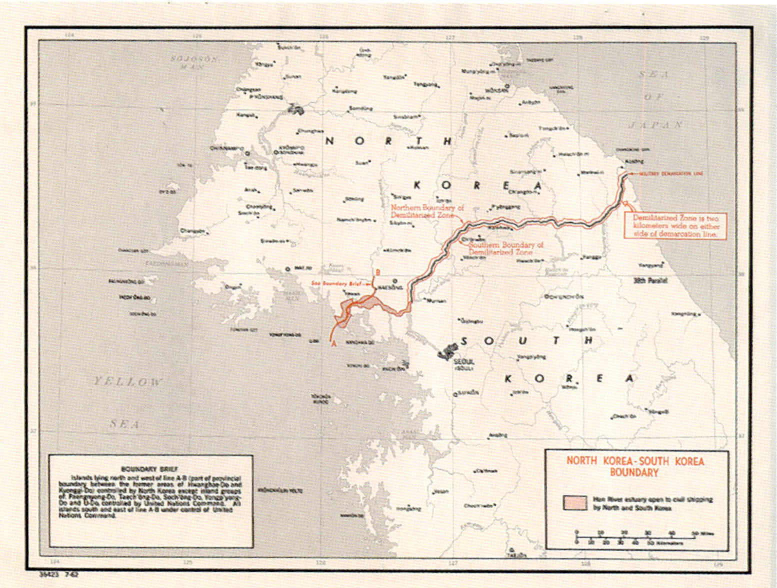

RIGHT: Produced by the US State Department in 1963, *North Korea–South Korea Boundary* depicts the DMZ as a precisely defined but apparently barren borderland.

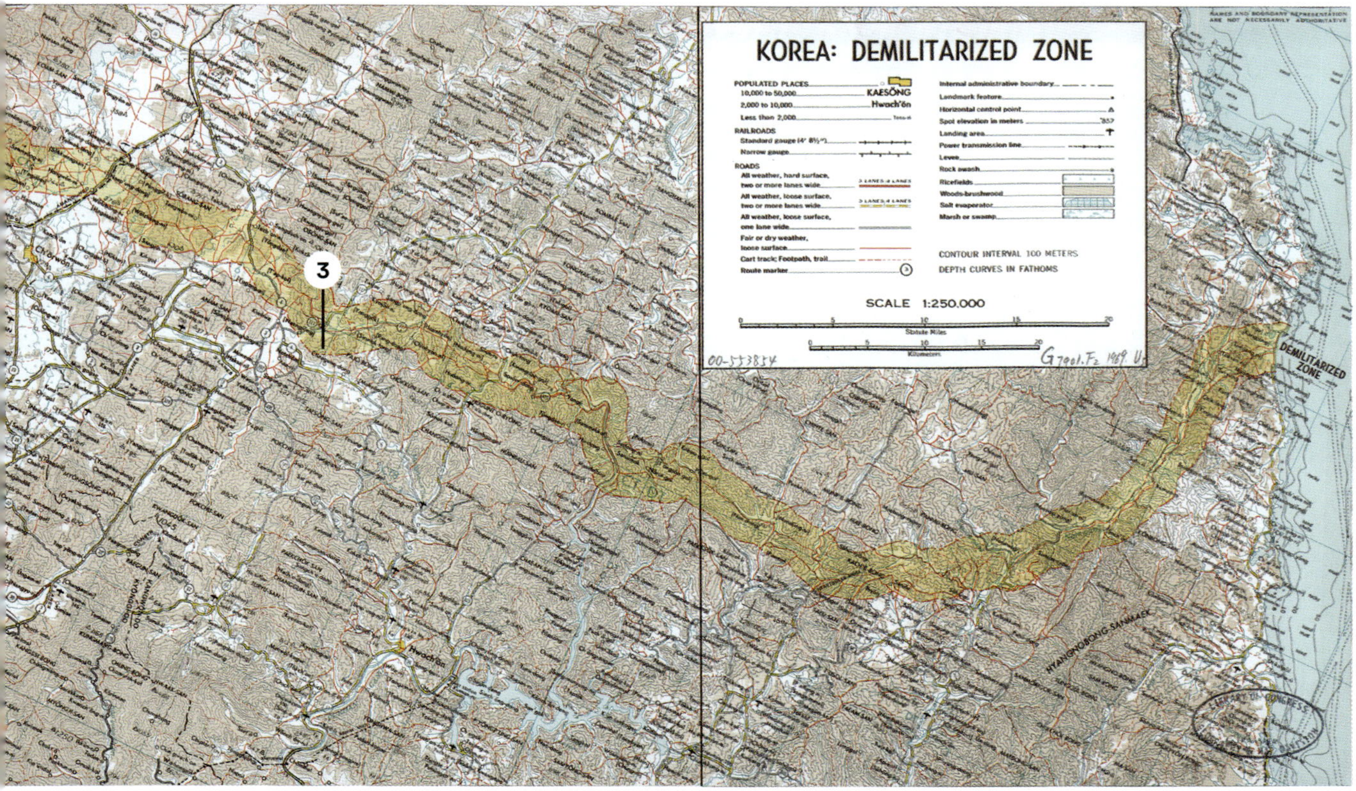

and antitank traps line its borders. Hundreds of thousands of land mines are strewn about its interior. Individuals caught inside the Zone have been kidnapped, shot at, and, in one horrible incident, even hacked to pieces by North Korean soldiers who didn't like how a detail of American and South Korean personnel were pruning a poplar tree.

But no matter how inhospitable it might be, a place this heavily politicized, starkly defined, and relentlessly patrolled was destined to inspire a classic political map.

Korea was a united, largely isolationist kingdom for hundreds of years, until the late nineteenth century. Like so many partitions around the globe, its division is a legacy of colonialism and war. In this case, Japan annexed Korea in 1910, and subjected it to imperial rule: government by military officials, no freedom of association or speech, massive land seizures, Korean-language education in schools replaced by Japanese pedagogy. In 1945, following Japan's defeat in World War II, Soviet and American forces moved into Korea. And as they did in Germany and Austria, the winning countries divided their occupied territory, in this case along the 38th parallel of latitude. To the north, the USSR and China backed a communist regime, while the United States and its allies supported anticommunist nationalists who formed a government in the south. After five years of increasing tensions between the two states, North Korea tried to take the whole peninsula by force in June 1950, sending 75,000 troops across the parallel in a surprise invasion.

The Korean War raged for three extraordinarily bloody years, with the United Nations taking the side of the South[1] and China intervening to aid the North. At least 2.5 million people died, most of them civilians, and the peninsula became one of the most heavily bombed places in history. The conflict ground into a stalemate, and truce talks began in July 1951, then dragged on for two more years before the two sides agreed to back off and establish the DMZ.

If you've ever seen a map of the Zone, it probably looked like the one shown on page 97 (top), which was produced by the US State Department in 1963. Indeed, most maps of Korea as a whole look like this. It's a perfectly

1

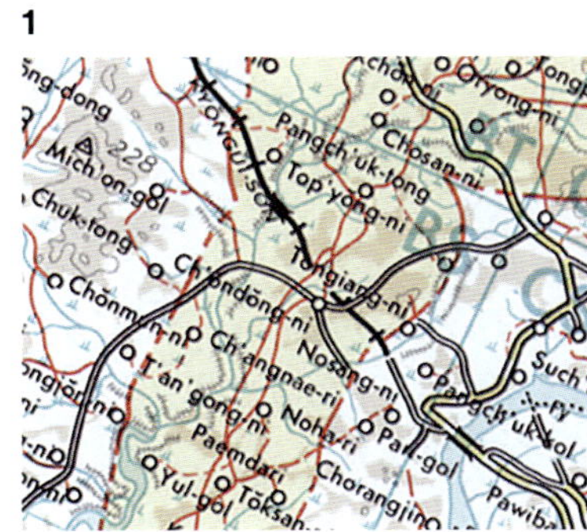

2

3

1 At the time war broke out, the Soviet Union was boycotting proceedings of the United Nations because of its refusal to recognize China. In the absence of the communist superpowers, the UN voted to assist the military defense of South Korea.

sensible map, as far as it goes—accurate and clear in labeling cities, rivers, coastlines, and bodies of water. But it shows the demarcation between North and South Korea in bright red and describes it in larger type. It essentially declares the most important feature of the Korean peninsula to be the borderland drawn across its midst. And that's pretty standard fare.

But in 1969, the US Central Intelligence Agency compiled an utterly different look at the DMZ. This map (pages 96–97, bottom, and opposite) has an unusual orientation: north points toward its upper right, so that the DMZ snakes horizontally across the plot. It is incredibly detailed, showing cities and towns with fewer than 2,000 people; highways, railroads, and airfields; and topographic features like hills, levees, and swamps.

But the map names very few active population centers in the Zone. It also shows the roads inside the DMZ as mostly loose-surface pathways, and the main railway through the Zone as abandoned. Indeed, the CIA map, embeds a story: It depicts the DMZ as emptied, not just empty.

When this map was produced in 1969, overt hostilities were closer to re-erupting in Korea than at any time since the end of the war. North Korea seized a US Navy intelligence ship in international waters in 1968 and sent thousands of agents across the DMZ on commando raids in the following months, including an assassination squad targeting the president of South Korea. But those provocations failed to trigger either an uprising among South Koreans or the withdrawal of American troops.

In 1978, a subterranean explosion revealed a tunnel under the DMZ, extending about a quarter of a mile into South Korea. North Korea tried to pass it off as part of a coal mine, though there's no coal in the region. The tunnel could have conveyed 30,000 troops per hour in a surprise attack, and for a while, it was one more flashpoint in the Cold War.

But while North Korea has remained an unpredictable and absurdly totalitarian state, and the DMZ is still extremely dangerous today, younger generations of Koreans have come to regard the Zone as a curiosity, even a tourist attraction.[2] And with its houses, farms, and villages crumbling away, the DMZ has reverted to nature. Rare black bears now roam its territory while endangered cranes spend their winters there.

1 The 1969 CIA map shows the main rail line through the Korean DMZ is abandoned.

2 Villages listed in parentheses were evacuated upon the stoppage of the Korean War.

3 Its coloration shows most of the Zone as wooded, and its tightly packed contour lines reveal it to be hilly. Intentionally or not, it portrays Korea, particularly the DMZ, as a very hard place to wage war.

---

2 By 2020, the *Royal Society Journal of the History of Science* reported, a sculpture stood at the tunnel site: a statue of two Amur gorals, long-tailed, goatlike mammals. The animals had become a tourist attraction. So had the tunnel.

1 MAJA
ŚWIĘTO
CAŁEGO
NARODU
Wydawnictwo Artystyczno-Graficzne,
Warszawa
Dom Słowa Polskiego

The Maps of the Most-Erased Country in the World

For centuries, maps have told the story of Poland's subjugation, destruction—and endurance.

In one of the prettiest political maps you'll ever see, *1 Maja Święto Całego Narodu* (shown opposite), Poland is depicted as a red carnation. Created by Roman Cieślewicz in 1956, this poster carries a brief message. Translated to English, it reads: "May 1, a Celebration for the Entire Nation."

There's a long association between red carnations, May 1 (May Day), and protest movements, particularly those supporting workers' rights. For example, antimonarchists wore flaming-red flowers during the French Revolution, as did residents of the short-lived Paris Commune in 1871. In the United States, the American Federation of Labor called a general strike on May 1, 1886, to demand an eight-hour workday, and international socialist organizations soon began holding annual demonstrations on that date. After the Russian Revolution—during which supporters sometimes wore cardboard badges fashioned into red carnations—many countries with communist governments established May Day celebrations, often combining ostensible support for workers with shows of military force.

So it would be easy enough to interpret the *1 Maja* poster as just another bit of Cold War hype, demanding that viewers celebrate a thoroughly red Poland. In an interview three years before he died in 1996, Cieślewicz himself called Wag, the organization that published the posters, a "propaganda agency." But Cieślewicz and his colleagues could sometimes subvert the communist government's intended messages—or at least leave them open to interpretation. For example, Cieślewicz designed a poster for the 1967 production of a nineteenth-century Polish play called *Dziady*, or *Forefathers' Eve*. This long, poetic work dramatized the suffering of the Polish people under czarist Russian rule, but modern audiences quickly saw it as a metaphor for life under Russian-patrolled

Made by Polish artist and graphic designer Roman Cieślewicz and printed in 1956, *1 Maja Święto Całego Narodu* (May 1, a Celebration for the Entire Nation) shows a bold red carnation incorporating the country's cities and administrative districts.

communism.[1] As a 2009 exhibit at New York's Museum of Modern Art put it: "Although state controlled, the posters . . . of the Polish Poster School . . . characterized by sophisticated imagery and surreal tendencies . . . often carried powerful, oblique commentaries on the designers' political surroundings."

1 Maja, then, with its spare use of language, could be a salute to Polish nationalism. It could be a call for greater rights for workers. In heavily Catholic Poland, it could even honor Saint Joseph, the earthly father of Jesus and the patron saint of workers and craftsmen, whose feast day just so happens to be May 1. The poster mentions no leaders, shows no soldiers, deploys no communist euphemisms (such as the country's official name, the "Polish People's Republic"). And of course, red, the color that fills its map and seems to drip from its southern borders, can symbolize blood. Despite its production as propaganda, *1 Maja* can also be seen as just one in a line of maps that signify Polish resistance to subjugation.

And the line is long indeed, because Poland has been obliterated from world maps only to reappear on them more often than any surviving country in history.

Poland's life as an independent kingdom began in 1025, and for a while in the sixteenth and seventeenth centuries, Poland and Lithuania formed a commonwealth that was one of the biggest nation-states in Europe. But Poland has long suffered greatly for being surrounded by ambitious powers—and for lying mostly on plains that are easy to invade. In 1772, Austrian, Prussian, and Russian troops all entered the Commonwealth from different directions and forced it to cede territories that each neighboring empire wanted. After giving up resource-rich provinces such as Royal Prussia in the north and Galicia in the south, Poland lost about 30 percent of its land, an even larger share of its population, and a huge chunk of its foreign trade.

This partition was memorialized in a satirical 1773 engraving called *The Troelfth Cake*[2] (shown opposite). It depicts the leaders of the three

---

1 Cieślewicz's black-and-white placard featured a large, veined, mummy-shaped form with a stark hole ripped open at its chest.

2 In English, the title was probably a misspelling of "Twelfth Cake," another name for Three Kings Cake, a baked good celebrating the Epiphany, or arrival of three kings to visit the baby Jesus, in Christianity.

The Troelfth Cake, originally illustrated by the French artist Jean-Michel Moreau le Jeune and published in 1773, depicts three imperial leaders—Catherine the Great of Russia; Joseph II, the Holy Roman Emperor and leader of Austria; and Frederick the Great of Prussia—wrangling over a large map of Poland with Polish King Stanisław II August Poniatowski.

imperial powers surrounding Poland negotiating with its distressed king, Stanisław II August Poniatowski. As Frederick the Great of Prussia thrusts his sword at the coveted city of Gdansk, Catherine the Great of Russia stares at Stanisław, who used to be her lover and with whom she shared a daughter. But an overwrought Stanisław is looking away, can barely keep his crown on his head, and seems ready to flee. In this work, war and soap opera both play out across a political map.

In 1792, Russia invaded Poland again and secured an agreement with Prussia to divvy up even more Polish land. This second partition saw Russia annex another huge swath of eastern territory, and Prussia extend so deeply into Poland that it took control of Warsaw. Afterward, Polish reformers led by Tadeusz Kościuszko (best known to Americans as a military hero in the Revolutionary War) rose up to oppose ongoing foreign interference in their country. But that only compelled Austria, Prussia, and Russia to wipe out the Commonwealth altogether. They put down the rebellion in 1794, and the following year agreed to split what was left of Poland and even to suppress any mention of its name. In the Third Partition of Poland, each of the occupiers seized areas with at least 1 million remaining residents; Russia's take included Lithuania. King Stanisław fled to St. Petersburg, where he lived at the Marble Palace as Catherine's prisoner-cum-guest. "Poland," as Ryan Moore, a cartographic specialist at the Library of Congress wrote, "was a memory."

More than a century later, the First World War led Polish nationalists to hope their country could rise again. One of them was a cartographer

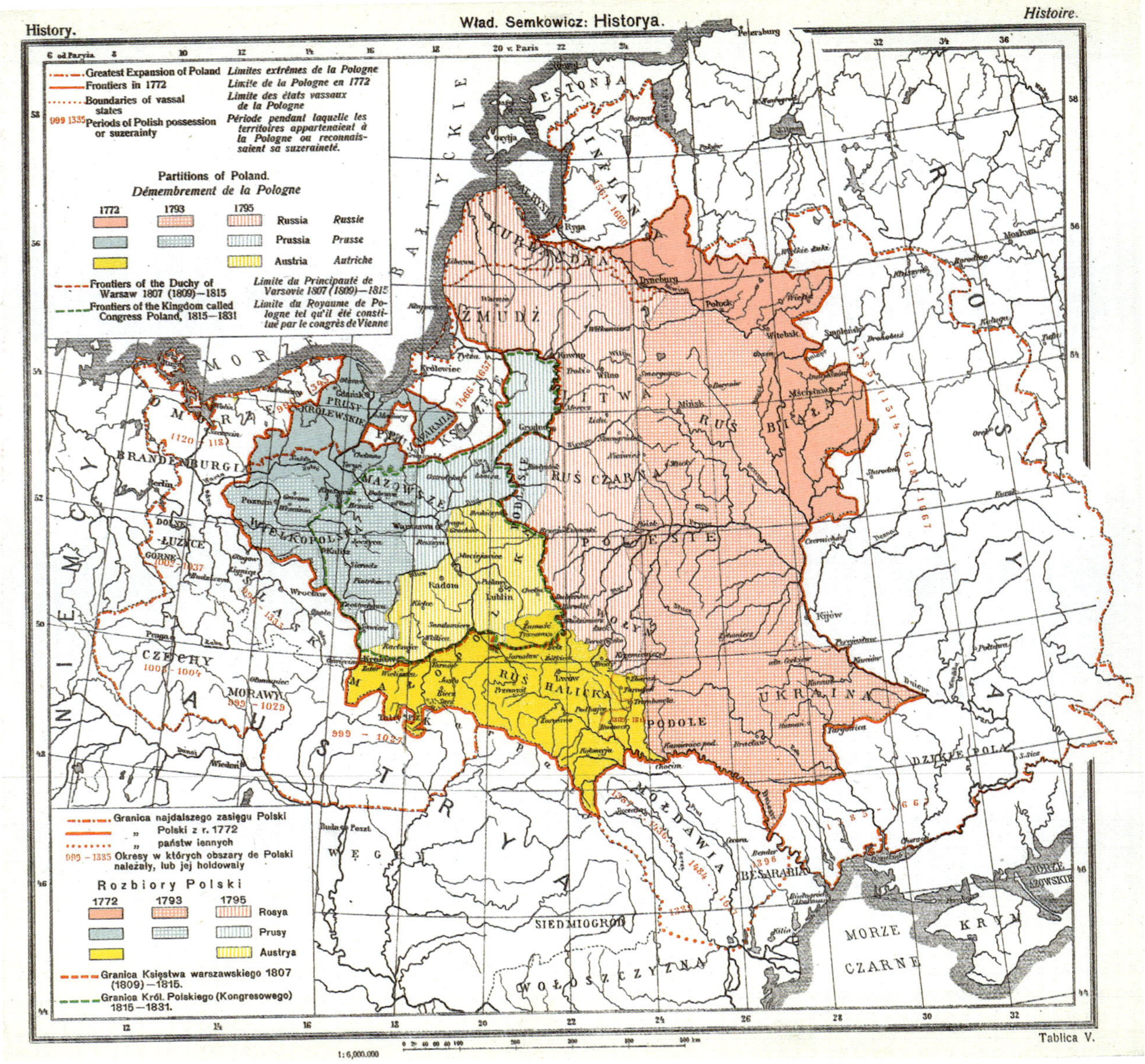
History.
Wład. Semkowicz: Historya.
Histoire.
Greatest Expansion of Poland
Limites extrêmes de la Pologne
Frontiers in 1772
Limite de la Pologne en 1772
Boundaries of vassal states
Limite des états vassaux de la Pologne
999 1335 Periods of Polish possession or suzerainty
Période pendant laquelle les territoires appartenaient à la Pologne ou reconnaissaient sa suzeraineté.
Partitions of Poland.
Démembrement de la Pologne
1772
1793
1795
Russia
Russie
Prussia
Prusse
Austria
Autriche
Frontiers of the Duchy of Warsaw 1807 (1809)—1815
Limite du Principauté de Varsovie 1807 (1809)—1815
Frontiers of the Kingdom called Congress Poland, 1815—1831
Limite du Royaume de Pologne tel qu'il été constitué par le congrès de Vienne
Granica najdalszego zasięgu Polski
„ Polski z r. 1772
„ państw lennych
989 – 1335 Okresy w których obszary de Polski należały, lub jej hołdowały
Rozbiory Polski
1772
1793
1795
Rosya
Prusy
Austrya
Granica Księstwa warszawskiego 1807 (1809)—1815.
Granica Król. Polskiego (Kongresowego) 1815—1831.
MORZE BAŁTYCKIE
ESTONIA
INFLANTY
KURLANDYA
ŻMUDŹ
LITWA
RUŚ BIAŁA
RUŚ CZARNA
POLESIE
WOŁYŃ
PODOLE
UKRAINA
RUŚ HALICKA
MAZOWSZE
WIELKOPOLSKA
PRUSY KRÓLEWSKIE
POMORZE
BRANDENBURGIA
ŚLĄSK
CZECHY
MORAWY
NIEMCY
AUSTRYA
WĘGRY
SIEDMIOGRÓD
WOŁOSZCZYZNA
MOŁDAWIA
BESARABIA
DZIKIE POLA
ROSYA
MORZE CZARNE
KRYM
MORZE AZOWSKIE
Tablica V.
1:6,000,000

named Eugeniusz Romer, who used data he unearthed from Austrian government archives to resuscitate public knowledge of Polish borders, demographics, and geography. In 1916, during the middle of the war, Romer published the *Geographical and Statistical Atlas of Poland*, which included thirty-two maps and detailed text in Polish, French, and German. One plate, simply titled *Historya* (*History*), opposite, depicts Poland's borders over time, using color and shading to show how the nation's neighbors partitioned it out of existence.

German and Austrian officials tried to ban Romer's atlas. But within two years, Germany and Austria-Hungary lost on the battlefields of World War I, and Russia was embroiled in revolution. Copies of the atlas made it to the United States, where President Woodrow Wilson included an independent Polish state in the "Fourteen Points" he declared necessary for postwar peace. And when the Paris Peace Conference of 1919 accepted a Polish delegation, Romer was a member.

The Treaty of Versailles, which ended the war between the winning Allies and defeated Germany, re-created the country of Poland, and returned substantial portions of land that Germany had expropriated during the partitions to the new republic. Poland then spent two more years fighting the Soviet Union, Ukraine, and Lithuania in wars that are poorly remembered today to establish its eastern frontiers.

They didn't last long. In the summer of 1939, German Foreign Minister Joachim von Ribbentrop went to Moscow to meet Soviet Foreign Minister Vyacheslav Molotov and sign a nonaggression pact between Nazi Germany and the USSR. Eight days later, Germany invaded Poland, triggering the Second World War. And a little more than two weeks after that, the Soviet Union invaded from the opposite side.

A map of the time (shown on page 107) demonstrates the Nazi-Soviet deal to carve up Poland was hardly a secret. On September 18, 1939, one day after the Red Army entered eastern Poland, *Izvestiya*, the official Soviet newspaper, printed an illustration showing Poland already cut in two. At the map's lower left-hand corner, its legend describes the thick, fuzzy double track that runs North-South through Warsaw and splits the nation: It's a "line of demarcation between the German and Soviet armies established by the German government and the government of the USSR."

The double invasions reprised the old partitions, but with lethally updated weapons, and crushed the Poles in a matter of weeks.

In 1941, Hitler violated the nonaggression pact and invaded the Soviet Union, opening a brutal new front in World War II. By mid-1943,

Historya (*History*), from *Geograficzno-Statystyczny Atlas Polski* (*Geographical and Statistical Atlas of Poland*) by Eugeniusz Romer, was published in 1916. It superimposes all the eighteenth-century partitions on one map, showing how foreign powers gobbled up Poland in three stages.

Russian troops were beating back the Germans, and by the summer of the following year, they were pushing back through Poland. But Soviet forces halted their advance outside Warsaw, and refused to reinforce Poles who were rising up against the Nazis, or to provide them with air or artillery support. The Germans then killed some 15,000 members of the resistance and more than 150,000 civilians, systematically burned down buildings across the city, and deported another 650,000 residents to labor camps. Once the insurgency failed, supporters of a free Poland were left unable to resist the administrative and military units the Soviets set up as they occupied the country. As World War II drew to an end, the USSR's Joseph Stalin made it clear to the US and Great Britain that the Soviets intended to stay in eastern Poland—and the Baltics, and parts of Finland and Romania—and the western Allies had little choice but to consent.

The Soviets ultimately kept most of the Polish land they had occupied in 1939, essentially snatching away the eastern third of the interwar republic. As compensation, the Allies assigned parts of eastern Germany and the Baltic coast to Poland. All told, the once-again-new country sustained a net loss of nearly 29,000 square miles, or 19 percent of its prewar territory, plus the staggering costs of displacing millions of people from the so-called Recovered Territories that shifted borders. Its new boundaries essentially became the ones shown in the carnation on the *1 Maja* poster, and remain in place today, more than thirty years after the collapse of the Iron Curtain.

From founding to invasions, through world war, precarious independence, and communist rule, political maps have told the story of Poland's survival—and its stubbornly nationalist character.

"Poland's modern history . . . is one of a recurrent loss of independence," the analysts Jarosław Kuisz and Karolina Wigura wrote in a *New York Times* opinion piece in 2023. "This tragic inheritance, never far away, explains the government's energetic response to the war in Ukraine: The future must not repeat the past. . . . A glance at the map is enough to see that the countries most muscular in their defense of Ukraine are those affected by the 1939 Nazi-Soviet pact. . . . Theirs is a solidarity based on the trauma of Russian imperialism."

To quote the play *Dziady*: "Our nation is like lava. On the top it is hard and hideous, but its internal fire cannot be extinguished even in one hundred years of cold."

Or one thousand.

On September 18, 1939, the day after the USSR invaded Poland, *Izvestiya* published a map showing Poland partitioned again, this time by the Nazis and Soviets.

БАЛТИЙСКОЕ МОРЕ
ЛИТВА
ГЕРМАНИЯ
ВОСТОЧНАЯ ПРУССИЯ
СССР
РУМЫНИЯ
Кенигсберг
Данциг
КАУНАС
Вильно
МИНСК
Белосток
ВАРШАВА
Брест-Литовск
Познань
Быдгощ
Лодзь
Калиш
Люблин
Каттовицы
Краков
Львов
КИЕВ
МАСШТАБ:
0 100 200 км.
Демаркационная линия между германской и советской армиями, установленная Германским Правительством и Правительством СССР.

Southern Sudanese Independence Referendum, 2011
Red Sea
Northern
River Nile
Ad Damir
North Darfur
Khartoum
Khartoum
Kassala
Kassala
North Kurdufan
Gezira
Wad Medani
Gedarif
El Fasher
Al Ubayyid
West Kurdufan
White Nile
Sennar
West Darfur
South Darfur
South Kordufan
Blue Nile
Upper Nile
Malakal
North Bahr-al-Ghazal
Unity
Warap
West Bahr al-Ghazal
Waw
Jungoli
Lakes
West Equatoria
Eastern Equatoria
Juba
Central Equatoria
Legend
International Boundary
Disputed Boundary (Line of Seperation)
Proposed Boundary between Northern and Sourthern Sudan
Wilayat (State) Boundary
Nicholas A. Jackson, Cartographer
Congressional Cartography Program
Library of Congress, Washington, DC
January 10, 2011
Source: US State Department and BBC.
1:9,000,000
LIBRARY OF CONGRESS

The Sad Map of the World's Newest Country

Establishing the borders of South Sudan helped create a new nation—but could not prevent the ceaseless woe that followed.

Following two long civil wars (the first stretched from 1955 to 1972, the second from 1983 to 2005), Sudan created an autonomous region from its southern lands, as shown on the map, opposite. And it agreed to put secession for ten southern states on the ballot. In February 2011, southern Sudanese voted overwhelmingly to create their own country. In July, South Sudan became independent. It's the 193rd and still most recently admitted member of the United Nations.

It has also been immersed in nearly continuous bloodshed since the moment of its birth.

The referendum map is marked by clean lines and plain text. Except for a couple of disputed bits between Sudan and external neighbors, all its boundaries seem quite orderly. A bright pink border cordons off the southernmost third of the country, representing what negotiators hoped would be a clean break between North and South.

An unusually broad array of stakeholders backed independence, including power players in the United States. Evangelicals sympathized with Christians in southern Sudan, who had been oppressed by Sudanese governments dominated by Islamist northerners. President Barack Obama and his administration viewed diplomacy in South Sudan as an important alternative to the military interventions on which America had embarked in Afghanistan and Iraq. Liberal internationalists everywhere saw a chance to set right a former British colony whose borders had been sutured together in the nineteenth century without regard for the Indigenous people who lived within them. On Independence Day in 2011, the US sent Susan Rice, its ambassador to the United Nations, to attend, and she brought her then-thirteen-year-old son; hope was in the air.

But things went very wrong very quickly. In December 2013, a battle broke out in the new capital of Juba between forces loyal to President Salva Kiir and backers of Vice President Riek Machar, and the fighting spread so fast that it displaced more than 400,000 people from their homes in a month. Soon, South Sudan was plunged into a full-scale

Southern Sudanese Independence Referendum was created by cartographers at the US Library of Congress early in 2011, just before a vote to determine the fate of ten states in Sudan, then Africa's largest country by area.

civil war of its own. The conflict was partly tribal—Kiir is a member of the Dinka ethnic group, while Machar is Nuer—and quickly became surpassingly brutal. Both sides targeted civilians, including children, for castration, rape, and murder, and attacked international aid workers too. The warring parties reached a peace agreement in 2015, only for it to collapse.

South Sudan also happens to be the country in the world most affected by climate change, according to World Food Program USA, which says the nation is "simultaneously drowning and drying," as it's hit in different regions by rising floods from the Nile River and by drought. And as fighting raged across the country, violence and natural disasters together destroyed any chance for many South Sudanese, 95 percent of whom depend on subsistence farming, herding, or fishing to make a living or even to eat. Famine struck in 2017.

Kiir and Machar agreed to another deal in 2018 and declared the war "over" in 2020, and this brought a shaky peace to South Sudan at the national level. But elections were scheduled for December 2024, then put off until 2026. And local violence is still widespread. The humanitarian situation is still dire—the United Nations estimated that 7.1 million people in South Sudan, more than half its population, faced crisis levels of hunger in 2024. And corruption is still endemic. South Sudan has substantial oil revenues, but independent observers say its politicians and generals have long siphoned off huge portions of them. "The government can't even pay its own workers," according to Alan Boswell, a senior analyst at the International Crisis Group, a conflict-prevention organization based in Brussels, Belgium. "The heart of the problem is that the oil money coming into the government is disappearing."

When South Sudan became a nation on paper in 2011, its map traced the need for its existence and the reach of its aspirations. But even the best political maps can't show whether elites will share resources, rivals fighting against a common foe will unite for a common cause, or institutions will strengthen borders. They are the first, not the last, step in partitions.

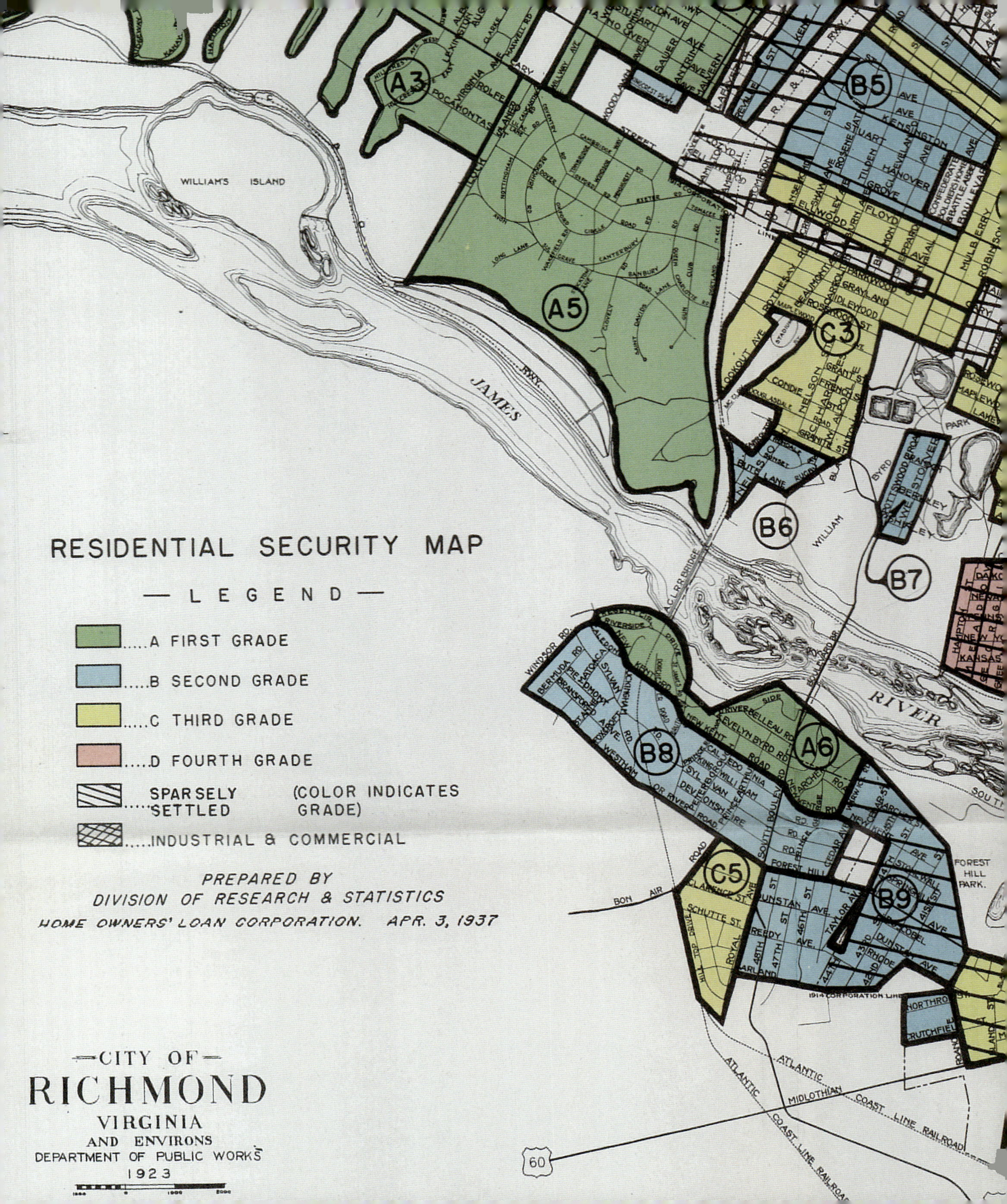
RESIDENTIAL SECURITY MAP
— LEGEND —
A FIRST GRADE
B SECOND GRADE
C THIRD GRADE
D FOURTH GRADE
SPARSELY SETTLED (COLOR INDICATES GRADE)
INDUSTRIAL & COMMERCIAL
PREPARED BY
DIVISION OF RESEARCH & STATISTICS
HOME OWNERS' LOAN CORPORATION. APR. 3, 1937
CITY OF
RICHMOND
VIRGINIA
AND ENVIRONS
DEPARTMENT OF PUBLIC WORKS
1923
WILLIAM'S ISLAND
JAMES
RIVER
A3
A5
A6
B5
B6
B7
B8
B9
C3
C5
FOREST HILL PARK
ATLANTIC COAST LINE RAILROAD
60

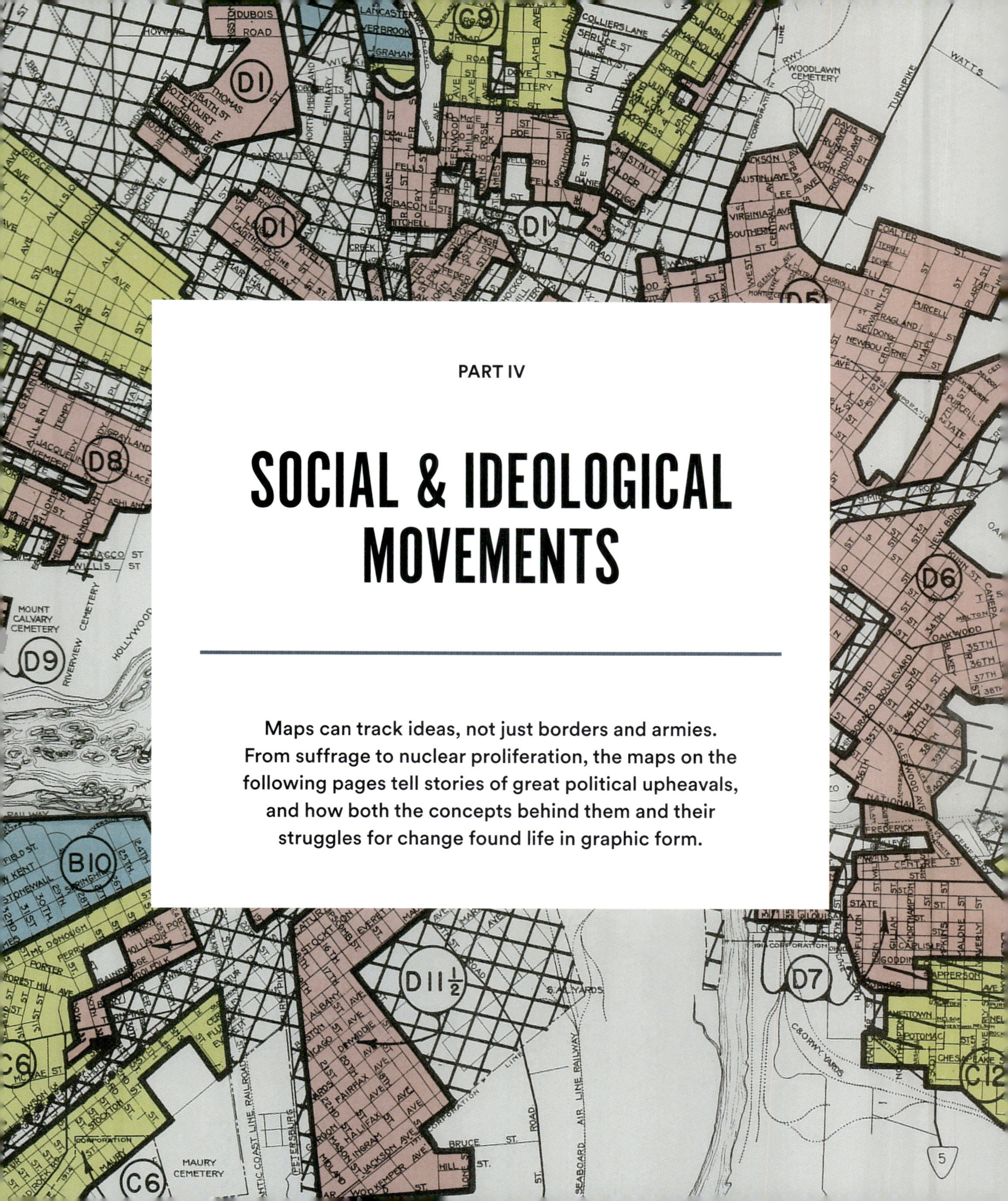

PART IV

SOCIAL & IDEOLOGICAL MOVEMENTS

Maps can track ideas, not just borders and armies. From suffrage to nuclear proliferation, the maps on the following pages tell stories of great political upheavals, and how both the concepts behind them and their struggles for change found life in graphic form.

JOHN C. FREMONT.

REYNOLDS'S
POLITICAL MAP OF THE UNITED STATE

DESIGNED TO EXHIBIT

THE COMPARATIVE AREA OF THE FREE AND SLAVE STATES,

AND THE TERRITORY OPEN TO SLAVERY OR FREEDOM BY THE REPEAL OF THE MISSOURI COMPROMIS

WITH A COMPARISON OF THE PRINCIPAL STATISTICS OF THE FREE AND SLAVE STATES, FROM THE CENSUS OF 1850.

NEW YORK: Published by WM. C. REYNOLDS, No. 195 Broadway, and J. C. JONES, No. 1 Spruce Street. CHICAGO: RUFUS BLANCHARD, No. 52 La Salle S

BRITISH AMERICA

WASHINGTON TER.

OREGON TER.

MINNESOTA

TERRITORY OF NEBRASKA

UTAH TERRITORY

CALIFORNIA

TERRITORY OF KANSAS

MISSOURI COMPROMISE LINE 36° 30'

TERRITORY OF NEW MEXICO

INDIAN TERRITORY

TEXAS

IOWA

WISCONSIN

MICHIGAN

ILLINOIS

INDIANA

OHIO

MISSOURI

KENTUCKY

TENNESSEE

ARKANSAS

ALABAMA

GEORGIA

SOUTH CAROLINA

NORTH CAROLI

FLORIDA

THE ELECTION OF PRESIDENT.

The Presidents and Vice-Presidents.

POST-OFFICE STATISTICS FOR A SINGLE YEAR.

FREEDOM VS. SLAVERY: COMPARISON OF THE CHIEF STATISTICS OF THE FREE STATES AND OF THE SLAVE STATES, ACCORDING TO THE U. S. CENSUS OF 185

E. MENDENHALL, MAP, BOOK & PRINT SELLER, CINCINNATI, OHIO.

The Road Maps to the US Civil War

Political maps lured Americans westward, showed the nation disintegrating over slavery, and reflected persistent divides after Reconstruction.

The greatest political maps of the nineteenth century show the United States reckoning with its foundational sin of slavery while expanding all the way across the continent of North America.

Even before the Declaration of Independence asserted that "all men are created equal," some Americans wondered whether their national ideals could withstand the reality of legal slavery.[1] For more than eight decades, the political answer to that question was a tenuous "yes," through a long series of messy bargains, often involving maps.

In 1787, for instance, the Constitution decreed that congressional representatives would be apportioned to states by population—and that each state's number of inhabitants would include three-fifths of its enslaved persons, even though the enslaved could not vote. Another example: The Missouri Compromise of 1820 admitted Missouri to the union as a slave state and Maine as a free state. It also split territories farther west along the 36°30' parallel, which runs between Missouri and Arkansas, banning slavery north of that latitude and allowing its expansion south of the line. These provisions, and many others involving the boundaries of slavery, were fiercely negotiated and hugely controversial.

Reynolds's Political Map of the United States, published in 1856, shows the country riven by slavery. Split starkly into pieces that are about to go to war with each other, it shows free states in pink, slave states in gray, and American territories in blue (leaving Kansas uncolored to highlight its unresolved status).

1 For example, in 1774, Richard Wells, a Quaker merchant from Philadelphia, wrote a series of "reflections" where he asked "whether we can reconcile the *exercise of* SLAVERY with our *professions of freedom*."

A New Map of
TEXAS OREGON
AND
CALIFORNIA
WITH THE REGIONS ADJOINING.
COMPILED
from the most recent authorities
PHILADELPHIA
Published by S. Augustus Mitchell
N.E. CORNER OF MARKET & SEVENTH STREETS.
1846
BRITISH POSSESSIONS
OREGON
PACIFIC OCEAN
MISSOURI TERRITORY
GREAT INTERIOR BASIN
UPPER OR NEW
OF CALIFORNIA
CALIFORNIA
TEXAS
CHIHUAHUA
DURANGO
GULF OF MEXICO
EXPLANATION.
EMIGRANT ROUTE FROM MISSOURI TO OREGON.

Meanwhile, the nation continued to grow, as would-be settlers from North and South alike eyed the vast stretches of the Louisiana Purchase, and then the lands beyond. The federal government encouraged them, in part by displacing the people who were already there. The Indian Removal Act of 1830, for example, expelled Indigenous peoples from their lands east of the Mississippi River.

After Mexico gained its independence from Spain in 1821, Americans streamed into the northeastern part of that new country, often to establish cotton plantations—and kept going even after Mexico banned slavery and outlawed emigration from the United States. In 1836, Texas declared its own independence and asked to join the US, which annexed the fledgling republic in 1845.

That was the year newspapers started using the phrase "Manifest Destiny"—the idea that God Himself ordained the expansion of the United States from Atlantic to Pacific. To the settlers heading west, the concept must have seemed plausible if not obvious. Migrants kept pushing, and not just into Mexico. In 1843, a wagon train of a thousand pioneers set out on the Oregon Trail, which eventually carried nearly half a million farmers, miners, ranchers, and tradespeople northwest.

By 1846, travel was booming—and so were maps. And in *A New Map of Texas, Oregon, and California*, opposite, Samuel Augustus Mitchell provided a detailed guide for trekking Americans while capturing the United States at the peak of its territorial hunger.

Mitchell, born in Bristol, Connecticut, was a teacher whose dislike of old, inaccurate classroom maps drove him to move to Philadelphia and start his own publishing company.[2]

Mitchell's 1846 map highlights the three huge chunks of land coveted by President James K. Polk, an ardent expansionist, and many of the pioneers: Texas, "Upper California," and the Oregon Territory.

American settlers in Oregon had already pushed far north. Some were agitating for the United States to grab land all the way to the border of Alaska, which was then owned by Russia. And they rallied to a slogan that soon became famous: "54°40' or Fight!"—indicating the latitude they wanted as a boundary. So at the time Mitchell published the first edition

Samuel Augustus Mitchell's 1846 *A New Map of Texas, Oregon, and California* shows three vast territories targeted by America settlers and expansionists: Texas in green, with a southern border of the Rio Grande River; "Upper California" in pink, stretching to the Pacific Ocean; and the Oregon Territory in yellow, extending almost 500 miles into what is now British Columbia.

---

2 Mitchell didn't draw maps himself, but relied on a fleet of top-notch cartographers and engravers. They issued maps, travel guides—and, yes, a school atlas.

of his map, the US faced the prospect of wars with both Mexico to the south and England (which ruled Canada) to the north.

But the map suggests only opportunity. It displays rivers, mountains, and towns. It shows caravan and expedition routes, distances between outposts on the way from Missouri to Oregon, plus "chief points of interest." Colorful, clear, and accurate, it measured 21.5 by 22 inches, but also folded to pocket size for easy travel. It was, in short, a wonderful lure to Americans looking for new lives in the West.[3] And it sold incredibly well, staying in print until 1894.

The US avoided violence over Oregon by agreeing to split the territory at the 49th parallel of latitude, which still traces the familiar borderline between the United States and Canada today. But President Polk got the fight he wanted. In 1846, he sent American troops into a disputed area of Texas, triggering two years of conflict with Mexico. Many northerners, including a young congressman named Abraham Lincoln, opposed the war as naked aggression on behalf of enslavers. But by the time it was over, Mexico had retreated from Texas and ceded 55 percent of its territory, including what are now the states of Arizona, California, and New Mexico, plus parts of Colorado, Nevada, and Utah—to the US. That's all of "Upper California" on Mitchell's map.

As the United States continued to expand, the issues of whether and where to allow slavery became harder and harder to finesse. In 1854, Illinois Senator Stephen Douglas, a prominent Northern Democrat, won passage of an act that organized Kansas and Nebraska as territories but left it to the residents of those regions to resolve the question of legalizing slavery. Douglas hoped to soothe tensions by making slavery a matter of local control, or, as he put it, "popular sovereignty."[4] Instead, pro- and antislavery factions flooded into Kansas, where they set up separate capitals, legislatures, constitutions, and militias, and ultimately broke into

---

3 Among the seekers: members of the Mormon Church, many of whom used Mitchell's map as a guide when they relocated to Utah.

4 Douglas also hoped to bolster national unity and his own chances of becoming president by opening the West to homesteaders and a transcontinental railroad, which he wanted to run through Chicago. He is best known today for his debates with Lincoln, whom he defeated in 1858 to win a third Senate term and lost to in the 1860 presidential election.

open warfare against each other: Civil war broke out in Kansas more than five years before it went nationwide. And as the fighting continued, the Democratic administrations of Franklin Pierce and James Buchanan supported the enslavers, even after it became evident that most residents of Kansas wanted it to enter the union as a free state.

The battles over Kansas inflamed antislavery Northerners, many of whom came to believe the federal government was out to push slavery across the entire country. Some of these opponents abhorred slavery on moral or religious grounds. Others were more concerned that slave lords who already had massive plantations and literally owned their own laborers would take control of the choicest lands in the West if they were allowed to invade whatever territories they pleased. Activists from both groups came together and launched the Republican Party. And in June 1856, this new caucus nominated John C. Frémont, a California senator and former western explorer, as its first candidate for president. His campaign slogan: "Free Soil, Free Labor, Free Speech, Free Men, and Frémont!"

Just three weeks after Frémont's nomination, a publisher named William C. Reynolds took out a front-page ad in the *New-York Tribune* announcing the sale of *Reynolds's Political Map of the United States*, (pages 114–115) supporting the Frémont campaign. Its price: 25 cents for a 29-inch by 31-inch sheet, or 50 cents for a pocket version. This was the first widely published document in American history to call itself a political map, and it vividly illustrates the exceptionally high stakes of its moment. Free states are pink, slave states are gray, and the result is a jigsaw puzzle that looks as though the gaping maw of slave power, with Missouri and Texas for jaws, is about to chomp Kansas on its way to swallowing up everything west of the Mississippi River.

And it's not just the map's color scheme leaving that impression. Many of us are familiar from our school days with the Mercator map (see pages 32–33), which shows the globe as though a light inside the earth is projecting outward onto a sheet of paper. Mercator maps get very distorted near the poles; most notoriously, they incorrectly show Greenland as being larger than Australia. But there are lots of different ways to translate a round surface to a flat plane. An orthographic projection, for example, shows a hemisphere as it would look from outer space. In contrast to Mercator maps, orthographic maps bulge in the middle, where land is most visible to a distant view.

Now, notice the lines of longitude on Reynolds's map: They're farther apart in the South, and convergent in the North. We don't know whether they were actually drawn so they would meet at the North Pole, as they would in an actual orthographic map, or just shrunk somewhat for propaganda purposes. But the effect is clear: southern regions look bigger—and more threatening. The slave state of Florida, for example, appears to be roughly the size of the free state of Michigan, even though Michigan actually covers nearly 50 percent more ground.

The fine print on Reynolds's map is unusually important. Six text blocks are tiered around the southern United States. And while these appear cut and pasted, they comprise a detailed, quite sophisticated argument: that slavery was retarding the progress of the South, yet persisted because of its special political protections.

Two tables across the bottom of the map, for example, use 1850 census data to show that while slave states covered more acreage than free states, free states had more valuable property and farms, and far more infrastructure, newspapers, and public libraries. One chart points out that only a small fraction of white Southerners were enslavers and fewer than three hundred held two hundred or more enslaved persons, yet "this faction controls every branch of the Federal Government, and wields its influence for the increase and perpetuation of Slavery." Why? Another chart explains: Slave states, while less populous than free states, were nevertheless entitled to two US senators apiece—a stipulation that still frustrates egalitarians today. And they were apportioned members of the House of Representatives based on numbers that partially included enslaved persons among their populations.

Reynolds's map carries no author's credit, but its text was probably written by John Jay, an abolitionist whose grandfather was the founder of the same name (and who served as the first chief justice of the Supreme Court of the United States). The younger Jay wrote analogous captions for a similar map, also published in 1856, adding a dollop of sarcasm.[5] Posters, handbills, even German-language maps for immigrants, were all over the

---

5 Noting on that map that slave states cost the federal government more in mail delivery than they collected in postage, while free states ran a surplus, Jay said that "all goes to prove how the suffering South is oppressed by the North."

campaign of 1856, and their message was stark: Enslaver oligarchs were undermining American democracy, and would soon destroy it altogether.

Frémont lost the 1856 election to Democrat James Buchanan, one of the very worst presidents the United States has ever had to endure. In 1857, the Supreme Court confirmed many Northerners' worst nightmares by ruling in *Dred Scott v. Sandford* that Blacks were not and could not be American citizens, and that Congress didn't have the authority to outlaw slavery in US territories. The country slid further into conflict, which became full-blown civil war after Abraham Lincoln was elected president in 1860 and eleven states seceded from the union.

The US Civil War generated a nearly endless (and still ongoing) flow of military maps, used during the war for strategic planning and afterward in everything from textbooks to battlefield reenactments. But the most important political map of the war didn't show any armed forces at all. Rather, it was a *Map Showing the Distribution of the Slave Population of the Southern States* (pages 122–123).

This map was produced by the US Coast Survey, which was originally established by President Thomas Jefferson in 1807 to help define and defend America's borders, and which remains the country's official maker of nautical charts. By the time of Lincoln's election, the Coast Survey was the federal government's top scientific agency. Its work helped the North blockade ports across the South, and in its maps of slavery, it advanced a relatively new kind of cartography that combined mapping with statistics. Cloropleth maps, invented in France in 1826, use colors or tones to indicate the quantity or value of data within particular areas. This was an early and important example in America: Cartographer Edwin Hergesheimer created a density map that showed Southern states subdivided into counties, with each small region shaded according to the percentage of its population that were enslaved persons, according to the 1860 census. The darker the county, the greater the enslaved proportion.

The result is extraordinary: Belts of blackness, sometimes across state lines, draw your attention to areas with high concentrations of—and dependence on—slavery in places like the counties on both sides of the Mississippi River Valley. As an extreme example, enslaved people made up 90.8 percent of the population of Tensas Parish in Louisiana, where census data reveals that just 340 enslavers held 14,592 enslaved people. At the same time, other regions on the map, like most of Appalachia, are hardly shaded at all.

For President Lincoln, this slavery density map affirmed two of his core beliefs: First, that the South had gone to war to preserve slavery, not "states' rights." Surely it was no coincidence that the most heavily shaded areas—where white citizens relied the most on slave labor and slave profits—were most committed to rebellion. Indeed, the map shows that the six states whose populations were more than 40 percent enslaved had been the first six to secede from the union.

Lincoln also thought there were plenty of places where Southerners were not particularly attached to slavery, and which he could hope to break apart from the Confederacy. In December 1861, for instance, he called on Congress to fund a railroad connecting "the loyal regions of east Tennessee and western North Carolina . . . with Kentucky and other faithful parts of the Union." Look at the Hergesheimer map and you'll see that east Tennessee and western North Carolina are two of its very lightest regions.

We know how much Lincoln valued this map partly because of an artist named Francis Bicknell Carpenter. Carpenter was inspired by the Emancipation Proclamation, and wanted to paint a grand tableau of the president reading the document to the members of his cabinet for the first time. Lincoln allowed sketches by Carpenter—and then also let him stay for six months at the White House, where he set up a studio in the State Dining Room. In his memoir, Carpenter noted Lincoln's attachment to the map, saying it "usually leaned against a leg of his desk or table, and bore the marks of much service."

"Wishing to introduce this map into my picture, I carried it off one day, without the President's knowledge," Carpenter wrote. Some time later, Lincoln entered the studio to check on the artist's progress, and, as Carpenter put it, "his eye fell upon the map." Carpenter continued:

"'Ah!' said he, '*you* have appropriated my map, have you? I have been looking all around for it.' And with that, he put on his spectacles, and, taking it up, walked to the window; and sitting down upon a trunk began to pore over it very earnestly."

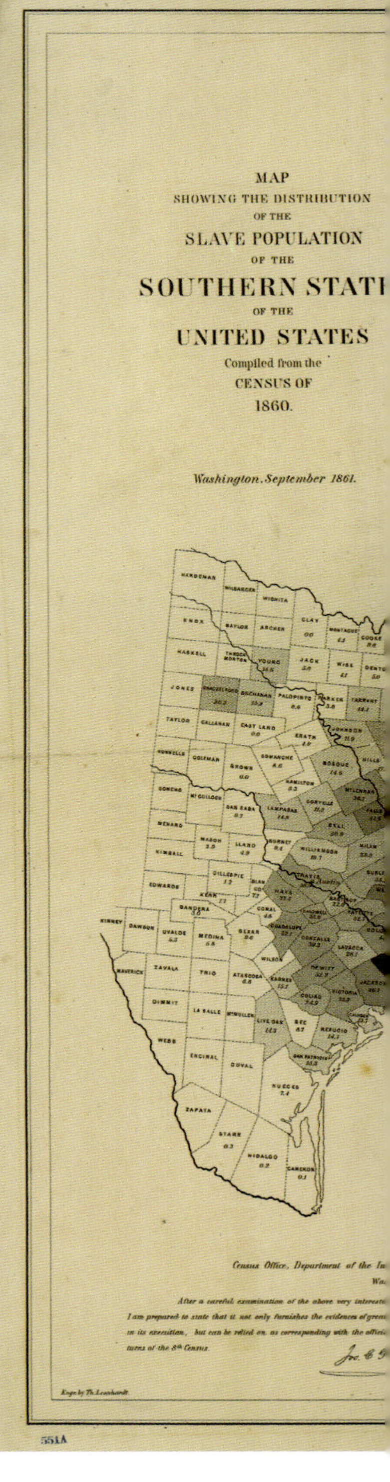

In 1861, Edwin Hergesheimer, working for the US Coast Survey, created this density map, officially named *Map Showing the Distribution of the Slave Population of the Southern States of the United States*. It showed the percentage of the population that was enslaved persons in counties across Southern states, according to 1860 census data. The darker the county, the greater the share of slaves.

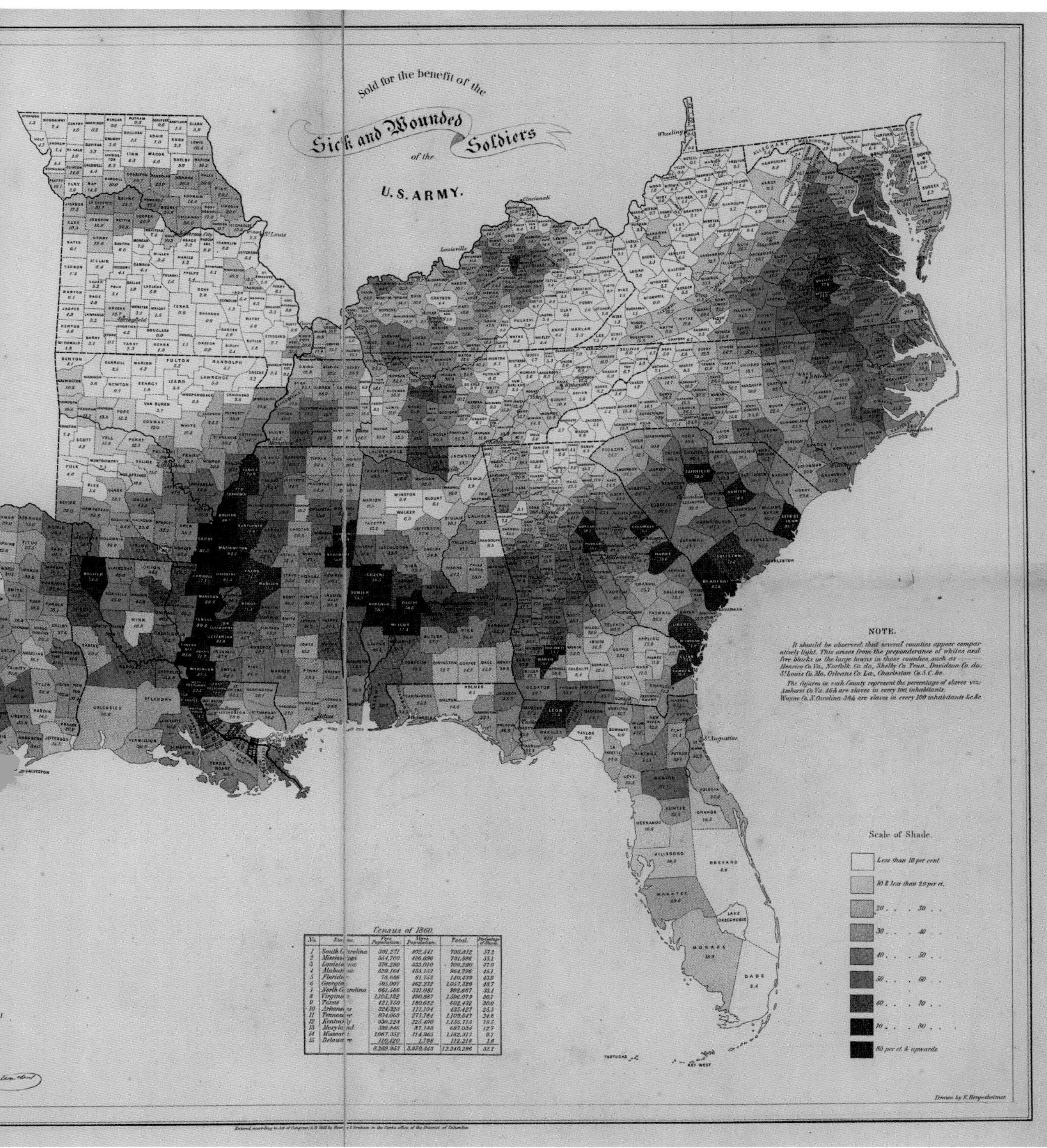

Census of 1860.

No.	States.	Free Population.	Slave Population.	Total.	Percentage of Slaves.
1	South Carolina	301,271	402,541	703,812	57.2
2	Mississippi	354,700	436,696	791,396	55.1
3	Louisiana	376,280	333,010	709,290	47.0
4	Alabama	529,164	435,132	964,296	45.1
5	Florida	78,686	61,753	140,439	43.9
6	Georgia	595,097	462,232	1,057,329	43.7
7	North Carolina	661,586	331,081	992,667	33.4
8	Virginia	1,105,192	490,887	1,596,079	30.7
9	Texas	421,750	180,682	602,432	30.0
10	Arkansas	324,323	111,104	435,427	25.5
11	Tennessee	834,063	275,784	1,109,847	24.8
12	Kentucky	930,223	225,490	1,155,713	19.5
13	Maryland	599,846	87,188	687,034	12.7
14	Missouri	1,067,352	114,965	1,182,317	9.7
15	Delaware	110,420	1,798	112,218	1.6
		8,289,953	3,950,343	12,240,296	32.2

Examining one of the dark areas of the map, Lincoln remarked that a recent Union incursion could liberate many enslaved residents. "We ought to get a heap of them," the president said.

Carpenter unveiled his 9-foot by 14.5-foot oil painting, called *First Reading of the Emancipation Proclamation by President Lincoln*, in July 1864 (above). Tucked into the somber group portrait, in its lower-right corner, is an image of the slavery density map.[6]

Of course, abolitionists were right to believe in a future without slavery. But it was hard to foresee just how long sectional disputes would

First Reading of the Emancipation Proclamation by President Lincoln, created by painter Francis Bicknell Carpenter in 1864, shows a seated Lincoln, proclamation in hand, flanked by his advisers. And in its bottom right-hand corner, leaning against the table, is the slavery density map (see pages 122–123).

---

6 *First Reading* is probably most famous today as the picture on the cover of Doris Kearns Goodwin's 2005 presidential biography *Team of Rivals: The Political Genius of Abraham Lincoln*—but that image is truncated and doesn't show the map. The painting now hangs above the west staircase outside the Senate floor at the US Capitol.

persist in American politics and culture. After Lincoln was assassinated in 1865 and the United States pursued a twelve-year-long but ultimately abortive attempt at Reconstruction in the South, a classic Gilded Age map illustrated this point. In 1883, Henry Gannett, chief geographer of the US Census, and historian Fletcher Hewes published *Scribner's Statistical Atlas of the United States*. And this 260-page compendium of census data contained *Popular Vote: 1880* (pages 126–127), which gave the nation a whole new way of visualizing its political preferences.

This map presented the results of the 1880 presidential election—and, like the Coast Survey map, displayed its data county by county using cloropleth shading.

The 1880 election was extraordinarily close. Republican James Garfield defeated Democrat Winfield Scott Hancock by fewer than 10,000 votes out of more than 9 million cast. And the map's level of detail, still impressive today, was incredible for its era: For the first time, Americans could see the local patterns that added up to state- and national-level results. In particular, there were areas with significant Democratic support in Northern states that Garfield won, including New York (which the Republican carried by less than 2 percentage points), Pennsylvania, and Ohio. This foreshadowed the politics of the late nineteenth and early twentieth centuries, when urban and immigrant voters increasingly trended Democratic.

But sometimes trees are important for what they tell us about forests. Look closely at the Southern states on the Gannett map, and you'll find Republican blue in just a few areas. They include the Mississippi River Valley and delta, the fertile-soil belt across southern Alabama, and coastal South Carolina. These were the areas whose cultures and economies were most dominated by slavery—precisely the regions colored darkest on the slavery density map in 1861. By 1880, freedmen could vote, and they turned out for the Republican Party of Abraham Lincoln and Ulysses S. Grant. The blue counties in the South also include east Tennessee and western North Carolina—the very same areas where the 1861 map showed relatively low reliance on slavery, and where Lincoln thought residents would stay loyal to the Union.

After Reconstruction, however, Southern states, one after another, snuffed out Black voting rights; and Republican support shrank to isolated pockets. Gannett's map does display local political variation very impressively. But what it really reveals is the birth of bloc voting by the "Solid South"—the start of an eighty-year period where, despite the Civil

War, national elections were virtually whites-only in the states of the old Confederacy.

US parties switched roles in the 1960s, when the Democratic administrations of John F. Kennedy and Lyndon B. Johnson supported federal intervention to guarantee civil rights for Black Americans. But many of the old political divides remain. Ten of the sixteen free states shown in red on Reynolds's map in 1856 voted for Kamala Harris in 2024. And of the fifteen blue states, twelve voted for Donald Trump (and one, Virginia, splintered in 1863 into two states, one ending in each 2024 camp). Flip the colors on the right-hand side of Reynolds's map, or keep them the same on Gannett's map, and you might think they were drawn yesterday, not more than 140 years ago.

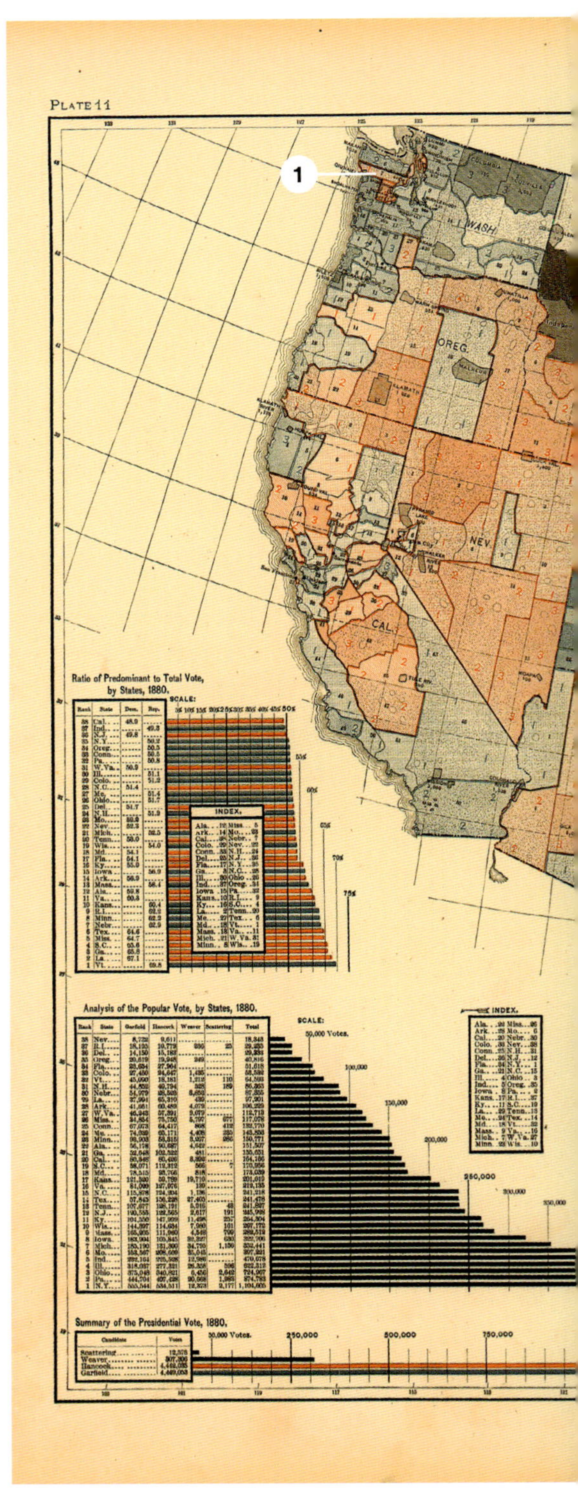

Popular Vote: 1880, created by Henry Gannett and Fletcher Hewes in 1883, showed the results of the 1880 presidential election at the county level. With patches of partisanship that look (and were) very evenly divided, it brings home just how tight the race was.

1 The map displays Democratic areas in red and Republican in blue (the opposite of today's usage).

2 Like the Coast Survey map (see pages 122–123), it deploys cloropleth shading: The greater a party's share of the vote, the darker its color.

3 Just a few regions in Southern states are Republican blue. These include freed areas where slavery had been most dominant—and which had been colored darkest on the 1861 Coast Survey map.

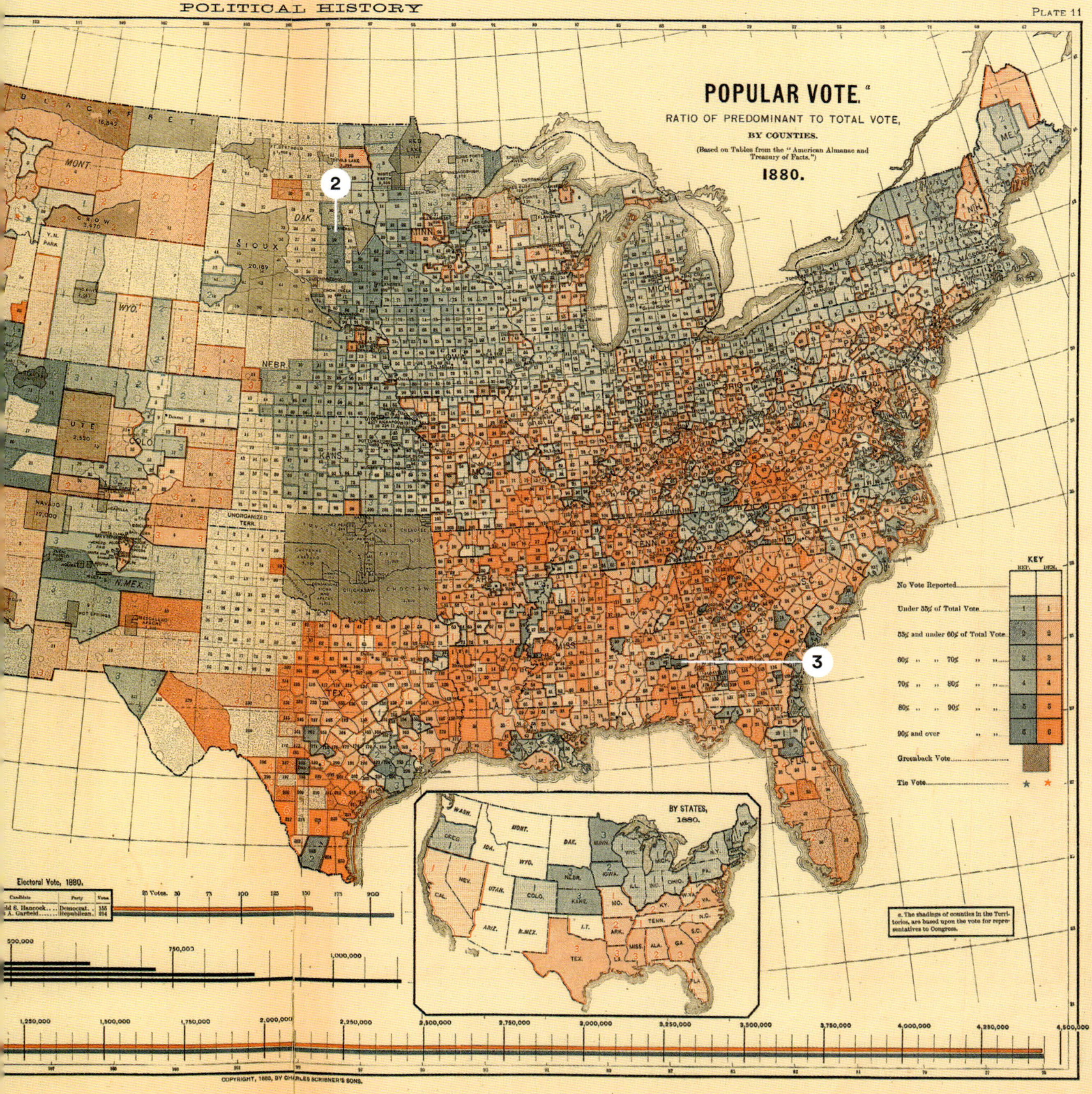

2

POPULAR VOTE.[a]

RATIO OF PREDOMINANT TO TOTAL VOTE,

BY COUNTIES.

(Based on Tables from the "American Almanac and Treasury of Facts.")

1880.

KEY

	REP.	DEM.
No Vote Reported		
Under 55% of Total Vote	1	1
55% and under 60% of Total Vote	2	2
60% ,, ,, 70% ,, ,,	3	3
70% ,, ,, 80% ,, ,,	4	4
80% ,, ,, 90% ,, ,,	5	5
90% and over ,, ,,	6	6
Greenback Vote		
Tie Vote	★	★

3

BY STATES, 1880.

a. The shadings of counties in the Territories, are based upon the vote for representatives to Congress.

Electoral Vote, 1880.

Candidate	Party	Votes
...ld S. Hancock	Democrat.	155
...A. Garfield	Republican.	214

Look forward, women, always; utterly cast away
The memory of hate and struggle and bitterness;
Bonds may endure for a night, but freedom comes with the day,
And the free must remember nothing less.

Forget the strife; remember those who strove—
The first defeated women, gallant and few,
Who gave us hope, as a mother gives us love,
Forget them not, and this remember, too;

How at the later call to come forth and unite,
Women untaught, uncounselled, alone and apart,
Rank upon rank came forth in unguessed might,
Each one answering the call of her own wise heart.

The Maps That Doubled America's Voting Population

Suffrage maps, the most influential maps of persuasion ever deployed in America.

Suffrage maps, which called for women to get the right to vote, combined powerful appeals with broad reach. And *The Awakening* (shown here) is the most sensational example.

Printed across a full two-page spread of *Puck* magazine in 1915, the imagery—and indeed, the very title—of the map equate the cause of women's suffrage with intellectual and moral enlightenment.

Beneath the image is a heroic poem by the feminist writer Alice Duer Miller. A sample verse:

Women untaught, uncounseled,
alone and apart,
Rank upon rank came forth in
unguessed night,
Each one answering the call of her
own wise heart.

The Awakening, created by Hy Mayer and published in 1915, is an outstanding example of a US suffrage map.

1 Lady Liberty wears a cape emblazoned with the words *Votes for Women*.

2 Torch aloft, she is striding from white-colored western states, which had already granted women the right to vote, eastward.

3 In the darkened regions of the rest of the country, feminine figures reach out toward her, grasping for freedom.

The Awakening was published at a critical point in the long fight for women's voting rights. Many suffragists had been bitterly disappointed by the changes to the US Constitution enacted after the Civil War. The Thirteenth Amendment banned slavery. But the Fourteenth disallowed abridging the right to vote only for adult male citizens. Which meant that the first mention of gender ever placed into the federal constitution actually privileged men. And the Fifteenth declared the right to vote would not be denied "on account of race," without mentioning gender. Advocates for equal rights then had to embark on an extended slog, trying to convince state governments one at a time to let women vote. And by the end of the nineteenth century, only a handful of states had done so.

For several overlapping reasons, the suffragists started having more success in the 1890s. Western states and communities realized they needed to attract families of settlers, not just male ranchers and miners (who had been recruited in some cases to dilute the impact of nonwhite voters). And as the Progressive Era dawned, all kinds of reformist ideas became more popular around the country. Finally, women's rights groups had begun adopting new, politically shrewder tactics to take their movement, as Christina Dando, professor of geography at the University of Nebraska Omaha, has put it, "from the parlors to the streets." This meant more public parades, rallies, and advertisements. In some places, it led to alliances with populists or socialists; in others, to targeting state and local elections, like bond issues and primaries.

Maps soon became a crucial new weapon for the suffragists. In December 1907, journalist Bertha Damaris Knobe published a map showing the status of women's voting rights legislation around the country, and it was quickly reprinted, then updated and repurposed for years afterward. These suffrage maps were much plainer than *The Awakening*. But with their shading—from dark times to a brighter future, with intermediate grays or hatching for partial suffrage—they made a simple and strong argument: The expansion of women's voting rights was inevitable and a sign of progress.

From 1910 to 1914, nine states, including California, extended full voting rights to women. By then, suffrage maps were appearing everywhere from billboards to baseball game programs, paper fans to window cards.

In February 1913, as voting rights groups undertook an "Empire State campaign" targeting New York, the editors of *Puck* dedicated an entire issue of their publication to supporting women's suffrage. *Puck*—named

By the early 1910s, suffrage maps could be found on all kinds of commonplace objects. This paper fan, entitled "Keep Cool!" was published by the Massachusetts Women Suffrage Association in 1915.

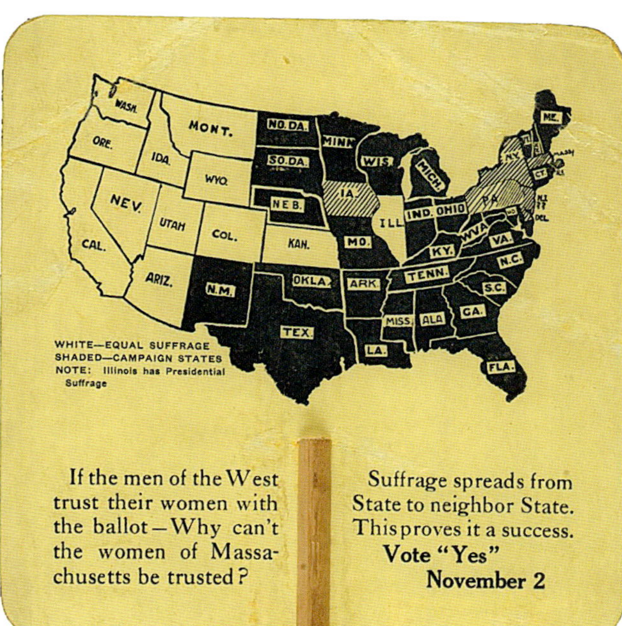

for the mischievous spirit who says, "What fools these mortals be!" in *A Midsummer Night's Dream*—was founded in 1876 and quickly became America's most popular and influential humor magazine. It skewered robber barons and corrupt politicians throughout the Gilded Age. And, capitalizing on rapid improvements in printing technology, it ran reams of colorful and detailed cartoons and illustrations.

For the centerpiece illustration of its suffrage issue, *Puck* turned to its chief cartoonist, Henry "Hy" Mayer.[1] Born in Germany, Mayer drew for magazines in Munich, Paris, and London before joining *Puck* in 1914. He also illustrated, wrote, or directed nearly two hundred short films from 1913 to 1936. But *The Awakening* remains by far his best-known work.

New York did not enact women's suffrage immediately after the Empire State campaign, but voters approved it in 1917. Catalyzing that momentum, the suffragists pressed for an amendment to the federal constitution, and in 1919, both houses of Congress passed the Nineteenth Amendment; three-fourths of states ratified it by August 1920. It stated: "The right of citizens of the United States to vote shall not be denied or abridged by the United States or by any State on account of sex."

Bertha Damaris Knobe doesn't often get counted among the great leaders in the fight for women's voting rights. But she was onto something when she said: "I hope everybody in the country will assiduously take to the making of suffrage maps, for it is a most effective way to advertise the cause."

---

1 To manage the special issue, *Puck* put together two special boards, including half a dozen leading voting rights activists as well as male editors at other publications who were also active in the Men's League for Woman Suffrage in New York.

2

4

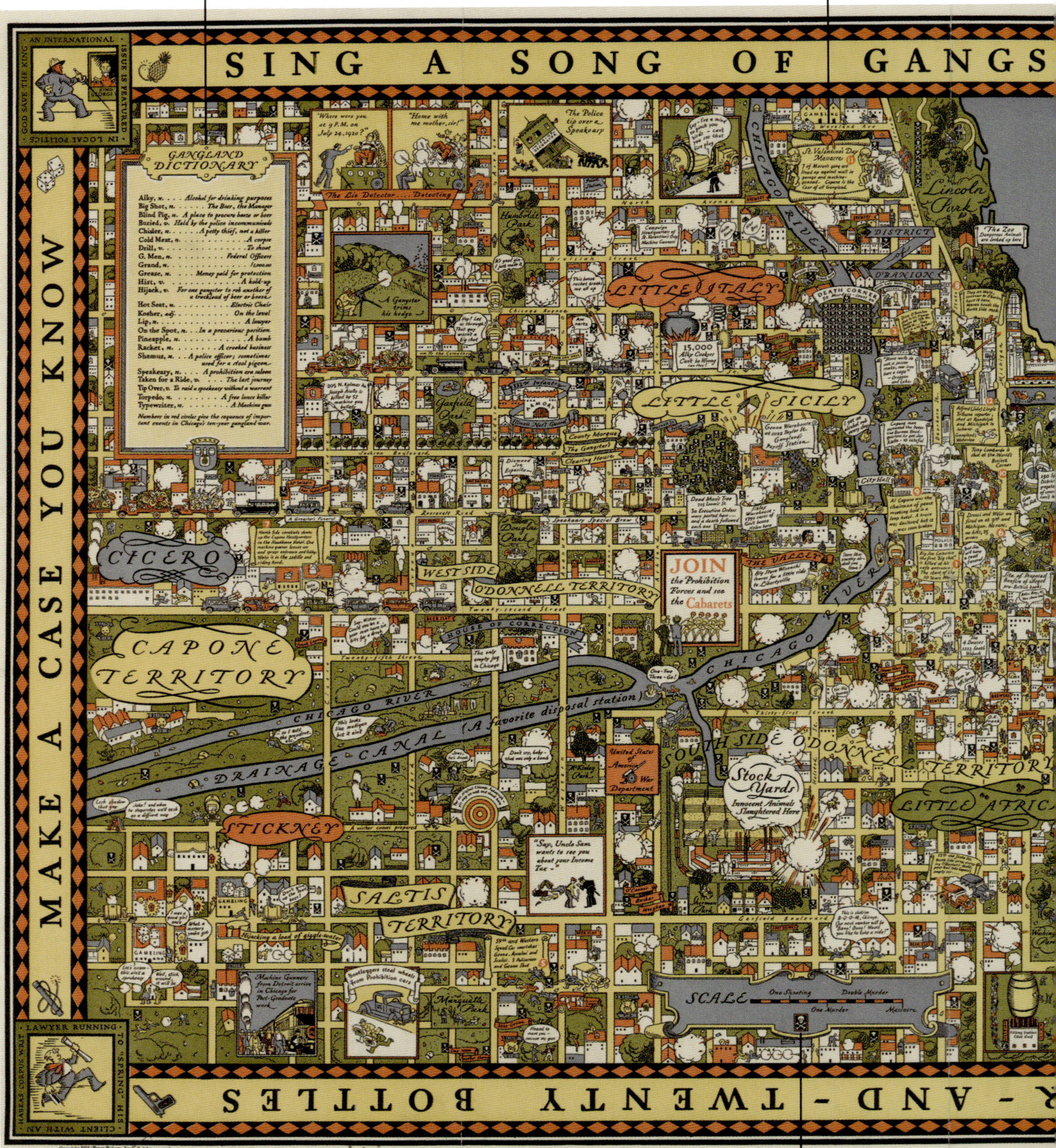

SING A SONG OF GANGS
MAKE A CASE YOU KNOW
TWENTY BOTTLES
AN INTERNATIONAL ISSUE IS FEATURED IN LOCAL POLITICS
GOD SAVE THE KING
LAWYER RUNNING TO "SPRING" HIS CLIENT WITH AN HABEAS CORPUS WRIT
GANGLAND DICTIONARY
Alky, n. . . . Alcohol for drinking purposes
Big Shot, n. . . . . . The Boss, the Manager
Blind Pig, n. A place to procure booze or beer
Buried, v. Held by the police incommunicado
Chisler, n. . . . . . A petty thief, not a killer
Cold Meat, n. . . . . A corpse
Drill, v. . . . . To shoot
G. Men, n. . . . . Federal Officers
Grand, n. $1,000.00
Grease, n. . . . Money paid for protection
Hist, v. . . . . A hold-up
Hijack, v. For one gangster to rob another of a truckload of beer or booze
Hot Seat, n. . . . . Electric Chair
Kosher, adj. . . . . On the level
Lip, n. . . . . A lawyer
On the Spot, n. . . In a precarious position
Pineapple, n. . . . . A bomb
Racket, n. . . . . A crooked business
Shamus, n. . . A police officer; sometimes used for a stool pigeon
Speakeasy, n. . . . A prohibition era saloon
Taken for a Ride, v. . . . The last journey
Tip Over, v. To raid a speakeasy without a warrant
Torpedo, n. . . . . A free lance killer
Typewriter, n. . . . . A Machine gun
Numbers in red circles give the sequence of important events in Chicago's ten-year gangland war.
"Where were you at 9 P.M. on July 24, 1930?"
"Home with me mother, sir!"
The Lie Detector . . . Detecting
The Police tip over a Speakeasy
St. Valentine's Day Massacre
CHICAGO RIVER
Lincoln Park
The Zoo
DISTRICT
O'BANION
LITTLE ITALY
DEATH CORNER
Humboldt Park
A Gangster trims his hedge
15,000 Alky Cookers Can't be Wrong
LITTLE SICILY
Garfield Park
County Morgue
City Hall
CICERO
WEST SIDE
O'DONNELL TERRITORY
JOIN the Prohibition Forces and see the Cabarets
THE VALLEY
HOUSE OF CORRECTION
CAPONE TERRITORY
CHICAGO RIVER
DRAINAGE CANAL (A favorite disposal station)
SOUTH SIDE O'DONNELL TERRITORY
Stock Yards
Innocent Animals Slaughtered Here
United States of America War Department
LITTLE AFRICA
STICKNEY
"Say, Uncle Sam wants to see you about your Income Tax —"
SALTIS TERRITORY
Hijacking a load of giggle water
Machine Gunners from Detroit arrive in Chicago for Post-Graduate work
Bootleggers steal wheels from Prohibition cars
Marquette Park
SCALE
One Shooting
Double Murder
One Murder
Massacre
Copyright 1931 Bruce-Roberts, Inc. all rights reserved

1

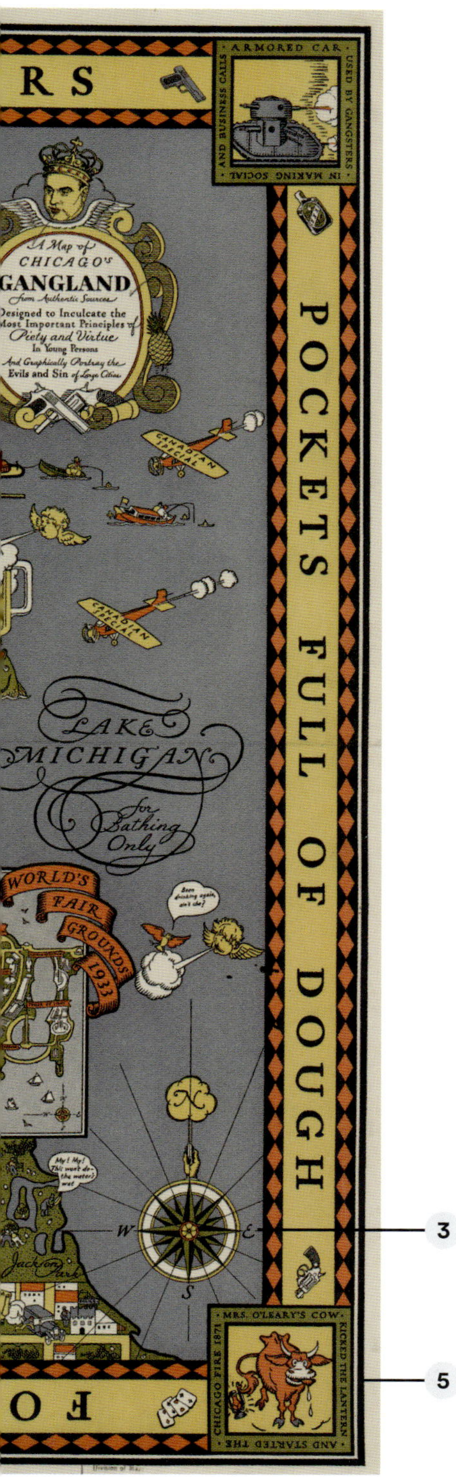

The Map That Whacked Itself

This pictorial classic invites readers to "Sing a song of gangsters, pockets full of dough."

Not too many political maps are funny—at least not intentionally—but *A Map of Chicago's Gangland* is a laugh-out-loud exception. Published in 1931, it's a pictorial map festooned with dozens of detailed, comic book–like illustrations of life overrun by organized crime.

Chicago's Gangland says it's "designed to inculcate the most important principles of piety and virtue in young persons and graphically portray the evils and sin of large cities." But that's just Prohibition-era snark. The street-level depiction of the city is surrounded by a border whose text is a corruption of an old nursery rhyme: "Sing a song of gangsters, pockets full of dough, four-and-twenty bottles make a case you know." The map's four corners depict amusing snippets of Chicago life, like Mrs. O'Leary's cow, which supposedly kicked a lantern to ignite the Great Fire of 1871, and a lawyer who's clutching a writ of habeas corpus rushing to spring his client. A crowned head of Al Capone sits just above the map's title, while underneath, "Canadian Special" planes are flying smuggled liquor across Lake Michigan.

The map shows the city divided by the Chicago River (plus its drainage canal, which the map calls "a favorite disposal station") and clumped into territories controlled by various gangsters. Almost every block shows some vignette of violence, bootlegging, or gambling. Many of these are sarcastic or exaggerated for humorous effect. In one illustration, a gangster uses a mounted machine gun to trim his hedges; in another, a voice from a speakeasy says, "I was a good girl once," and gets the response, "What a memory you've got!"

Amid all its guns and barrels and dice, the map weaves an actual history of Chicago's gang wars into its depictions of landmarks. It details

A Map of Chicago's Gangland, printed in 1931, is packed with illustrations of the city's underworld.

the St. Valentine's Day Massacre of 1929, but its pictorial survey of gangster life extends to a vast range of less-remembered incidents, too. Just above its center, for example, the map marks the "Dead Man's Tree" at 725 South Loomis Street. During Chicago's "Alderman's Wars" from 1916 to 1921, a period when local politicians literally went to war against one another, then names of thirty people were carved into a poplar tree at this site. All thirty were murdered.

Chicago's Gangland first appeared in 1931, a local election year, and just two years before Chicago was due to host a world's fair that would showcase a "Century of Progress" to an international audience. And some reports say that new mayor, Anton Cermak, wanted copies of this map, with its hyperactive portrayal of a violent city, rounded up and destroyed. Whether or not that's true, we know this much: There's no evidence that Bruce-Roberts Inc., the publishing company that printed *Chicago's Gangland*, did business again after August 1931. The map became so rare that only a handful of originals still existed when reproductions started to give it a new life five decades later. Mayor Cermak himself was gunned down by an assassin who was trying to kill President-elect Franklin Roosevelt in March 1933. And even now, we don't know who illustrated or wrote *Chicago's Gangland*. No author ever came forward.[1]

At least not in time to claim credit.

1 The scale of *Chicago's Gangland* isn't in feet or miles, but in distances measured from "one shooting" to "massacre."

2 A gangland dictionary tells readers that a lip is a lawyer, a pineapple is a bomb, and a torpedo is a freelance killer.

3 Its compass points north with a hand holding a gun.

4 Numbered red circles—accompanied by skulls and crossbones where appropriate—annotate key events in mob bosses' struggles to control the city. Number 11 (pictured) describes the St. Valentine's Day Massacre of 1929.

5 Among the map's many caricatures of Chicago legends: Mrs. O'Leary's cow, whose lantern-kicking allegedly started the Great Fire of 1871.

---

1 Some sources attribute this map to an Arthur Erickson, but Mr. Erickson doesn't seem to have created any other cartographic work.

1

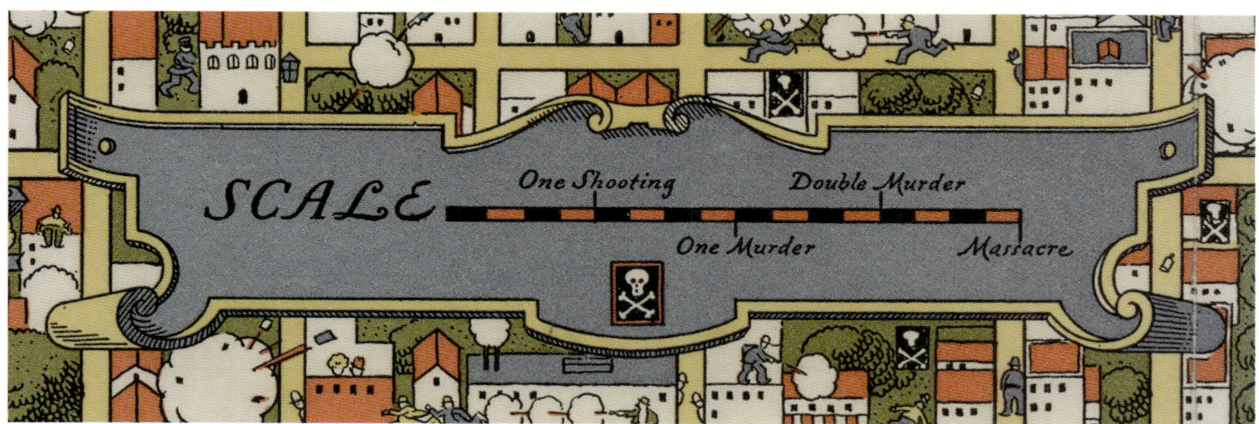

2

GANGLAND DICTIONARY

Alky, *n.* . . . . *Alcohol for drinking purposes*
Big Shot, *n.* . . . . . . *The Boss, the Manager*
Blind Pig, *n.* *A place to procure booze or beer*
Buried, *v.* *Held by the police incommunicado*
Chisler, *n.* . . . . . *A petty thief, not a killer*
Cold Meat, *n.* . . . . *A corpse*
Drill, *v.* . . . . *To shoot*
G. Men, *n.* . . . . *Federal Officers*
Grand, *n.* *$1,000.00*
Grease, *n.* . . . . *Money paid for protection*
Hist, *v.* . . . . *A hold-up*
Hijack, *v.* *For one gangster to rob another of a truckload of beer or booze*
Hot Seat, *n.* . . . . *Electric Chair*
Kosher, *adj.* . . . . *On the level*
Lip, *n.* . . . . *A lawyer*
On the Spot, *n.* . . *In a precarious position.*
Pineapple, *n.* . . . . *A bomb*
Racket, *n.* . . . . *A crooked business*
Shamus, *n.* . . . *A police officer; sometimes used for a stool pigeon*
Speakeasy, *n.* . . . . *A prohibition era saloon*
Taken for a Ride, *v.* . . . . *The last journey*
Tip Over, *v.* *To raid a speakeasy without a warrant*
Torpedo, *n.* . . . . *A free lance killer*
Typewriter, *n.* . . . . *A Machine gun*

Numbers in red circles give the sequence of important events in Chicago's ten-year gangland war.

3

4

5

• MRS. O'LEARY'S COW • KICKED THE LANTERN • AND STARTED THE • CHICAGO FIRE 1871

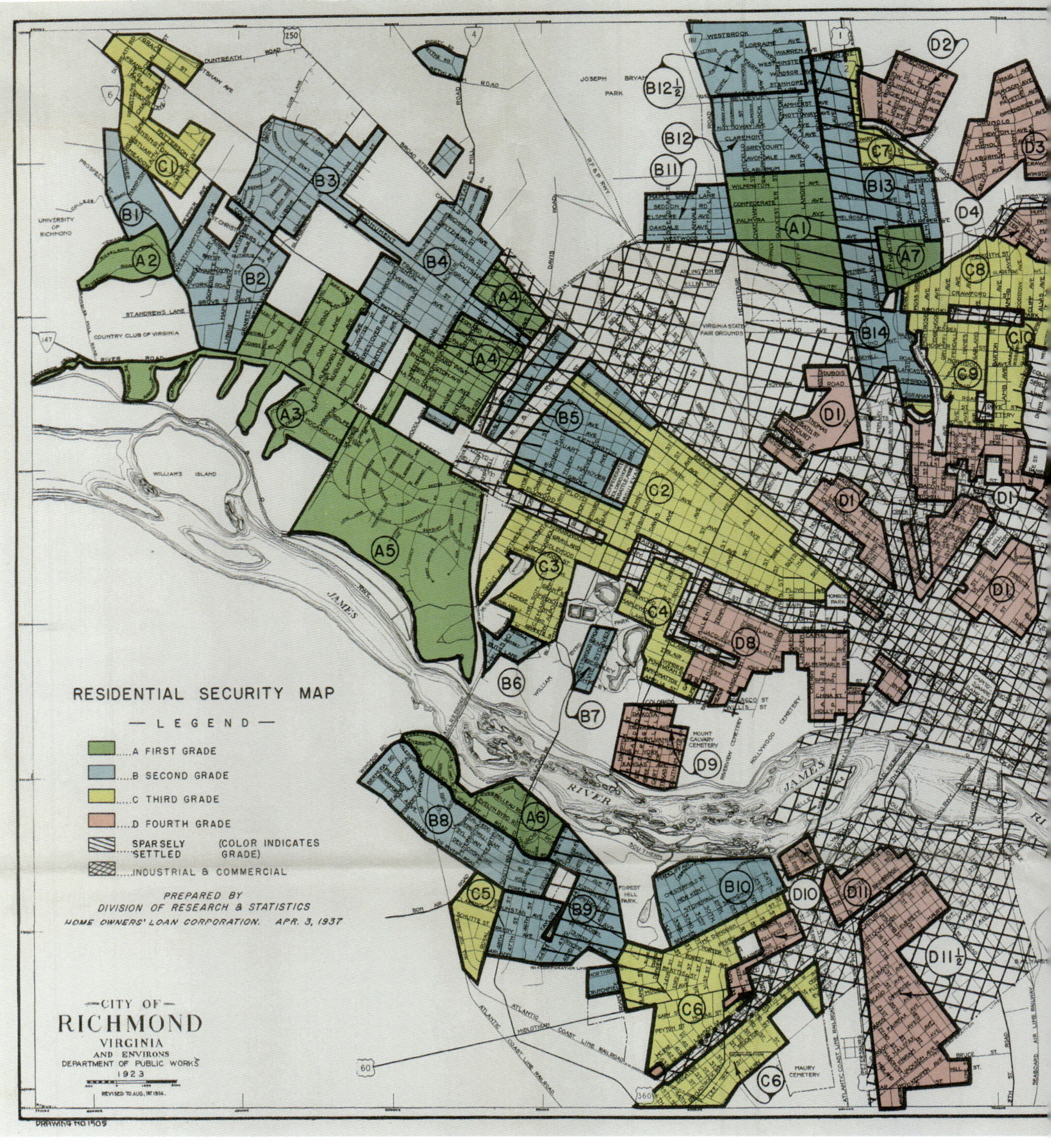
RESIDENTIAL SECURITY MAP
— L E G E N D —
A FIRST GRADE
B SECOND GRADE
C THIRD GRADE
D FOURTH GRADE
SPARSELY SETTLED (COLOR INDICATES GRADE)
INDUSTRIAL & COMMERCIAL
PREPARED BY
DIVISION OF RESEARCH & STATISTICS
HOME OWNERS' LOAN CORPORATION. APR. 3, 1937
CITY OF
RICHMOND
VIRGINIA
AND ENVIRONS
DEPARTMENT OF PUBLIC WORKS
1923
JAMES
RIVER
WILLIAMS ISLAND
UNIVERSITY OF RICHMOND
COUNTRY CLUB OF VIRGINIA
VIRGINIA STATE FAIR GROUNDS
JOSEPH BRYAN PARK
HOLLYWOOD CEMETERY
MOUNT CALVARY CEMETERY
MAURY CEMETERY
FOREST HILL PARK
DRAWING NO 1505

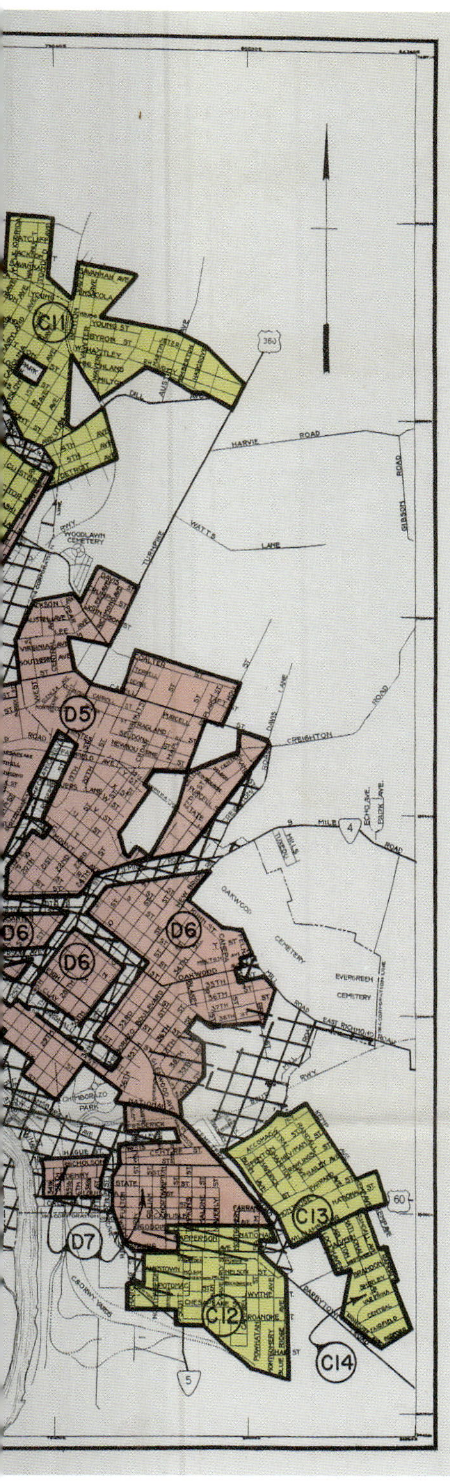

The Maps with Red Lines

Maps made by the US government used race to help determine where homebuyers moved in American cities.

This *Residential Security Map* was one of many created by the US Home Owners' Loan Corporation (HOLC) as part of a project that surveyed major American cities.[1] It's color coded, in more ways than one.

The Great Depression was a catastrophe for American homeowners. In 1933, when President Franklin D. Roosevelt took office, an average of 1,000 residential mortgages a day suffered foreclosure. By the beginning of the following year, half of urban homeowners were delinquent on their mortgage loans. To try to stem the flood of defaults and encourage homebuying, FDR's New Deal launched the HOLC, which sold bonds, used the proceeds to buy mortgages from banks, and then refinanced those mortgages. The HOLC ultimately refinanced $3.1 billion in loans before closing up shop in 1951, helping the owners of one of every ten non-farm dwellings in the country.

After its initial emergency efforts, the HOLC also worked with local mortgage bankers, developers, and appraisers to assess the creditworthiness of various areas across the country. Its officials depicted their findings in a series of "security maps" that purported to show the

Residential Security Map, City of Richmond, Virginia was created in 1937 by the US Home Owners' Loan Corporation (HOLC) as part of an initiative that surveyed real estate in 239 American cities between 1935 and 1940. These maps used color codes to rate the supposed safety of offering mortgages in various neighborhoods, ranging from green (the most attractive properties) to blue to yellow to red ("hazardous").

1 Researchers and developers at the University of Richmond have collected and annotated the HOLC maps and placed them online at an outstanding site called Mapping Inequality.

relative safety of offering mortgages on a neighborhood-by-neighborhood basis. HOLC maps displayed four grades, each with its own color: A, or green, for the best properties; B, or blue, for places that were still desirable; C, or yellow, for communities in decline; and D, or red, for zones deemed "hazardous."

The authors of the HOLC maps looked at a variety of data to make their appraisals: the age and quality of housing stock; sales and rental prices; and, relentlessly and repeatedly, race and demographics. Their collective outlook reflected the real estate industry's deep-rooted belief in a racialist "life cycle" theory of community degeneration: Americans of Western and Northern European descent would be replaced by ethnic whites and ultimately by people of color, triggering economic and social decay in central cities. Just as a few examples, HOLC maps noted the "infiltration" of "Greeks and Italians" in a section of Birmingham, Alabama, "Slovaks" in a district of Akron, Ohio, "Jewish families" in a Los Angeles, California, neighborhood. These areas escaped with yellow grades, unlike a red region in Sacramento, California, where the HOLC map found "a sprinkling of Mexicans, Negroes and Orientals," and wrote: "The subversive character of population constitutes the area's principal hazard."

On this security map of Richmond, Virginia, the HOLC has coded every Black area in the city red, while assigning its poorest grade to just one of more than thirty white neighborhoods. Further, the map's "clarifying remarks" warn against investment in the frontier between Black and white, using language that would be shocking today. Describing the central district marked C4, the map says: "This area is yellow, largely because the school for white children is in the negro area, D-8, and because the negroes of D-8 pass back and forth for access to the William Byrd Park which lies to the west." About another district to the north (C7), it comments: "Respectable people but homes are too near negro area D2."

The HOLC maps have been fairly notorious since historian Kenneth T. Jackson unearthed them in the 1970s. But as striking as they are as political documents, we shouldn't be so naive as to think that any one set of maps created by a relatively obscure federal agency could be responsible for the history of housing discrimination in America. By the time this map was created, Richmond—formerly the capital of the Confederate States of America—had been segregated for a long time. For decades, its leaders had used zoning codes, restrictive housing covenants, and the state of Virginia's "racial integrity" law to keep Black residents in particular neighborhoods. Further, the HOLC had closed the vast majority of its mortgage refinancings by the time it started making the security maps, and did not disseminate the maps widely.

The HOLC did, however, collaborate with the Federal Housing Administration (FHA), also established by the New Deal. The FHA took on the enormously powerful task of insuring home mortgages (and still does so today). And it created its own set of similar maps for appraising lending risk, leading to the widespread denial of credit to otherwise deserving applicants because of their race. As the US Federal Reserve itself has admitted, "The FHA was the architect of federally sponsored redlining from 1934 until the 1960s." The FHA maps just aren't as well-known as the HOLC security maps because the agency destroyed most of them during the Nixon Administration!

Fundamentally, the HOLC, and the FHA, and their maps, took local real estate customs that kept communities divided and both normalized and standardized them for banks, real estate agents, states, and cities. They turned racist procedures into best practices.

And the results cast a very long shadow. The redlining sanctioned by the federal government in these security maps trapped millions of Black Americans in distressed neighborhoods and deprived them of the chance to build home values and pass greater wealth to future generations. It's now been nearly ninety years since the HOLC created its maps and more than five decades since the federal government banned housing discrimination in 1968. But research shows that even today, living in the communities marked red on the security maps of the 1930s correlates with higher rates of premature birth, infant mortality, asthma, COVID-19, high blood pressure, and kidney disease. And the red neighborhoods are still hotter in temperature, because they are covered with more concrete and lined with fewer trees than are the green areas.

At a time when millions of Black Americans were moving into cities and billions of investment dollars were up for grabs, the security maps made the fear of what might happen so vivid that they became century-long self-fulfilling prophecies.

The Maps That Rewired America

Interstate highways opened and connected the United States—and devastated many inner cities.

National System of Interstate Highways (opposite) shows nothing less than the rerouting of America's entire landscape. The US government first hatched plans to link and expand highways around the country during the New Deal. After consulting with state agencies and the Department of Defense, federal transportation officials, led by Thomas MacDonald, the longtime commissioner of the Bureau of Public Roads, produced this map in 1947. MacDonald had been evangelizing for better roads for more than a quarter of a century—he saw them as a basic human right as well as a way to revitalize distressed cities. And his vision inspired the connections on this map, a template for the network that was built after the Federal-Aid Highway Act became law in 1956.

Americans spent the years following World War II buying as many cars as they could climb into and driving from inner cities to the outer rungs of metropolitan areas. The share of US families that owned automobiles jumped from 54 percent in 1948 to 74 percent in 1959. The proportion of Americans living in suburbs climbed from less than 20 percent in 1940 to more than 30 percent in 1960. And as their commutes began to choke the country's byways, they had in Dwight Eisenhower a president who believed the nation needed to modernize its roads, and not just for the sake of convenience.

As a young lieutenant colonel in 1919, Eisenhower took part in a military caravan that crossed the United States to highlight the need for better motorways; it took the three-hundred-man group two months to make it from Washington, DC, to San Francisco, California. When he was supreme commander of Allied forces

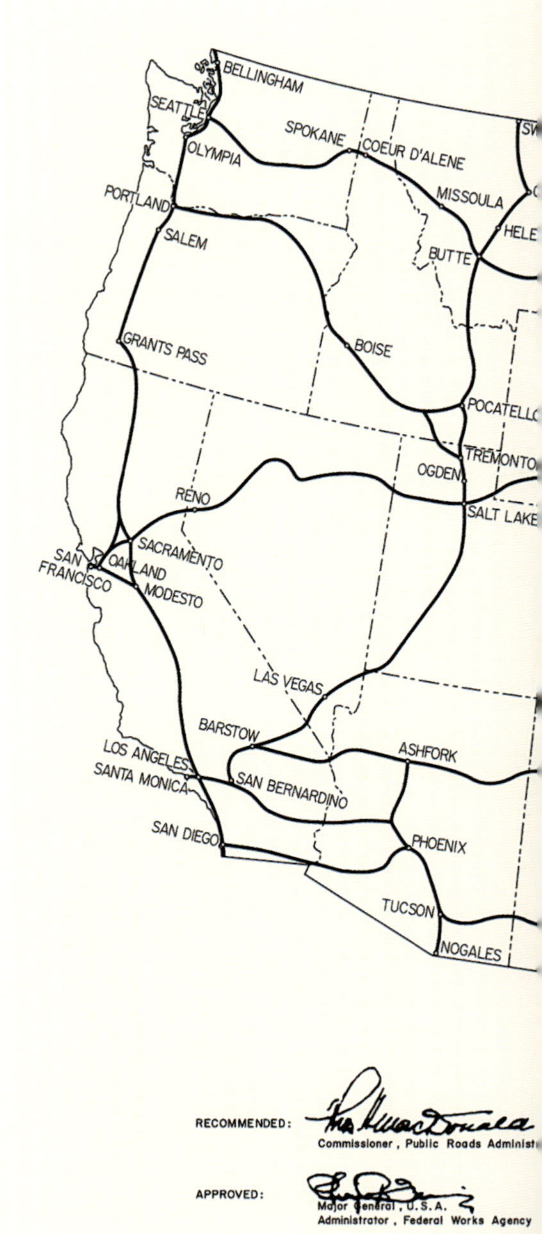

National System of Interstate Highways, spearheaded by Thomas MacDonald (the longtime commissioner of the Bureau of Public Roads) in 1947, shows the blueprint for what became the biggest public works project in history.

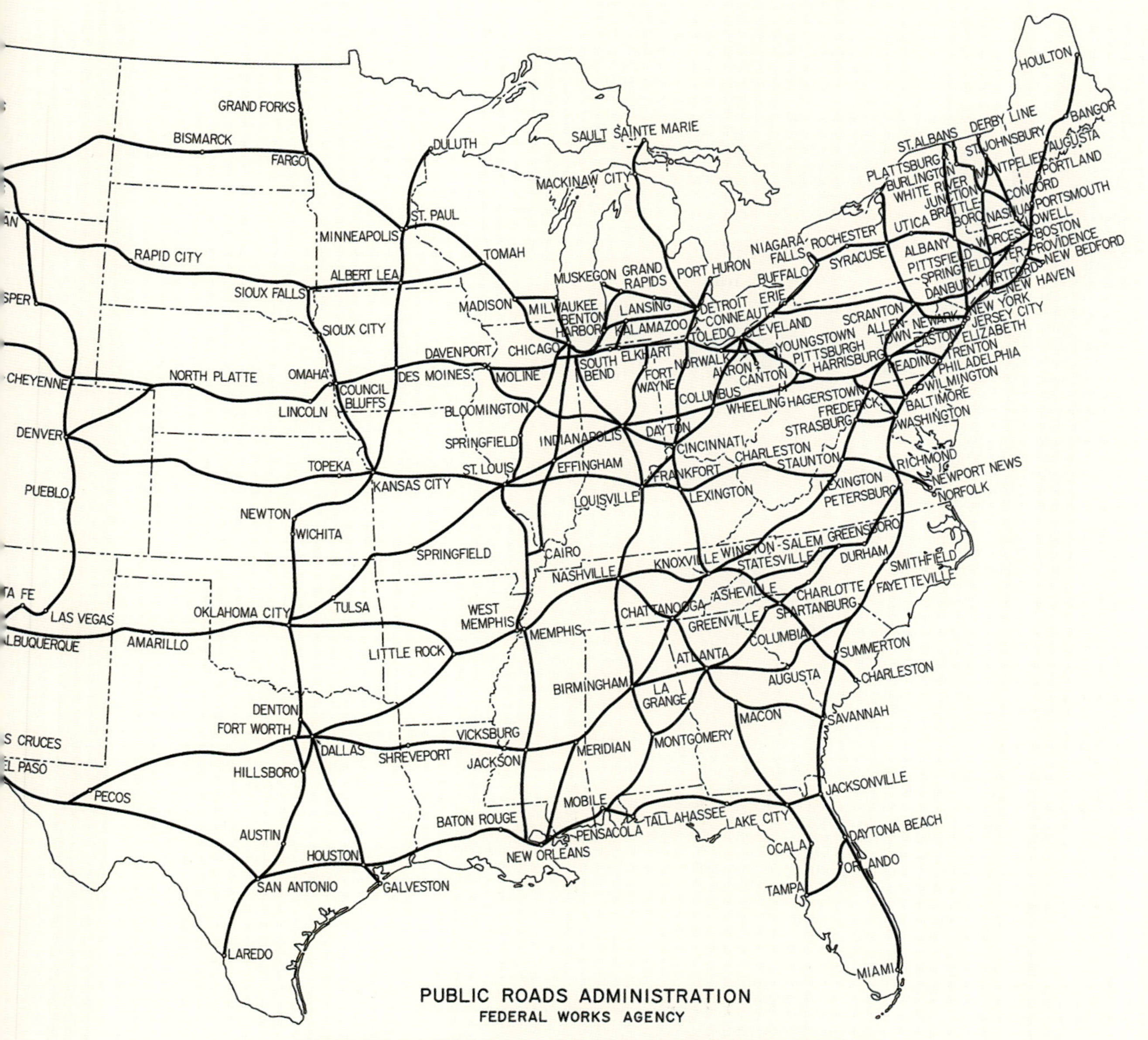

PUBLIC ROADS ADMINISTRATION

FEDERAL WORKS AGENCY

NATIONAL SYSTEM OF INTERSTATE HIGHWAYS

SELECTED BY JOINT ACTION OF THE SEVERAL STATE HIGHWAY DEPARTMENTS
AS MODIFIED AND APPROVED
BY THE ADMINISTRATOR, FEDERAL WORKS AGENCY
AUGUST 2, 1947

in World War II, Eisenhower appreciated the logistical advantages the enemy gained from what he called "the superlative system of German *Autobahnen*," or highways.

And as president, Eisenhower said: "Our unity as a nation is sustained by free communication of thought and by easy transportation of people and goods. . . . Together, the united forces of our communication and transportation systems are dynamic elements in the very name we bear—United States. Without them, we would be a mere alliance of many separate parts." Under the law he signed in 1956, the federal government would pay 90 percent of the cost of building out a system of more than 40,000 miles of interstate and national defense highways.

The Interstate Highway System turned into the largest public works project in history, and as an engine of economic growth, it was an astounding success. The project was a huge boon to construction workers and truckers, mines and quarries, heavy machinery producers and oil refiners, and eventually gas stations, motels, and big-box stores.[1]

Interstate highways made long-distance driving much easier and safer. As roads expanded through the 1960s and '70s, millions of people were able to visit places never before accessible to them. Businesses shipped materials and delivered products cheaper and faster. Public agencies reached disaster areas more quickly and effectively.

On a deeper level, by literally increasing mobility, the Interstate Highway System connected Americans, eased the regional differences among them, and left fewer places isolated from the mainstream of national life.

With the exception of one huge archipelago.

Take a close look at the Interstate Highway map,[2] and consider what happens at each of the many dozens of cities it names: The planned roads run straight through every one of them. It was "one of the . . . program's basic assumptions—that the interstates had always been planned to cut

---

1 Every $1 spent building the system generated $1.80 in economic activity over the following fifteen years, according to a doctoral dissertation by economist Daniel Leff Yaffe.

2 The version shown on pages 140–141 was digitally and painstakingly reconstructed from an original in 2014 by Cameron Booth, who runs the Transit Maps website.

into and through the cities as well as circle them on interstate beltways," as a 2002 report by the Poverty and Race Research Action Council put it.

Urban areas were increasingly clogged with traffic in the 1950s, and "urban interstates," or intracity expressways, promised to relieve that congestion. But at a time when the entire thrust of American politics and culture was to encourage single-family home ownership in emerging suburbs, the new wide, fast-moving interstates shown on this map would connect municipal cores to each other and to those greenbelts—and leave downtowns behind. Indeed, a 2007 study by Nathaniel Baum-Snow, now a professor of economic analysis and policy at the University of Toronto, found that every new highway built through an urban center from 1950 to 1990 reduced that city's population by an average of about 18 percent.

Further, while the federal government paid for almost all the cost of the new roads, state and local officials decided what routes the roads would take. Some cities combined highway construction with plans to redevelop aging buildings and impoverished neighborhoods—"slum clearance," in the parlance of the day. Others simply sited interstates through precincts with the least political power to oppose them. Often those alternatives led to the same result: the destruction of Black communities. From Syracuse to New Orleans, Detroit to Los Angeles, interstate highways razed and ripped through Black areas.

As just one example of how all this played out, consider the Twin Cities of Minnesota, where the numbers of cars on local roads zoomed by about 60 percent in the years immediately after World War II. As it became more important to relieve the gridlock of getting back and forth between Minneapolis, the state's largest city, and St. Paul, its capital, civic leaders moved forward on long-debated plans for building an expressway between them. George Herrold, the St. Paul city engineer, recommended joining the Capitol and the University of Minnesota (in Minneapolis) with a highway that would run next to railroads already in place, rather than through local neighborhoods. This idea is preserved on a map (shown on the following page) from the 1965 book *The City Planning Process: A Political Analysis* by Alan Altshuler, an urban policy and planning professor now at Harvard University.

The bulk of city and state officials disagreed, preferring a more direct route farther south, which they estimated would be more convenient for drivers and less costly to maintain. This is the thicker line on the map, named the "St. Anthony Route" after the central avenue the new corridor would traverse. This plan had powerful political backing from many

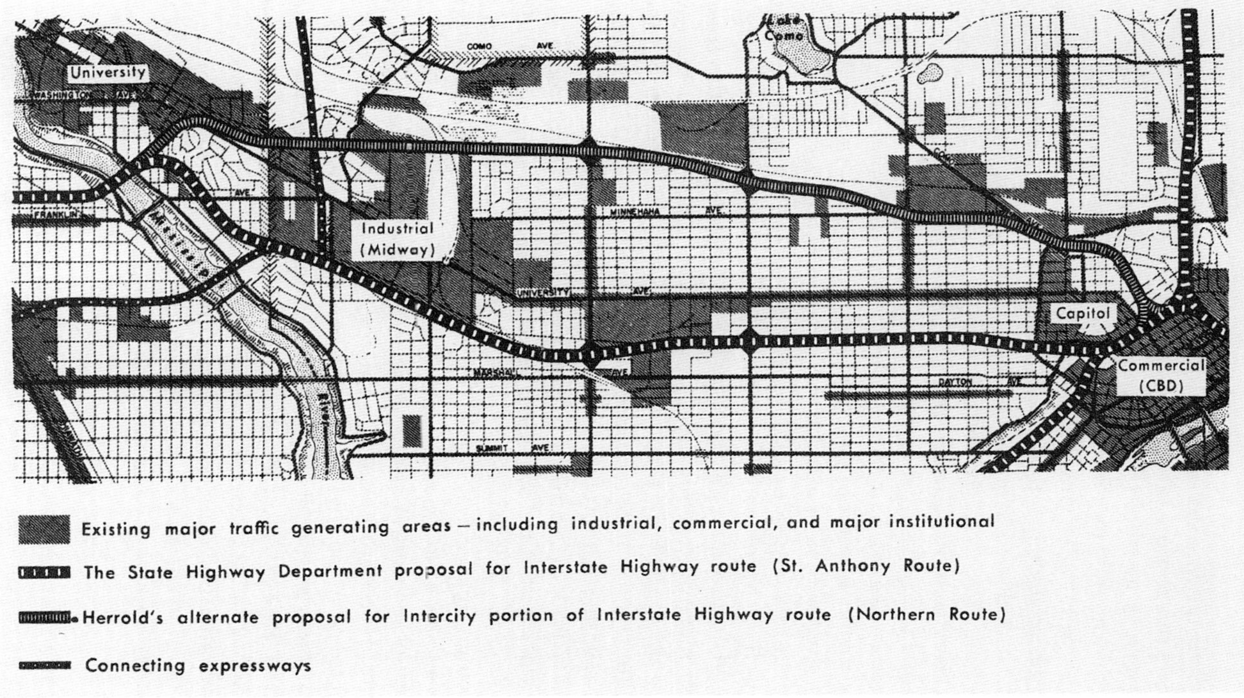

politicians, businesses, and labor leaders, and it's the one that moved forward.

In 1956, the federal highway program began, and construction started on the St. Anthony Route. Three years later, a new state law took away the power local officials had to veto highway projects, and essentially made the extension of I-94 connecting Minneapolis and St. Paul inevitable. It took 12 years and $80 million to finish the 7.5-mile road; beauty queens from each city tied a ribbon across the new expressway to mark its completion. Afterward, you could drive from one downtown to the other in 10 minutes.

But the new six-lane freeway sliced the venerable Minneapolis neighborhood of Prospect Park into two pieces. It demolished a third of an area called Seward and blocked that locale's access to nearby Riverside Park. In St. Paul, it walled the state Capitol off from the city's central business district. And it plowed right through Rondo, the capital's largest Black community.

Rondo was a largely integrated, culturally vital neighborhood, home to at least three Black newspapers, the Minnesota chapter of the National Association for the Advancement of Colored People (NAACP), and many

Alternative Proposals for the Intercity Route, St. Paul, appears in the 1965 book *The City Planning Process: A Political Analysis* by Alan Altshuler. It shows an alternative, less destructive approach to building an expressway between Minneapolis and St. Paul. A highway, shown as the "Northern Route," could have run alongside existing railroads, rather than through local neighborhoods.

Black-owned businesses. Unfortunately, the path taken by the interstate destroyed hundreds of Rondo's properties, and with them, its identity. Black residents lived in nearly three-fourths of the buildings torn down for the new highway. And when the dust cleared, "one in eight African Americans in St. Paul lost a home to I-94," as a University of Minnesota report put it in 2006. In many ways, Rondo has never recovered.

Today, with many city highways aging and jammed, municipalities around the US are reconsidering their transportation planning. And Rondo has become a recurring example brought up in debates over how to reconnect communities divided by earlier rounds of roads. Local organizers have crafted a plan to build a land bridge over part of the I-94 expressway, but funding is scarce.

"Transportation can connect us to jobs, services, and loved ones," then-Secretary of Transportation Pete Buttigieg said in 2022. "But we've also seen countless cases around the country where a piece of infrastructure cuts off a neighborhood or a community because of how it was built. . . . We can't ignore the basic truth that some of the planners and politicians behind those projects built them directly through the heart of vibrant, populated communities."

It's true. Highway maps are very often political maps.

The Map of Enduring Hope

Before the United Nations could get to work, it needed a logo.

In April 1945, 850 delegates from 50 nations, representing more than 80 percent of the world's population, gathered in San Francisco to draft the charter of the United Nations. The representatives hoped to create a framework for countries to cooperate in maintaining peace and security around the globe after World War II. But first, they needed ID badges. Or at least some kind of seal that would identify them as conference attendees.

US Secretary of State Edward Stettinius Jr., who chaired the American delegation, saw an opportunity: He thought that even a lapel pin, if it were powerful enough, could become the permanent symbol of the new organization. So he set up a committee to create the first UN insignia.

The design its members came up with soon became the United Nations' official emblem—and one of the world's most recognizable logos.

Oliver Lincoln Lundquist, an industrial designer from Westbury, New York, supervised the group. The design committee had to devise a symbol that could fit onto a button that was just 1¹⁄₁₆ inches in diameter alongside the words *United Nations Conference on International Organization* and *San Francisco, 1945.* And Donal McLaughlin, a Manhattan-born architect who led the team reporting to Lundquist,[1] disliked some of the initial ideas the committee fit into those constraints. One early design for the UN badge featured countries yoked together, supposedly to symbolize new connections. McLaughlin commented: "Linked in peace, but also a world in chains."

Ultimately, McLaughlin himself came up with the winning idea: a map of the world as seen from above the North Pole, with all the

---

1 McLaughlin was already well versed in the art of communicating critical information concisely. In his prior work with the Office of Strategic Services (precursor to the CIA), he created wartime instructions for how to derail German trains, which were printed on cigarette packs for US troops.

1

2

continents splayed around it, the whole thing crisscrossed by circular lines of latitude and straight, radial lines of longitude (above left). Another team member suggested swaddling the globe with laurel branches, a sign of victory; McLaughlin changed that to olive branches, a sign of peace. The world would be in a simple, round field, with no extra text. And the whole thing would be blue—"the opposite of red, the war color," as Lundquist later explained.

McLaughlin's image made it onto delegates' lapel pins in San Francisco, and at the conclusion of the conference in June 1945, it was stamped in gold on the United Nations Charter. Afterward, he made some changes: The updated logo (above right) extended its field of vision to include several new countries, such as Argentina, which wasn't a member of the UN when McLaughlin created his first map. And it de-emphasized the position of the United States.

In December 1946, the UN adopted this design as its official seal and emblem, and has used it—and the distinctive shade now known as "United Nations blue"—ever since. It's the most enduringly hopeful political map ever made.

McLaughlin lived to the age of 102. After a very long career that included designing Tiffany's flagship store in New York and teaching at prominent universities, his favorite work was still the project he called his "button." About the United Nations emblem, he said: "It's like an old, warm friend."

1 In his design for the first insignia for the United Nations, created for its inaugural meeting in April 1945, architect Donal McLaughlin sketched out a polar map of the world framed by olive branches.

2 The revised logo, adopted in 1946, extends its projection farther into the Southern Hemisphere and decentralizes the United States.

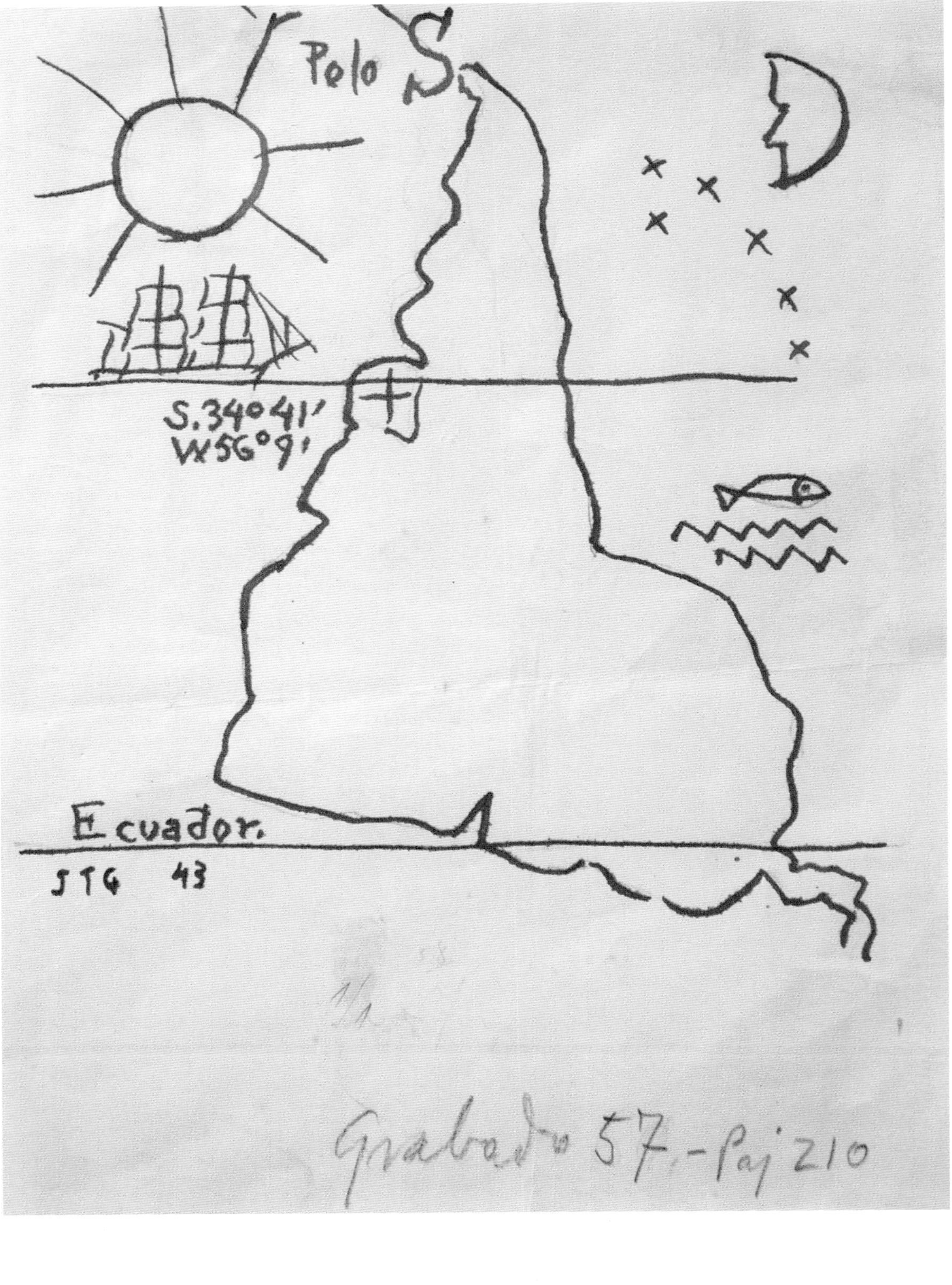

Polo S

S. 34°41'
W 56°9'

Ecuador.

JTG 43

Grabado 57.-Paj 210

The Map That Turned the Americas Upside Down

Placing a particular direction at the top of a map can make a political statement.

It's hard to imagine a simpler political map: *América Invertida* (Inverted America), opposite, is a black-ink-on-white-paper sketch of South America created in 1943 by Uruguayan artist Joaquín Torres-García, with very few extra lines or decorations and no internal borders at all. But on this map, the southern extreme of Tierra del Fuego nearly touches the shining sun, the equator is low on the page, and Panama juts toward the rest of Central America at the bottom. Torres-García reversed the continent's polarity—and his work has led generations of viewers to consider just how much it means that on traditional maps, *north* means upward.

Torres-García was born in Montevideo, the capital of Uruguay, in 1874, then moved with his family to Spain when he was a teenager. He spent more than forty years in Europe building a career as an artist, working in Barcelona, Brussels, and Paris and socializing with Marcel Duchamp, Pablo Picasso, and Joseph Stella. He maintained a passion for pre-Columbian Latin American culture. And he developed a style called "Constructive Universalism," where he created often grid-like structures from geometric patterns and natural symbols that would be at home in native South American art as well as experimental modern works.

In 1934, Torres-García returned to his native Montevideo, where he delivered lectures, broadcast a radio show, and launched the Taller Torres-García (TTG), or Torres-García Workshop. There he urged other artists to work independently from northern—North American, European, "modern"—traditions, expectations, and demands. Torres-García included an early version of the inverted America map in a 1935 manifesto, "The School of the South": "I have called this 'The School of the South' because in reality our north is the south. There must not be north for us, except in opposition to our south. Therefore, we now turn the map upside down, and then we have a true idea of our position, and not as the rest of the

In *América Invertida* (Inverted America), a sketch of South America he created in 1943, Uruguayan artist Joaquín Torres-García flipped the traditional compass for maps, challenging viewers to appreciate the artistic and cultural importance of the South.

world wishes. The point of America, from now on, forever," he declared, "insistently points to the South, our north."

Torres-García drew the version of *América Invertida* shown on page 148 in 1943 for inclusion in his book *Universalismo Constructivo* (*Constructive Universalism*), which he published the following year. And notice he doesn't rotate *everything* on his map. Its inscriptions for the equator and South Pole are right side up (as are Torres-García's own initials). It shows a ship and fish that seem to be atop water. It still uses traditional latitude and longitude to situate Montevideo at its center of attention. All of which underscores how our traditional perspective is neither inevitable nor dictated by anything in science or nature. There's no gravity pulling north upward, just habit. This map wants us to move down to travel north, to turn left to look east—and to navigate by the stars of the Southern Hemisphere, which it shows alongside an ancient Incan symbol of a half-moon.

Torres-García died of a heart attack in 1949, but his calls for an autonomous Latin American culture have far outlived him and even the particular style of art he advocated. His inverted map has become famous enough that you can find it on T-shirts and mugs—just the kind of inauthentic artifacts he disliked. But his influence has transcended the kitsch that so often comes with fame.

As just one example of his influence, consider *Global Optimization Diagram*, opposite, a 2012 painting by Ana Vizcarra Rankin. She says her subjects are "travel and cartography." And this worldwide map not only inverts the traditional positions of the hemispheres, it shows milky drips—representing resources? Blood? Lives?—leaking down a flattened Mercator map (see pages 32–33) toward "El Norte."

Gloomy but vivid, this canvas intentionally uses inversion and distortion to carry on the project that Torres-García launched. It makes it impossible to unthinkingly accept the assumptions embedded in so many traditional maps: that north points up, and further, that country sizes and shapes are accurate, bigger is better, and globalization is natural.

Torres-García's work helped inspire other artists to challenge colonial and exploitative perspectives, including Ana Vizcarra Rankin (also born in Uruguay, now based in Philadelphia), who painted *Global Optimization Diagram* in 2012.

EL NORTE

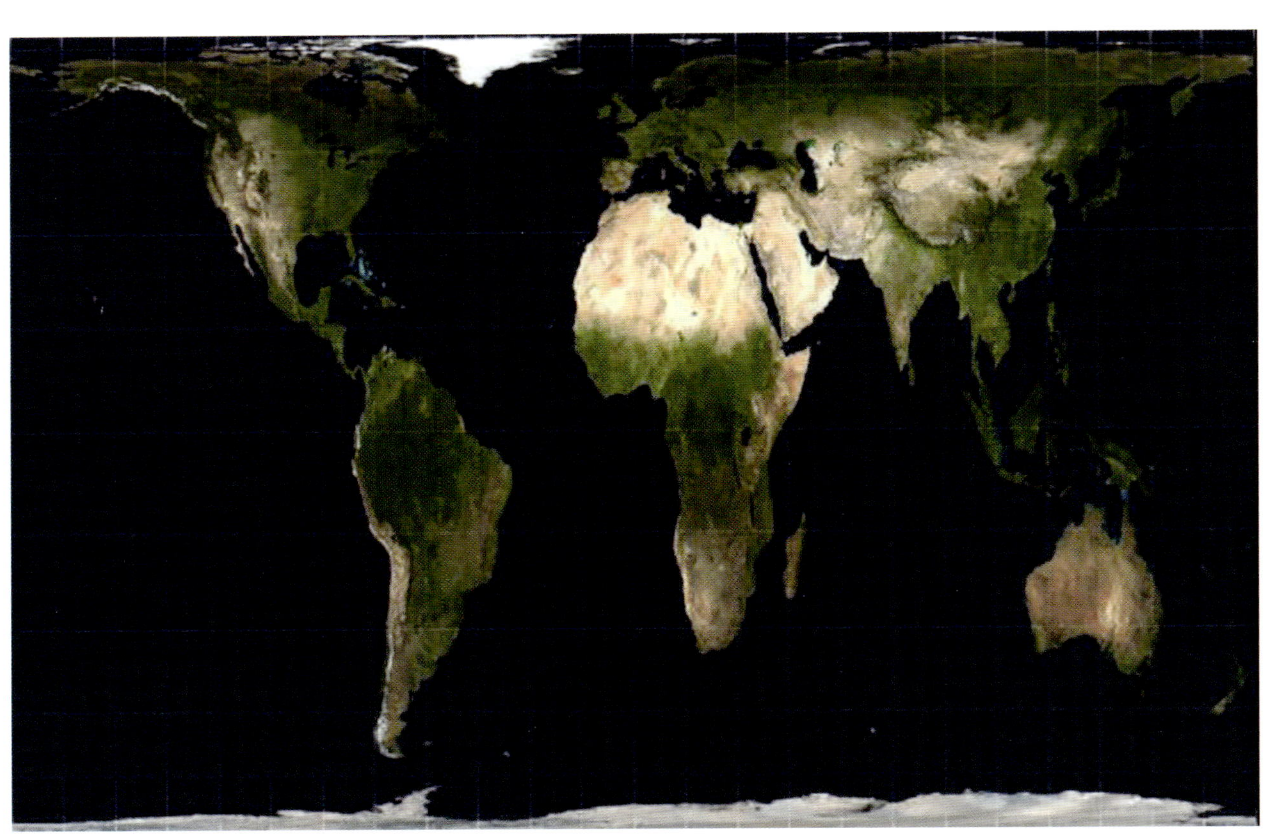

The Map That Freaked Out the World of Maps

Since the 1970s, maps showing the true areas of global surfaces have challenged the long-dominant perspective of the Mercator projection.

Very few modern cartographers have erupted into mainstream celebrity. But that's exactly what happened in May 1973, when a German historian named Arno Peters addressed a press conference in Bonn, Germany, and attacked the world-famous Mercator map.

"Mercator presents a fully false picture, particularly regarding the non-white-peopled lands," Peters told an assembly of more than three hundred journalists, public officials, and researchers. "It over-values the white man and distorts the picture of the world to the advantage of the colonial masters of the time." And as he dropped that rhetorical bomb, he presented a replacement standard: his own *Peters projection*. Peters wanted this new map to clear away old biases and begin a long overdue process of reeducating people about how our world actually looks. The results were eye-popping. Mercator-trained minds had grown used to seeing Scandinavia as bigger than Italy, the Soviet Union as larger than Africa, and North generally privileged over South. Suddenly they beheld a world map whose "lower" continents were huge—while most of Europe appeared to be tiny.

Peters, born in Berlin in 1916, was a filmmaker, journalist, and, as one 2002 obituary put it, "advocate of equality in all things." In 1952, he and his first wife, Anneliese, published a synchronoptic world history that gave equal portions of its timeline charts to all parts of the globe and each era of the preceding 3,000 years. His early study of movies as propaganda and his historical research then drove a new mission, in cartography.

"The quest for the causes of arrogance and xenophobia," he wrote in 1983, "has led me repeatedly back to the global map as being primarily responsible for forming people's impression of the world. . . . It became clear to me that existing global maps were worthless for an objective representation of historical situations and events."

The Gall-Peters projection, popularized in the 1970s by German historian Arno Peters, was intended to wipe out the biases of the Mercator map (see pages 32–37) and restore neglected and undervalued landmasses to their proper sizes. It does so, however, by severely vertically stretching places near the equator and squashing those close to the poles, creating its own distortions.

To make a fairer world map, Peters started, as Mercator did, with a cylindrical projection of the earth onto a flat surface. But where Mercator wanted to convey angles accurately, Peters wanted to show *areas* as equivalent to their real sizes. To achieve this, he used mathematical formulas to deform zones of the globe by elongating North-South distances at the equator and compressing them at the poles. This had its intended effect: A rectangle covering 1,000 square miles on a Peters map represents 1,000 square miles on the earth.

Peters had a friendly manner, sympathy for underdogs, left-wing politics, and shrewd marketing skills. And his work dovetailed with an increasing focus on international development by Western reformers. As he kept up yearslong attacks on Eurocentric cartography, he and his map gained headlines and the support of important nonprofits and public agencies. The National Council of Churches in the US adopted the Peters map, as did Oxfam, UNICEF, and many other groups with millions of followers and donors. The map became an international bestseller.

But Peters himself often acted like the atheist who argues that all absolute faith is wrong except for their own absolute faith that God doesn't exist. He dismissed the history of cartography since Mercator and proclaimed his own projection to be "revolutionary," "objective," and "the single greatest advance in mapmaking in over four hundred years." He played up his own political aims. He had created an equal-area map of the earth precisely because, as he wrote in 1979, he "didn't want to mitigate the Eurocentric character of our geographical worldview, but rather overcome it." He was also a verbose, often opaque writer.

All this infuriated academics, and fueled what historians have called "the map wars." Critics objected to Peters's math, his historical arguments, and his aesthetics. They called his efforts "polemic propaganda," "preposterous," and "pretentious," and those are just a fraction of the insults they hurled his way. Making matters worse, it turned out that Peters's projection had been actually devised by James Gall, a Scottish cartographer, back in 1855. Peters said he didn't know about that work, but many cartographers now call his map the *Gall-Peters projection*.

It was absurd for Peters to claim he had found one true way to correct Mercator and make an accurate world map. In deciding how to make a rectangular map faithful to areas, not to angles, distances, or shapes, he landed on a particular arrangement among an infinite variety

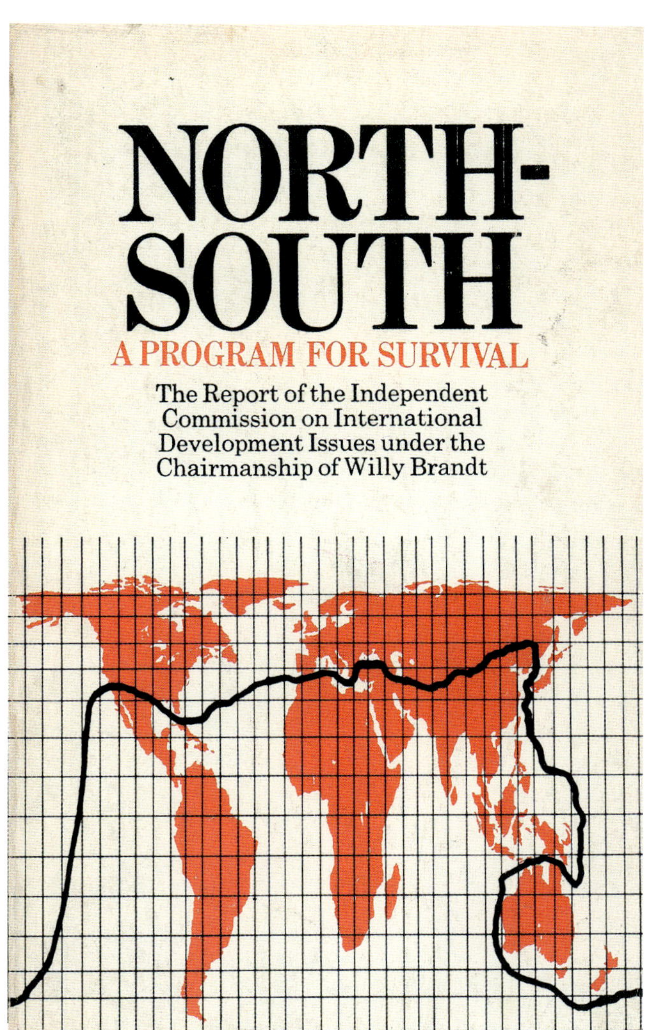

In 1980, a highly publicized report by the Independent Commission on International Development Issues led by Willy Brandt, former chancellor of West Germany, put a vivid red version of the Gall-Peters map on its cover, with the "developed" North and "developing" South separated by a bold black line.

of possibilities—and one whose continents are vertically distended, often severely.[1]

The original Peters map was also centered, like many traditional maps, on the prime meridian, which runs through England. And its shadings grouped various continents together, applying different hues to the nations within them. (Europe and Asia were pink, North and South America were green, and so forth.) *Like every map*, its projection and decoration embodied a series of choices and expressed a range of suggestions, whether it intended to or not.

Arno Peters was an elder expert ready to challenge the establishment through popular engagement—a description that fits figures of the 1970s as diverse as futurist Buckminster Fuller, philosopher Herbert Marcuse, and pediatrician Benjamin Spock. We can appreciate how each of these men had their moments, and how their inquiries opened minds, without taking all of the advice they offered.

Similarly, the Peters map struck a chord in the late-twentieth-century West. It tuned into an emerging sense that better ways were needed to portray the world than Mercator maps. That sense persists: In 2023, the city of Boston began putting Peters maps into social studies classrooms.

The effect of seeing the Peters map for the first time persists too. An episode of *The West Wing* captured it in a scene where a (fictional) group called the Organization of Cartographers for Social Equality meets with White House Press Secretary C. J. Cregg. Its spokesman tells her: "When Third World countries are misrepresented,

---

1 Arthur Robinson, an American cartographer and longtime geography professor at the University of Wisconsin-Milwaukee, wrote: "On the 'Peters projection' the landmasses are somewhat reminiscent of wet, ragged, long, winter underwear hung out to dry on the Arctic Circle."

they're likely to be valued less. When Mercator maps exaggerate the importance of Western civilization, when the top of the map is given to the Northern Hemisphere and the bottom is given to the Southern, then people will tend to adopt top and bottom attitudes."

He then stuns her by showing her an inverted version of the Peters map.

"Yeah, but you can't do that," she says.

"Why not?" he asks.

"'Cause it's freaking me out," she replies.

But there's no reason to accept any one map's trade-offs as mandatory. Or to push it far beyond the purposes for which it's best suited, as Mercator was to sea navigation or Peters was to shock value. Especially today, when computers make it easier than ever to test misperceptions and find projections that strike globe-approximating compromises between angles and areas. (You can try it yourself at the Digital Atlas Project online.)

The Peters map set out to show that we don't live in a one-map world. Its enduring lesson is that we don't live in a two-map world, either.

CRUISE THREATENS PEACE AND BREAKS THE LAW

9th Nov '83

GREENHAM WOMEN AGAINST CRUISE

take President Reagan to Court in the USA

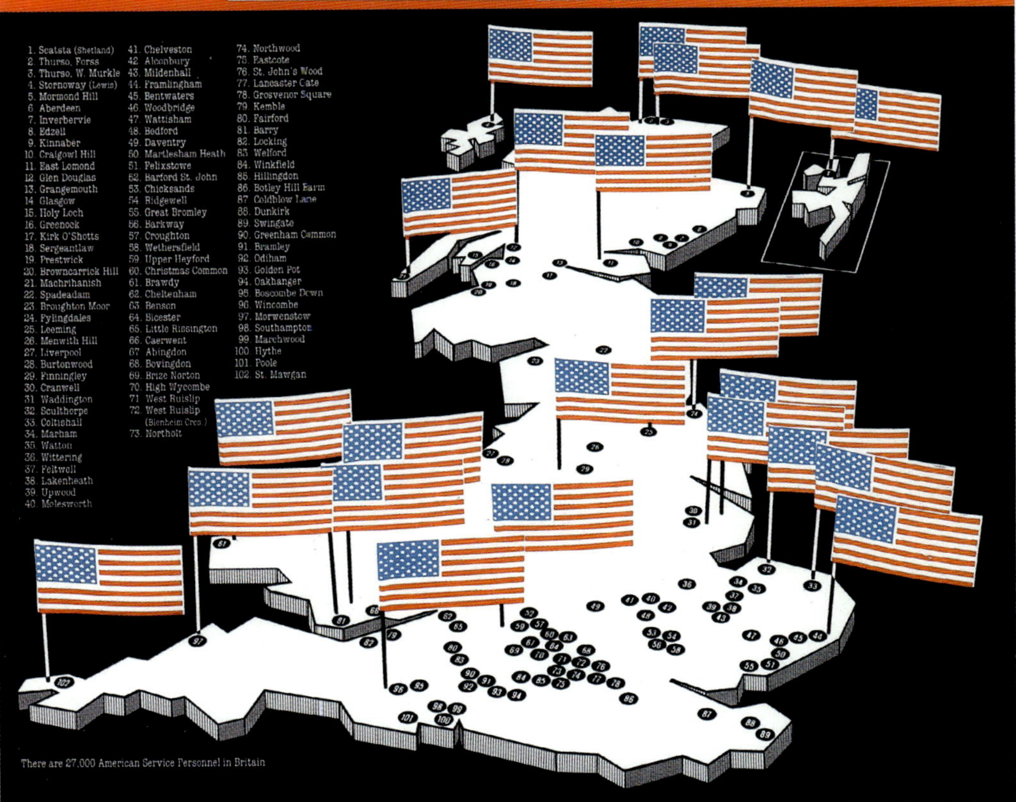

There are 102 US bases in Britain.

On 9th November '83 there will be 102 Peace Camps one at each base.

The Map That Tried to Stop Nuclear Missiles

Late in the Cold War, women sustained a movement that fought the installation of cruise missiles in Great Britain.

By vividly marking a place as well as a time, an effective political map can remind us of an event or movement that might otherwise be overwritten by mainstream history. Case in point: the *Greenham Women Against Cruise* map, a protest map from 1983.

Greenham Common was the site of a Royal Air Force base, opened in 1942, located about 55 miles west of London, England. During World War II and afterward, American forces used the base for everything from stationing troop carriers to sorting mail to running air shows. In 1980, when NATO decided to boost its deployment of nuclear weapons in Western Europe, it decided to put American-made cruise missiles there.

Cold War tensions were then at a dangerously high point. For years, the USSR and its Warsaw Pact allies had maintained conventional forces in Europe that were much larger than those of the United States and its NATO allies. But both superpowers were deterred from starting a third world war by the threat to each of their homelands from the other's intercontinental ballistic missiles. In the late 1970s, though, the Soviets began deploying a new class of intermediate-range SS-20 missiles, which could accurately strike Western Europe without necessarily triggering all-out war with the US. In 1979, the USSR invaded Afghanistan. In 1980, following a half decade of American foreign policy disasters from Vietnam to Iran, Ronald Reagan was elected president of the United States. Reagan, who advocated a huge military buildup, wasn't just a longtime avowed anticommunist. He was easy to caricature as a warmonger. He would go on to call the Soviet Union "the focus of evil in the modern world" and (wrongly) claim there is no word for "freedom" in Russian.

But in the Cold War, decisions about weapons development and the relationships between global strategy and military technology were still subject to public pressure, in a way they really haven't been since the rise of the "Global War on Terrorism" after September 11, 2001. And quite unexpectedly, Greenham Common became a focal point for that pressure. In September 1981, a group from Wales called Women for Life on Earth staged a march at the base to oppose the deployment of cruise

In stark shades of white, blue, and black, this protest map, created in 1983 by the Greenham Women Against Cruise, shows American flags pinned all over Britain, telling UK readers their autonomy is being swamped by more than a hundred US bases.

missiles. Soon afterward, protesters began staying in the area, creating the Greenham Common Women's Peace Camp, which became both an ongoing campaign against nuclear weapons and a female-only commune. Women came, demonstrated, sang, and sometimes got evicted; when they left, for a remarkably long time, others came in their place.

In 1983, the protesters sued the US government in a case called *Greenham Women Against Cruise Missiles vs. Reagan*, claiming the deployment of first-strike nuclear weapons in Great Britain violated the US Constitution and international law. Showing scores of American flags on a black-and-white field, this map protests the 102 US bases planted across UK soil. (Greenham Common is shown as No. 90.) And it calls for "peace camp" protests at each of those bases on November 9, 1983, the day the lawsuit was filed. Its typewriter font carries the feel of breaking news, and its language is plain and strong: "Cruise Threatens Peace and Breaks the Law."

The legal case advertised by the map was dismissed on the grounds that it involved issues that American courts could not decide. As the Center for Constitutional Rights, which helped bring the suit, put it: "The issue of nuclear destruction was the prerogative of the elected branches of government." But over time, activists blockaded Greenham Common, held "Embrace the Base" events where they joined hands and surrounded the entire station, and even formed a 14-mile-long human chain from Greenham to a nearby weapons factory. From 1981 to 2000, more than 70,000 women took part in activities at the Greenham Peace Camp. They formed the largest female-led protest movement in the UK (and maybe anywhere) since women had campaigned for the right to vote.

"I was drawn to the idea of Greenham because . . . close relationships between women became normalized, with the possibility of alternative relationships opening up to women who might never have considered it," feminist advocate Julie Bindel wrote in 2021, nearly forty years after she joined protests at Greenham. "This was a time when homophobia was rampant . . . and lesbians were losing custody of their children to violent spouses. Another appeal was how activists made connections between policing, militarism, war, and everyday male violence toward women."

The Greenham Peace Camp and the antinuclear movement it symbolized offered another kind of hope, too. Ronald Reagan was indeed a hardliner against communism, and the protests did not stop him from deploying missiles at Greenham. But Reagan also dreamed of ridding the world of nuclear weapons. And demonstrations in Europe and the

US helped embolden the faction of American officials—including, as it turned out, the president himself—who believed in using the missiles for bargaining chips, as opposed to saber-rattling or preparing for (or waging) war. In the 1987 Intermediate-Range Nuclear Forces (INF) Treaty negotiated by Reagan and Soviet leader Mikhail Gorbachev, the US and USSR agreed to eliminate all of their medium-range missiles. This was the first time the superpowers consented to wipe out an entire category of nuclear weapons. Both the cruise missiles and the SS-20s were destroyed.

It's almost completely forgotten today, with Reagan widely lionized for being the man who "won" the Cold War, but the American president was then savaged by the political right. Conservative columnist George Will, for example, said December 8, 1987, when Reagan and Gorbachev signed the treaty, was the day the US lost the Cold War.

That was remarkably stupid, seeing as how it was actually the day America won the Cold War.[1] Getting rid of nuclear weapons was—and is—a vision worth fighting for.[2]

"Some of you who have been on the committee long enough will remember Greenham Common and some of the other sites in England and Germany where we had such trouble," Colin Powell testified to the US Senate when he was about to become secretary of state in 2001. "But lo and behold . . . within a few years after we met and checked the Soviet challenge, those missiles were on their way out again, and the Soviet Union was on its way out."

---

1 I am indebted to the late, great writer Richard Reeves for this formulation—and many, many other ideas.

2 In 2019, President Donald Trump pulled the US out of the INF Treaty.

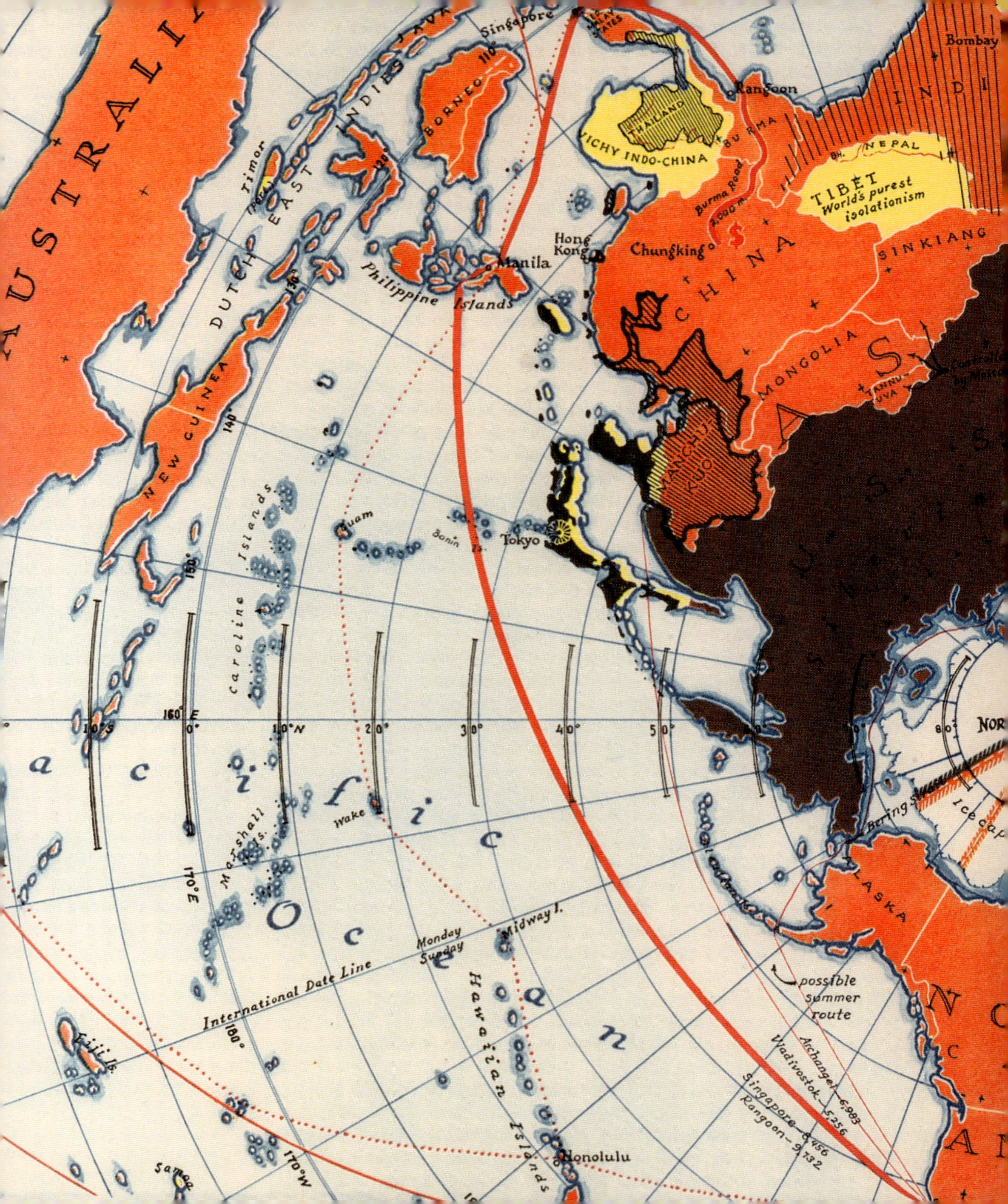

AUSTRALIA
Singapore
JAVA
DUTCH EAST INDIES
Timor
BORNEO
NEW GUINEA
Philippine Islands
Manila
Hong Kong
VICHY INDO-CHINA
THAILAND
BURMA
Rangoon
Burma Road
Bombay
INDIA
NEPAL
TIBET
World's purest isolationism
Chungking
CHINA
SINKIANG
MONGOLIA
MANCHUKUO
Caroline Islands
Guam
Bonin Is.
Tokyo
Marshall Is.
Wake
Pacific Ocean
International Date Line
Monday
Sunday
Midway I.
Hawaiian Islands
Honolulu
Fiji Is.
Samoa
Bering St.
ALASKA
possible summer route
Archangel—6,983
Wadivostok—5,256
Singapore—8,456
Rangoon—9,732

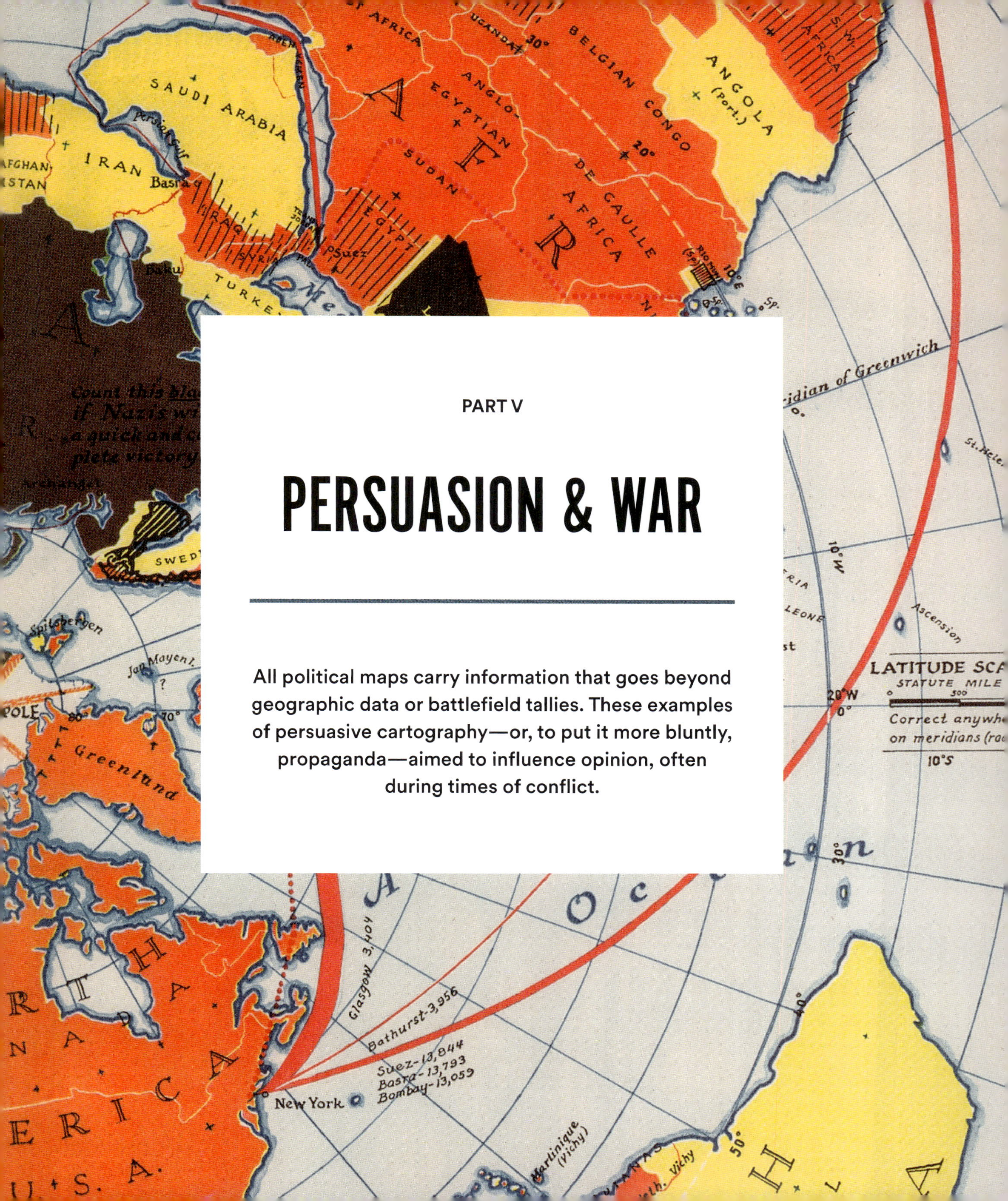

PART V

PERSUASION & WAR

All political maps carry information that goes beyond geographic data or battlefield tallies. These examples of persuasive cartography—or, to put it more bluntly, propaganda—aimed to influence opinion, often during times of conflict.

REVISED EDITION
SERIO-COMIC WAR MAP
FOR THE YEAR 1877.
BY F. W. ROSE.
ERKLÄRUNGEN.
Der nördliche Kolosz—Russland—ist repräsentirt in der Form eines wild aussehenden Octopus, dessen Kopf den grösseren Theil des europäischen Russland's einnimmt, während er mit seinen ausgestreckten Krallen sich wunderbar nach allen Richtungen ausdehnt und bereits verschiedene Länder festhält.
Die Türkei liegt hingestreckt unter ihm. Der Kopf und die Brust eines Türken umfassen die europäische Türkei, während sein Unter-Körper Klein Asien darstellt. Der Bosphorus, das Marmora Meer, und die Dardanellen bilden zusammen einen Gürtel an der Figur, während der lüsterne Preis, Constantinopel, als seine goldene Uhr repräsentirt ist. Griechenland, in der Gestalt eines Krebses beunruhigt den Türken im Süden.
Eine Kralle des Octopus umringt Bulgarien, und scheint die umliegenden Distrikte zu bedrohen. Eine Andere hat die Krimm umfaszt, welche aber noch eine schlimme Wunde bei Sebastopol zeigt. Eine dritte Kralle hat den Fusz des Türken ergriffen (Armenien); eine Vierte dehnt sich weiter nach unten zu dem lange beneideten Gelobten Land; eine Fünfte umarmt den Schah von Persien und eine Sechste umringt Khiva und die anderen Eroberungen in Asien. Eine siebente Kralle scheint Polen ganz erwürgt zu haben, weil die Achte, Finnland umfäszt, welches bei einem Feuer das Wenige genieszt was Russland ihm gelassen.
Ungarn ist nur von seiner Schwester, Oesterreich, davon zurückgehalten seinen Nachbar Russland anzugreifen.
England und Schottland beobachten aufmerksam die Scene, letzteres bewaffnet mit Dolch und Schwert. Irland ist als Mönch abgebildet. Alle Drei aber scheinen ganz entschieden wenigstens des Türken goldene Uhr zu retten.
Frankreich ist der Marschall Mc Mahon mit einer Mitrailleuse auf seinen Nachbar zielend.
Deutschland zeigt seinen Kaiser in Uniform, von Kugeln und Kanonen umgeben, ein Zeichen dass es sich für jeden Nothfall bereit hält.
Spanien ist der junge Alphonso welcher sich von seinen Anstrengungen ausruht.
Italien ein junges Mähchen freut sich seiner neu errungenen Freiheit. Den Papst erkennt man in Rom. Der reiche König von Belgien bewacht seine Schätze. Dänemark's Fahne zwar nur klein, doch ist es stolz darauf. Sicilien ist als drei Wein Fäszer dargestellt, und in Aegypten zeigt sich der Kopf einer Figur, welche dem Khedive und der Sphinx ähnlich sieht.
NORWAY
SWEDEN
FINLAND
G. OF BOTHNIA
G. OF FINLAND
ST PETERSBURG
RU
BALTIC SEA
SKAGERRACK
CATTEGAT
DENMARK
BRITISH ISLES
IRISH SEA
ST GEORGES CHANNEL
INDIA
NORTH SEA
ENGLISH CHANNEL
POLAND
GERMANY
Die heilige Schrift
FRANCE
BAY OF BISCAY
PORTUGAL
SPAIN
STRAIT OF GIBRALTAR
CORSICA
SARDINIA
SICILY
ITALY
ADRIATIC SEA
AUSTRO HUNGARY
BULGARIA
CRIMEA
BLACK
TURKISH EMPIRE
Constantinople
BOSPHORUS
SEA OF MARMORA
DARDANELLES
ASIA MIN
ARCHIPELAGO
GREECE
CANDIA
MEDITERRANEAN SEA
MOUTHS OF THE NILE
EGYPT
ALL RIGHTS RESERVED
REFERENCE.
The Northern Colossus—Russia—is represented in the form of a vicious-looking Octopus, the head of which occupies the greater portion of European Russia, while, with its outstretched arms, it is extending marvellously in every direction, and embracing many countries in its grasp.
Turkey lies prostrate beneath it. The head and bust of a Turk make up European Turkey, while the lower vestments stretch over Asia Minor The Bosphorus, Sea of Marmora, and the Dardanelles, form together a girdle for the figure, whilst the coveted prize, Constantinople, is seen in the shape of a gold watch. Greece, shown as a crab, is annoying the Turk on the south.
One of the arms of the Octopus encircles Bulgaria, and seems threatening the surrounding districts. Another envelopes the Crimea, but this arm shows a bad wound at Sebastopol. A third arm has seized hold of the Turk's foot (Armenia). A fourth is stretching far down to the long-coveted Holy Land, while a fifth is giving the Shah of Persia a gentle embrace as it curls round his neck. A sixth is encircling Khiva and the other acquisitions in Asia. A seventh seems to have wrung all life out of Poland while the eighth arm passes round Finland, who is warming up and making the most of what little Russia has left him. Hungary is only prevented from attacking his neighbour Russia through being held back by his sister Austria.
England and Scotland are eagerly watching the scene, from afar, the latter armed with a dagger and claymore. Ireland is shown as a hooded monk, with an indication of "Home Rule" on the brain. All three look fully determined to save at least the Turk's watch.
France is Marshal MacMahon pointing a mitrailleuse towards his neighbour.
Germany is represented by her Emperor, in uniform, surrounded by shells, cannons, and shot, indicating her readiness for any emergency which may arise.
Spain is young Alfonso sleeping after his recent exertions.
Italy is a young girl rejoicing in her newly acquired liberty. The Pope's triple crown is seen at Rome. The wealthy King of the Belgians is taking care of his treasure. Denmark's flag is small, but she is evidently proud of it. Sicily is made up of three wine barrels, and in Egypt is seen a figure suggesting both the Khedive and the Sphinx.
1
2
3
4
5
6

The Half-Serious Map That Made the Octopus a Celebrity

"Seriocomic" maps bring issues of national security and war to life in cartoon form.

In the *Serio-Comic War Map for the Year 1877*, British illustrator Fred W. Rose ingeniously depicts the geopolitical tensions of the era:

1 Russia is a sinister-looking octopus, and dominates the map from the East. Its tentacles are entangled with Turkish interests in the Balkans and Middle East, and grasp a defeated Poland and compliant Finland.

2 Greece is a small crab, harassing the Turks, while 3 Spain's king is asleep.

4 Germany and France have masses of weapons facing each other.

5 England observes the continent from a distance, with the Suez Canal and India on its mind, while 6 Ireland thinks of "home rule," or self-government.

SERIOCOMIC IS AN important word in the history of political maps, but it's not a technical term like *azimuthal* or *orthographic*. It literally means part serious and part funny. And its master was Fred W. Rose, an artist from Victorian England whose maps portrayed issues of national security and war in cartoon form, sometimes using animals to stand for countries.

Rose, who was born in London in 1849, spent more than forty years as a British civil servant, during which he freelanced as an illustrator and journalist and even wrote a couple of pulpy novels. His early years were a particularly fraught time for Europe, where the empires that had emerged in previous decades entered into conflicts. Many of these are little remembered and poorly understood today, but were deadly nonetheless, such as the Crimean War between Great Britain, France, and the Ottoman (Turkish) Empire on one side and Russia on the other (1853–56), and the Franco-Prussian War between France and the states that became Germany (1870–71).

Rose captured the tensions of the time in his *Serio-Comic War Map for the Year 1877*, (pages 164–165), which brilliantly fits all kinds of symbols into national borders. Representing Russia, a huge, creepy, ochre-colored octopus looms over the eastern portion of the map. And the spaces for other territories are filled with clever, telling details. Bulgaria, where Turkish forces had slaughtered civilians at the town of Batak in 1876, is shown as a skull. Sardinia and Corsica are depicted as the pope and his miter hat, Sicily as three barrels of wine. The overall effect is indeed serio-comic.

The Octopus map built on work by other artists, but came along at the right time for Rose to score a huge hit. Parliament was engaged in a series of sharp debates over Russia, Turkey, and Eastern Europe, and the English public was increasingly interested in national politics and international affairs. Rose's map humorously and colorfully conveyed current events, and was easy to understand—and if anyone missed any of its symbolism, Rose himself had written an attached "Reference" section explaining its contents. The map sold so well that in the summer of 1877, G. W. Bacon, its publisher, brought out a revised edition, for which Rose added details and enlarged the Russian octopus. (This is the version shown on pages 164–165.) In various forms and languages, the Octopus map found an audience in places ranging from San Francisco to Denmark to Persia (now Iran).[1]

Rose went on to identify himself as "Author of the 'Octopus' Map of Europe." But sadly, the events he covered with such a sharp eye and hand ultimately cost him his family. His sons Ronald and Launcelot, both officers in the British Army, were killed in World War I in the fall of 1914. Fred Rose died shortly afterward.

Rose published only five[2] seriocomic maps over thirty-three years of work as an artist. But they were all popular, and his work cast a long shadow. Ever since, illustrators have deployed images of octopuses to suggest scary, lurking evil. Peter Barber, former head of map collections at the British Library, has written (seriocomically, if you will): "Once Fred W. Rose . . . created the 'Octopus' map of Europe, it proved difficult to rid propaganda maps of them."

Indeed, after Rose's career, England, Germany, Japan, and the United States all showed up as octopuses on various widely publicized maps, as did the Standard Oil Company and individuals ranging from Winston Churchill to Arthur Brisbane, a conservative editor for William Randolph Hearst's publishing empire. *Indie Moet Vrij!*, meaning "The Indies must be free!" in Dutch, is a striking example (shown on the next page). It was printed in 1944 in London for the Netherlands' government-in-exile that took refuge there during World War II. All any reader needed to know to understand it was that the Dutch had colonized Indonesia long before the war. By the time the map was published, the rest—with the dark head of a scary octopus replacing the rising sun of Japan, its tentacles spread throughout the East Indies—was self-explanatory.

More generally, in the late nineteenth century and into the early twentieth, it became more common for artists to caricature nations as animals to create satirical maps. One famous map published at the height of US territorial ambitions in 1898, shown on page 169, portrayed an American eagle with wings stretching from Manila to Puerto Rico.

---

1 When Russian troops arrived in the Turkish town of San Stefano (now Yeşilköy) at the end of the Russo-Turkish War and found a French copy of the map, even they enjoyed it enormously, according to the *London Daily News*.

2 Or seven. Historians are still arguing over two that are generally attributed to him.

Pat Keely
INDIE MOET VRIJ !
WERKT EN VECHT ERVOOR!

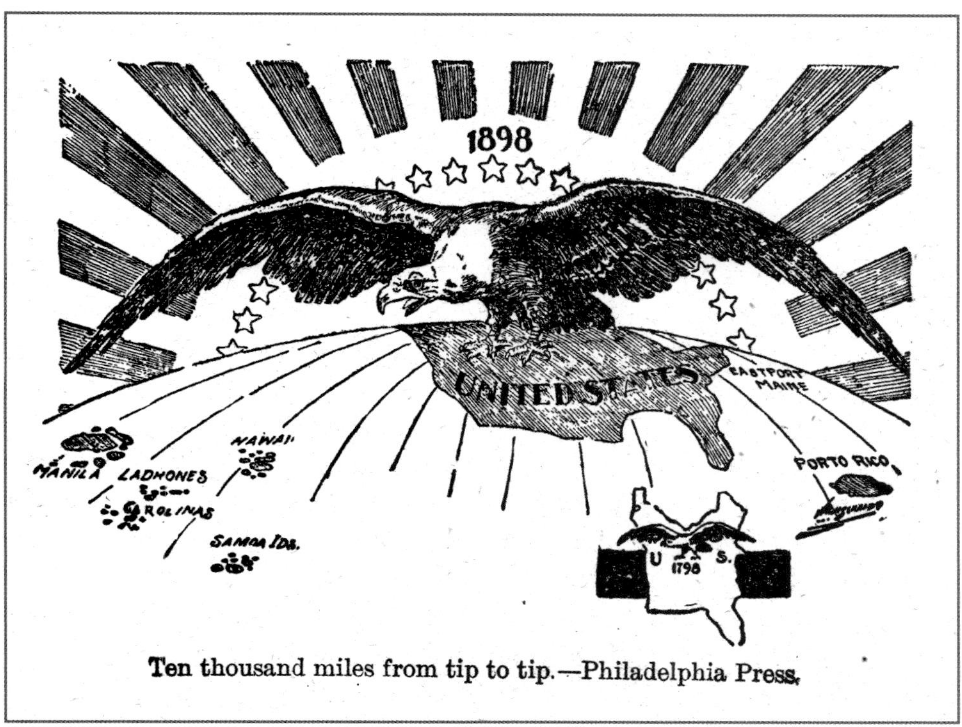

The Situation in the Far East (page 171) is a zoomorphic masterpiece from the same era but a very different cultural context. Tse Tsan-tai (Xie Zuantai), a Chinese revolutionary and writer, created it in 1899 to show how imperial powers were threatening China, and to awaken fellow patriots.

In this map, animals represent various foreign powers: A Russian bear marauds through Manchuria and Mongolia in the northeast, and a British lion prowls along the east (with its tail labeled "Sausage Ambitions" and curled like a casing around the German-colonized port of Tsingtao (now called Qingdao). A French frog occupies Indochina in the southeast, and an American eagle hovers off the coast, above the Phillippines. The rising sun of Japan casts hostile rays across Korea and has Taiwan hooked on a fishing line, while other imperial animals line up at the bottom of the map for their chance to devour territory for themselves. Meanwhile, Chinese officials in the interior of the country appear decadent and doddering, interested only in celebration, money, wine, and sleep.

By the time Tse (Xie) published this map, the decaying Qing dynasty, which had ruled China since 1644, had suffered a series of body blows.

OPPOSITE: Translating to "The Indies Must Be Free!" *Indie Moet Vrij* (created by Patrick Cokayne Keely and published in 1944 by the Netherlands' government-in-exile) depicts a scary cephalopod head in place of Japan's rising sun, its tentacles spread deep into the Malay Archipelago.

ABOVE: Published in 1898 by *The Press* (Philadelphia) after the Spanish-American War, *Ten Thousand Miles from Tip to Tip* portrays US influence as an eagle with wings spanning from the Philippines to the Caribbean.

Beginning in the 1840s, imperial powers forced the opening of Chinese ports to international trade, including the sale of opium, took control of important cities such as Hong Kong and Macau, and seized large chunks of Chinese territory outright, such as Taiwan and parts of Manchuria. In response, nationalist and revolutionary groups were emerging across the country, and Tse's (Xie's) images were an important call to take down the Qing government.

Tse (Xie) was an interesting character. He was born in Australia in 1872, moved to Hong Kong as a teenager, and designed an airship while he was in his twenties. He persisted as a revolutionary despite the failure of an early uprising in 1895 and the assassination of one of his close comrades in 1901. In 1903, he cofounded the *South China Morning Post*, an English-language newspaper in Hong Kong that's still in business today. Tse (Xie) also claimed he could demonstrate the Garden of Eden was located in China. And *The Situation in the Far East* may be the very first example of Chinese *manhua*, or comic drawing, whose Japanese variant became manga. Although he lived until 1938, Tse (Xie) did not join the republican government that replaced the Qing dynasty after revolution came to China in 1911.

But this map, which has remained Tse's (Xie's) best-known work, has reverberated inside China as a national rallying cry for more than one hundred years. In 2013, Jennifer He, a student at the University of Richmond, wrote on that school's *Mappenstance* blog: "Personally, I still remember writing answers such as 'Bear in mind the past and create a bright future' for questions like 'What did you learn from this map?' on plenty of tests in school."

"In general," she continued, "Chinese take this map as part of their complex national identity: They were the weak and vulnerable nation suffer[ing] under corrupted government, both haughty and scared of the western powers. But the 'sleeping giant' has now awakened."

Created in 1899 by Tse Tsan-tai (Xie Zuantai), a Chinese revolutionary and writer, *The Situation in the Far East* shows how imperial powers were dividing and destroying China.

時局圖

一目了然

不言而喻

6
SUPPLEMENT TO THE "GRAPHIC" JULY 24TH 1886.
FREEDOM
FRATERNITY
GREENLAND
BAFFIN BAY
DAVIS STRAIT
ARCTIC
2
MAP OF
SHOWING THE EXTENT OF THE BRI
DOMINION OF CANADA
HUDSON BAY
BERING SEA
BRITISH COLUMBIA
NORTH AMERICA
BRITISH ISLANDS
NORTH SEA
1
3
EUROPE
ASIA
INDIA
NORTH ATLANTIC OCEAN
PACIFIC OCEAN
WEST INDIA ISLANDS
BRITISH GUIANA
SOUTH AMERICA
SOUTH PACIFIC OCEAN
SOUTH ATLANTIC OCEAN
AFRICA
ARABIAN SEA
INDIAN OCEAN
CAPE COLONY
4
WORLD
5
IMPERIAL FEDERATION, MAP OF THE WORLD SHOWING THE EXTENT OF THE BRITISH EMPIRE IN 1886.
STATISTICAL INFORMATION FURNISHED BY CAPTAIN J.C.R. COLOMB, M.P. FORMERLY R.M.A. BRITISH TERRITORIES COLOURED RED
COPYRIGHT

The Maps of an "Empire of Good Intentions"

At its peak, the British Empire ruled over—and was on a mission to civilize—a quarter of the Earth's land.

Imperial Federation Map of the World Showing the Extent of the British Empire in 1886 was created by English artist and illustrator Walter Crane in 1886.

1 It portrays Great Britain and its territorial possessions in red, while barely naming most other places.

2 An inset shows the (much smaller) reach of the British Empire one hundred years earlier.

3 Lines trace major sea routes within the empire, such as London to Bombay.

4 Britannia—a trident-wielding woman warrior whose image has stood for Britain since Roman times—sits atop a world globe.

5 The globe is held up by the titan Atlas wearing a banner that reads, "Human Labour."

6 Figures labeled "Freedom," "Fraternity," and "Federation" wear red caps, symbols of liberty.

THE HISTORY OF political maps is filled with works that carefully blend particular scales, colors, symbols, and shadings to convey political ideas without necessarily making them explicit. The maps here, on the other hand, loudly and proudly declare the greatness of the British Empire at its maximum domain—and the very British message that its reign benefitted its subjects, not just their rulers.

The first (pages 172–173) was created by the Imperial Federation League, a group that sought permanent unity in the Empire through closer relationships between England and its colonies, and was published as a magazine supplement in 1886, a year before the fiftieth anniversary of Queen Victoria's ascension to the throne. It's a Mercator projection (which increases the enormity of Canada) centered on the United Kingdom. Its colors highlight Great Britain and its territorial possessions. Its insets list area, population, shipping, and trade data for various colonies. Lines show major sea routes within the Empire, such as London to Bombay and Quebec to Liverpool.

Living symbols of the empire are arrayed around all along the bottom three edges of the map. There's an elk, seal, and Indigenous North American in a headdress to the northwest; an elephant, tiger, and woman waving a fan decorated like a peacock representing India; a half-clad Indigenous woman and kangaroo for Australia. At first glance, it's all fantastic—literally. As Felix Driver, professor of human geography at the University of London, has written, this map brings together in one image "the infrastructure of empire . . . and imperial fantasy (especially . . . statuesque human bodies, flora and fauna around its crowded margins to denote whole continents, races, and landscapes)." It seems the map is reminiscent of G.K. Chesterton's poem "Geography," without any of its intended irony:

The world is a place on which England is found,
And you will find it however you twirl the globe round;
For the spots are all red and the rest is all grey,
And that is the meaning of Empire Day.

But there's a bit more to the story. The creator of the Imperial Federation map went unrecognized for more than one hundred years, until a researcher named Pippa Biltcliffe published a paper in 2005 identifying it as the work of Walter Crane, an English artist who was a prominent illustrator of children's books. Crane was a socialist, too, which helps explain a few fascinating twists on this map. At top, the figures representing "Freedom," "Fraternity," and "Federation" are donning pieces of red headgear. These are Phrygian caps, symbols of emancipation from slavery in ancient Rome, radicalism in revolutionary France, and liberty in general.[1] And Atlas is wearing a banner that says, "Human Labour."

So it's probably best to read the map as trying to celebrate empire without fully advocating imperialism, however paradoxical that might seem. As its power expanded to govern a quarter of the world's population, Victorian-era Britain took itself to be a divinely inspired force for good, spreading "Christianity, commerce, and civilization," in the phrasing used by famed missionary and explorer David Livingstone. It proclaimed it wanted its subjects to graduate from disease, ignorance, and poverty to self-rule. Many Britons of different political stripes shared at least some pride in that mission—even socialists, who were committed to building an international movement of workers, and members of the Imperial Federation League, who wanted more autonomy for Britain's colonies.

"We would take whole cultures crippled by those maladies and stand them on their own two feet," English historian Simon Schama, who has called Britain "the empire of good intentions," said in 2002. "In the fullness of time, so the theory went, the millions would become civilized enough to govern themselves, and we would leave them, the children of our liberal dream."

There's a similar tension brewing in *The Flags of a Free Empire, Showing the Emblems of British Power Throughout the World* (shown on the following pages). It announces what it wants you to know: "This picture helps us understand the wonderful way in which the British Empire is established throughout the world."

These are the words of Arthur Mee, a British writer who isn't widely remembered today but was extremely popular across the English-speaking world a century ago. Beginning in 1908, he edited *The Children's Encyclopaedia*, which issued magazine-like installments every two weeks, and which published *Flags of a Free Empire* in 1910. Though Mee himself admitted he didn't know much about children, he was intensely interested in helping young citizens develop civic and moral virtues. And his work

---

1 In our time, we know Phrygian caps as the hats known by the cartoon characters the Smurfs.

spread so far and wide that his biographer Keith Crawford has estimated that between its British and American editions, 5 million sets of *The Children's Encyclopaedia* were sold; he even called it "the early-twentieth-century version of the internet."

Mee struck such a chord because he both embodied and made accessible the key beliefs that Victorian England held about its place in the world. (Appropriately enough, he made his last notable appearance in popular culture when Monty Python named the host of the "All-England Summarize Proust Competition" after him in a 1972 comedy sketch, nearly thirty years after he died.)

Every part of *Flags of a Free Empire*, from its borders to its banners to its annotations, comprises an extended argument that the map's very title is perfectly sensible, rather than a contradiction in terms. "The flag that flies over the British Isles . . . is the Union Jack, under which no slave can breathe," Mee writes in his inscription. "But the flags that wave over other parts of the empire have all another sign . . . which generally means that those places, though they are loyal to the British flag, have a nationality or government of their own."

Across the twenty-first-century version of the internet, you can still find echoes of those assertions. Plenty of academics and politicians credit the British Empire for globalizing key elements of modern civilization, such as the rule of law and the English language, around the world. Of course, it was also a myth, however strongly rooted in his national identity, for Mee to claim that Great Britain granted freedom to its colonial subjects as soon as they were able to govern themselves. The United Kingdom acquired many of its colonies by force—a 2012 study found that at one time or another over its long history, England had invaded nearly 90 percent of the world's countries. And it clung to those territories for as long as keeping them served its interests.

Imperial Britain, after all, fought one war to try to prevent the United States from breaking away and two to keep opium markets open for sales from its colonial possessions to Chinese drug users. It not only suppressed independence movements in India and Ireland for many decades, but its fanatic adherence to free-market economics made devastating famines in those lands far worse.

The people living under the flags on this map were supposed to end up "grateful, devoted, peaceful," said Schama. "And—this was the bonus for the modern world—free."

"It didn't exactly work out like that," he continued. "Did it?"

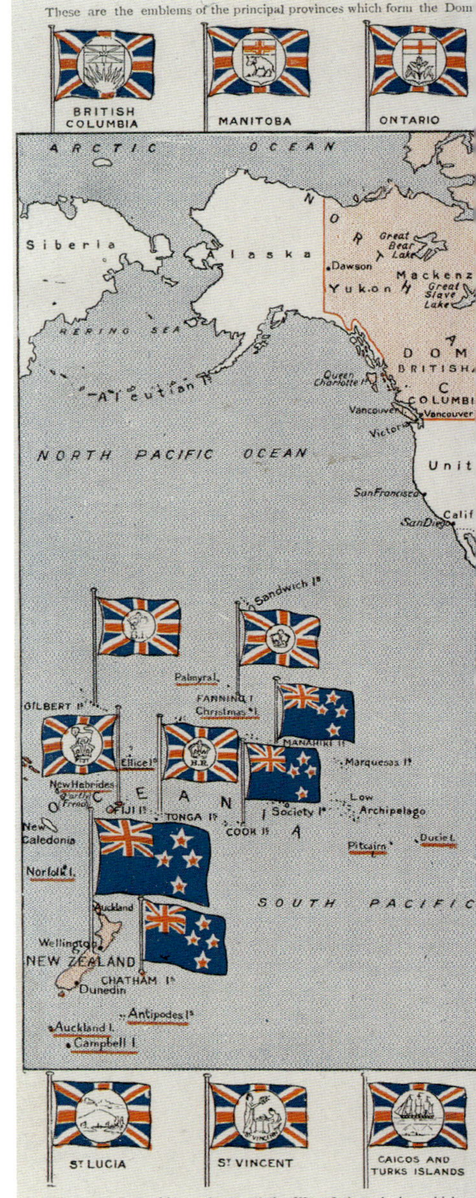

The Flags of a Free Empire, Showing the Emblems of British Power Throughout the World, was published by Englishman Arthur Mee in *The Children's Encyclopaedia* in 1910. It makes its intentions plain: "This picture helps us understand the wonderful way in which the British Empire is established throughout the world."

The Map of America After a German Takeover

What changes would a German victory in the First World War have brought to the United States? Welcome to a map of "Schlauterhaus" and "Pilsener Laker."

Life magazine published *My Country, 'Tis of Thee* (opposite) in February 1916, eighteen months after World War I (then called the Great War) erupted, but while the United States was still neutral in the conflict.

Isolationist feelings ran strong in the US at that time, as did anti-British sentiment among many German and Irish Americans. *Life* dedicated what it called a Get-Ready Number to arguing the opposite side of the case for war. Its editorial in this issue commended President Woodrow Wilson's moves to boost US military preparedness, and warned of the dangers of "hyphenated Americans." And it put *My Country, 'Tis of Thee* on its cover, offering readers a sarcastic version of what the United States might look like after an invasion and takeover by Germany and its allies.

On this map, the US has become "New Prussia" and the names and places of its cities and geographical features have been Germanized. Many of the substitutions the map makes are really quite clever: Washington, DC, has turned into New Berlin, Boston into Kulturplatz, and Chicago into Schlauterhaus. New York is now New Potsdam, rather than its old name of New Amsterdam, and New Orleans has taken the name of another great port city and become New Hamborg, while Bismarck, North Dakota . . . remains Bismarck. The Great Lakes are now named after varieties of beer. Various slices of the continent have been lopped off for allies of Germany, including Florida ("Turconia") for the Ottoman Empire; Baja, California ("Austriana"), for Austria-Hungary; and the West Coast for Japan ("Japonica," including the cities of Nagaseattle and Yokohanjalee). And a small "American Reservation" sits in desert lands of the Southwest, presumably for anyone who doesn't like the new order.

Life didn't credit an illustrator for the map, but their excellent satire drew a lot of attention. Two weeks after its publication, *The Fatherland*, a pro-German periodical based in New York, ran a rip-off–cum-parody

My Country, 'Tis of Thee (New Prussia) was published by *Life* magazine in February 1916, a year and a half after World War I broke out. It showed readers what changes a victory by Germany and its allies might bring to the United States.

GET-READY NUMBER

Life

PRICE 10 CENTS
Vol. 67, No. 1737. February 10, 1916

"MY COUNTRY, 'TIS OF THEE"

on its cover, like an answer song in pop music. Its title: *New Map of the D.S.E.—Dependent States of England—Formerly U.S.A. with No Apologies to "Life."* The *Fatherland* map (right) wasn't as detailed as the *Life* map, and never became as famous, but it too was pretty funny. It showed a subservient America called "New Britain," with Washington as London on the Potomac, New Orleans as New Liverpool, and the Atlantic Ocean renamed Lake Winston Churchill.

The American Rights Committee, a group dedicated to supporting England and France and opposing German militarism, then reprinted the *Life* map as a leaflet—probably to distribute at a large rally the committee held at Carnegie Hall in mid-March. The trends in political mapping that started around the Civil War and continued with fights over women's suffrage accelerated during the Great War: Maps were gaining wider circulation and figuring more directly into American political debates.

Shortly after *Life*'s map appeared, *The Fatherland* published this response, satirizing a possible British victory in the Great War.

Just over one hundred years later, the *Life* map resurfaced on the cover of another magazine—this time, the Winter 2017 issue of *The Portolan*, which is the journal of the Washington Map Society. Inside was a long essay about "persuasive cartography" by the noteworthy map collector PJ Mode, who chose the *Life* map to represent the massive changes political maps underwent in the early twentieth century.

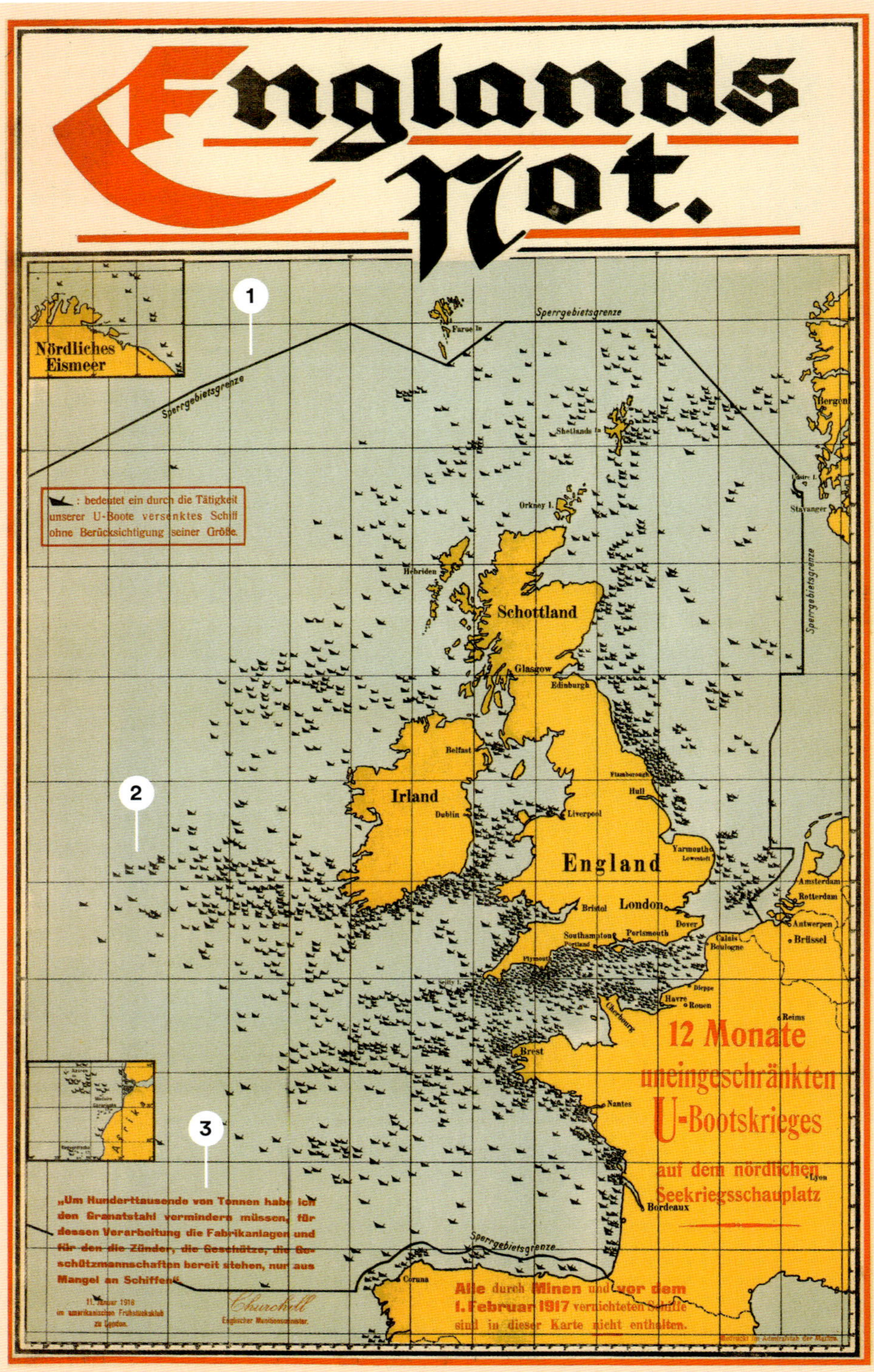
Englands Not.
1
2
3
Nördliches Eismeer
Sperrgebietsgrenze
: bedeutet ein durch die Tätigkeit unserer U-Boote versenktes Schiff ohne Berücksichtigung seiner Größe.
Faroe
Shetlands
Orkney I.
Hebriden
Bergen
Stavanger
Schottland
Glasgow
Edinburgh
Belfast
Irland
Dublin
Flamborough
Hull
Liverpool
England
Yarmouth
Lowestoft
London
Bristol
Dover
Southampton
Portsmouth
Portland
Plymouth
Calais
Boulogne
Amsterdam
Rotterdam
Antwerpen
Brüssel
Dieppe
Havre
Rouen
Cherbourg
Reims
Brest
Nantes
Bordeaux
Lyon
Coruna
12 Monate uneingeschränkten U-Bootskrieges auf dem nördlichen Seekriegsschauplatz
„Um Hunderttausende von Tonnen habe ich den Granatstahl vermindern müssen, für dessen Verarbeitung die Fabrikanlagen und für den die Zünder, die Geschütze, die Geschützmannschaften bereit stehen, nur aus Mangel an Schiffen".
11. Januar 1918
im amerikanischen Frühstücksklub zu London.
Churchill
Englischer Munitionsminister.
Alle durch Minen und vor dem 1. Februar 1917 vernichteten Schiffe sind in dieser Karte nicht enthalten.

The Maps of Wartime Desperation

Germany created skillful propaganda maps in service of a losing cause in World War I.

About 110 years ago, political maps, often carrying striking propaganda, began showing up on posters. Thanks to two colliding trends, they became instruments of mass marketing on a scale that dwarfed their previous influence.

For one thing, posters of all kinds zoomed in popularity just before the turn of the twentieth century. In the mid-1800s, French artist Jules Chéret led massive breakthroughs in the technology and adaptation of lithography.[1] Artists no longer had to spend their time hand-coloring every engraving they produced, and began printing posters filled with vivid imagery, intense colors, and bold typefaces.

Chéret championed those results; he organized the first group exhibit of posters (in 1884) and wrote the first book on posters as art (in 1886). And the wildfire spread of posters kicked off the eras known as the Belle Epoque in France (think of Henri de Toulouse-Lautrec's work) and Art Nouveau across Europe, when posters became accepted as fine art—but were still inexpensive enough that middle-class Europeans and Americans could collect them. It also launched the modern age of advertising.

At the same time, the strongest powers in Europe were on a collision course for war. Specifically, after unifying into one country in 1871, Germany rapidly grew into an empire ready to forcefully and sometimes violently challenge the manufacturing, shipping, colonial, and military might of England and France. And when war among them exploded in 1914, it engulfed more countries in more destructive combat than the world had ever seen.

Englands Not (England's Misery), produced by the admiralty staff of the German navy a year after Germany had declared unrestricted warfare in the area around the British Isles, shows the destruction that attacks had wrought since they began in February 1917.

1 The war zone is demarcated with a line and labeled *Sperrgebietsgrenze*, or "border of the restricted area."

2 Hundreds of little tilted ships all around England indicate vessels sunk by German U-boats.

3 The map features a grim quote (in German) from Winston Churchill, then the United Kingdom's Minister of Munitions, to bolster German hopes that terror on the seas would choke off England's capacity to wage war.

---

1 Lithography is a printing process where an illustrator uses a water-repellent medium (like crayon) to draw an image on a smooth slab of rock or a metal plate, then treats the surface with water and ink. The design soaks up the ink while shunning the water, and can then be transferred to paper. Chéret figured out how to use three blocks of limestone to create a wide range of colors.

Amid the carnage, national governments needed a way to quickly and directly rally political, financial, and material support from their peoples. In an era before radio or newsreels, let alone television or the internet, countries from Austria-Hungary to Australia turned to posters, issuing thousands about topics ranging from recruitment to food conservation. Their efforts pulled in some of the world's greatest advertising illustrators and designers, including Britain's John Hassall, who was known as the Poster King, and Lucian Bernhard of Germany. The United States didn't enter the war until 1917, but still produced more posters than any nation—including James Montgomery Flagg's iconic image of Uncle Sam pointing at readers and saying, "I want YOU for US Army."

Showcasing easily understood and often lively images of territorial gains, losses, and threats, maps were all over these posters. In fact, World War I was probably the peak era for political maps, at least as propaganda. Medium turbocharged message, with enormously effective results. "For the first time," as map collector and historian PJ Mode has written, "four great nations [England, France, Germany, and the United States] were competing in the production of persuasive maps on the same subject, some of them through newly established state propaganda agencies. The result was a marked increase in both the amount of persuasive cartography and its quality."

Toward the end of the conflict, German maps grew louder, as poster makers tried to convince citizens their forces were gloriously winning battles they were actually precariously close to losing. In February 1917, Germany, facing the dire effects of a British naval blockade, declared unrestricted warfare inside a zone around the United Kingdom. A year later, *Englands Not*, or "England's Misery" (shown on page 182), depicted the results of its attacks: hundreds of ships sunk by U-boats. The map adds a quote from Winston Churchill, at that time the minister of munitions in the British government, about how the sea war was damaging England's military production. "I have had to reduce by hundreds of thousands of tons the shell steel for which factories are used," Churchill said. "And for which tinder, guns, and gun crews are available, simply because of the lack of ships."

This map, like many classic German posters, makes heavy use of distinctive type and vivid but flat colors, relying on contrasts rather than showing inclines or textures to make its elements stand out. And it flat out revels in the destruction of the enemy—civilians as well as military. All of this is also true of *Die brennende Wunde Frankreichs*, or "The burning wound of France," left, printed in the spring of 1918. On this map, the Western Front has been ripped open from Ostend in Belgium to Verdun in France, where the longest battle of the war had been waged—and Paris is being shelled by German cannons.

In its description of the "burning wound," the text in the upper-right-hand corner achieves a kind of murderous eloquence: "Large areas of ruins of formerly flourishing towns and villages, dead industrial sites, fields riddled with iron that no plow can furrow anymore!"

It continues, blaming the British and French prime ministers for the destruction: "The wound grows bigger and bigger every day, the fire continues greedily, fanned by the warmongers [Prime Ministers] Clemenceau and Lloyd George. . . . Germans, thank our field grays who protect you and your homeland from the same fate."

These are lurid, desperate political maps. Few have ever been more powerful. Despite their bravado, they are also stories of failure. Initially, the U-boat campaign portrayed by *Englands Not* was a great success, and exacted a huge toll on Britain, whose reserves of wheat sank to just a six-week supply by the spring of 1917. But unrestrained submarine attacks led the United States to enter the war on the side of the Allies in April—a decisive turning point against Germany. And German cannon attacks did reach Paris in 1918, as shown on "The burning wound." But the German spring offensive that year, launched around the time the map was published, led to enormous losses—something like 250,000 casualties on each side. Germany's most massive attempt to deepen the "burning wound" depleted its army, and accelerated its loss of the war.

Die brennende Wunde Frankreichs, or "The burning wound of France," was printed in the spring of 1918 by the German Military Department of the Office of Foreign Affairs. A jagged bright red area suggests a gash has been ripped across the Western Front, with the nearly twenty cities shown in its path left in flames.

БУДЬ НА СТРАЖЕ!

The Map That Saved the Russian Revolution

Vivid propaganda helped Vladimir Lenin and Leon Trotsky overcome inconceivable odds in their battle to control what became the Soviet Union.

The conditions leading to the creation of this map, in Russia in 1920, were some of the most chaotic that any place on the earth has ever endured. To begin with, as the First World War had ground to a brutal, exhausting conclusion, Russia's military, economy, and government had all collapsed. After staggering losses to the highly efficient and mechanized armies of Germany and facing rebellion by soldiers and workers, Czar Nicholas II abdicated in 1917, ending more than three hundred years of dynastic rule by the Romanov family. The Provisional Government that replaced them lasted for just under eight months before it too was overthrown, by revolutionary communists led by Vladimir Lenin, leading to civil war later that year.

Meanwhile, Germany and its allies, unable to overcome American intervention in the Great War, lost in the west. As a result, all along the vast frontier between the broken, depleted empires of Germany and Austria-Hungary on one side and Russia on the other, new conflicts broke out over the borders among various emerging states. From 1917 to 1922, Soviet Russia engaged in no less than fifteen wars, from intervening in the Finnish Civil War, to putting down a push for independence in Ukraine, to invading Armenia.

Inside Russia, the revolutionaries were trying to take hold of a realm where the Great War had just killed something like 1.5 million combatants and civilians while malnutrition and disease had claimed another 700,000 victims. Hunger, influenza, and typhus were still rampant. The factions that had opposed the czars were fighting each other. Countries such as Great Britain and the United States were intervening to fight the communists. Japan was landing troops in Siberia to seize parts of Asia. And resurgent nationalists from Latvia to Poland to Kazakhstan were trying to carve out their own countries. Almost inconceivably, the Leninists prevailed. They lost significant battles, but won enough to triumph in the Russian Civil War.

Bud' na strazhe! (*Be On Guard!*) was produced by Dmitriĭ Moor, a pioneer of Soviet political poster art, during war with Poland in the winter of 1920–21. It shows a larger-than-life figure (clearly meant to be Trotsky) taking the shape of Russia, wearing a Red Army coat, and swinging a bayonet as he fends off foreign interlopers.

The communists never built a popular movement broad enough to win an election, but they didn't have to. Under the leadership of Vladimir Lenin and Leon Trotsky, the most important architects of the Russian Revolution, they developed a disciplined, powerful military. And they maintained loyalty from its ranks as well as from many workers and peasants through the use of both propaganda and terror. The revolutionaries deployed posters the way that contemporaneous Western European and American political actors did—as key tools of persuasion. And some of their most influential messages were emblazoned with political maps, like *Bud' na strazhe!* (*Be On Guard!*), produced amid war with Poland during the brutal winter of 1920–21.

Trotsky, who founded the Red Army, was particularly effective at inspiring the troops as revolution turned into civil war. As the writer Christopher Hitchens once said, Trotsky "combined in himself the role of man of action and man of ideas. . . . He held forth on an amazing number of subjects, but he was a soldier as well as a revolutionary and a person of moral and physical courage." And he's all over the *Be On Guard!* map.

A huge figure in bright red dominates this map, taking the shape of Russia west of the Ural Mountains, wearing a Red Army overcoat and forage cap and swinging a bayonet. While he is not named explicitly, this superman's eyes, nose, and mustache clearly indicate it is Trotsky himself, fending off foreign invaders.

Further, the text below is derived from a communiqué Trotsky issued at the end of the Russo-Polish War: "We do not know whether it will be the supporters of peace or the criminal incendiaries who will get the upper hand in Poland this winter or next spring. We must be prepared for the worst. . . . The Red Army is redoubling its work of military preparation. No turn of events will take the Red Army by surprise!"

Be On Guard! was designed by Dmitriĭ Stakhievich Moor (1883–1946), a founding father of Soviet political poster art. After the failed first Russian Revolution of 1905, Moor began publishing satirical drawings and anti-czarist caricatures. During the Revolution of 1917, when the communists needed a cheap, visceral way to reach audiences that included people who couldn't read, Moor came up with colorful and succinct posters. He also helped design the first "agit-trains"—decorated railroad cars that the Bolsheviks started sending around the country in 1918 to bring information to people in far-flung areas of Russia. *Be On Guard!* perfectly captures Moor's style.

One feature of this map marks it as specifically a Marxist effort. Notice that the small forms standing in opposition to the giant Trotsky don't caricature or even symbolize the countries they're from. Rather, the Finnish and Estonian and Latvian foes all look alike—they're all fat cats, in tuxedos and tails. (One exception is the figure behind the Polish adversary, who appears to be a sneaky Frenchman, instigating conflict.) *Be On Guard!* doesn't attack other nationalities per se. It warns against all members of the upper classes who oppose revolution.

Still, those capitalist figures *do* look like they're trying to tread on Mother Russia. Moor was didactic, but never overly theoretical or wordy. And it was his genius in *Be On Guard!* to connect Trotsky and his comrades with a huge audience that might never have read Marx or Lenin but approved of protecting the homeland and preserving the empire's boundaries. Look at *Be On Guard!* and, whether or not you recognize Trotsky or grasp the intricacies of the Lithuanian Wars of Independence, your first reaction is likely to be that it's positively a *Russian* map.

The map proved to be hugely influential. In 2010, Peter Barber, then head of map collections at the British Library, even ranked it No. 1 on his list of 10 of the greatest maps that changed the world. Describing it, the London *Daily Mail* wrote: "The infant USSR was threatened with invasion, famine, and social unrest. . . . Using a map of European Russia and its neighbours, Moor's image of a heroic Bolshevik guard defeating the invading 'Whites'[1] helped define the Soviet Union in the Russian popular imagination."

That's true, and by 1922, Lenin, Trotsky, and their comrades had either killed or absorbed their enemies or driven them out of the Soviet Union. It's also true that by using weapons like this map, they succeeded at least as much by appealing to Russian nationalism as to any communist concept of class struggle or international revolution.

---

1 In this context, "Whites" refers to the multiple groups opposing Lenin, Trotsky, and the Red Army. They included anticommunist reformers, splinter factions of socialists and communists, loyalists to the czars, and nationalists of various ethnicities—a diverse and ultimately hopelessly uncoordinated coalition.

87 545 000
Deutsche in Europa
Der deutsche Bevölkerungs- und Kulturanteil in den Staaten Europas
Entwurf und Gestaltung nach Angabe des Amtes für Schulungsbriefe im Hauptschulungsamt der NSDAP. von A. Hillen-Ziegfeld unter Mitwirkung von Prof. Dr. K. C. von Loesch und Dr. Dr. Friedr. Lange — Nachdruck verboten!
Es ist auf die Dauer für eine Weltmacht von Selbstbewußtsein unerträglich, an ihrer Seite Volksgenossen zu wissen, denen aus ihrer Sympathie oder ihrer Verbundenheit mit dem Gesamtvolk, seinem Schicksal und seiner Weltauffassung fortgesetzt schwerstes Leid zugefügt wird!
Der Führer am 20. 2. 1938
Die ostwärtigen Pfeile kennzeichnen die Ausbreitungsrichtung der deutschen Stadtrechte im Mittelalter (Schulungsbrief 1/38)
Deutscher Volksboden
Deutschtum in der Verstreuung
Seit der Abtrennung: Mischgebiet
Grenzdeutsche mit andersvölkischem Einschlag
Alpenromanen im deutschen Kulturbereich
Städte deutsch. Rechtsgründg. im Ostraum
Die Reichsgrenze als Scheidegrenze innerhalb d. deutschen Volksraumes
Die Reichsgrenze als Volksgrenze
Das Stärkeverhältnis d. Deutschen zur Gesamtbevölkerung des betreff. Staates
70000 Deutsche Volkstums-Zahlen
DEUTSCHES REICH
67 000 000
SCHWEDEN
6000
DÄNEMARK
60000
OSTSEE
ESTLD.
20000
LETTLAND
70000
LITAUEN
190000
400000
HOLLAND
115000
BELGIEN
150000
290000
FRANKREICH
1700000
SCHWEIZ
3000000
ITALIEN
270000
TSCHECHOSLOWAKEI
3500000
6 200 000
UNGARN
600000
POLEN
1200000
RUMÄNIEN
800000
JUGOSLAW.
700000
Stockholm
Reval
Dorpat
Riga
Libau
Dünabg.
Memel
Kauen
Tilsit
Königsbg.
Allenstein
Danzig
Stolp
Kopenhagen
Tondern
Flensbg.
Lübeck
Hambg.
Bremen
Stettin
Schneidemühl
Thorn
Posen
Warschau
Lodsch
Berlin
Hannover
Magdebg.
Frankfurt
Oder
Weichsel
Amsterdam
Calais
Brüssel
Lille
Aachen
Eupen
Malmedy
Köln
Dortmund
Wuppertal
Kassel
Erfurt
Leipzig
Dresden
Liegnitz
Breslau
Oppeln
Beuthen
Reichenberg
Eger
Prag
Iglau
Budweis
Olmütz
Troppau
Teschen
Bielitz
Krakau
Lembg.
Rowno
Luxembg.
Metz
Mainz
Frankfurt
Saarbrücken
Mannheim
Nürnbg.
Stuttgart
Straßburg
Basel
München
Donau
Linz
Salzbg.
Wien
Preßbg.
Ödenbg.
Graz
Klagenfurt
Gmünd
Innsbruck
St. Moritz
Bern
Zermatt
Salurn
Tarvis
Marbg.
Budapest
Fünfkirchen
Essegg
Neusatz
Werschetz
Belgrad
Temeschbg.
Hermannstadt
Kronstadt
Bistritz
Sathmar
Tschernowitz
Leutschau
Bukarest
Paris
Seine
Maas
Rhein
Main
Elbe
Lyon
Rhone
Po
Etsch
Genua
Gottschee
Agram
Sau

The Map of the Worst Idea Ever

Maps were a key medium for Nazi rhetoric of extermination.

87 545 000 Deutsche in Europa, or "87,545,000 Germans in Europe," expresses in map form history's most noxious concept: *lebensraum*, or "living space."

At first, lebensraum simply referred to the ways geography can shape culture, particularly how a society can feel the need to spread physically as it grows. In the early twentieth century, German scientists and political leaders adopted the term to justify German colonialism and to target Eastern Europe as a place into which expansion could help Germany overcome its defeat in World War I. Then Adolf Hitler and the Nazis took the idea to genocidal extremes. For them, lebensraum meant a call to unite all Germanic peoples, take new territory, and expel or liquidate anyone in the way.

"87,545,000 Germans" (left), printed in 1938, displays German populations across Europe. Its definition of *German* encompasses citizens living on German soil, "Germans in the dispersion" of emigration to other countries stretching from Holland to Turkey, and peoples "in the German cultural sector," or close enough to German for them to count for the Nazis, such as Alpine Italians.

With its powerful red colors and its precisely plotted blots connected by arrows, "87,545,000 Germans" argues it's the reach of the mass of victimized *Volksdeutsche*—people of German ethnicity or culture, wherever they might

87 545 000 Deutsche in Europa (87,545,000 Germans in Europe), printed in 1938 at the direction of the Nazi Party Office of Training, shows German populations across Europe in shades of red varying by their density. It maps historical dispersion—but, replete with a quote from Adolf Hitler, also future conquests.

live—that really matters, not the national boundaries of the present moment. As Hitler himself put it in a paranoid quote at the upper-left-hand corner: "In the long run, it is unbearable for a world power . . . to have compatriots who are constantly being inflicted with the most severe suffering because of . . . their connection with the entire people, their destiny, and their worldview!" So while the map's vectors ostensibly indicate the eastward movement of Germans since the Middle Ages, they look ominously like invasion routes of the future.

"87,545,000 Germans" was created by Arnold Hillen-Ziegfeld, who was probably Germany's leading maker of political maps. He had been a Nazi since 1921, and was dedicated to propaganda maps, which he called "suggestive cartography." For this map, he was assisted by two professors, including Friedrich Lange. Fifteen years earlier, Lange had produced a map showing "separate and withheld areas" with the unsubtle title *Das ganze Deutschland soll es sein!* or "It should all be Germany!" This time around, he obtained the population statistics Hillen-Ziegfeld used, and, in keeping with the team's racist philosophies, made sure to exclude Jews from their numbers.[1]

As much as "87,545,000 Germans" looks like—and was—a blueprint for World War II, no map that focuses purely on territories and numbers can fully capture the menace of Nazi Germany's cartographic propaganda. Nazi leaders understood the authoritative and visceral power of maps, and used them often in relentless campaigns to whip up popular resentments and political support, both in Germany and abroad. Maps helped blast the full range of Nazi messages: Germany had been treated unfairly after the Great War; its exiles abroad were oppressed; Britain and France were aggressors; the United States should stay home—and the enemies of German purity deserved extermination.

Hitler got his most lurid support from a tabloid called *Der Stürmer* (The Stormer), which was published by a virulent antisemite named Julius Streicher from 1923 to 1945. Streicher, an early backer of Der Führer, was a "thoroughly unsavory character, unpopular even with many fellow Nazis," according to his biographer Randall Bytwerk. At *Der Stürmer*, Streicher published a nonstop litany of malevolent, often pornographic, screeds.

---

1 Lange also had two doctorates, and demanded the fatuous title of "Dr. Dr.," as he is called in the credit box beneath the map's title.

A horrifying 1944 cover from the German publication *Der Stürmer*, entitled "Das Ungeziefer," or "Vermin." Its hideous image of Judaism joins American capitalism and Soviet communism and infests Europe.

He regularly slandered Jews as greedy, subhuman creatures out to pollute German blood, murder Christian children, and seize world power. Monstrous illustrations by Philipp Rupprecht, a caricaturist who went by the pen name "Fips," amplified Streicher's raging words. As early as 1927, a Streicher-Rupprecht collaboration showed a Nazi Party member pumping poison into the roots of a tree surrounded by dead rats representing Jews. And their work sold well: By 1937, *Der Stürmer* had a weekly circulation of more than 480,000, and reached many more Germans through its large red display cases, which showcased its front pages and became popular around the country.

In September 1944, when Allied forces had liberated France and were advancing toward Germany, Streicher and Fips unveiled a vile *Der Stürmer* cover called "Das Ungeziefer," or "Vermin" (left). It shows a giant, hairy, hook-nosed, segmented louse crawling across the Northern Hemisphere of the globe, with a dollar sign in one of its huge eyes and a hammer and sickle in the other. It's a repellent vision of Judaism supposedly uniting American capitalism and Soviet communism and infecting Europe. To the upper left, an inscription inside a Star of David perverts a biblical quote to guide the beast: "You shall devour the people of the earth."

Below, Streicher's doggerel says: "Life is not worth living, / When one does not resist the parasite, / Never satisfied as it creeps about. / We must and will win."

They didn't.

After the end of the war in Europe, Streicher was arrested, tried by the Allies at Nuremberg for crimes against humanity, and sentenced to death. Nasty to the end, as he stood on the gallows, Streicher screamed, "Purim Fest, 1946!"—invoking the Jewish holiday that marks the hanging of Haman, who had planned to annihilate the entire Jewish population of the Persian Empire in ancient times.

"Vermin" is figuratively and literally the most skin-crawling political map in history. It's incitement to mass murder, the end result of lebensraum.

The Map That Put the United States at the Center of the World

Unconventional mapmakers like Richard Edes Harrison gave Americans a global perspective during the Second World War.

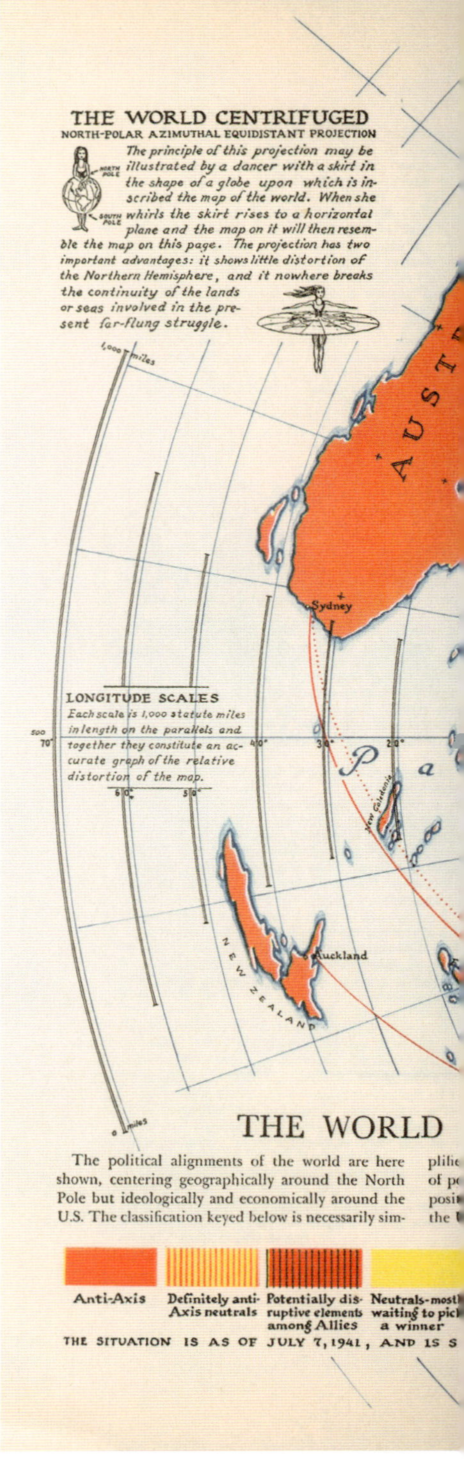

Fortune published Richard Edes Harrison's *The World Divided* in August 1941. The map uses an unusual polar view, and every visual element brings home its central point: Only the United States was in a position to stop a worldwide fascist takeover.

1 The US, in bright red and smack in the center of global action, stands opposite the dark forces swarming ominously from 2 the swastika shown in the middle of Europe and 3 the islands of Japan. Meanwhile, 4 Britain and 5 China each appear isolated.

6 Lines extend from the United States like tentative tentacles to show routes of the Lend-Lease program, through which the US loaned military supplies to allies. 7 Dollar signs signify American foreign aid, and 8 peaked caps denote American military bases.

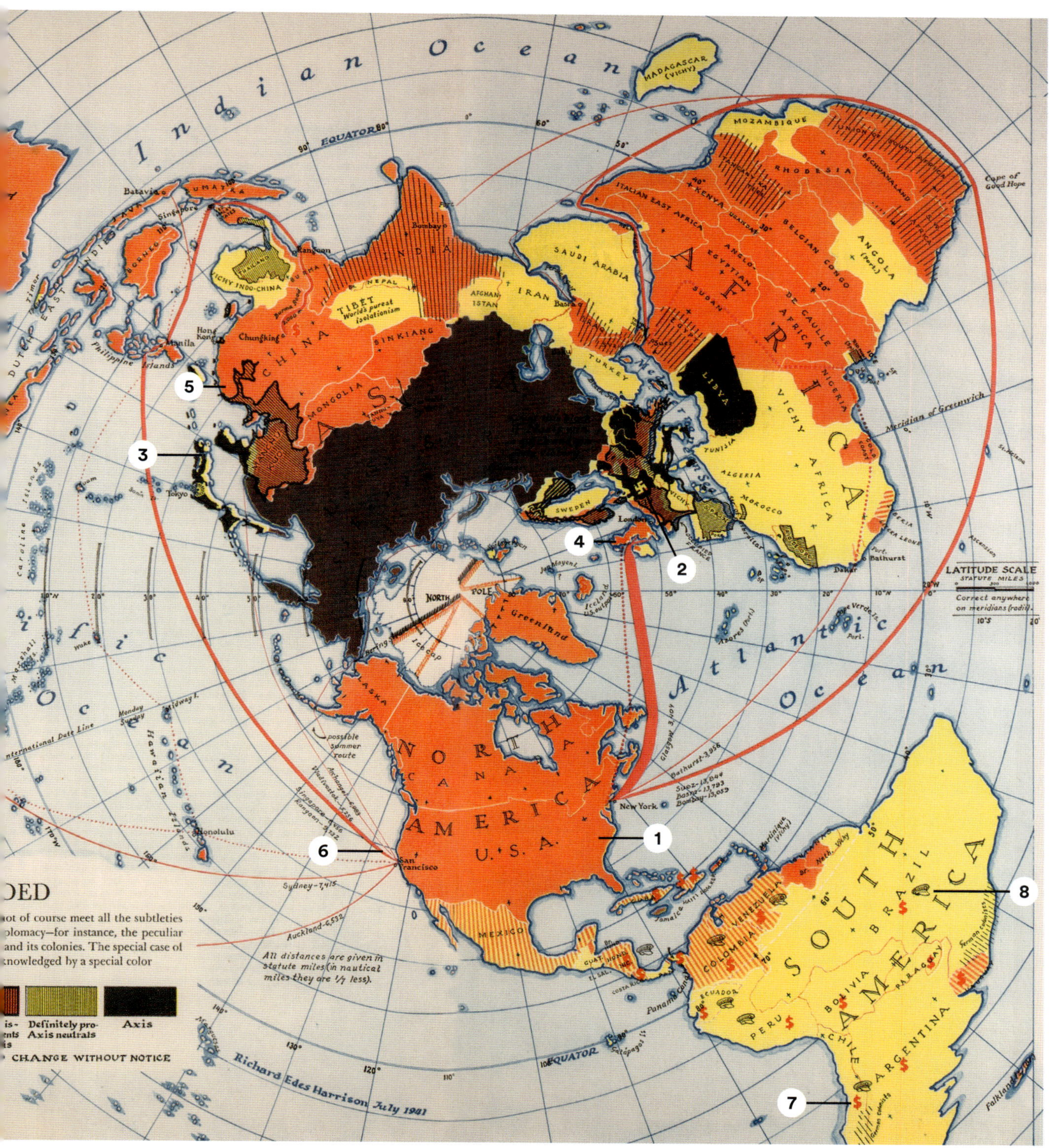

Indian Ocean
MADAGASCAR (VICHY)
EQUATOR
MOZAMBIQUE
UNION OF SOUTH AFRICA
RHODESIA
BECHUANALAND
Cape of Good Hope
ITALIAN EAST AFRICA
KENYA
BELGIAN CONGO
ANGOLA (Port.)
ANGLO-EGYPTIAN SUDAN
DE GAULLE AFRICA
AFRICA
SAUDI ARABIA
IRAN
INDIA
Bombay
NEPAL
TIBET World's purest isolationism
AFGHANISTAN
SINKIANG
CHINA
Chungking
MONGOLIA
ASIA
VICHY INDO-CHINA
Rangoon
Singapore
Batavia
Manila
Philippine Islands
Hong Kong
Tokyo
TURKEY
LIBYA
VICHY AFRICA
TUNISIA
ALGERIA
MOROCCO
NIGERIA
Meridian of Greenwich
SWEDEN
London
Dakar
Bathurst
LATITUDE SCALE
STATUTE MILES
Correct anywhere on meridians (radii).
NORTH POLE
Greenland
Iceland
Atlantic Ocean
Pacific Ocean
NORTH AMERICA
CANADA
U.S.A.
New York
San Francisco
Honolulu
Midway I.
Hawaiian Islands
International Date Line
possible summer route
Glasgow 3,10?
Bathurst-3,956
Suez-13,064
Basra-13,793
Bombay-15,059
Sydney-7,415
Auckland-6,532
All distances are given in statute miles (in nautical miles they are 1/7 less).
MEXICO
Jamaica
Martinique (Vichy)
VENEZUELA
COLOMBIA
ECUADOR
PERU
BOLIVIA
PARAGUAY
CHILE
ARGENTINA
BRAZIL
SOUTH AMERICA
Falkland Is.
Panama Canal
Galápagos Is.
EQUATOR
Richard Edes Harrison July 1941
DED
not of course meet all the subtleties
plomacy—for instance, the peculiar
and its colonies. The special case of
knowledged by a special color
Definitely pro-Axis neutrals
Axis
CHANGE WITHOUT NOTICE
1
2
3
4
5
6
7
8

BACK IN 1797, as George Washington was leaving office, he asked: "Why, by interweaving our destiny with that of any part of Europe, entangle our peace and prosperity in the toils of European ambition, rivalship, interest, humor, or caprice?"

Washington's Farewell Address reflected the kind of isolationism that has always run through American politics: a proud belief that the United States was no mere tribe, but a free nation that had created itself, stood apart, and had no need to get stuck in the squabbles of the "Old World." And for many decades, the United States, separated from Europe, Africa, and Asia by thousands of miles of oceans, had the luxury of essentially being able to avoid any war not of its own choosing. By and large, most of its citizens wanted to keep to their own affairs—even in the 1930s, when fascist governments in Germany and Japan brutally annexed and attacked neighboring countries. The week after Adolf Hitler triggered World War II by invading Poland in September 1939, a Gallup poll found that 84 percent of Americans opposed sending armed forces abroad to fight Germany.

But the world was shrinking! By the end of the 1930s, 83 percent of US households had a radio, more than double the number who had one at the start of the decade. Americans were flying 840 million passenger-miles a year, up from barely 100 million in 1930. Quite suddenly, people, goods, information, news, and entertainment were all traveling great distances at previously unimaginable speeds. So were military forces, typified by the Nazi doctrine of *blitzkrieg*, meaning "lightning war."

Many leaders of the Eastern Establishment—keepers of the old-school financial institutions and elite universities clustered in the northeastern United States—came to believe the country had a duty to engage the world more fully. Some were idealists who wanted to protect the concept of democracy. Others were pragmatists who sought to promote American strategic and commercial interests. Several of the most important, including President Franklin D. Roosevelt, were both. And these internationalists found their most powerful expression in the magazines run by Henry Luce, whose stable included *Time*, *Life*, and *Fortune*.

In those pre-internet, pre-television days, magazines *were* the national media, and the Luce publications dominated their industry. They were written in accessible language and a distinctive omniscient tone, and in the 1930s they became not only incredibly popular, but widely influential—a way for Americans to make sense of the world changing around them.

These magazines insisted on the need for the US to assert itself in global affairs. And late in the decade, an illustrator named Richard Edes Harrison carried that project into the maps these magazines published.

Born in 1901, Harrison studied architecture at Yale but landed in New York City looking for work in the middle of the Great Depression. He took what illustration and design jobs he could get, and drew objects ranging from lighting fixtures to matchbook covers to artificial breasts. In 1932, a copyeditor at *Time* asked Harrison to fill in on short notice for a mapmaker who had gone missing (apparently on a drinking binge), and he went on to join the staff of *Fortune* three years later, then started his own cartography business three years after that. With no formal training in the field, the talented draftsman felt free to try the boldest methods he could dream up to compel readers' attention. He quickly became a pioneer in using dramatic colors and unusual perspectives to deliver the message of his assignments.

In 1940, for instance, Harrison drew *Three Approaches to the US* (page 198), a set of maps displaying the curved surface of the earth from three very different vantage points, each with a direct line from a foreign power into the United States. With airplanes zooming overhead, there was neither Atlantic nor Pacific refuge in Harrison's reckoning; he stunned Americans into seeing paths from Berlin to Detroit, Tokyo to Seattle, Caracas to New Orleans. And he supported his images with gut-punching prose: "If an enemy should ever establish himself on the northern shore of South America or in the mazes of the West Indies," he wrote about that first example, "he would cut first at the US G-string, the [Panama] Canal, then rip at its soft belly here displayed."

Harrison developed *The World Divided* (pages 194–195), his greatest masterpiece, during the summer of 1941, after Nazi Germany had overrun Poland, France, Norway, and the Balkans and was striking deep into Russia. His text left no doubt about his mission. It begins, "This is a map of a world struggle that will mark a turning point in civilization."

This map uses an unusual, eye-catching perspective to look at the world from the North Pole outward. And it places the United States smack in the center of global action. The US, in bright red, stands against the dark forces of Nazi Germany and Imperial Japan. Britain and China each appear lonely and vulnerable.

Again and again, Harrison portrays the US as connected to, not isolated from, the rest of the world: Red lines extend from the United States to show routes of the Lend-Lease program, through which the US

THREE APPROACHES TO THE U.S.
Map 9
. . . FROM BERLIN
A great-circle route from Berlin here passes through Detroit. The fanciful can see, if they wish, a pincers movement extending from Newfoundland down the New England coast and down the St. Lawrence to the continent's heart; a third arm reaching to the south shore of Hudson Bay, where the terrain permits quick construction of landing fields. And there is no east-west highway north of the Great Lakes.
Map 10
. . . FROM TOKYO
The direct line from most Asiatic ports, as shown on Map 7, approaches the U.S. from this angle. The coastal valleys seem temptingly remote from the U.S. center of population, 2,000 miles away across mountains, badlands, and plains. But the map does not reckon with a transportation system that could put a fully equipped army of half a million men into Seattle in a matter of days—if we had the army.
Map 11
. . . FROM CARACAS
If an enemy should ever establish himself on the northern shore of South America or in the mazes of the West Indies, he would cut first at the U.S. G-string, the Canal, then rip at its soft belly here displayed. For the Gulf Coast—with oil, salt, sulfur, coal, and gas—is becoming a great chemical stewpot nourishing, shaping, and extending industry, a modern analogue to the earlier iron-ore economy of the Great Lakes.
MEXICO
CENTRAL AMERICA
Gulf of Mexico
New Orleans
Chicago
Detroit
Washington
New York
Ottawa
Montreal
Quebec
Boston
Bermuda
Atlantic Ocean
West Indies
CANADA
Hudson Bay
Hudson Strait
LABRADOR
NEWFOUNDLAND
NOVA SCOTIA
Botwood
Great Slave L.
Great Bear L.
Magnetic Pole
Baffin Island
Davis Strait
Baffin Bay
GREENLAND
Seattle
Pacific Ocean
Denver
Salt Lake City
San Pedro
San Francisco
Bremerton
ALASKA
Great Lakes
Lake Winnipeg
Mississippi River
Galveston
Norfolk
Gulf of Mexico
Key West
Havana
CUBA
Bahamas
JAMAICA
HAITI
Caribbean Sea
Lake Nicaragua
Panama Canal

loaned equipment to allies well before it entered the war. Red dollar signs show recipients of American foreign aid. Peaked caps indicate US military bases. Harrison is telling his audience the United States, however much it aspired or pretended to neutrality, was already fighting the war all over the world. And now it was time, as he put it, "to become realistic for the future."

In the top left-hand corner, Harrison explains the projection he used for this map. Imagine a dancer wearing a globe-shaped skirt, he writes. As she spins, the skirt billows upward into a horizontal plane, and everything on it will appear flat. Harrison enjoyed funky perspectives, and liked to say that anyone could improve their geographical sense just by taking a map and turning it sideways or upside down. *The World Divided* does something more: It forces us to leave behind our Mercator classroom wall map biases, recognize the world's curved surfaces, and consider the earth as an orb.[1]

Harrison's office in the 1940s was so cluttered with maps, atlases, and encyclopedias that friends found it amazing he could get anything done. For perspective maps, like *Three Approaches to the US*, he worked with globes. Typically, he would photograph sections of them from 6 feet away, establishing a vantage point equivalent to a distance of 40,000 miles from Earth. He then produced sketches and eventually illustrations from those pictures.

Distortions did crop up in Harrison's work. The southern parts of *The World Divided*, for example, are broadened and squashed. Many of his aerial maps show the earth's curvature along with features like mountains and rivers, which would be impossible to actually see all at once from any single perspective. For such transgressions, he drew harsh criticism from some traditional cartographers. Charles C. Colby, who chaired the geography department at the University of Chicago, sniffed that Harrison's maps were "messy in appearance and confused in detail," and told him, "Most of the exhibits which you call maps are not maps at all."

But they were maps, and great maps at that. Every mapmaker trades some aspects of accuracy for emphasis and impact, because every map

In *Three Approaches to the U.S.*, published in 1940, Harrison produced a group of maps showing the curved surface of the earth from three vantage points, each displaying a direct line from a threatening foreign region into the United States.

1 To see how hard that can be even today, ask yourself: Does the shortest flight from the United States to India go due east, across Europe, or due west, across Asia? The answer is neither. It goes north, over the Arctic!

is but some kind of scaled-down representation of reality. Projection, perspective, title, orientation, terrain, symbols, labels, borders—these are all up for grabs before a map fills a canvas. One basic task in studying a finished map is to understand the choices made by its creator. And the fundamental question for assessing any map is whether, within the context of those choices, it brings us new insights. Harrison succeeded in making his maps accessible, appealing, and influential. And after December 1941, when Japanese forces attacked Pearl Harbor and Hitler declared war on the United States, another adjective joined the list, too: prophetic.

Franklin Roosevelt and the internationalists were right about World War II: It would take America's entry to decisively defeat the Axis powers. FDR knew that many Americans wanted to believe they could avoid the horrors of a second global conflict. But he literally had a different perspective, and saw it as part of his mission to change theirs. Like George Washington, Thomas Jefferson, and Abraham Lincoln, Roosevelt had an intense interest in cartography. Unlike those predecessors, he never worked as a surveyor, he just loved maps from the time he was an international-stamp-collecting child. "Franklin D. Roosevelt's mind saw in maps," according to Sarah Navins, an archivist at the FDR Presidential Library in Hyde Park, New York.

In 1939, *National Geographic* gave large map cabinets to Roosevelt and British Prime Minister Winston Churchill. FDR kept his in his Oval Office study, concealed by blown-up photos. He could see any region of the world up close just by rolling maps out from the case. In January 1942, after the US entered the war, the president turned a basement coatroom in the White House into an extremely limited-access war headquarters called the Map Room. From this early version of the White House Situation Room, Roosevelt tracked the movement of US forces around the world on maps and communicated with other leaders such as Churchill and the Soviet Union's Joseph Stalin.

The following month, he delivered a "fireside chat" national radio address where he laid out his vision:

> I have asked you to take out and spread before you a map of the whole earth, and . . . follow with me. . . . The broad oceans which have been heralded in the past as our protection from attack have become endless battlefields. . . . We must all understand and face the hard fact that our job now is to fight at distances which extend all the way around the globe. . . . Those Americans who believed

that we could live under the illusion of isolationism wanted the American eagle to imitate the tactics of the ostrich. Now, many of those same people, afraid that we may be sticking our necks out, want our national bird to be turned into a turtle. But we prefer to retain the eagle as it is—flying high and striking hard.

Later that year, the US Office of Strategic Services—forerunner of the CIA—developed the President's Globe (left) to give full expression to the "whole earth" that Roosevelt described. This was a huge wooden sphere, measuring 50 inches in diameter and weighing 750 pounds. It sat on a base that contained rubber balls inside, allowing the globe to rotate in any direction. And it was inscribed with the names of 17,000 places.[2] FDR got his globe as a Christmas present in 1942—others went to Churchill and George C. Marshall, the US Army chief of staff—and he put it right behind his chair in the Oval Office.

Along with Roosevelt's exhortations, the many battles of the war inspired an explosion of public interest in cartography. With frontlines changing daily in 1942, *Newsweek* called Washington, DC, a "city of maps." And by the time the US and its allies invaded France, newspapers across America were making maps an integral part of their coverage. The *Los Angeles Times*, featuring the work of Charles H. Owens, is an outstanding example.

Owens was born in San Francisco in 1881 and had little formal education or training; he said he graduated from third grade with "more or less honor," and later spent one year at art school. But he had talents that made him perfect for newspaper illustration: He loved to sketch, he drew accurately and plentifully, and he incorporated arresting, oblique perspectives into his work. Owens broke into the business as an errand boy, then moved to New York, where he gained attention for

The US Office of Strategic Services built the President's Globe in 1942 to show the worldwide scope of the war and the curved surfaces of its transportation routes and supply lines.

2 The OSS cartographers who designed this project didn't sign their work; instead, they placed their hometowns on the globe.

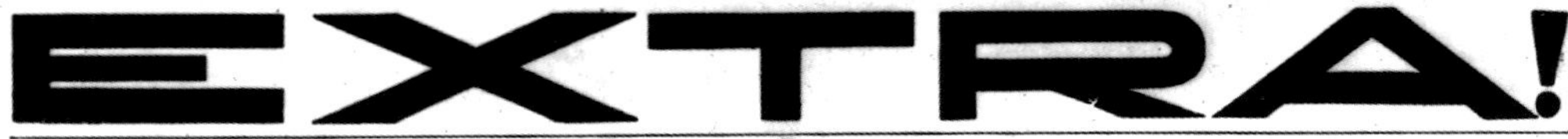

9 A.M. FINAL

Los Angeles Times

EQUAL RIGHTS — LIBERTY UNDER THE LAW — TRUE INDUSTRIAL FREEDOM

9 A.M. FINAL

VOL. LXIII ★ TUESDAY MORNING, JUNE 6, 1944 DAILY, FIVE CENTS

INVASION!

WHERE ALLIES STRUCK—Arrows show major points where invasion army hit France.

4000 Ships and 11,000 Planes Hit at French Coast

SUPREME HEADQUARTERS, ALLIED EXPEDITIONARY FORCE, June 6. (AP) Allied forces landed in Northern France early today in history's greatest overseas operation, designed to destroy the power of Hitler's Germany and wrest enslaved Europe from the Nazis.

The German radio said the landings were made from Le Havre to Cherbourg, along the north coast of Normandy and the south side of the bay of the Seine.

Prime Minister Churchill told the House of Commons today that more than 4000 ships with several thousand smaller craft had carried Allied forces across the Channel. He added that 11,000 first-line aircraft are sustaining the operations and said that massed airborne landings had been made successfully behind the German lines.

Allied headquarters did not specify the locations, but left no doubt whatever that the landings were on a gigantic scale.

Eisenhower Issues Statement

Ringing in their ears, the American, British and Canadian forces who made the landings had these words from their supreme commander, Gen. Dwight D. Eisenhower:

"You are about to embark on a great crusade. The eyes of the world are upon you and the hopes and prayers of all liberty-loving peoples go with you . . .

"We will accept nothing less than full victory."

The German radio filled the air with invasion flashes for three hours before the formal Allied announcement came at 7:32 a.m. Greenwich mean time (12:32 a.m., Pacific War Time.)

It acknowledged deep penetrations of the Cherbourg Peninsula by Allied parachute and glider troops in great strength.

The assault was supported by gigantic bombardments from Allied warships and planes which the Germans admitted set the coastal areas ablaze.

A senior officer at Supreme Headquarters said rough water caused "awful anxiety" for the sea-borne troops, but

Turn to Page 2, Column 1

LAST MINUTE INVASION BULLETINS

LONDON, June 6. (AP)—The German radio reported today that four British parachute divisions had landed between Le Havre and Cherbourg in France. This was four times the size of the Nazi parachute force dropped on Crete in the Mediterranean.

BY THE ASSOCIATED PRESS

The Berlin radio broadcast a D.N.B. dispatch today saying that one Allied cruiser and a large landing vessel carrying troops had been sunk in the area of St. Vaast la Hougue, 15 miles southeast of Cherbourg.

SUPREME HEADQUARTERS, ALLIED EXPEDITIONARY FORCE, June 6. (AP)—United States battleships are supporting the Allied landings in France and U.S. Coast Guard units also are participating in the operations, it was announced today. American marines likewise are in the fighting, manning secondary guns aboard the big ships.

NEW YORK, June 6. (AP) The Berlin radio, in a broadcast recorded by N.B.C., said this morning that strong Allied air attacks have been launched in the Dieppe area.

LONDON, June 6 (Tuesday.) (U.P.) — The German Transocean agency broadcast a report, unconfirmed by Allied sources, of heavy fighting with "invasion" forces in the area of Caen, about 8½ miles south of

Turn to Page 2, Column 7

Special Invasion Edition

Times readers will note that this is an unusual edition of The Times—made necessary by the greatest news story of all time—the invasion of Europe! Not a single line of advertising appears in this issue. Every inch of available space has been devoted to invasion news, maps, pictures.

This is in keeping with The Times policy of serving, above all else, the interests of this newspaper's readers. The Times regrets that it must omit the messages of its many advertisers and hopes those advertisers will realize, as The Times does, that a newspaper's foremost obligation must be to its readers!

making detailed sketches of the Great Earthquake of 1906, relying only on incoming bulletins and his own understanding of San Francisco. Returning to California, Owens joined the *Los Angeles Times* in 1921, and became staff illustrator.

Owens, who modestly called himself "just a newspaper craftman," turned out reams of sketches to illustrate daily stories for the *Times*, created a series of magnificent pictorial maps in the 1920s, and drew tourist maps and painted landscapes. In the last great act of his career, after he turned sixty, Owens brought World War II to the *Times*' readers.

Owens's war maps—influenced, like Harrison's, by the global nature of the conflict as well as air travel—feature bird's-eye views, curved earths, arrows demonstrating action, and plentiful blocks of annotations. And readers loved them. Indeed, the *Times* began running Owens's maps across full pages and in color every week in 1942. As vivid and lively as all his great work, his D-Day cover for the *Times* (opposite) took up the front page of the paper's special "Extra" edition—headlined "INVASION!"—on June 6, 1944. Owens kept churning out what the *Times* called his "action maps" until the war was over fifteen months after that; he retired from the paper in 1953, and died five years later.

For his part, Richard Edes Harrison gained popularity and even a bit of fame from his work. *Life* magazine profiled him in 1944, and when he published an atlas called *Look at the World* that year, it sold out almost instantly. The US Armed Forces used Harrison's maps to help train bomber pilots, and reprinted 250,000 copies of them for members of the army and navy. After the war, he enjoyed a long career as a college lecturer and consulted for institutions ranging from the State Department to *Smithsonian Magazine*. Through it all, he maintained little regard for the cramped rules of traditional mapmaking. Eminent map expert Susan Schulten interviewed Harrison in 1993, a year before he died.

Call him an artist, he told her, not a cartographer.

Charles H. Owens's D-Day cover for the *Los Angeles Times* took up the front page of the paper's special "Extra" edition on June 6, 1944.

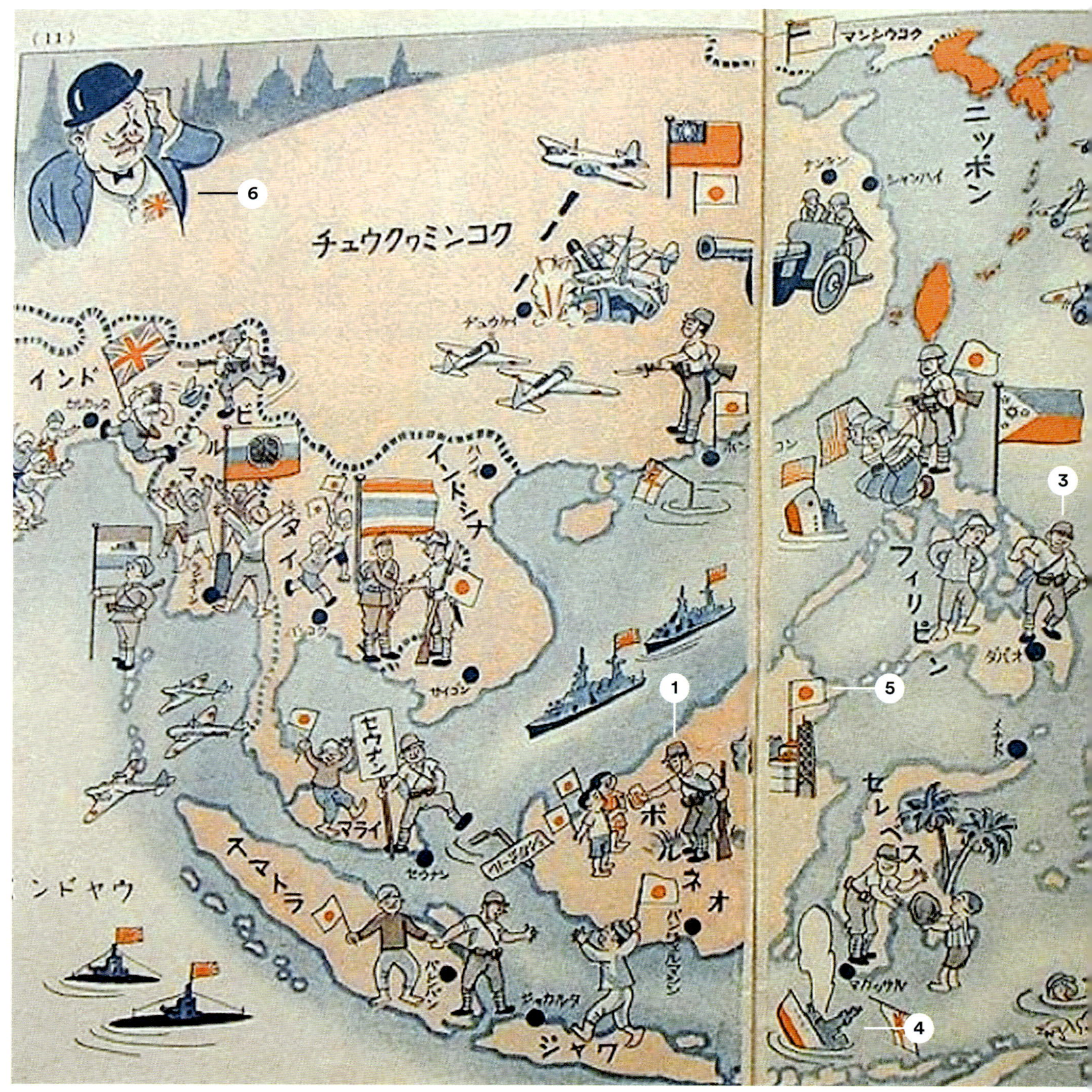

〈11〉
マンシウコク
ニッポン
ナンキン
シャンハイ
チユウクヮミンコク
ヂユウケイ
インド
ビルマ
タイ
インドシナ
ハノイ
バンコク
サイゴン
フィリピン
ダバオ
マライ
セウナン
ボルネオ
スマトラ
パレンバン
ジャカルタ
ジャワ
セレベス
マカッサル
ンドヤウ
1
3
4
5
6

The Maps of a Would-Be Pacific Empire

Imperial Japan was as ambitious and ruthless as any world power.

It's easy to think of the word *imperialist* as a synonym for "Western." But in the late nineteenth and first half of the twentieth centuries, the Empire of Japan was as aggressive and ruthless a conqueror as any nation in Europe or America. It was also a high-volume propaganda machine that often used maps and posters as tools of public relations.

Japan industrialized rapidly following the Meiji Restoration of 1868, which ended nearly seven hundred years of rule by shoguns, or hereditary military commanders, and recentralized the role of the Japanese emperor. And it soon embarked on a series of military interventions so frequent that historian Hiyama Yukio has called the era from 1894 to 1945 Japan's "Fifty-Year War." The Japanese empire occupied Taiwan in 1895. It crushed Russia in the Russo-Japanese War (1904–05), a conflict famously settled through negotiations mediated by US President Theodore Roosevelt. It annexed Korea in 1910. And it took control of and vastly expanded the South Manchuria Railway, also known as Mantetsu, in northeastern China.

Mantetsu wasn't just a railroad company, it was a conduit for Japanese colonization. It brought Japanese settlers deep into Manchuria and built hotels, schools, and utilities for them. It also opened coal mines, invested in metal refineries, built harbors, exported soybeans. In September 1931, a bomb went off near one of its stations in Mukden (now Shenyang, China), a city in Manchuria. Japan quickly condemned China for the act, and used the incident as a pretext to invade Manchuria and set up a puppet state loyal to the Empire called Manchukuo, sometimes transliterated "Manchuokuo." (The explosion turned out to be the work of Japanese soldiers.)

In 1942, Dai Nihon Yubenkai (the "Great Japan Debate Society"), a nationalist publishing house, produced a booklet called *A Declaration for Greater East Asian Co-operation*. Filled with cartoonlike illustrations and simple language, it was designed to put across the message of pan-Asian unity.

Imperial Japan's emergence as a first-rate military and economic power impressed Western political and financial leaders, and for a while, it sought accommodation with and investment from them. For example, at the 1933 World's Fair in Chicago, Japan held an exhibit where an illustrated Mantetsu map boasted of "The Progress of Manchuria" and compared Japanese emigrants there to American pilgrims. "They found a land of peace and plenty until their war lords taxed and exploited them to the limit," it read. "So they declared their independence, as did the Americans in 1776."

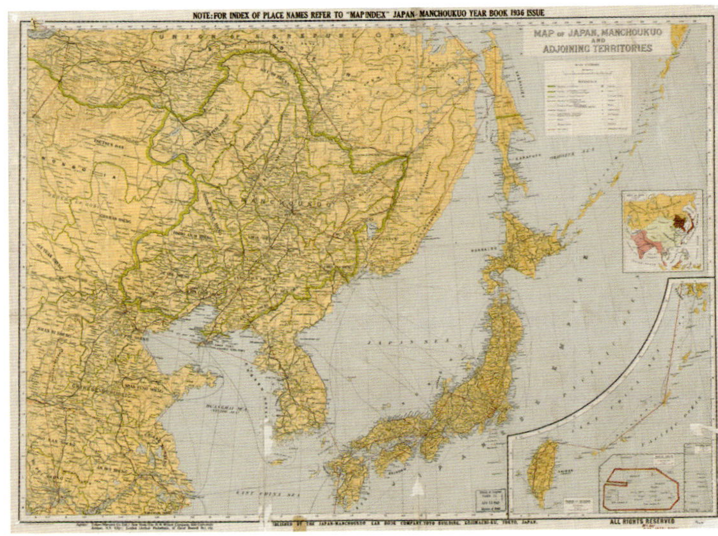

Soon, a very unusual dichotomy in political maps emerged. On one hand, knowledgeable outsiders tended to portray East Asia as a powder keg. In February 1935, *Fortune* magazine published *A Militarist's Map of Manchukuo* (page 207), showing the Japanese-occupied state in bright yellow, almost completely surrounded by the USSR in red, Japan in tan, and the flat (and vulnerable) plains of Mongolia in blue. "Most observers," a journalist for *Fortune* wrote, "seem to think there will be . . . a war between Japan and Soviet Russia . . . before long." The map highlighted various potential flashpoints: fishing grounds and oil fields to the far northeast, frontier military bases, old battle sites from the Russo-Japanese War. It also showed major railroads, and its text emphasized the importance of transportation and communication networks across such vast territory.

"Already Manchukuo has, per square mile, many times the railway mileage of China, and new construction is going ahead faster than in any other country in the world," *Fortune* noted. "The Japanese are pushing lines out to the borders—toward Inner Mongolia, toward the Amur River in the north, toward Korea, to provide more avenues into the country for troops from Japan."

At the same time, however, many Japanese maps were very quiet about the land of more than 30 million people that the Empire of Japan now controlled. For instance, in the 1930s, the East Asiatic Economic Investigation Bureau, a Tokyo intelligence network that began as part of the Mantetsu railroad, published the *Manchukuo Year Book*, an annual

Map of Japan, Manchoukuo, and Adjoining Territories was included in the 1936 edition of the Japanese *Manchukuo Year Book*, an annual catalog of companies in Manchuria. This Japanese view of Manchuria is monochromatic and placid, even boring.

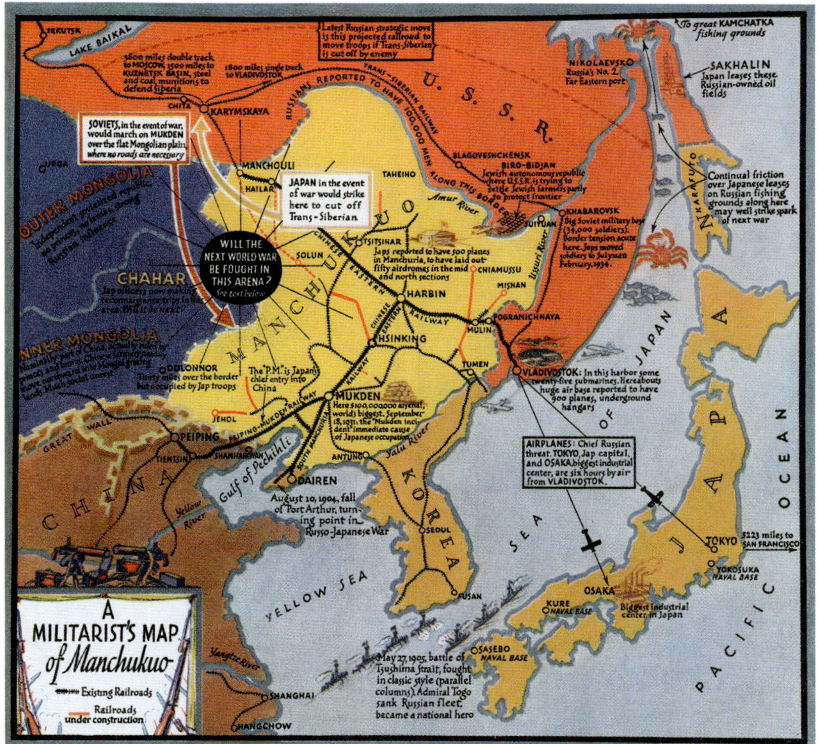

In February 1935, *Fortune* published *A Militarist's Map of Manchukuo*, showing the Japanese-occupied state as a potential battleground between Japan and Soviet Russia.

English-language listing of companies in Manchuria. The 1936 edition came with a map, (page 206), showing Japan, Korea, and Manchuria, with insets for Taiwan and various islands. A thick line surrounds Japan's client state of Manchukuo, but except for one small box showing various empires in Asia, everything is the same color, and no disruptions or disputes are evident. Imperial Japan and its possessions, and in fact the places it might conquer next, are all one big stretch of developing Asia, ready to do business with readers. It's basically the most boring political map of all time.

In reality, Japan's exploitation of Manchuria was brutal from the beginning. As just one example, by the time of that World's Fair brochure, about 100,000 Chinese had died after being forced to work in Mantetsu-run coal mines. And things took a far darker turn after Japan invaded China again in July 1937. Japanese troops captured the Chinese capital of Nanjing in December, then went amok during a six-week spree of murder, rape, torture, and wanton destruction called the Nanjing Massacre.

Western democracies were slow to respond, but the United States began slapping economic sanctions on Japan in 1940. By the following year, Japan was facing an oil embargo. But the Empire's territorial aspirations hadn't been checked yet, and Dutch-controlled Indonesia, with huge oil and rubber reserves, and British-controlled Malaya, with rice and tin, beckoned. In December 1941, Japan not only bombed Pearl Harbor in Hawai'i, it struck the Philippines and invaded Burma and Malaya, and took control of Indonesia three months later.

With full-scale war on against the US, Great Britain, and their allies, the Empire made much greater use of a phrase its leaders first mentioned in 1940: Fascist Japan would create a "Greater East Asia Co-Prosperity Sphere" of political and economic cooperation by standing with people from neighboring countries and liberating colonial possessions. As a US intelligence report noted, the idea expressed both "high idealism and frank opportunism," as Japanese officials described Greater East Asia as "an international order based upon common prosperity" but also a mechanism for "the development of the Japanese race."

In 1942, a nationalist publisher issued a striking call for solidarity in a comic-style booklet named *A Declaration for Greater East Asian Co-operation*. Its cover shows smiling children of various nationalities and skin colors in front of a map of East Asia. Inside, one drawing shows a solitary Japanese soldier holding off American and British tanks and planes as they try to move into China. And deeper inside, one of the great propaganda maps of World War II (shown on pages 204–205 and opposite) takes up two very busy and colorful pages.

This map is teeming with scenes showing Japanese troops helping native children and fighting off enemy soldiers. While anxious Western leaders look on, Japan's forces are occupying their former colonies and sinking their ships.[1]

Unfortunately for the Empire, it had less time to consolidate its gains than its leaders imagined. Heavy losses at the naval battles of Midway and Guadalcanal forced Japan into a defensive posture against the United States before the end of 1942, and the war never stopped going downhill afterward.

As for Greater East Asia, it turns out that Imperial Japan placed its key outfit for developing biological warfare weapons, the notorious Unit 731, at a location near Harbin, a city in Manchuria. From 1936 to 1945, the Japanese bioweapons program tested more than two dozen methods of causing disease in civilians and prisoners, and murdered hundreds of people a year. Japan's troops poisoned more than 1,000 Chinese wells with infectious diseases and released fleas infected with plague into Chinese rice fields and over Chinese cities.

The forces of Imperial Japan, in other words, found so much solidarity in "co-prosperity" that they used their fellow Asians as human guinea pigs.

In a dozen vignettes placed across Asia, *A Declaration for Greater East Asian Co-operation* shows Japanese troops coming to the assistance of natives. In some cases 1, they are helping children, while in others 2 they're using bayonets to drive enemy soldiers to the ground or 3 into the sea.

4 As Japanese planes stream from the top of the page, Allied ships are sinking toward the bottom.

5 Red-dotted Japanese flags are planted in eight countries occupied by the Empire since the outbreak of the Second World War.

Overlooking the whole scene from the top corners of the map are very worried caricatures of 6 Winston Churchill and 7 Franklin Roosevelt. 8 The inscription under FDR says it all: "Japan stood up to take back Greater East Asia into our hands."

---

1 More than seventy years later, a Reddit user named "hairway2steven" saw the map and offered this juvenile but apt response: "If I was a kid in Japan in '43 this would be on my wall."

1

2

3

4

5

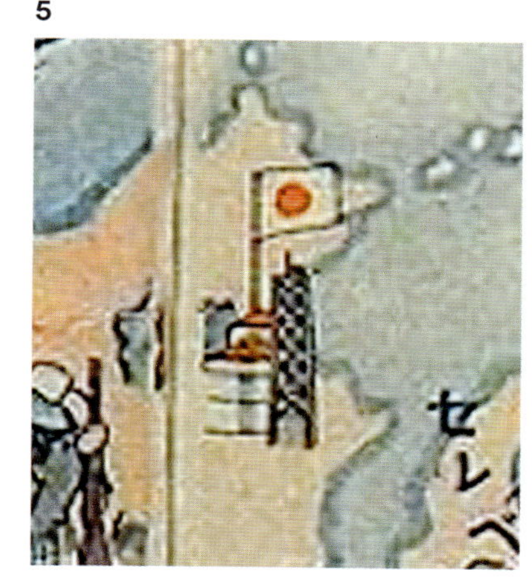

6

7

8

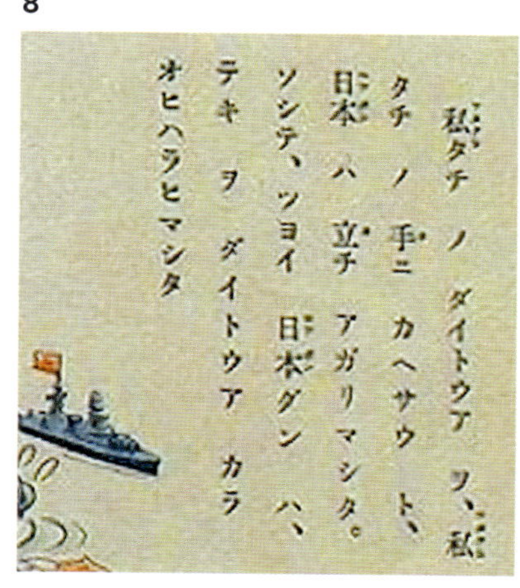

私タチ ノ ダイトウア ヲ、私
タチ ノ 手ニ カヘサウト、
日本 ハ 立チ アガリマシタ。
ソシテ、ツヨイ 日本グン ハ、
テキ ヲ ダイトウア カラ
オヒハラヒマシタ

THE ATLANTIC CHARTER
FIRST, their countries seek no aggrandisement, territorial or other.
SECOND, they desire to see no territorial changes that do not accord with the freely expressed wishes of the peoples concerned.
THIRD, they respect the right of all peoples to choose the form of government under which they will live; and they wish to see sovereign rights and self-government restored to those who have been forcibly deprived of them.
FOURTH, they will endeavour, with due respect for their existing obligations, to further the enjoyment by all States, great or small, victor or vanquished, of access, on equal terms, to the trade and to the raw materials of the world which are needed for their economic prosperity.
FIFTH, they desire to bring about the fullest collaboration between all nations in the economic field, with the object of securing for all improved labour standards, economic advancement and social security.
SIXTH, after the final destruction of Nazi tyra
to all nations the means of dwelling in safety with
all the men in all the lands may live out their liv
SEVENTH, such a peace should enable all m
EIGHTH, they believe all of the nations of the
the abandonment of the use of force. Since no
continue to be employed by nations which thre
they believe, pending the establishment of a
disarmament of such nations is essential. The
measures which will lighten for peace-lo
1
2
NORTH AMERICA
SOUTH AMERICA
AFRICA
PACIFIC OCEAN
ATLANTIC OCEAN
IND
GREENLAND
ICELAND
BRITISH ISLES
NEWFOUNDLAND
Hudson Bay
Davis Strait
CANADA
DOMINION
ALASKA
Arctic Circle
Tropic of Cancer
Equator
Tropic of Capricorn
MEXICO
Bahama Islands
WEST INDIES
Caribbean Sea
VENEZUELA
COLOMBIA
ECUADOR
PERU
BOLIVIA
BRAZIL
CHILE
URUGUAY
ARGENTINA
Falkland Is.
Cape Horn
New York
Washington
Bermudas
Azores
FRANCE
SPAIN
PORTUGAL
MOROCCO
ALGERIA
LIBYA
EGYPT
FRENCH WEST AFRICA
ANGLO EGYPTIAN SUDAN
ABYSSINIA
ARABIA
INDIA
KENYA
TANGANYIKA TERRITORY
ANGOLA
RHODESIA
SOUTH WEST AFRICA
MADAGASCAR
UNION OF SOUTH AFRICA
Gulf of Guinea
Rio de Janeiro
Arabian Sea
St. Helena
Ascension
They shall beat their swords into plowshares, and their spears into pruninghooks: nation shall not lift up sword against nation, neither shall they learn war any more.
ISAIAH
The only excuse for war is that we may live in peace unharmed
But the real and lasting victori are those of peace, and not of w
SYMBOLS
Aluminium
Apples
Butter & Cheese
Cattle & Beef
Citrus Fruits
Coal
Coffee
Copper
Corn
Cotton
Flax
Gold
Iron
Lead
Maize
Manganese
Petroleum
Pigs
Precious Stones
Rice

The Map of Swords into Plowshares

The principles for which the Allies fought in World War II were codified in the Atlantic Charter—and on this map.

The global scope and massive stakes of World War II pulled some of the world's most influential illustrators into persuasive cartography. Leslie MacDonald Gill, for example, virtually invented the twentieth-century pictorial map. Born in Brighton, England, in 1884, Gill, who was known as "Max," began his career as an architect and calligrapher. Max carried his talents for design and inscription to mural painting and making posters. In 1914, he created a map of the London Underground that was packed with cheerful details and humorous annotations, and which became so popular that legend says many missed their trains because they were staring at it so intently, and the London Underground began selling it commercially. Historians credit *The Wonderground Map of London Town* with boosting ridership—and its cheerfulness and sheer density influenced pictorial mapmaking for decades.

Gill subsequently worked on a range of interesting projects. He designed the alphabet and typeface for England's military headstones after World War I, and more than one hundred years later, the country still uses his lettering on graves. He created posters for the General Post Office showing wireless stations and steamship routes for mail delivery. He illustrated a popular map called *Tea Revives the World*, which presented scads of data about which parts of the globe produced and consumed England's lifeblood drink.

In this 1942 illustration for *Time & Tide*, Leslie MacDonald Gill commemorated the Atlantic Charter—a statement of "common principles" developed by US President Franklin Roosevelt and British Prime Minister Winston Churchill. Looking toward the postwar world, the Charter expressed the right of all people to self-determination, and supported global cooperation.

After the Second World War broke out, Gill created one more masterpiece (pages 210–211): He illustrated the Atlantic Charter for *Time & Tide*, a British political and literary magazine.[1]

In August 1941, US President Franklin Roosevelt and British Prime Minister Winston Churchill met on an American warship off the coast of Newfoundland, and put together a statement of "common principles" for the world to come. They included the right of all people to self-determination and support for freer trade and reduced armaments. "After the final destruction of Nazi tyranny," the document said, "they hope to see established a peace which will afford to all nations the means of dwelling in safety within their own boundaries and assure that all the men in the lands may live out their lives in freedom from fear and want."

The Atlantic Charter, as it was soon called, boosted the hopes for independence of colonized peoples around the world (though Churchill argued it applied specifically to territories conquered by Nazi Germany). By promising access to trade and raw materials for "all States, great or small, victor or vanquished, on equal terms," the Charter also promised no repeat of the harsh economic terms the Allies had imposed on Germany after World War I. Essentially, the Atlantic Charter took the first few steps in creating what would become the United Nations.

Gill reproduced the Charter verbatim across a worldwide map showing endless bounty in free trade and travel. The sun beams out from behind the Charter, pushing clouds away to each side. The globe's lands are filled with resources and its oceans with ships, all surrounded by quotes celebrating peace. One particularly nice touch: After Roosevelt and Churchill parted from that 1941 meeting, they continued to negotiate final revisions to the Charter, so it was never actually signed by both men.[2] But each leader provided his handwritten signature on slips of paper for this map, and Gill included them beneath the text of the Charter. There is a somewhat backward-looking feel to the *Time & Tide* map. Even in 1941, its decorative framing, classical allusions, and whimsical elements

1 *Time & Tide* was founded and funded by Margaret Haig Thomas (1888–1958), a viscountess and suffragist. From 1920 to 1987, the writers it published ranged from D. H. Lawrence to C. S. Lewis, George Orwell to Virginia Woolf.

2 FDR joked that the nearest thing to a formal document of the Charter would have to come from the radio operators on his and Churchill's ships.

1 Ships steam from continent to continent, all filled with lands where Gill marked the presence of more than thirty natural resources, from apples to zinc.

2 There are pro-peace quotes from various figures key to Anglo-American history, including Cicero, Alexander Pope, and Ralph Waldo Emerson.

3 Roosevelt and Churchill kept negotiating revisions to the Charter after they parted ways, so the document was never actually signed. But each provided his handwritten signature for this map, and Gill included both.

1

2

3

-ld, for realistic as well as spiritual reasons, must come to
-ure peace can be maintained if land, sea or air armaments
, or may threaten, aggression outside of their frontiers,
-er and permanent system of general security, that the
-ll likewise aid and encourage all other practicable
g peoples the crushing burden of armaments.

Franklin D Roosevelt Winston S. Churchill 1941

hearkened back to earlier, pre-fascist eras. While laying out some earth-shaking ideals, the map has an antirevolutionary vibe. Its whole design suggests that winning the war would restore and extend liberty and prosperity already delivered by Anglo-American traditions. Stephen Hornsby, a professor of geography and Canadian studies at the University of Maine, has written: "Although it is one of Gill's most arresting designs, full of art deco tropes such as the sunburst . . . the muscular worker . . . and the stylized motif forming the border, the map appears dated." But at the time the Atlantic Charter was signed, Germany was still bombing British cities, and the US was months away from entering the war. Using an old-school Mercator projection to depict natural wealth and project an optimistic future, this great map offers propaganda as comfort food. Like the Charter itself, it was designed not just to communicate the Allies' aims, but to boost readers' morale.

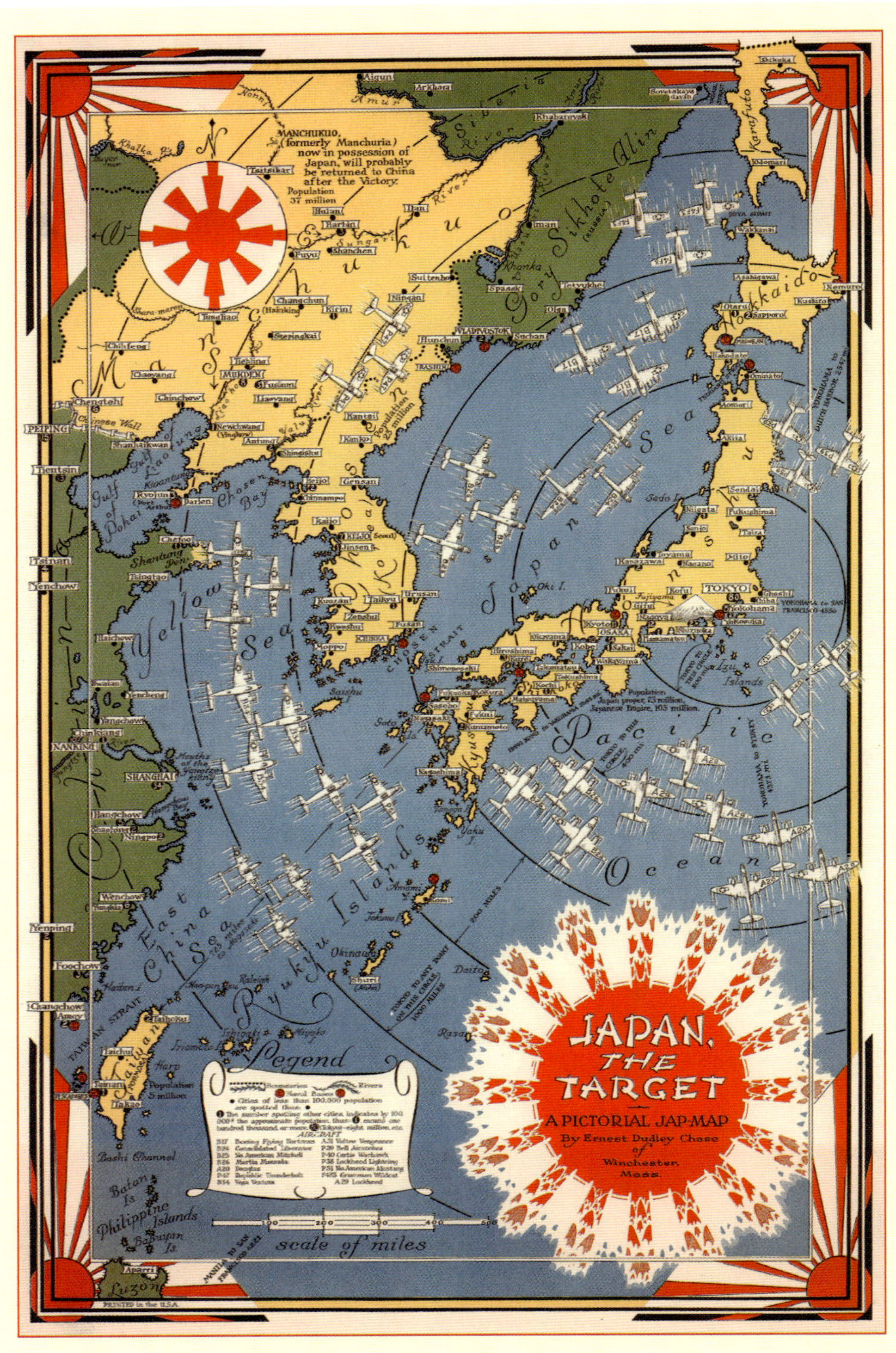
JAPAN, THE TARGET
A PICTORIAL JAP-MAP
By Ernest Dudley Chase of Winchester, Mass.
MANCHUKUO, (formerly Manchuria) now in possession of Japan, will probably be returned to China after the Victory.
Population 37 million
Population 23 million
Population Japan proper, 73 million, Japanese Empire, 105 million.
Population 5 million
Legend
Boundaries
Rivers
Naval Bases
Cities of less than 100,000 population are spotted thus:
The number spotting other cities indicates by 100,000's the approximate population, thus 1 means one hundred thousand or more, 68 sixty-eight million, etc.
AIRCRAFT
B17 Boeing Flying Fortress
B24 Consolidated Liberator
B25 No. American Mitchell
B26 Martin Marauder
A20 Douglas
P47 Republic Thunderbolt
B34 Vega Ventura
A31 Vultee Vengeance
P39 Bell Airacobra
P40 Curtis Warhawk
P38 Lockheed Lightning
P51 No. American Mustang
F4F3 Grumman Wildcat
A29 Lockheed
scale of miles
100
200
300
400
500
Yellow Sea
East China Sea
Japan Sea
Pacific Ocean
Ryukyu Islands
Hokkaido
Honshu
Kyushu
Korea
Manchukuo
China
Siberia
Karafuto
Sikhote Alin
Izu Islands
TOKYO
OSAKA
KOBE
KYOTO
NAGOYA
YOKOHAMA
SHANGHAI
NANKING
PEIPING
MUKDEN
KEIJO (Seoul)
VLADIVOSTOK
Harbin
Tsitsikar
Changchun
Dairen
Taiwan (Formosa)
Philippine Islands
Luzon
Okinawa
Shuri (Naha)
TOKYO TO ANY POINT ON THIS CIRCLE 1000 MILES
200 MILES
MANILA TO SAN FRANCISCO 6821
YOKOHAMA TO SAN FRANCISCO 4536
YOKOHAMA TO DUTCH HARBOR 2547 mi
PRINTED in the U.S.A.

The Map of the Pacific Bull's-Eye

Ernest Dudley Chase's greatest map is a case study in devastation.

As in England, World War II drew artists in the United States into making propaganda, none greater than Ernest Dudley Chase. Born in 1878, Chase grew up in Lowell, Massachusetts, where his father, who designed wallpaper, taught him how to sketch. He worked at printing companies as a young man, then started his own publishing company, which in 1921 merged with a Boston publishing house called Rust Craft. Chase was an executive there for more than thirty years, leading its design of greeting cards. All the while, he traveled widely around the world, and loved to draw, photograph, and film the sights he saw. In his fifties, he began putting his passions to work creating pictorial maps, which he drew and published on his own.

Using a magnifying glass to work at a minuscule scale, Chase painstakingly stippled small illustrations, dot by dot, of one scene after another. In many of Chase's maps, the results vibrate like Piet Mondrian's greatest paintings, except instead of primary-colored shapes drawing your eyes from space to space, it's tiny tableaux.

Chase's creations were signature works of the heyday of pictorial maps, offering deluges of visuals and text to readers who were hungry to learn about the far reaches of the world. "There's just so much to love on each one of Chase's maps," writes Jason Forrest, editor in chief of *Nightingale: Journal of the Data Visualization Society*. "The more-is-more aesthetic makes these among the most slow of visualizations, perfect for enjoyment over time."

Chase marketed twenty-five of his works via a pamphlet called *The Ernest Dudley Chase Decorative Novelty Pictorial Maps*, which described his studies of subjects such as the US, various European countries, "world wonders," and the history of flying as "designed and drawn with infinite care." In most cases, readers could order a poster-sized map for $1 and receive it autographed and gift-wrapped in a mailing tube. One was a selection Chase simply called the *Peace* map, which laid out his profound belief in progress. Completed in 1944, its full name is *Mercator Map of the World United: A Pictorial History of Transport and Communications and Paths*

Japan, the Target, published in 1944, is pictorial map artist Ernest Dudley Chase's most arresting work. Japan is surrounded by waves of American bombers, and its national symbol of the rising sun refashioned into an exploding core.

to Permanent Peace, and it portrays all its titular subjects as intertwined. Chase shows better and faster means of travel and transmission shrinking the world while communities around the globe are growing in size and complexity, from families to cities to countries to the United Nations. "No spot on earth is more than forty flying hours from your local airport," says a band around the equator. "Nations can no longer live unto themselves alone," blares a separate banner. And individual illustrations provide a multitude of examples, from radio towers broadcasting news to millions to a New York–Bombay air route to Australians watching movies. As Chase put it: "Science marches on toward a better world."

It might seem wrong to remember someone so forward-looking for his wartime propaganda. But Chase's optimism was very American—scientific, internationalist, and commercial. He inscribed "Peace Spells Plenty" twice on the *Peace* map. On a later map of "World Freedom," he also wrote at the Marianas Trench, the deepest point of the world's oceans: "This would be a suitable place to sink all communistic ideas and concepts." When Chase adopted the American cause, he did so with gusto.

And that's how Chase's most vivid work came about in 1944: the brilliant *Japan, the Target*—which he unfortunately called the "Jap map" (page 214).

It's almost a disservice to use words to describe as visceral an image as *Japan, the Target*. Like other works of art with highly immediate impact, from graphic design to pop music, it hits you, and you get it. Japan is ringed with American bombers; its national symbol of the rising sun is repurposed into an exploding hub.

Three further elements of its design are worth noting. First, the map as a whole is off-center. It's expansive enough to portray not only Japan, but lands to the west and south that the Japanese empire had conquered, including Korea and Taiwan—and to show their liberation as part of the US war effort. Second, the outcome of that effort is a foregone conclusion. The map shows naval bases and cities subject to attack by fourteen different kinds of American aircraft, but no Japanese troops or planes defending them. And one annotation says flat out that Manchuria, "now in possession of Japan, will probably be returned to China after the Victory."

Finally, the title of *Japan, the Target* is rendered in a stereotypically chopstick-like typeface—what publishers call a "wonton font." This is partly just a reflection of the casual, thoroughgoing racism of Chase's

Alaska: Death-Trap for the Jap was created by the Federal Art Project, a New Deal program, for the US Navy during World War II. Nothing subtle about this map: Japan is a rat, with blood dripping from its overbite, approaching an "Army-Civilian-Navy" mousetrap as it threatens the territory of Alaska. It was drawn by Edward Grigware, who later became known for painting murals for Mormon churches.

time.[1] (For an example of full-on racist propaganda during this period, consider *Alaska: Death-Trap for the Jap*, a US map produced around 1942, shown at left.)

The lettering on Chase's map also adds to the overwhelming feeling that *Japan, the Target* conveys—that the winner of this war was bombing the holy hell out of the loser, and could impose whatever brand of civilization it wanted on whatever remained.

The US forces that occupied Japan after the war did take important steps to preserve nonmilitary aspects of Japanese culture while the country rebuilt from the devastation Chase's work foretold. But the presence of Hiroshima and Nagasaki on this map make it more prophetic than he could ever have imagined.

1 In *The War*, a book published in 1960, historian Louis Snyder wrote that after the Japanese attack on Pearl Harbor, "Thousands of . . . Americans reacted in precisely the same way: 'Why, the yellow bastards!' Others exploded with variations of 'We'll stamp their buck teeth in!'"

"GULAG"—SLAVERY, INC.

THE FIRST COMPREHENSIVE, SELF-AUTHENTICATED DOCU-MAP OF FORCED LABOR CAMPS IN SOVIE

Prepared by The Editors of PLAIN TALK

GULAG—the Soviet Slave Labor Trust—is an abbreviation of **Glavnoye Upravlenye Lagerei,** or Office of Penal Labor Camps, a department of the MVD, the Ministry of the Interior (formerly known as the NKVD—Russian equivalent of the Gestapo).

There are over 14,000,000 forced laborers in GULAG, scattered through scores of penal colonies each a Devil's Island at its worst, living in unspeakable wretchedness, on the edge of death by starvation and disease, and slaving twelve hours a day under arbitrary taskmasters.

The existence of this state monopoly in expendable human flesh has been known for many years and recognized as a chief source of revenue for the Communist regime. As far back as 1930, the U.S. Treasury clamped an embargo on Soviet pulpwood and matches as products of "forced labor." But for the first time, **incontrovertible proof** of the GULAG system and its vast ramifications has been brought out of Russia.

During the period of the Stalin-Hitler Pact, about 1,600,000 Poles—men, women and children—were deported by the Soviet authorities to GULAG colonies in the Far North and in Siberia. On August 12, 1941, as a result of the Polish-Soviet Agreement, an amnesty was granted to the Polish internees in Russia. 114,000 of these released Poles eventually reached Iran, forming the backbone of the Polish Army which fought gloriously in Italy.

Legend

The dotted circles represent GULAG forced labor colonies, each a sprawling area comprising a constellation of concentration camps under a separate administration.

The ringed dots denote individual concentration camps operated by municipalities under the control of local NKVD authorities.

PENAL LABOR COLONIES, BY ADMINISTRATIVE AREAS

The following list details the types of industries operated by GULAG—the Penal Labor Trust of the Soviet Government. Although complete on the basis of available documentary evidence, the forty-odd colonies shown here do not exhaust al geographic divisions of GULAG known to exist in the Soviet Union today.

- **Sorokski**—Light metal mines; construction of railways, tunnels, canals, electric works and airfields; brickworks; quarries, timber camps and fisheries. **Severo-Nickel,** south of Murmansk: aluminum, nickel, copper, lead and zinc mines. **Belomor-Baltiski,** construction and maintenance of the White Sea-Baltic Canal.
- **Solov ki, Onega, Kargopol, Sev-Dvina, Kuloyski, Vytegra, Ust-Vym, Unzha**—Timber and paper industry; railway and canal construction; quarries and brickworks; farming; settlement building; construction of airfields; road making.
- **Northern Railway Camps**—Construction and maintenance of railroad from the Dvina River to the Arctic.
- **Volgastroy, Ukhta, Pechora, Vorkutstroy, Vyatka**—Construction and maintenance of the Volga-Baltic Canal; power stations and railways; petroleum, cement, and pig iron works; coal and asphalt mines; heavy water (A-bomb) project; road building; timber and farming; brickworks and quarries; construction of airfields.
- **Ussolski, Bezymyanski-Samara, Osobstroy, Temnikovski, Yuj-Kavkaz**—War industries; construction of underground airfields and fortifications; dyke and road building; women's labor camps; manufacture of wood products; timber and farming; quarries and brickworks; railway construction.
- **Ivdel, Sverdlovsk and Northern Urals, Narym, Tobolsk, Norylsk, Camps of Complete Isolation**—Iron, coal and precious metal mines; airplane factories; airfield construction; metallurgical industry; railway and road construction; timber and farming; quarries and brickworks.
- **Karaganda, Sibirski (including Tomasin), Krasnoyarski, ski**—Coal, iron and light metal mines; construction of facto settlements; textile industries and tanneries; distilleries; qua brickworks; farming and timber; railway and road construc
- **Yakutsk, Sev-Vostochni (Magadan-Kolyma), Chukotski, K ka**—Gold, platinum and lead mines; road and airfield cons timber industry; quarries; fisheries and canneries.
- **Burenski, Dalne-Vostochni, Nijni-Amur, Sakhalin**—Harbo railway and road construction; fortifications and airfields; installations.
- **Novaya Zemlya**—Coal mines and fisheries in the most area in Soviet Russia, an island in the Arctic Circle.

SOURCES

NEARLY 14,000 affidavits, plus other documentary evidence and crude maps made by ex-inmates of Soviet prisons and concentration camps, served as the basis of this Docu-Map. All of these came from the liberated inmates, many of whom supplemented their affidavits with detailed statements of their experiences as Soviet captives. Photostatic reproductions of the official "passports" furnished to the amnestied men and women by the various GULAG administrations, bearing the seals and signatures of camp commanders, have been reproduced here to furnish graphic proof of the number and magnitude of Slavery, Inc., as operated by the Soviet Government. A typical "passport" will be found over the upper lefthand corner of the map, of the Sorokski Administration, in the territory adjoining northern Finland. It reads in translation: "U.S.S.R.—Peo missariat of Internal Affairs (NKVD)—Administration of Railroad Construction ski Correctional Labor Camp—December 15, 1941—number 4/58024/16—Cit morsk." The seals and signatures of the commanders, Kliuchkov and Georgeye pended.

The numbers on these "passports" stand for all the registered communic papers issued from each administrative center. The highest of these exceed the figure, and enable us to gauge the turnover of human cargo in the different pen

A Reward of $1,000 Will Be Paid by PLAIN TALK for Evidence Disproving the Authenticity of the Soviet Documents Here Re

The Maps of Peace That Was No Peace

During the Cold War, the world's superpowers battled through proxy fights, economic competition, Olympic sports—and cartographic propaganda.

"Gulag"—Slavery, Inc. described itself as "The First Comprehensive, Self-Authenticated Docu-Map of Forced Labor Camps in Soviet Russia." Isaac Don Levine published it in the May 1947 issue of the New York–based magazine *Plain Talk*.

1 Labor camps appear as red dots, a reminder of their communist origins, surrounded by bigger, powdery circles, representing the colonies' administrative regions and indicating that the prison system occupies huge swaths of land.

2 The camps bleed off the map to the north and into Poland to the west, suggesting they can't be contained.

3 The map is surrounded by a dozen "passports," or papers carried by prisoners during their time in the camps, stamped and signed by Soviet administrators.

4 A small inscription tells us that these severely emaciated youths are "typical examples of thousands of children upon their release from Soviet concentration camps."

FOR SHEER DRAMA of imagery combined with high-stakes impact, it's hard to beat the best political maps of the Cold War. As the United States and the USSR vied for global supremacy, they never directly came to blows.[1] Instead of nuclear war, the superpowers channeled their energies into political and economic competition, proxy conflicts—and persuasive cartography.

Upon the end of the Second World War, the winning alliance between the Americans and Soviets deteriorated rapidly into an escalating standoff. Following the Russian army's push across much of Eastern Europe, communist forces set up governments in Poland, Romania, and Bulgaria. The US rushed aid to prevent similar outcomes in Greece and Turkey, then extended massive assistance called the Marshall Plan to help rebuild Western Europe, and President Harry Truman declared it would be American policy to "support free peoples who are resisting attempted subjugation by armed minorities or by outside pressures." Nevertheless, communist regimes took over Hungary, then Czechoslovakia in 1948, and, most stunning to Americans, mainland China in 1949, the same year the Soviet Union detonated its first A-bomb.

In this tense environment, maps became an important tool in the ideological battles between supporters of the US and USSR. The most influential was *"Gulag"—Slavery, Inc.* (shown on pages 218–219), which appeared in 1947.

"Gulag" had its origins in a 1945 book published in Rome by two Polish military officers, who compiled information from Soviet documents and former prisoners. Almost from the time of the Russian Revolution, the Soviet Union had thrown common criminals, war prisoners, and enemies of its communist leadership into a vast network of penal colonies, where convicts were put to work in mines or on construction or lumber projects. Those who refused were subject to starvation or summary execution. Many who complied died anyway from the horrible working conditions and harsh climate. By 1940, there were more than four hundred such camps across the USSR.

---

1 The Cold War fulfilled the prophecy of George Orwell, who wrote just after the end of World War II that the likely long-term outcome would be "monstrous super-states, each possessed of a weapon by which millions of people can be wiped out in a few seconds, dividing the world between them . . . prolonging indefinitely a peace that is no peace."

Isaac Don Levine, a Russian émigré to the US who became a journalist, then brought the map of those camps to wide circulation. He printed *"Gulag"—Slavery, Inc.* in the May 1947 edition of *Plain Talk*, a New York–based anticommunist journal he edited. But first he made changes that, taken together, could serve as a textbook for creating compelling propaganda.

Many political maps have an element or two of persuasion. *"Gulag"* has at least half a dozen. Consider its title: It introduced American readers to the word *gulag*. With *slavery*, it tied the penal camps it portrays to both the worst horror of American history and to the fascists the US had just defeated. And with *Inc.*, it mocked Soviet communists, who claimed to be anticapitalists, as merchants of serfdom.

The Soviet Union itself swells across the map in a giant, thick arc that stretches from the Barents Sea to the Bering Sea. The map shows the labor camp districts as red dots, collectively taking up a huge area. A series of "passports," or prisoner documents, testify to its authenticity, which is further bolstered by $1,000 offered to anyone who can disprove the map's claims. The passports are also stamped and signed by Soviet administrators, which adds to the overall feeling that this map is letting you peer into a bureaucracy of death.

And then there are the children. In a semicircle (again outlined in bold red), the lower-right portion of *"Gulag"* shows three youngsters, so gaunt their shoulders are hollowed and their ribs visible. The middle child stares straight ahead while wearing a crucifix. The map's text tells us they are victims of the camps. Really, though, no words are necessary to convey what godlessness communism has perpetrated here.

"The producers of *'Gulag'—Slavery, Inc.* are careful not to arrange their facts in an overly scientistic way," writes Timothy Barney, professor of rhetoric and communication studies at the University of Richmond and author of the book *Mapping the Cold War: Cartography and the Framing of American Power*. "[T]he overall crudeness of the presentation lacks the emphasis on cartographic technique and technology found, for instance, in the *National Geographic*'s Cold War–era maps. . . . [I]t looks almost as if it [*'Gulag'*] had been produced *by* a camp survivor." Exactly: *"Gulag"* wants to be the ultimate you-are-there map without seeming like it's trying to convey any deeper agenda.

"Gulag" was a smashing success, both at spreading news about the camps and rousing Americans against them. The *Chicago Tribune* ran an editorial that said it "exposed more perfectly than a million words could

do the essential character of the rulers of Russia and the creed they espouse." In distinct contrast to their European counterparts, most major American unions were staunchly anticommunist, and the American Federation of Labor (AFL), the leading voice of unions in the US, used the map to campaign against forced labor in the USSR. In fact, the head of the AFL's Free Trade Union Committee was an American intelligence asset, and the CIA funded an updated edition of *"Gulag,"* which the AFL printed in poster and pamphlet form. (And which used hammers and sickles to denote the labor camps.) The AFL soon found itself flooded by requests for copies of the map from local schools, unions, and churches around the country.

In September 1951, the map made it into *Time* magazine, which reported a story from a conference that month in San Francisco where delegates from nearly fifty countries gathered to conclude a peace treaty between the World War II Allies and Japan. At one meeting, a Missouri congressman named O. K. Armstrong approached Andrei Gromyko, the deputy minister of foreign affairs for the USSR, and asked, "Would the Soviet delegate . . . like to see a map of Russia?"

"I'd be delighted," Gromyko replied.

In 1951, the French Communist Party issued *Voici les bases américaines dans le monde* (Here are the American bases throughout the world). This powerful anti-American map asks (in French), "Who is the aggressor? Who is the menace?" And it delivers an answer in the form of dozens of heavy arrows extending from American military bases around the world's edges into the hearts of communist nations.

AMÉRICAINES DANS LE MONDE
DEPUIS L'ÉCRASEMENT D'HITLER, PAS UN SOLDAT DE L'U.R.S.S. OU DES DEMOCRATIES POPULAIRES N'A TIRÉ UN SEUL COUP DE FUSIL EN DEHORS DES FRONTIÈRES DE SON PAYS
ALASKA
POLE NORD
OENLAND
SLANDE
SPITZBERG
ALEOUTIENNES
U. R. S. S.
JAPON
MONGOLIE
CORÉE
OKINAWA
CHINE
FORMOSE
GUAM
Hong Kong
PHILIPPINES
MER NOIRE
URQUIE
IRAN
MER ROUGE
ARABIE
INDE
VIET NAM
OCÉAN INDIEN
AUSTRALIE
Qui est l'agresseur? Qui menace?
« LE DISPOSITIF MILITAIRE SOVIÉTIQUE EST ESSENTIELLEMENT DÉFENSIF. » (DÉCLARATION DE MAC ARTHUR DEVANT LE SÉNAT AMÉRICAIN).
ÉDITÉ PAR LE PARTI COMMUNISTE FRANÇAIS

"It happens to contain," Armstrong said, "an accurate portrayal of every slave labor camp in the Soviet Union." He then unrolled the new version of *"Gulag"* for the Soviet minister. Gromyko glanced at the map and muttered, "No comment." One of his assistants threw it aside.

"It would be interesting to know," Gromyko said later, "what capitalist slave is the author of this map." It's not clear whether he was contesting the language of "Slavery, Inc." or repeating it inadvertently, but the map's title got in his head.[2]

To be sure, there was another side to the global story, and in that same year of 1951, the French Communist Party published the most powerful anti-American map of the early Cold War: *Voici les bases américaines dans le monde* (Here are the American bases throughout the world) (pages 222–223).

The map's globe is tilted toward the south, so that the menace of American power also projects from Alaska and Canada across the North Pole. One block of text announces: "Two million American soldiers are making war or preparing for it outside America in all countries of the world." This echoes a common, and fair enough, left-wing critique that the United States was ringing the globe with outposts that, along with monetary and trade agreements, would ensure its dominance in the postwar era.

Using persuasive perspective, shading, typography, the Bases map packs quite a punch. And it raised legitimate questions about how the expanding reach of American influence and capitalism would affect the lives of anyone reading it.[3] But it's weakest where it can't be truthful: Only by depicting Eastern European nations as democracies within its

---

2 The following month, American officials planned to release copies of *"Gulag"* in Vienna, which at that time was still divided among the Allied nations of World War II. But when word got out that one of the final stages of printing was taking place in the Russian sector, Soviet military police seized 500,000 copies by force. Until then, a *New York Times* editorial noted, there had been "no denial of the map's accuracy, no invitation to foreigners or UN observers to visit these places and check for themselves." Grabbing the half-million sheets, the *Times* claimed, was "the most eloquent proof that the map was irrefutable with logic or with facts."

3 And the Communist Party got 26 percent of the popular vote in the 1951 elections for the French National Assembly, the most of any party.

threatened zone—rather than the Soviet puppet states they really were—can it portray the military posture of the USSR as purely defensive.

The *"Gulag"* map, on the other hand, is most powerful because it's exposing the horrible reality of the Soviet labor camps, not just because it's expertly manipulative. It's rather old-fashioned these days to assess any cultural artifact by the value of its content, rather than its production or context. But propaganda often has more impact when it's *true*.

The gulag system went into decline after the death of Joseph Stalin in 1953, and Soviet Premier Nikita Khrushchev abolished it in 1960. Aleksandr Solzhenitsyn, a Nobel Prize–winning writer and Soviet dissident who spent eight years in the camps, brought the word back into public discourse with his book *The Gulag Archipelago* in 1973. The USSR threw him out of the country the following year. In a 1975 speech, he said that "when wise men of the West, who had forgotten the meaning of the word 'liberty,' were swearing that in the Soviet Union there were no concentration camps at all, the American Federation of Labor published . . . a map of our concentration camps, and on behalf of all the prisoners of those times, I want to thank the American workers' movement."

EUROPE FROM MOSCOW
Atlantic Ocean
AFRICA
ALGERIA
TUNISIA
FR. MOROCCO
SP. MOROCCO
Casablanca
PORTUGAL
Lisbon
Madrid
SPAIN
Mediterranean Sea
FRANCE
Paris
EIRE
GREAT BRITAIN
London
SICILY
Rome
ITALY
BENELUX
Bonn
Rhine
WEST GERMANY
North Sea
AUSTRIA
Vienna
EAST GERMANY
Elbe
Berlin
DENMARK
Copenhagen
ALBANIA
YUGOSLAVIA
Belgrade
HUNGARY
Budapest
CZECHOSLOVAKIA
Prague
POLAND
Warsaw
NORWAY
Oslo
SWEDEN
Stockholm
Athens
GREECE
BULGARIA
Sofia
Danube
Bucharest
RUMANIA
Baltic Sea
TURKEY
Istanbul
Odessa
Kiev
Helsinki
FINLAND
Leningrad
Black Sea
Kharkov
Rostov
W.
S.
N.
E.
Moscow
U. S. S. R.
White Sea
TIME Map by R.M.Chapin, Jr.

The Maps of Worldwide War Gone Cold

Time's Robert M. Chapin popularized political maps for mid-twentieth-century audiences.

As Richard Edes Harrison introduced masses of Americans to a global view of conflict through his perspective maps in *Fortune* (see pages 194–198), Robert M. Chapin Jr. popularized international political perspectives through his pictorial maps in *Fortune*'s big brother publication, *Time* magazine. In doing so, he created some of the most influential and memorable cartography of World War II and the Cold War.

A 1933 graduate of the University of Pennsylvania, Chapin trained to be an architect, but (like Harrison) found little work in his intended field during the depths of the Great Depression. Instead, he retouched photos for a couple of years at *Newsweek*, where he also learned to draw maps. *Time* hired him away in 1937, just as a key editor there named Dana Tasker was revolutionizing its—and the entire publishing industry's—treatment of artwork.

Over the first fifteen years after its founding in 1923, *Time* ran black-and-white images of men on 694 of 782, or nearly 90 percent, of its covers. Tasker smashed that formula spectacularly in November 1941, with a color cover of a flame-haired and exceptionally long-legged Rita Hayworth. And in September 1944, just after the Allied powers recaptured Paris from Nazi invaders, *Time* ran its first graphic cover (page 228): a street map of the French capital,[1] surrounded by illustrations of the Arc de Triomphe, Eiffel Tower, and Notre Dame, all drawn by Chapin.

By then, Chapin was overseeing a department of five cartographers and researchers, who maintained a reference library of more than

This piece by Robert M. Chapin, from a March 1952 issue of *Time*, shows the Soviet Union from a westward-looking perspective as a bold red mass that seems to be thrusting everywhere all at once. Indeed, the map's compass is a red hammer and sickle centered on Moscow.

1 "PARIS," *Time*'s cover asked, "How long till her heart is warm and gay?" The question referenced *The Last Time I Saw Paris*, a popular song from 1940 by Jerome Kern and Oscar Hammerstein II. Hammerstein wrote the lyrics after the Fall of France: *The last time I saw Paris, her trees were dressed for spring / And lovers walked beneath those trees and birds found songs to sing . . . / The last time I saw Paris, her heart was warm and gay / No matter how they change her, I'll remember her that way.*

1,500 maps, charts, and photos, and who churned out up to half a dozen detailed maps every week to meet demand for information about the Second World War. Chapin kept two big globes (one showing the natural world, the other with political boundaries) hanging in his workplace, suspended with weights so he could rotate or photograph them at any angle. He also used an airbrush to give his work three-dimensional depth. Most crucially, he pioneered the infographic, piling images and facts onto his maps. Indeed, he developed a large library of standardized symbols, showing everything from bombs to flags to camels, that he could simply drop into his illustrations for quick, bite-sized effect. "I try to dramatize the news of the week," Chapin said, "not just to produce a reference map like those in an atlas."

In September 1944, *Time* ran this pioneering graphic cover: a map of Parisian streets and landmarks, drawn by Chapin.

Chapin produced lively battle maps at a prolific rate, conveying data to readers in figures as well as borders and arrows. His work mixed and matched natural phenomena, wartime events, and visual commentary, bringing together mountains and railways, oil fields and explosions, showing swastikas casting long shadows and American forces in the shape of a vise. He did all this in as close to real time as journalism of the 1940s got, and while laboring under national-security restraints. In August 1942, a *Time* correspondent sent a message from Hawaiʻi that said: "If Chapin is a wise man, he will know what to map in the Pacific." Recognizing the text was coded in some way, Chapin figured out it was a reference to Solomon, whose wisdom is legendary in the Bible, and worked up a map of the Solomon Islands. Four days later, the US announced that Marines had landed at Guadalcanal in the Solomons, marking a decisive shift in the Pacific theater of war, and *Time* was immediately able to detail the attack.

After global war turned cold, Chapin kept producing maps that were as striking as ever; he could appeal to imagination and ideology, not just illustrate battles and fronts. *Europe from Moscow* (page 226), from a March 1952 issue of *Time* (and reprinted in larger size for classrooms), is a most dramatic example. It shows the Soviet Union as a bulging bulk of red.

"The view from inside Russia looking out," warned *Time*, "is a pleasing vista of past opportunities promptly cashed in on and future prospects that may pay big dividends—if the capitalist West goes bankrupt." And by tilting the earth away from readers and shading non-communist countries in lighter colors, Chapin intensified that dire threat. As map collector PJ Mode has noted, "[T]he distance from Paris to Lisbon . . . appears to be about the same as the distance from Moscow to Leningrad, when in fact it is more than twice as great. . . . [I]t look[s] as if Soviet tanks could simply roll downhill into the heart of Western Europe."

In 1959, Chapin collaborated with Jeremiah Donovan, the artist who would succeed him as *Time*'s head of cartography eleven years later, to create a pictorial blockbuster called *It's an Interesting World in an Interesting Time* (pages 230–231). While it's not particularly characteristic of Chapin's canon, it captures a political and cultural moment as well as any map ever has.

For their work, Chapin and Donovan chose an "Armadillo projection," which was invented in 1943 by Erwin Raisz, a Hungarian cartographer who emigrated to the United States and ultimately joined Harvard's Institute of Geographical Exploration.[2] Raisz found that projecting the earth onto a torus (or doughnut shape) created plane-eyed perspective views while allowing viewers to see almost all of the planet's landmasses. The result had curved latitude and longitude lines that looked like the back of an armadillo—and also seemed three-dimensional. And while it distorted both angles and areas at its edges, most of the space it cut out or shortened was in the middle of the Pacific Ocean.

The Armadillo projection never really caught on with most cartographers or the public, but it was perfect for Chapin and Donovan, who wanted to cram as many illustrations as they could onto a single image of the inhabited globe. They decorated their torus with portraits of world leaders, shown in frames in their capital cities, including Dwight Eisenhower of the United States, smiling; Nikita Khrushchev of the Soviet Union, bellowing; Charles de Gaulle of France, swatting down revolution in Algeria; and Mao Zedong of China and Chiang Kai-shek of Taiwan, facing off against each other. Chapin and Donovan also packed the map with icons for various locations, some of which still make sense to modern eyes and some that now register as mere stereotypes (a kangaroo in Australia, scantily clad warrior figures in East Africa, a bowl of rice in China).

---

2 Raisz taught cartography, created logistics maps used by the US Army during World War II, and drew, by hand, some of the most beautiful landform maps the world has ever seen. But even his work could not stop Harvard, whose president sniffed that "Geography is not a university subject," from closing its program in 1948.

And this is just a partial list! You might say it's the tip of the iceberg, except that a torus has no tips.[3]

All of these items had one thing in common: They would interest *Time*'s audience—a huge group of mostly middle-class readers, generally optimistic but living with the dread of both nuclear weapons and communism, focused on America but restless and ready to make something of the world they had been engaging since the end of their fight against fascism. *The Twilight Zone* appealed to their curiosity and anxiety; JFK's New Frontier would seek to harness their energy. From its title to how it shows Sputnik and Vanguard satellites orbiting the earth to its bathing-beauty depiction of a woman who is either Gladys Zender of Peru (Miss Universe 1957) or Luz Marina Zuluaga of Colombia (Miss Universe 1958), *It's an Interesting World in an Interesting Time* conveys the spirit of the early Space Age.

In 1959, Robert M. Chapin and Jeremiah Donovan collaborated to create *It's an Interesting World in an Interesting Time*, loaded with small pictograms—forerunners of emojis—representing events of the late 1950s:

1 The admission of Alaska and Hawai'i to the United States in 1959

2 The Cuban Revolution, which ended in January 1959

3 The construction of Brasilia, the new capital of Brazil, which started in 1956

4 The people of Guinea voting *NON*—"no"—to a new French constitution that would have maintained Guinea's status as a colony in September 1958

5 Harvey Lavan "Van" Cliburn Jr., the American pianist who won the International Tchaikovsky Competition in Moscow in April 1958

6 Mushroom clouds from atomic bomb tests in Nevada, Siberia, and the South Pacific

---

3 Chapin and Donovan did give their world a truncated cap to show the North Pole—and also showed a *Nautilus* submarine traveling underneath it, which happened for the first time in August 1958.

TERESTING WORLD IN AN INTERESTING TIME
6
5
4
3
TIME Map by R.M. Chapin, Jr. and J. Donovan
© TIME Inc.

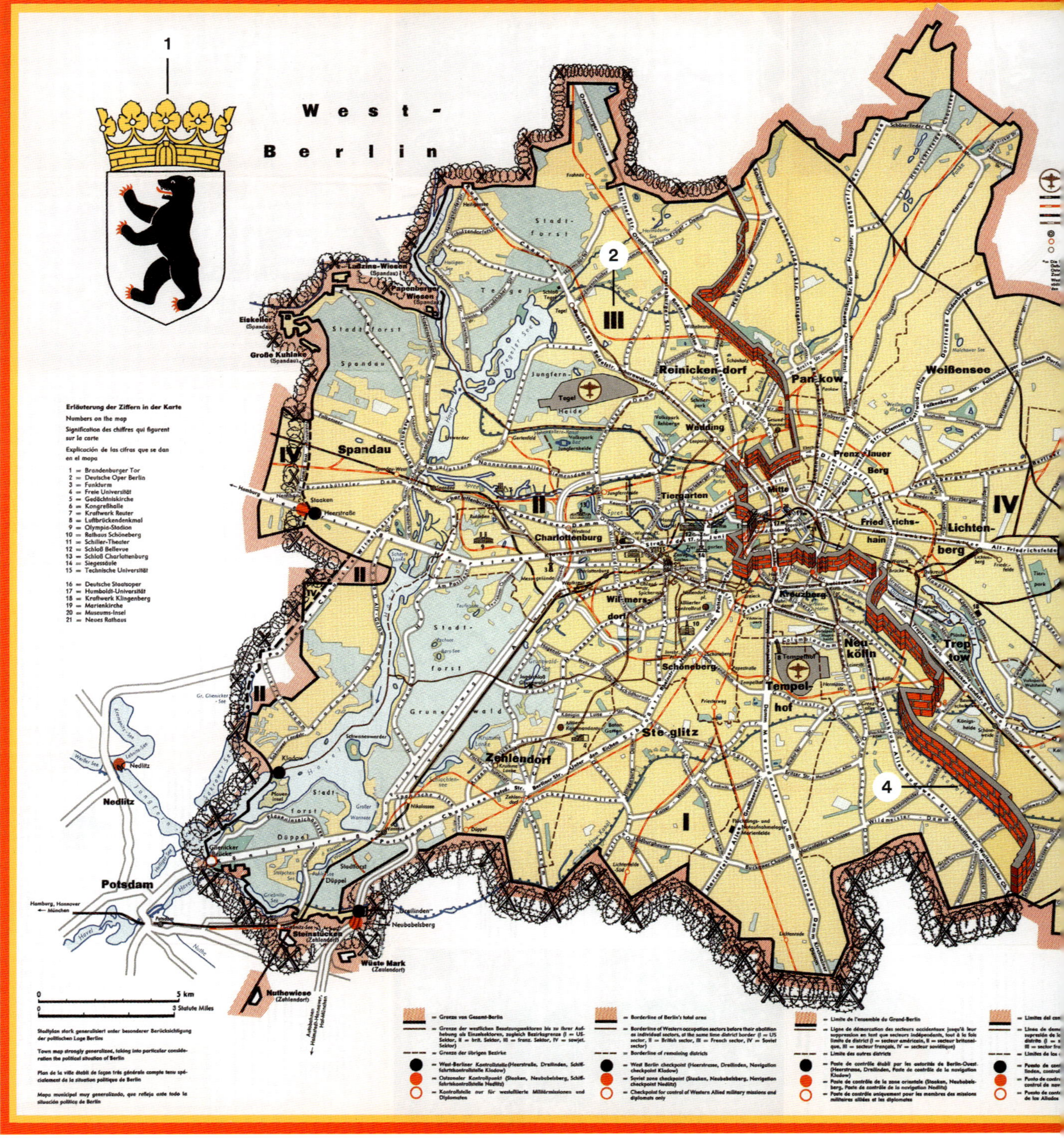
1
West-
Berlin
2
III
Erläuterung der Ziffern in der Karte
Numbers on the map
Signification des chiffres qui figurent sur la carte
Explicación de las cifras que se dan en el mapa
1 = Brandenburger Tor
2 = Deutsche Oper Berlin
3 = Funkturm
4 = Freie Universität
5 = Gedächtniskirche
6 = Kongreßhalle
7 = Kraftwerk Reuter
8 = Luftbrückendenkmal
9 = Olympia-Stadion
10 = Rathaus Schöneberg
11 = Schiller-Theater
12 = Schloß Bellevue
13 = Schloß Charlottenburg
14 = Siegessäule
15 = Technische Universität
16 = Deutsche Staatsoper
17 = Humboldt-Universität
18 = Kraftwerk Klingenberg
19 = Marienkirche
20 = Museums-Insel
21 = Neues Rathaus
Reinicken-dorf
Pankow
Weißensee
Wedding
Prenz-lauer Berg
Mitte
Spandau
Tiergarten
Charlottenburg
Fried-richs-hain
Lichten-berg
IV
II
Wil-mers-dorf
Kreuzberg
Neu-kölln
Trep-tow
Schöneberg
Tempel-hof
Steglitz
Zehlendorf
I
4
Tegel
Staaken
Heerstraße
Eiskeller (Spandau)
Große Kuhlake (Spandau)
Laszine-Wiesen (Spandau)
Papenberger Wiesen (Spandau)
Nedlitz
Potsdam
Steinstücken (Zehlendorf)
Dreilinden
Neubabelsberg
Wüste Mark (Zehlendorf)
Nuthewiese (Zehlendorf)
Glienicker Brücke
Kladow
Grunewald
Hamburg, Hannover ← München
5 km
3 Statute Miles
Stadtplan stark generalisiert unter besonderer Berücksichtigung der politischen Lage Berlins
Town map strongly generalized, taking into particular consideration the political situation of Berlin
Plan de la ville établi de façon très générale compte tenu spécialement de la situation politique de Berlin
Mapa municipal muy generalizado, que refleja ante todo la situación política de Berlin
= Grenze von Gesamt-Berlin
= Grenze der westlichen Besatzungssektoren bis zu ihrer Aufhebung als Einzelsektoren, zugleich Bezirksgrenze (I = US-Sektor, II = brit. Sektor, III = franz. Sektor, IV = sowjet. Sektor)
= Grenze der übrigen Bezirke
= West-Berliner Kontrollstelle (Heerstraße, Dreilinden, Schiffahrtskontrollstelle Kladow)
= Ostzonaler Kontrollpunkt (Staaken, Neubabelsberg, Schiffahrtskontrollstelle Nedlitz)
= Kontrollstelle nur für westalliierte Militärmissionen und Diplomaten
= Borderline of Berlin's total area
= Borderline of Western occupation sectors before their abolition as individual sectors, at the same time district border (I = US sector, II = British sector, III = French sector, IV = Soviet sector)
= Borderline of remaining districts
= West Berlin checkpoint (Heerstrasse, Dreilinden, Navigation checkpoint Kladow)
= Soviet zone checkpoint (Staaken, Neubabelsberg, Navigation checkpoint Nedlitz)
= Checkpoint for control of Western Allied military missions and diplomats only
= Limite de l'ensemble du Grand-Berlin
= Ligne de démarcation des secteurs occidentaux jusqu'à leur suppression en tant que secteurs indépendants, tout à la fois limite de district (I = secteur américain, II = secteur britannique, III = secteur français, IV = secteur soviétique)
= Limite des autres districts
= Poste de contrôle établi par les autorités de Berlin-Ouest (Heerstrasse, Dreilinden, Poste de contrôle de la navigation Kladow)
= Poste de contrôle de la zone orientale (Staaken, Neubabelsberg, Poste de contrôle de la navigation Nedlitz)
= Poste de contrôle uniquement pour les membres des missions militaires alliées et les diplomates

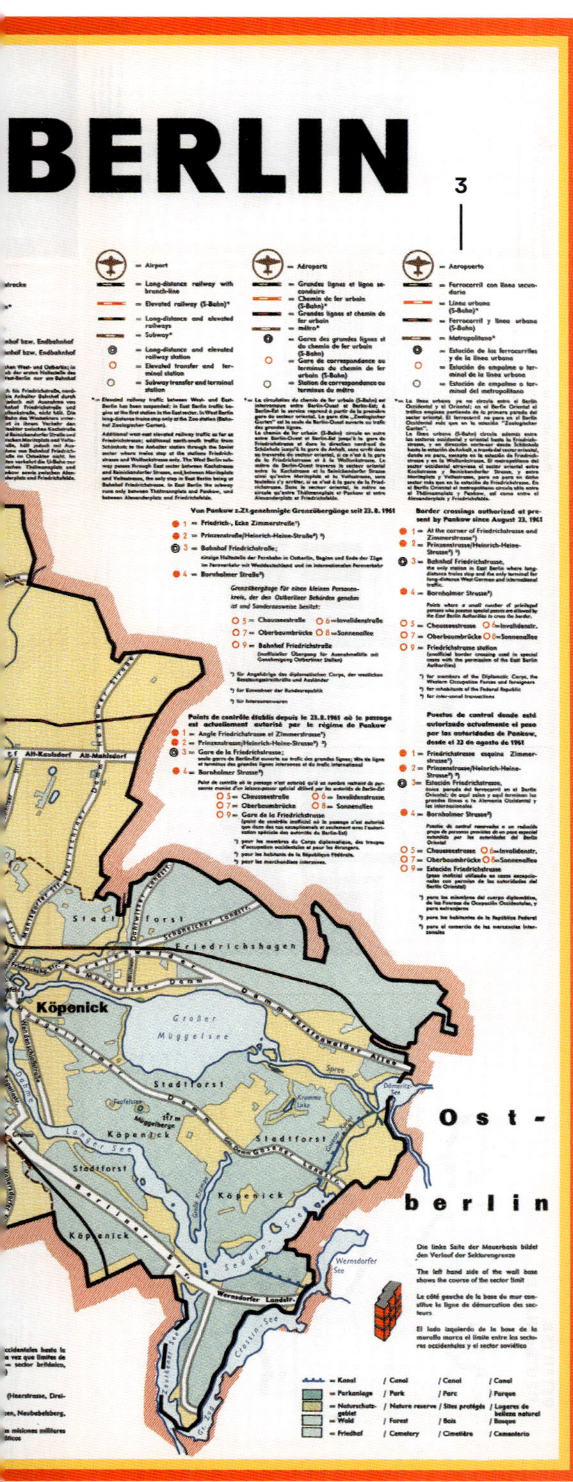

The Map—and Gap—of the "Wall of Shame"

Maps to contend with the significance—and embarrassment—of the Berlin Wall.

Credited to geographer Gustav Fochler-Hauke and cartographer Ernst Kremling, this map was published c. 1962 in what was then West Germany, and was probably designed to be used mostly by tourists.

1 The coat of arms of West Berlin, with its traditional Berliner black bear and five-crested crown

2 Allied zones of occupation are indicated with Roman numerals—I for American, II for British, III for French, IV for Soviet.

3 Information is given in four languages about border crossings

4 The thick brick wall and barbed wire highlight how oppressively they cut off West Berlin, and how harshly they separate East and West.

OF ALL THE human-made structures significant enough for political maps to include, the most notorious is probably the Berlin Wall, which ran through the biggest city in continental Europe and encircled its western districts from 1961 to 1989. You can see—you can virtually *feel*—its throttling effects in the pointedly out-of-scale, three-dimensional lines of red brick and black barbed wire on *Berlin*, a folding map published by the Press and Information Office of West Berlin around 1962.

Berlin was divided and increasingly dangerous for fifteen years before the Wall. At the end of World War II, the United States, the USSR, Great Britain, and France carved defeated Germany into four areas of occupation. They likewise split Berlin, located about 110 miles inside the Soviet zone, into four sectors. But they disagreed sharply about what should happen next. In June 1948, the USSR tried to choke off the outpost, cutting all land and water routes between western Germany and western Berlin. The remaining Allies responded with an 11-month, 280,000-flight airlift, supplying the city with food until the Soviets ended their blockade. The western powers then reorganized their territories into a federal republic, which became the country of West Germany, and which included the inland "island" of West Berlin. The USSR set up the German Democratic Republic of East Germany as a communist satellite state. And West Berlin remained a bone in its throat, both ideologically and materially.

While West Germany underwent one of history's great economic miracles in the 1950s, East Germany was suffering repression, paying massive reparations to the USSR, dealing with severe shortages brought on by the state-forced collectivization of its agriculture—and sustaining massive emigration. By 1961, it was clear that the Soviet Union would be compelled to stop the flow of refugees out of East Germany somehow. Global tensions ran extraordinarily high through the spring and summer of that year, as the world watched to see if the USSR would move on Berlin again, this time with more force, and what the American response would be.[1]

---

1 "West Berlin has been protected . . . by the fear that interference with the city, or with access to it, would result in war between the United States and the Soviet Union," former US Secretary of State Dean Acheson wrote in a memo to President John F. Kennedy in June 1961. "War," Acheson continued, "in this case means nuclear war."

While all-out war seemed perilously close for weeks that summer, the US under President John F. Kennedy found ways to signal to the Soviets that as long as they stayed on their side of the border, East Berlin and East Germany were effectively their business. And so it went. Soviet Premier Nikita Khrushchev put a plan that western intelligence services called Operation Chinese Wall into motion, and on August 13, East German paramilitary police began laying barbed wire, erecting blockades, and ripping up roads to close off all entry points from East to West Berlin. Neither East German nor Soviet forces attempted to take over West Berlin or interfere with its air corridors.

Global catastrophe was averted, but the Wall literally drove a murderous wedge through the heart of Berlin. Concrete blocks came soon after the barbed wire, and then watchtowers, guard dogs, anti-vehicle trenches and bunkers filled with guards. Eventually, the East Germans built a barrier 96 miles long, usually to a height of 12 feet, not just along the line dividing the city, but all the way around West Berlin. They also put up a second line of fencing, about 100 yards inside the first, clearing a zone called the Death Strip between the two barricades. In the years to come, defectors would occasionally succeed in tunneling, flying, or even ballooning their way to West Berlin. But the Death Strip really was no man's land.[2]

It might seem impossible for any one document to capture the extraordinary drama of this place and time. But the *Berlin* folding map (pages 232–233) does just that.

Designed by geographer Gustav Fochler-Hauke and cartographer Ernst Kremling, it was probably intended mainly for tourists, and one US Air Force unit included copies in its welcome kit for visitors. It shows the Allied zones of occupation, and it's dense with symbols for buildings, landmarks, roads, and airports. But the map is dominated by the boundaries of West Berlin. The heavily lined wall, twisting through the middle of the city, and thick spiral of fencing, enclosing the rest of

---

2 In August 1962, a teenaged apprentice bricklayer named Peter Fechter jumped out of a workshop window in East Berlin and ran across the Death Strip. But before he could scale the outer Wall, sentries shot him in the right hip. The guards on the eastern side wouldn't help Fechter, while those on the western side didn't want to start a war by intervening, and he bled out while crying for help.

the western boroughs, aren't just impossible to miss. These are purposely artificial, drawing attention to how oppressively they cordon off West Berlin, and how unnaturally they are separating the families and homes and businesses of East and West Berlin—which otherwise look completely similar on the map. With its tall wall an instant classic, this is truly a memorable artifact of Cold War mapmaking.

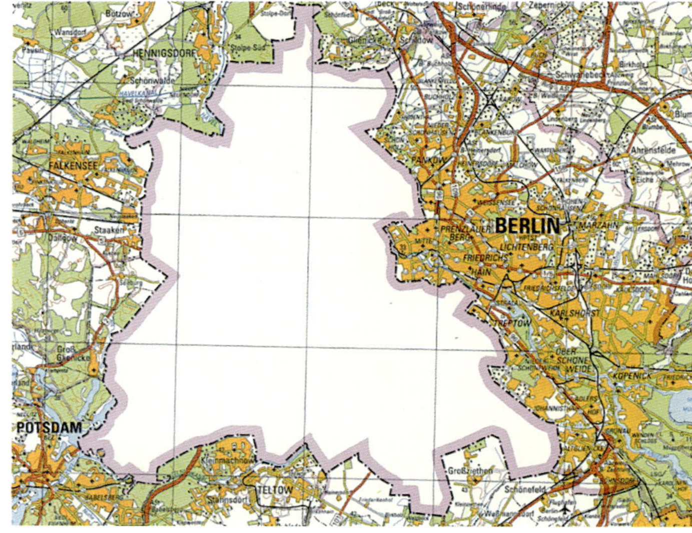

The Berlin Wall inspired a wide range of artists, from John le Carré, who set the climactic scene of *The Spy Who Came in from the Cold* at the Wall, to Lou Reed and David Bowie, who were each interested in the divided city as metaphor. It also handed Western politicians a never-ending propaganda triumph. "All free men, wherever they may live, are citizens of Berlin," Kennedy said to a huge crowd when he visited the city in 1963. "And therefore, as a free man, I take pride in the words, '*Ich bin ein Berliner*.'"

Twenty-four years later, at the Brandenburg Gate, Ronald Reagan spoke directly and memorably to the leader of the Soviet Union: "Mr. Gorbachev, tear down this wall!"

In the East, as the Wall grew ever more fortified over its lifetime, it persisted as a symbol of the dreary brutality of communist rule. And a map published in an East German atlas in 1988 (above) offered one way to respond: by simply ignoring anything on the other side of the Wall. This map shows East Berlin, labeled just as "Berlin," with districts and roads detailed. The city of Potsdam is to its west. And in between—nothing at all!

This is an extreme version of a trend that also showed up in various East Berlin transit maps from the same era. Those sometimes displayed West Berlin as a small, uninteresting patch, surrounded by East German trains and subways (which ceased making stops in West Berlin when the Wall went up). In the atlas map, West Berlin has disappeared altogether.

It's pretty funny at first glance, and definitely silly. And it's true that "all maps have to make decisions about what they do and do not include, depending on what they're for," as the popular YouTubers the Map Men said when commenting on this map. But maps can be wrong. And West Berlin did exist, even if East Germans didn't have access to it. Totalitarians

This map, published in an East German atlas in 1988, details East Berlin, which it calls "Berlin." But within the thick purple line marking the boundary of West Berlin, there's just a gaping white space.

try to erase what they don't want to acknowledge, and that's what's happening in this map.

The year after the atlas map appeared, mass protests returned to East Germany, and this time, the Soviets, exhausted and now seeking reforms, would not try to suppress public sentiment. "Life punishes those who arrive too late," Gorbachev told Erich Honecker, the longtime ruler of East Germany, in October 1989. Within two weeks, Honecker was out of office. Three weeks after that, crowds rushed the Wall—and made it through without getting shot. East German troops began official demolition of the Berlin Wall in 1990, the same year the two Germanys reunified.

Willy Brandt was mayor of West Berlin when the Wall went up, and called it the Wall of Shame. Later, he became chancellor of West Germany. At the age of seventy-six, he was suddenly able to say: "Now what belongs together will grow together."

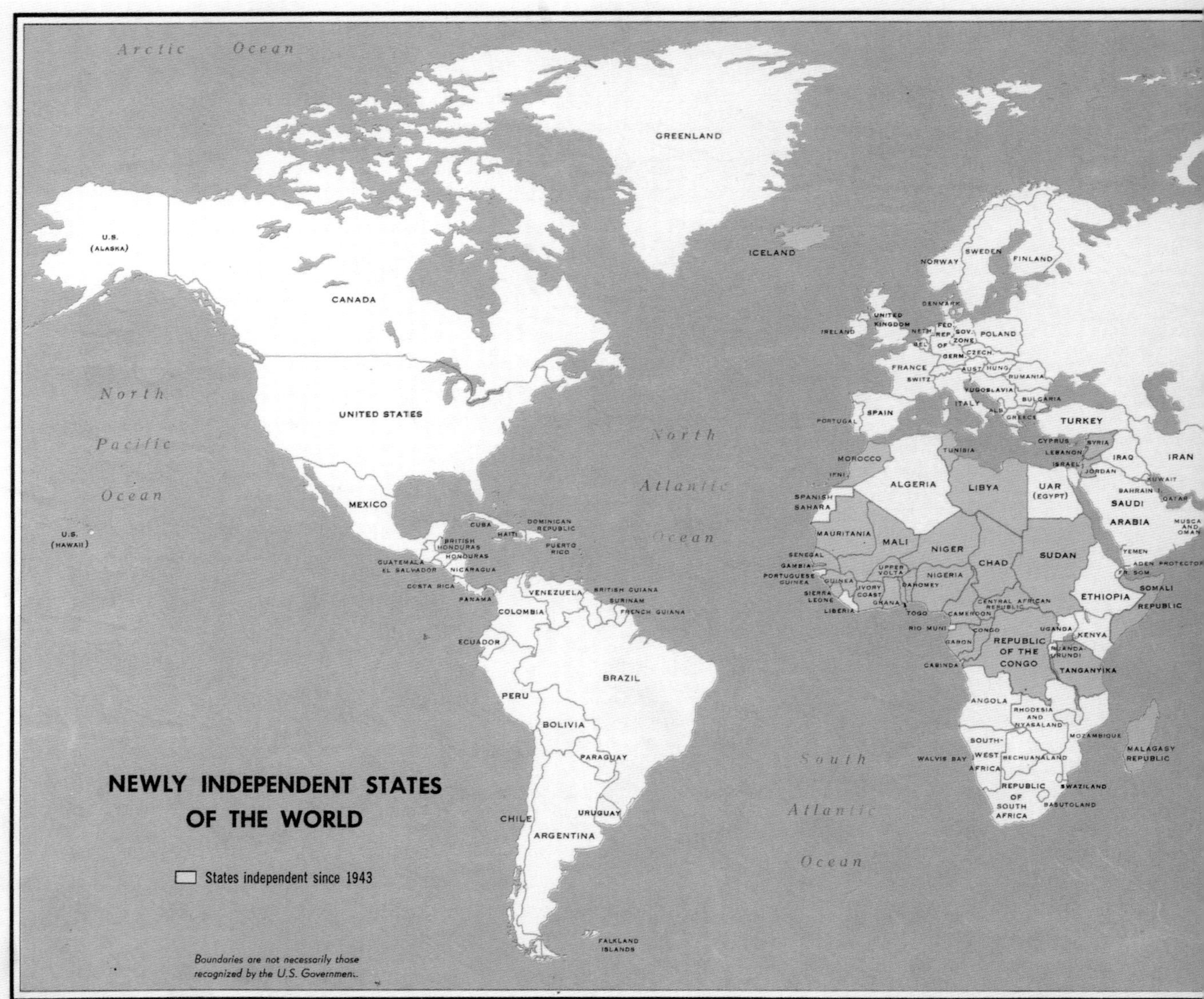
NEWLY INDEPENDENT STATES OF THE WORLD
States independent since 1943
Boundaries are not necessarily those recognized by the U.S. Government.
Arctic Ocean
North Pacific Ocean
North Atlantic Ocean
South Atlantic Ocean
GREENLAND
ICELAND
U.S. (ALASKA)
CANADA
UNITED STATES
MEXICO
U.S. (HAWAII)
CUBA
HAITI
DOMINICAN REPUBLIC
PUERTO RICO
BRITISH HONDURAS
HONDURAS
GUATEMALA
EL SALVADOR
NICARAGUA
COSTA RICA
PANAMA
VENEZUELA
BRITISH GUIANA
SURINAM
FRENCH GUIANA
COLOMBIA
ECUADOR
PERU
BRAZIL
BOLIVIA
PARAGUAY
CHILE
URUGUAY
ARGENTINA
FALKLAND ISLANDS
NORWAY
SWEDEN
FINLAND
DENMARK
UNITED KINGDOM
IRELAND
NETH.
BEL.
FED. REP. OF GERM.
SOV. ZONE
POLAND
CZECH.
FRANCE
SWITZ.
AUST.
HUNG.
RUMANIA
YUGOSLAVIA
ITALY
ALB.
BULGARIA
GREECE
PORTUGAL
SPAIN
TURKEY
CYPRUS
SYRIA
LEBANON
ISRAEL
JORDAN
IRAQ
IRAN
KUWAIT
BAHRAIN I.
QATAR
SAUDI ARABIA
MUSCAT AND OMAN
YEMEN
ADEN PROTECTORATE
FR. SOM.
SOMALI REPUBLIC
MOROCCO
IFNI
TUNISIA
ALGERIA
LIBYA
UAR (EGYPT)
SPANISH SAHARA
MAURITANIA
MALI
NIGER
CHAD
SUDAN
SENEGAL
GAMBIA
PORTUGUESE GUINEA
GUINEA
SIERRA LEONE
LIBERIA
IVORY COAST
UPPER VOLTA
GHANA
TOGO
DAHOMEY
NIGERIA
CAMEROON
CENTRAL AFRICAN REPUBLIC
ETHIOPIA
RIO MUNI
GABON
CONGO
REPUBLIC OF THE CONGO
CABINDA
UGANDA
KENYA
RUANDA URUNDI
TANGANYIKA
ANGOLA
RHODESIA AND NYASALAND
MOZAMBIQUE
MALAGASY REPUBLIC
SOUTH-WEST AFRICA
WALVIS BAY
BECHUANALAND
REPUBLIC OF SOUTH AFRICA
SWAZILAND
BASUTOLAND

The Map of Independence Across the World

In the decades following World War II, decolonization created new countries across the globe.

Newly Independent States of the World captures a remarkable moment in history, when dozens of nations across the globe were born around the same time and the era of colonialism died out. From 1945, when the United Nations was founded, to 1962, when the US Central Intelligence Agency created this map, membership in the UN more than doubled, from 51 states to 110. Seventeen new countries emerged in Africa just in the year 1960.

On one level, *Newly Independent States* is a product of its precise time. In keeping with American Cold War views, it shows East Germany, which had formally existed since 1949, as the "Soviet Zone" of Germany. It doesn't portray North Korea or North Vietnam at all. And it depicts some realms whose names would disappear from world maps within just a few years, such as Sarawak, which gained independence from Great Britain and became one of the founding states of Malaysia in 1963;

Newly Independent States of the World, created by the CIA in 1962, depicts a huge group of former colonies and occupied territories that had recently emerged as new nations. The map announces their arrival in calm colors and fonts—and doesn't show any contested borders amid all these new countries.

French Somaliland, which was renamed the French Territory of the Afars and Issas in 1967, won independence in 1977 and is now Djibouti; and Río Muni, which was controlled by Spain until 1968 and is now part of Equatorial Guinea.

But the map's central message is one of sweeping yet calm change. A large group of former colonies and protectorates, from Iceland in the North to the Malagasy Republic (Madagascar) in the South, as big as India and as small as Gambia, were, rather suddenly, becoming free. And this map shows their emergence in a placid tone of aqua blue and very plain type—no bursts of red or orange, no arrows for invasion routes or symbols for explosions or conflicts of any kind, not even any disputed borders. This map represents what mainstream historians called "polite decolonization," defined by the *World Almanac* as "the peaceful decline of European political and military power in Asia and Africa."

In reality, however, there were plenty of places where decolonization wasn't anything like peaceful or polite. Western empires had their military forces exhausted and their coffers drained by the Second World War, and retained diminished popular support afterward for controlling faraway colonies. But where those colonies possessed particularly rich resources, strategic importance, or cultural significance for their rulers, governing nations generally kept a tight grip as long as they could, only to evacuate suddenly, whatever the consequences. Great Britain held off the Indian independence movement until 1947, then hastily and disastrously partitioned the subcontinent and withdrew, leaving behind millions of refugees (see page 93). The British Empire tried to set the political borders of the Middle East until 1948, when it dumped issues that still aren't resolved today on the United Nations and left that region too. The Dutch waged war for four years after the end of World War II before relinquishing their claims to Indonesia in 1949. France battled communist nationalists for control of Southeast Asia until 1954 before withdrawing from Vietnam.

The era's tipping point came in 1956: In July of that year, Egypt, led by Gamal Abdel Nasser, a pan-Arab nationalist who had ousted his country's monarchy four years earlier, took control of the Suez Canal. Three months later, amid war between Israel and Egypt, Britain and France invaded the Sinai Peninsula, intending to retake control of the canal, which their countries had built in 1869. But under severe pressure from the United States, the European nations stood down and had to accept a ceasefire. After that calamity, it was all downhill for the colonials—though, even then, in often highly violent fits and starts. While France granted independence to many of its colonies during the late 1950s, it fought a bitter, unsuccessful war until 1962 to keep Algeria. Portugal engaged in bloody struggles until 1975 to maintain control of mineral-rich Angola and Mozambique.

The newly independent states of this map emerged into a bipolar world where two nuclear superpowers, both professing to oppose colonialism, vied for their allegiance. The United States provided support for democracy and access to vast markets—but wasn't averse to knocking over governments it decided it didn't like. (In the 1950s and '60s, the CIA tried to overthrow the leaders of several countries shown in blue on this map, including Indonesia and the Republic of the Congo.) The Soviet Union offered massive aid for industrial projects as well as ideological and military backing to Marxist allies.

At first, many leaders of the new nations tilted toward socialism—naturally enough, since they opposed colonial capitalism. Many also proved susceptible to autocracy. Again, that's fairly understandable, since they were often revolutionaries who suddenly needed to grasp control of the mechanisms of state power. But over the long haul, the combination proved depressingly hard to dislodge in large swaths of the so-called developing world. Following independence, many of the countries here were afflicted for decades by oppressive one-man rule as well as stagnating socialist economies.

Today, the meaning of "decolonization" is, as academics like to say, contested. Frantz Fanon, the Martiniquais philosopher whose 1961 book *The Wretched of the Earth* popularized the term, wrote that "colonialism is not a machine capable of thinking. . . . It is naked violence and only gives in when confronted with greater violence." Regrettably, there are modern leftists who take that as excusing the wanton slaughter of innocents. Najma Sharif, an American writer, posted this after Hamas's October 2023 attack on Israel: "what did y'all think decolonization meant? vibes? papers? essays? losers."

But while we struggle to decide who does and doesn't get to co-opt that word, *independence* is up for grabs in the post–Cold War world, too. For many of the countries on this political map, new nationhood circa 1962 turns out to have been a late ticket to the dance of globalization. And many of them are still in the process of figuring out just what that means.

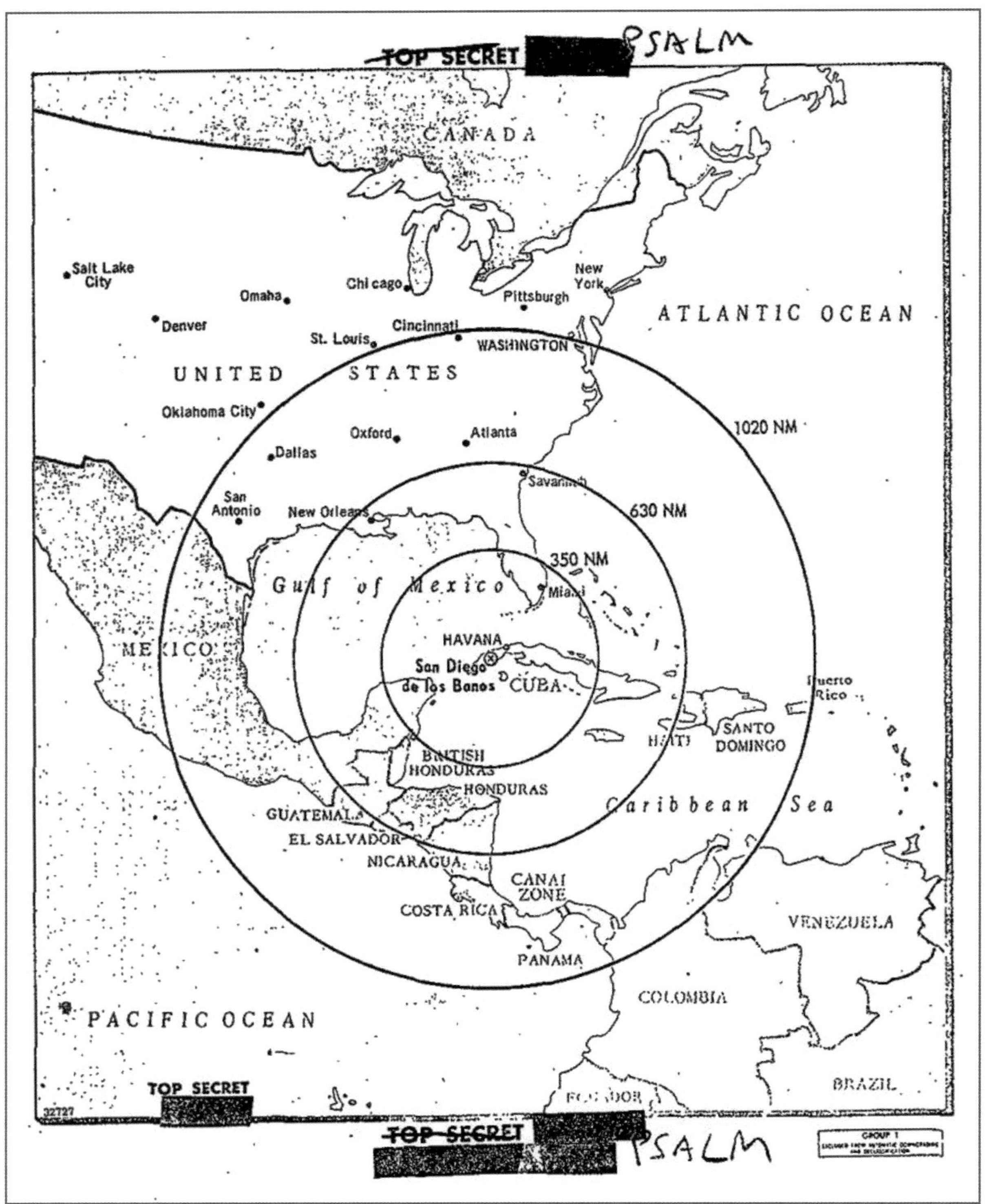
TOP SECRET
PSALM
CANADA
Salt Lake City
Omaha
Chicago
Denver
Pittsburgh
New York
ATLANTIC OCEAN
St. Louis
Cincinnati
WASHINGTON
UNITED STATES
Oklahoma City
Oxford
Atlanta
1020 NM
Dallas
San Antonio
New Orleans
630 NM
350 NM
Gulf of Mexico
Miami
MEXICO
HAVANA
San Diego de los Banos
CUBA
Puerto Rico
HAITI
SANTO DOMINGO
BRITISH HONDURAS
HONDURAS
Caribbean Sea
GUATEMALA
EL SALVADOR
NICARAGUA
CANAL ZONE
COSTA RICA
VENEZUELA
PANAMA
COLOMBIA
PACIFIC OCEAN
TOP SECRET
32727
BRAZIL
TOP SECRET
PSALM
GROUP 1

The Map of Nuclear Crisis

In the most dangerous moment of the nuclear era, maps revealed the Soviet Union had stationed missiles in Cuba.

On the morning of October 16, 1962, McGeorge Bundy, the national security advisor to US President John F. Kennedy, walked into JFK's White House bedroom. He found Kennedy in a nightshirt and slippers, reading papers and eating breakfast.

"Mr. President," Bundy said, "there is now hard photographic evidence, which you will see, that the Russians have offensive missiles in Cuba."

Cold War tensions between the United States and Soviet Union were running high. Rumors had been flying for months that the USSR was amping shipments of weapons to its ally Cuba—and that the US was planning to invade the island. But it seemed barely conceivable to almost all American officials that the Soviets would be so aggressive if not reckless as to move ballistic missiles to a location 90 miles off the Florida coast. When Attorney General Robert Kennedy learned the news, his one-word reaction was: "*Shit!*"[1]

JFK quickly assembled a secret executive committee of advisors, called ExComm. When they met for the first time later that morning, the CIA presented the president and his advisors with a map showing not just the estimated ranges of the Soviet missiles, but also some of the American locales they could incinerate. Potential targets included cities across the southern and southeastern US: Dallas, Texas; Miami, Florida; New Orleans, Louisiana—and Washington, DC.[2] Together with aerial photos of the missile sites, this scary map worked like an X-ray after a medical

Upon learning in October 1962 that the USSR had positioned weapons just 90 miles off the Florida coast, the CIA prepared a briefing memo called "Probable Soviet MRBM [Medium-Range Ballistic Missile] Sites in Cuba," and attached this map showing the estimated ranges of the missiles and the places they could strike.

1 Robert Kennedy had just been immersed in the battle to desegregate the University of Mississippi, which ultimately led the US government to send more than 30,000 troops to quell rioting by white residents and secure the safe admittance of James Meredith, a Black student, to Ole Miss. When he first saw photos of the missiles, RFK asked, "Can they hit Oxford, Mississippi?"

2 The map also showed Oxford, which intelligence analysts dutifully included in response to RFK's sardonic question.

diagnosis, visually confirming and reminding everyone involved of the stakes at hand.

John Kennedy was inclined at first to launch an air strike at the missile sites. But he asked at that first meeting, "How effective can the take-out be?"

"It'll never be 100 percent," replied Maxwell Taylor, chairman of the Joint Chiefs of Staff. "We hope to take out a vast majority in the first strike, but this is not just one thing, one strike, one day, but continuous air attack."

Then–Secretary of State Dean Rusk said: "I don't believe, myself, that the critical question is whether you get a particular missile before it goes off. Because if they shoot those missiles, we are in general nuclear war." And this horrifying fact echoed through the Executive Committee of the National Security Council's deliberations over the following thirteen days. On October 21, for instance, Kennedy's military briefers told him again that even under optimum conditions, "The best we can offer you is to destroy 90 percent of the known missiles."

"In other words," as the National Security Archive, a research center in Washington, DC, put it in a 2022 report, "one [missile] could very well survive the air strikes and be launched—in which case, boom goes Atlanta."

Kennedy decided to make public the existence of the missiles, demand the Soviets dismantle the launch sites, and blockade Cuba from receiving further weapons, while holding off on more drastic military action. And the standard history of the missile crisis says that strategy worked. It goes like this: The superpowers came closer to nuclear conflict than anytime before or since. But US ships enforced the quarantine. Kennedy gave Soviet Premier Nikita Khrushchev time to back down. And when Khrushchev sent the American president a long, emotional letter on October 26, followed by a harsher statement the next day, Kennedy replied to the first and ignored the second. Khrushchev then agreed to remove the missiles, in exchange for a guarantee that the US would not attack Cuba.

That's all accurate, though vast troves of new information have come to light since Kennedy Administration memoirs and Hollywood screenwriters established American conventional wisdom about the crisis. The US also had a far greater superiority over the Soviets in missiles than the American public realized at the time. The Kennedy Administration was also heavily invested in trying to overthrow Fidel Castro through secret programs of sabotage and assassination. The American government also let the Soviet Union know that the US would remove Jupiter missiles it had placed in Turkey—but kept that quiet. All of which means Khrushchev thought there were greater benefits to his missile bluff than were apparent at the time.

The real lesson of the Cuban Missile Crisis isn't about crisis management. It's that "the two at the center—Nikita Khrushchev and John Kennedy—realized that no politician in his right mind was going to use nuclear weapons first," as Richard Reeves wrote in his 1993 biography *President Kennedy: Profile of Power*. "The price was too high; the judgment of history would be too severe."

That mutual understanding might have led to some fascinating places. In the summer of 1963, for starters, the Americans and Soviets were able to negotiate a treaty outlawing atmospheric tests of nuclear weapons. But Kennedy was murdered in November of that year, and Khrushchev was deposed the next. It would take an entire generation before the US and USSR again had leaders (in Mikhail Gorbachev and Ronald Reagan) who could acknowledge the vulnerabilities of nuclear strength to each other. Until then, the contours of the world's political maps would largely remain where the threat of Cold War destruction had frozen them.

Map data © 2025 Google, INEGI

PART VI

NEW DIRECTIONS

In an era where climate change, pandemics, immigration, trade, and the computational power of Google Maps all cross international lines, how important can borders still be? Across the following examples, made by and for the players wielding contemporary maps most powerfully, the answer so far is: Extremely.

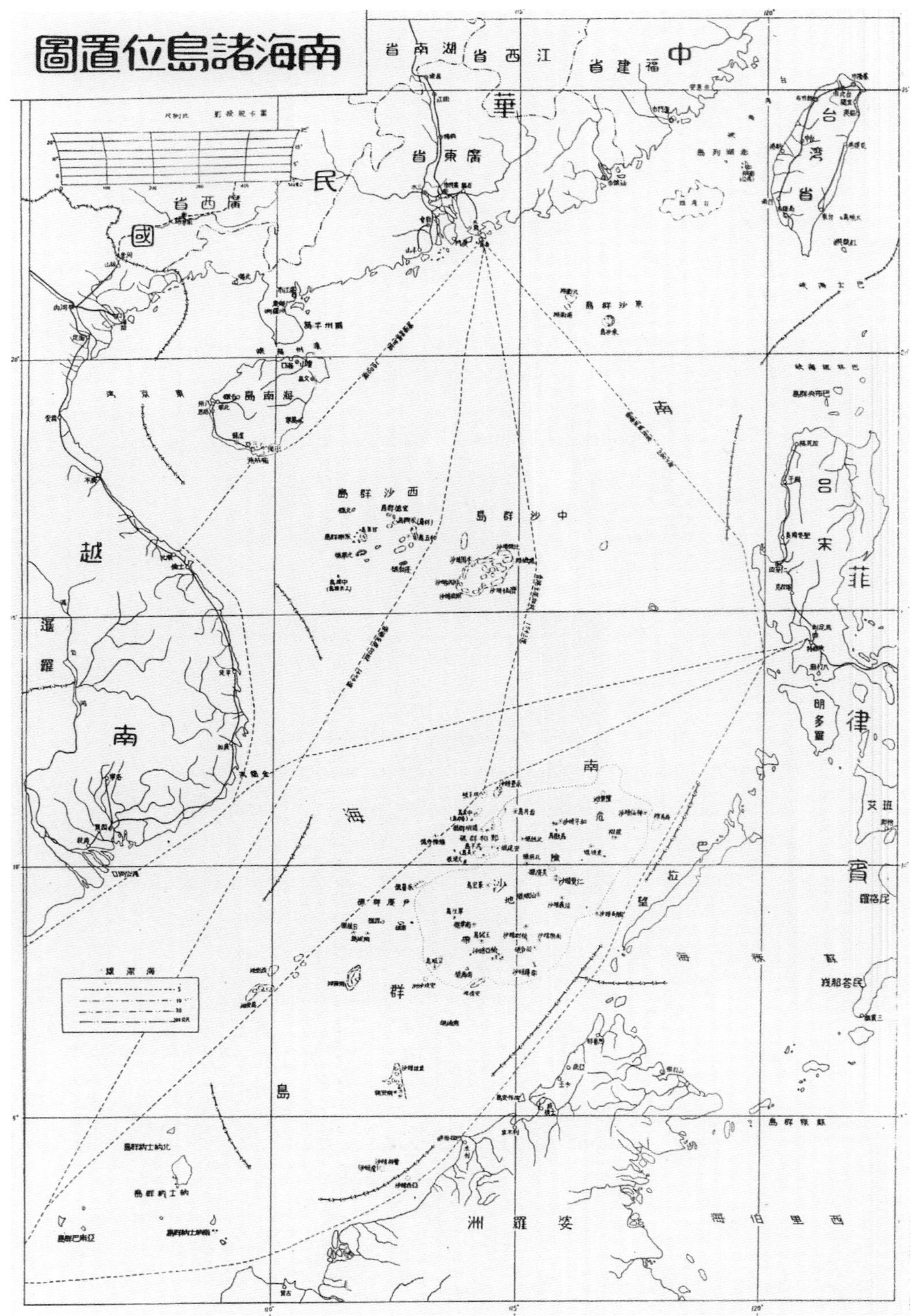

南海諸島位置圖
中華民國
湖南省
江西省
福建省
廣東省
廣西省
台灣省
越南
暹羅
菲律賓
呂宋
明多羅
海南島
東沙群島
西沙群島
中沙群島
南沙群島
南海
巴拉望
婆羅洲
西里伯海
蘇祿群島
北納土納群島
納土納群島

The Map That Could Start World War III

The cartography of the South China Sea is fuzzy, but Chinese intimidation there is real.

In today's Googlized world, it's easy to believe the value of maps lies in being useful rather than carrying meaning—after all, people mostly consult maps to see how to get to the airport or drive to dinner, not to learn about borders or territorial claims or migrations. But there are still places where a handful of markings on a plain old map can trigger huge political disputes. Like the South China Sea.

The South China Sea is an expanse covering nearly 1.5 million square miles of water surrounded by China, Taiwan, the Philippines, Malaysia, Brunei, Indonesia, and Vietnam. And China claims almost the whole thing, using a boundary of simple segments known as the Nine-Dash Line.

The Nine-Dash Line is older than most contemporary opponents of Xi Jinping's foreign policy probably realize. In the first half of the twentieth century, Chinese patriots began trying to reclaim the heritage and terrain that Western and Japanese imperialists had robbed from their country—including the South China Sea, which Chinese voyagers had explored nearly 2,000 years earlier. Markings similar to the Nine-Dash Line began showing up on privately printed maps in the 1930s. And the government of China issued the first official version of the line (opposite) in 1947, two years before that regime was overthrown by communist revolutionaries. The Nine-Dash Line has its roots in Chinese nationalism, not communist ideology.

That said, it has no standing under international law. The United Nations Convention of the Law of the Sea, which was negotiated for fifteen years and took effect in 1994, and which China ratified in 1996, lays out distances from shorelines for various types of maritime zones for all nations. And in a case between the Philippines and China, an arbitration tribunal ruled in 2016 that "any historic rights that China may have had to the living and non-living resources within the 'nine-dash line' were superseded . . . by the limits . . . provided for by the Convention."

China quickly rejected that ruling and has essentially proven it unenforceable. It has never spelled out exactly what the Nine-Dash Line

The Nationalist Government of China published the first official version of the Nine-Dash Line in a "Location map of South Sea Islands," or *Nanhai Zhudao*, in 1947—before the communist takeover of the country.

means. Does China claim the entire marine territory within the line, or sovereignty over the islands within it? Does it believe it's entitled to exclusive rights to, say, natural gas deposits inside the line? How do the dashes even connect? China hasn't said. Keeping things ambiguous means it's compelled to defend claims only when it can win, and it has gradually ratcheted up its strength in the region. China has built and militarized entire artificial islands within the Nine-Dash Line. In 2021, China reportedly demanded that Indonesia stop drilling for oil within the line and sent a Coast Guard patrol and four warships to the area near an Indonesian rig. And throughout 2023, Chinese vessels intercepted Filipino boats in contested regions of the South China Sea near the west coast of the Philippines, sometimes ramming or firing water cannons at them.

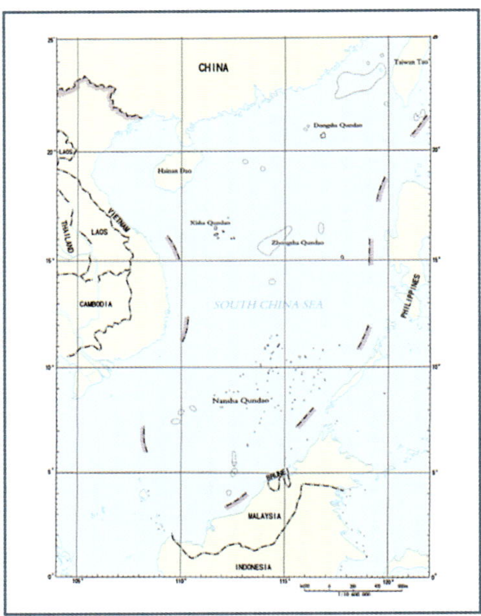

China claims almost all of the South China Sea, using a partially traced border. This illustration of the Nine-Dash Line was included in a statement it submitted to the United Nations in 2009.

The stakes are massive. The South China Sea is hugely important strategically and commercially: It connects the Pacific and Indian Oceans. A third of the globe's shipping passes through it every year. It's home to more than 3,000 species of fish and 55 percent of the world's fishing boats. The countries around it have long histories of disputes with China and have no desire to be pushed around by their powerful neighbor, including Vietnam, which calls the Nine-Dash Line the "cow's tongue line," and Indonesia and the Philippines, which have conducted military exercises with the United States. For all these reasons and more, when China issued a new national map including the line in 2014, *The Washington Post* ran a story with the headline, "Could This Map of China Start a War?"

China also uses its economic clout to bolster its political aims, including claims about its borders, through censorship. Foreign producers or publishers who want access to China's 1.4 billion consumers must earn green lights from the Chinese government. And since 2018, it's the propaganda department of the Communist Party that conducts film reviews. China has blocked many movies altogether, while studios have also cut their films or included scenes to please the censors. For instance, *Abominable*, a 2019 animated feature about a girl from Shanghai who finds a yeti on her rooftop, shows its main character in a room with a wall map that includes the Nine-Dash Line. The line doesn't have anything to do with the movie's plot—but *Abominable* was a collaboration between the American studio DreamWorks and Pearl Studio, a Chinese production company.

This whole process has infected American moviemaking, and caused further backlash among China's neighbors. It's enough to raise questions about portrayals of the Nine-Dash Line even when Chinese censorship isn't directly involved. In the 2023 blockbuster *Barbie*, for example, Barbie (played by Margot Robbie) briefly stands in front of a garish "real world map" when she first visits Weird Barbie (Kate McKinnon). Among the map's colorful, misshapen continents and symbols for boats, sunshine, and waves, a scribbly dashed line extends from the right side of Asia. And some viewers immediately saw the hand of China at work. Vi Kiến Thành, head of Vietnam's Cinema Department, said, "It contains the offending image of the Nine-Dash Line." His country soon banned *Barbie*.

In this particular case, Warner Bros., which produced *Barbie*, was almost certainly correct when it claimed the map "was not intended to make any kind of statement." The map in BarbieLand looks like it's written in crayon, and the team that designed it relied on maps drawn by children for inspiration. Other broken lines appear on the map, and at other times in the movie. And the line connecting to Asia has only eight dashes!

In this 2016 photo, a young visitor to a "national defence education center," or military instructional facility, in Nanjing, China, examines a map of the South China Sea that includes the Nine-Dash Line.

But storms keep brewing around the South China Sea for a reason. China is exerting pressure on everyone from Filipino fishing fleets to Hollywood screenwriters to bend toward accepting a border that it won't call a border, which we can see only as nine dashes on a political map.

The Map of the Red and the Blue

Today's most pervasive political maps distort power and exaggerate polarization—which make them very useful weapons.

"The Australian election map has been lying to you," blared the headline of a May 2022 story by the Australian Broadcasting Corporation (ABC). Just ahead of the country's federal election day, the piece showed a map of its voting patterns (shown on page 254) with districts colored according to the political groups leading in each region. Blue, standing for the Liberal Party, and green, representing the National Party (allied with the Liberals), completely dominated the image. For the most part, areas shaded red for the opposition Labor Party occupied just a few small spots of the map. Clearly Oz was heading for a landslide, right?

Not so fast. The coalition of Liberals and Nationals actually won a bare majority of seats in the Australian Parliament in 2019, and then lost, despite a very similar voting map, in 2022. Because while Australia is divided into 151 electorates with roughly equal populations, these regions vary widely by density. For instance, Durack covers more than half a million square miles of the northwestern part of the country. It looks huge on the map, but it's just one division. Meanwhile, Sydney and Melbourne, the largest metropolitan centers in Australia, are home to more than two dozen tightly packed seats apiece, many of which are hardly discernable on the map. So all that blue and green on the Australian map represents a lot of space, but not necessarily many voters—or a majority of public opinion. "All the seats in our big cities were basically invisible," the ABC story reported. "Which essentially means millions of voters were wiped off the map."

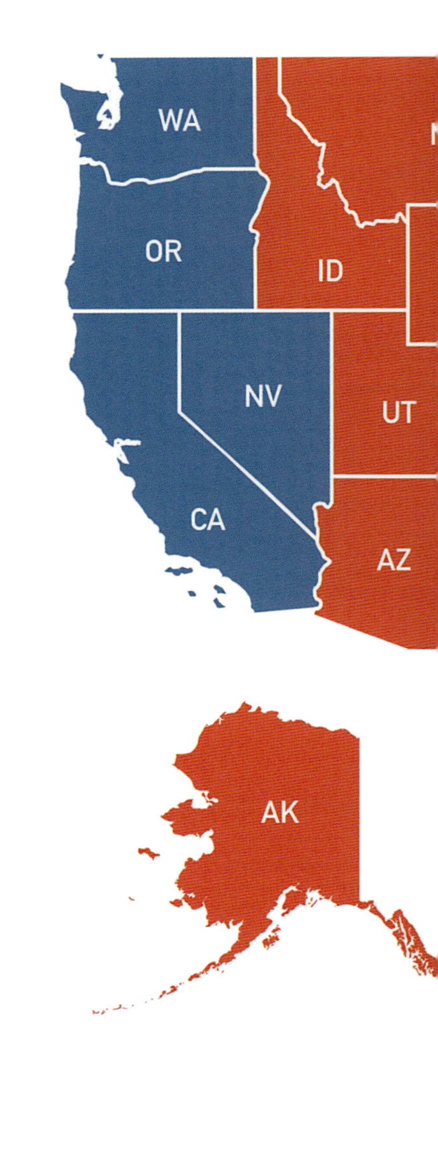

The Electoral College voting map of 2016 paints a picture of a red wave—despite the fact President Donald Trump trailed his opponent, former Secretary of State Hillary Clinton, by nearly 3 million votes nationwide. And the actual count of the final result was Trump 304, Clinton 227, thanks to a handful of "faithless electors," members of the Electoral College who voted for neither candidate.

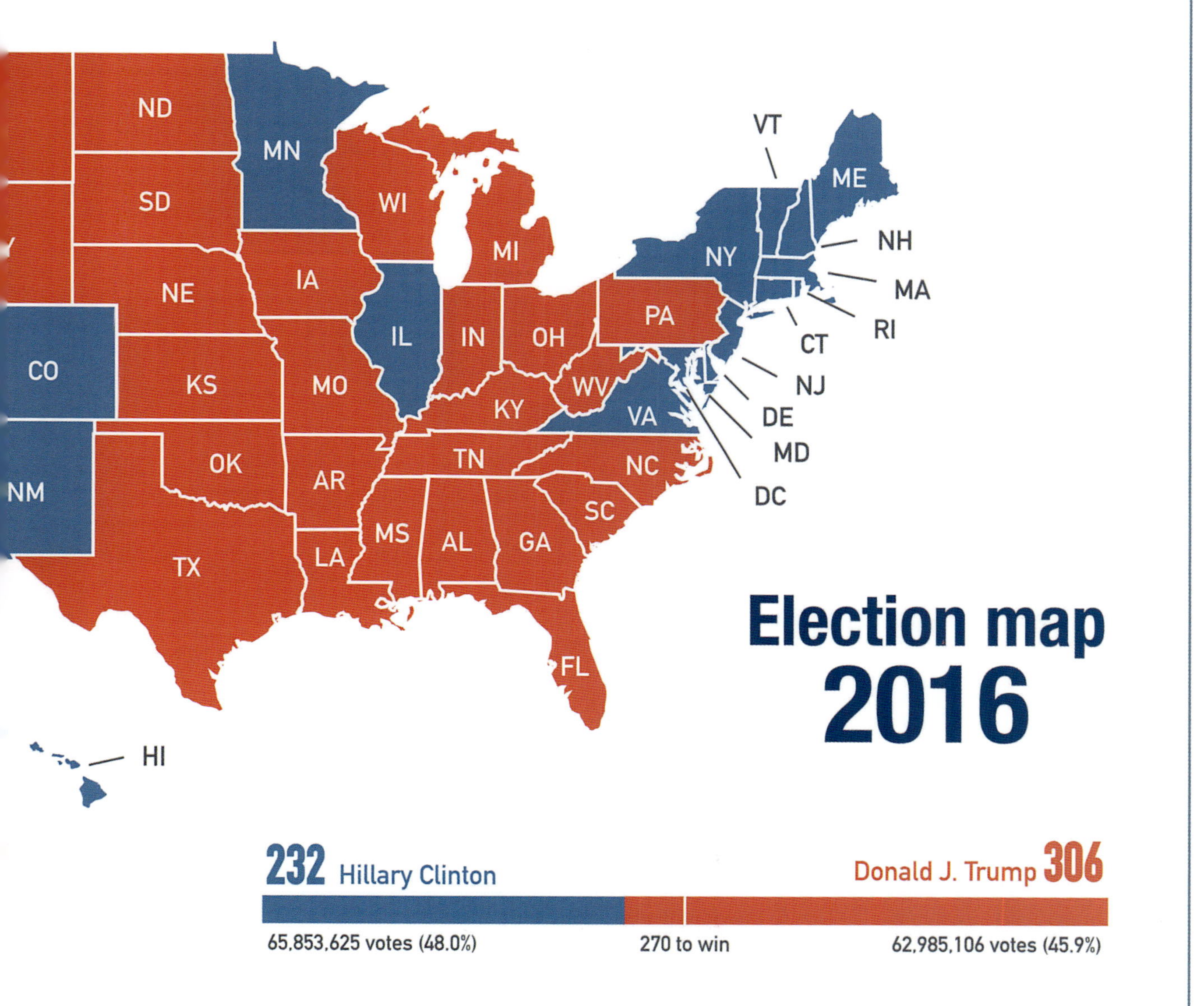
ND
MN
SD
WI
MI
NE
IA
CO
KS
MO
IL
IN
OH
PA
NY
VT
ME
NH
MA
RI
CT
NJ
DE
MD
DC
WV
VA
KY
TN
NC
SC
NM
OK
AR
TX
LA
MS
AL
GA
FL
HI
Election map
2016
232 Hillary Clinton
Donald J. Trump 306
65,853,625 votes (48.0%)
270 to win
62,985,106 votes (45.9%)

The case of Australia shows how, wherever citizens are concentrated much more heavily in some parts of a jurisdiction than others, voting maps can distort political authority by showing it as rooted in terrain rather than popular sovereignty. Since 2016, this antidemocratic potential has been weaponized by the leader of the world's most powerful democracy, as US President Donald Trump sees it as a feature, not a bug, of political maps.

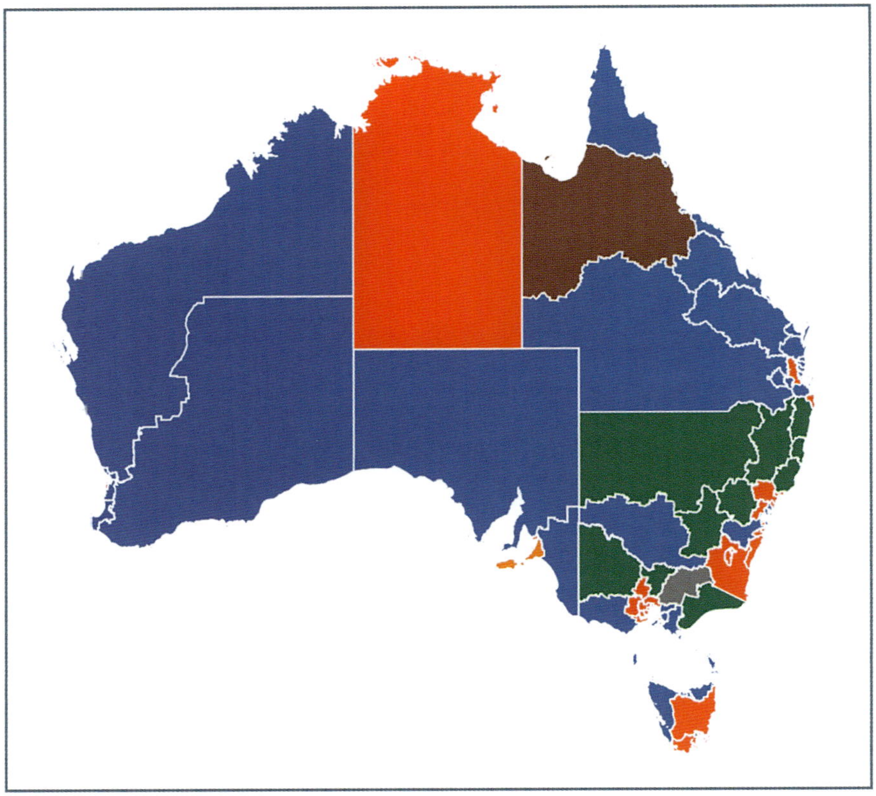

The United States chooses presidents via its Electoral College, which allocates votes to states according to how many members of Congress each has (and also gives three electors to the District of Columbia). Thus, spacious but sparsely populated states not only appear more important on typical American voting maps, they actually are disproportionately powerful: In addition to the electors that correspond to its population-based presence in the House of Representatives, every state gets two votes because of its senators. For example, more than 9 million people live in New Jersey, while fewer than 600,000 reside in Wyoming. But Wyoming has three electoral votes, about one for every 200,000 denizens, while New Jersey has fourteen, or just one for every 680,000. Wyoming is also more than ten times bigger geographically, and shows up as a large (and almost always red) rectangle on voting maps.

Further, the Electoral College is winner-take-all. In 2024, Trump won more than 2 million votes in Virginia (which he lost), and Kamala Harris earned more than 2.5 million in Georgia (which she lost), but these supporters don't register on maps that encode only red or blue. This itself tends to deepen polarization in the United States. Research has found

A 2022 map of Australia's voting patterns, with districts colored according to the political groups leading in each region, has distortions similar to the US red-and-blue map. Large swaths of blue and green represent areas that are geographically large but sparsely populated.

that exposure to two-color maps leads Americans to overestimate Democratic strength in blue areas and the Republican tilt of red regions—and to expect their own votes to matter less.

Now, suppose you were a presidential candidate who appealed most to precisely the Americans most overrepresented in contemporary red-and-blue maps: inhabitants of vast but lightly populated states, and swing voters in closely contested states. That's exactly what happened in 2016 with Trump: He had a lock on small, largely Republican states in the South and West, and ran well enough among disaffected rural and blue-collar white voters in the Midwest to eke out victories in Michigan, Pennsylvania, and Wisconsin. So even though Trump trailed his opponent, former Secretary of State Hillary Clinton, by more than 2 percentage points of the total vote, he prevailed in the Electoral College.

The popular vote and Electoral College had split on three earlier occasions in American history, most recently in 2000. But no new president ever embraced winning an election through losing the voters as affirmatively as Trump. He called his win a "massive landslide." And he and his supporters drew sustained validation from what he termed the "beautiful map" that illustrated it, awash as it was in red (shown on pages 252–253).

While talking about a completely unrelated subject with Reuters reporters in the Oval Office in 2017, Trump paused, then handed out copies of a red-and-blue map of the previous autumn's election. "Here, you can take that, that's the final map of the numbers," Trump said. "That's pretty good, right? The red is obviously us."

Nearly eight years later, the map and its divisions were still on Trump's mind as he celebrated winning a second term in the 2024 election. "The golden age of America has officially begun," he claimed the following February. "The red states [are] going to be leading the way to

US President Donald Trump launched his second term by making it clear that he wanted to redefine the identities of a range of places in the Western Hemisphere, beginning with changing the Gulf of Mexico to the Gulf of America. Google Maps quickly complied. *Map data © 2025 Google, INEGI* making our country richer and safer and stronger than ever before. The red states are going to do good. And the blue states—I don't know, maybe they'll totally disappear off that map."

Whether you're a fan of politics, cartography, or both, you have to reckon with the fact that MAGA and maps were made for each other. Trump, who has a knack for lurid imagery and a consistently underrated sense of humor, is a visceral communicator. He truly grasps the gut-level power of definition.[1] And when it comes to renaming places, big tech companies have bent to his wishes. It's a key lesson: When the gatekeepers of any medium, including Google Maps, become monopolies, they channel powerful interests.

Trump also has an outlook on world affairs that would have been at home at the turn of the last century, when nations asserted greatness through spheres of influence. He has said he wants to acquire Greenland, exert more control over the Panama Canal, and, by the by, absorb Canada. Americans could then see their nation reclaiming imperial power over the Western Hemisphere while leaving other places, like Ukraine, to their own devices. "As a state, it would be one of the great states anywhere," Trump said of Canada in March 2025. "This would be the most incredible country, visually."

Meanwhile, many Americans are now choosing to live near neighbors who share their political affiliations. And gerrymandering continues apace (see page 57). So blue (and heavily urban) America will probably keep getting both demographically denser and geographically smaller.[2] And voting maps will probably keep getting disproportionately redder.

On the evening of Thanksgiving 2024, Vice President–elect J. D. Vance posted an image to X (shown opposite) that repurposed *Freedom from Want*, a famous Norman Rockwell painting from 1943 that shows an older man and woman setting a holiday turkey upon a family dinner table. In this mockup a grinning headshot of Trump replaces the father figure's face, while Vance, also smiling, plays the role of his wife. And instead of bringing forth a stuffed bird, the couple is delivering a two-color voting

---

1 As Syracuse University geography professor Karl Offen told *Politico* in May 2025: "To name is to claim."

2 The share of US land covered by Democratic-voting congressional districts dropped from 39 percent in 2008 to just 20 percent over the following ten years, according to a 2019 report by the Brookings Institution.

In November 2024, J. D. Vance used social media to deliver this Thanksgiving message. It shows the Republican presidential ticket (with Vance in drag) bringing an overwhelming electoral bounty to a Norman Rockwell–drawn American family. Donald Trump and Vance earned 49.8 percent of the votes cast earlier that month.

map of the United States, apparently of the 2024 election broken down by county, that's drenched in red.

Like many Trumpian appeals, this tweet is crude, funny, and amazingly over the top (especially considering who posted it) in portraying subservience to the president. It puts Vance in women's clothes on the heels of an election where he, Trump, and their surrogates campaigned relentlessly against drag and other forms of transgender expression. And it appropriates a voting map to literally serve up the false impression of a landslide. Cheerfully misleading, winking at its own absurdity, but serious about restoring the morality of the early 1940s, this truly is a political image for our times.

Trump himself included versions of voting results in earlier tweets. In 2019, he posted a county-level map of the US, dominated by Republican red, with the caption, "Try to impeach this." Readers soon figured out that map was distorted, and not just because of population density. It showed Trump winning a batch of counties he had actually lost to Clinton.

As it turns out, you actually could impeach that. But conviction is a whole different question.

The Pentagon's New Map: War and Peace in the Twenty-First Century

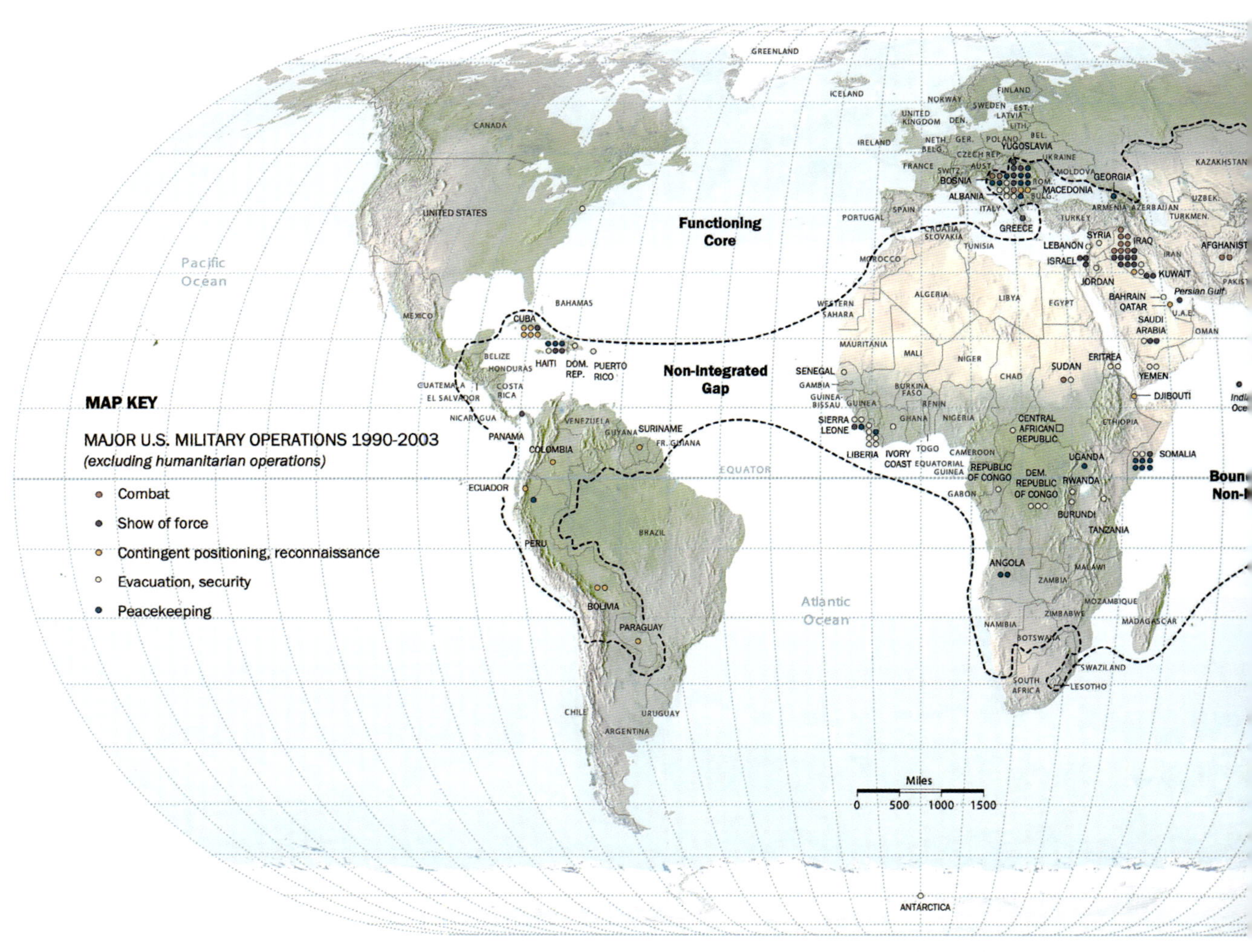

Response data source: U.S. Military Services via Dr. Henry Gaffney Jr. / The CNA Corporation

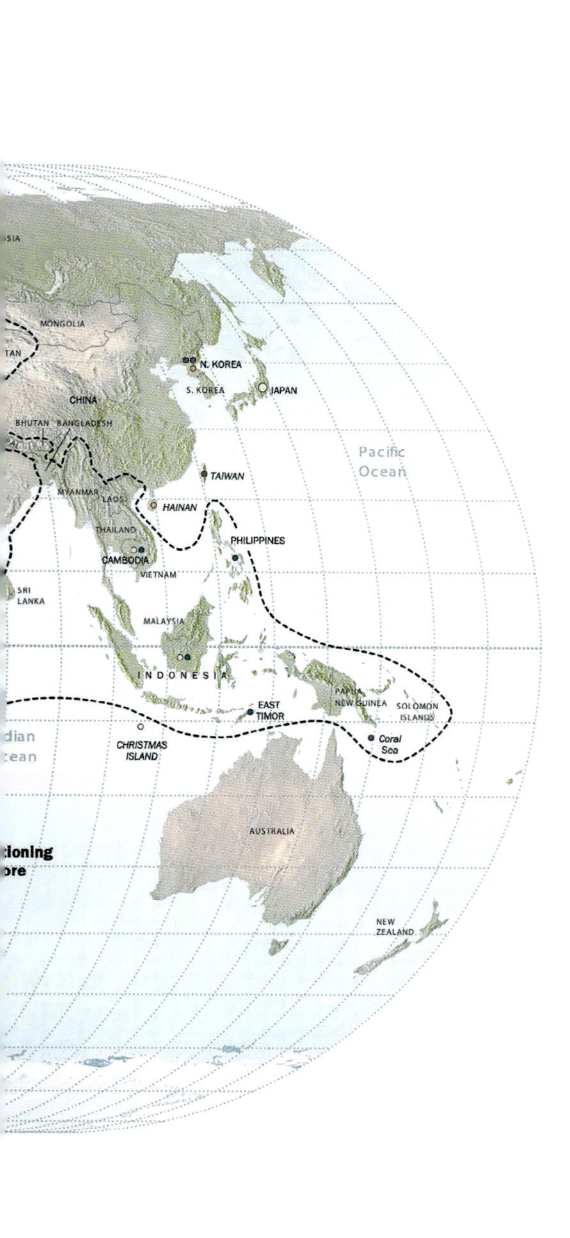

The Map of Globalization, Forestalled

In the 2020s, borders somehow mean both less and more than ever before.

The world has rarely needed new political maps as thoroughly and urgently as it did after the collapse of the Soviet Union, whose dissolution in 1991 set off changes that are still reverberating today. Fifteen new countries, from Estonia to Tajikistan, were born from the old USSR's breakup. And the entire configuration of international politics changed virtually overnight.

Throughout the twentieth century, strong states had grouped themselves into pairs of opposing lineups, and even took names like sports teams: The Allies fought the Central Powers in World War I and the Axis in World War II, and the "free world," anchored in NATO, confronted communist regimes, including members of the Warsaw Pact, during the Cold War. Once this bipolar confrontation imploded, it looked for a while like there was just one viable formula left for nations to keep themselves on the map: free elections plus free trade. Political scientist Francis Fukuyama famously wrote that "the universalization of Western liberal democracy" was "the final form of human government," and in fact "the end of history as such." In other words, game over!

Changes came fast in those heady days, and many of them seemed to show that old borders and barriers meant less and less. Western nations cut military spending, reduced tariffs, and liberalized immigration rules. East and West Germany

For *The Pentagon's New Map*, which he first produced in 2003, geostrategist Thomas P. M. Barnett drew a line around its most troubled areas of the world. He identified the zone inside as the "Non-Integrated Gap," and pinned its challenges on the fact that globalization is thinning or absent in its regions.

reunified in 1990. The European Union launched in 1993. The worldwide number of democracies passed the number of autocracies for the first time around 1995. NATO admitted Poland, the Czech Republic, and Hungary as members in 1999. Global trade grew nearly twice as fast as economic output throughout the 1990s, and China joined the World Trade Organization in 2001.

After the terrorist attacks of September 11, 2001, shocked Americans into realizing they still had enemies, many analysts, across the political spectrum, concluded that the opponents of globalization were rejecting modernity itself. Policymakers and cartographers sought frameworks to both understand and represent a new reality: Political, commercial, and technological life in the twenty-first century seemed to require democratic capitalism, but that hadn't spread everywhere just yet. Geostrategist Thomas P. M. Barnett delivered just such a template with *The Pentagon's New Map*, which grew out of briefings he gave to the US Department of Defense and intelligence agencies after 9/11.

Barnett took a world map, centered on Africa, and drew a single line around its most troubled countries, as though he were carefully stringing a set of beads. He was guided, though not exclusively, by identifying areas where the US conducted non-humanitarian military operations after 1990. (Which is to say, where American force had been required to keep some kind of order just since the end of the Cold War.) Chile, Finland, South Africa, and New Zealand were outside the boundary. Haiti, Serbia, Somalia, and East Timor were inside. Barnett called the former the "Core" and the latter the "Gap," and he described how much the places within each had in common.

"Show me where globalization is thick with network connectivity, financial transactions, liberal media flows, and collective security, and I will show you regions featuring stable governments, rising standards of living, and more deaths by suicide than murder," he wrote about the Core. "But show me where globalization is thinning or just plain absent," he continued about the Gap, "and I will show you regions plagued by politically repressive regimes, widespread poverty and disease, routine mass murder, and—most important—the chronic conflicts that incubate the next generation of global terrorists."

Barnett believed it was imperative for the US to confront and reduce the "non-integrated" parts of the map. In a March 2003 piece for *Esquire*, he wrote that he supported going to war in Iraq because "the resulting

In this 2023 infographic map of the Russia-Ukraine conflict, Russia occupies the territory shown in red and launched missile strikes at cities marked in the same color. The data was compiled from the Institute for the Study of War, a Washington, DC, think tank; Vitaliy Koval, former governor of the Ukrainian province of Rivne; and President Volodymyr Zelenskyy of Ukraine.

long-term military commitment will finally force America to deal with the entire Gap as a strategic threat environment."

About a month after that story appeared, the United States and a coalition of its allies did in fact invade Iraq, and deposed the dictator Saddam Hussein within a matter of weeks.

And ever since, it's been one downhill lurch after another for the globalists.

The US had trouble subduing opposing forces in Iraq—its combat operations lasted until 2011—much less bringing democracy there, much less shrinking the Gap elsewhere. And the rapid descent of American foreign policy from hubris into exhaustion was just one shock to the post–Cold War international system. A financial crisis in the US housing market metastasized into a severe global recession that extended from 2007 to 2009. Looser immigration and freer trade policies by Western democracies triggered political backlash, particularly in the United Kingdom, which voted in 2016 to exit the EU, and the United States, which elected Donald Trump later that year. The COVID-19 pandemic struck in 2020. And countries in the Core have proven quite capable of retreating from democracy while pursuing trade and technology, as in the case of China. Or going to war against their neighbors: In February 2022, Russia invaded Ukraine—one of its biggest trading partners—launching a brutal war that by October 2025 had killed more than 250,000 combatants and civilians and which remained deadly and inconclusive (see a map of the conflict on the previous page).

It's all made for chaotic, confusing times. But in the mid-2020s, two opposing trends have become clear: Nationalism is as politically powerful as ever. There are more borderlines on world maps today than at any point in history, and the number of physical barriers between countries—walls, fences, blockades—grew from just twelve at the end of the Cold War to seventy-four in 2023. At the same time, the world is facing increasingly grave threats—climate change, mass migration, disease, instability among governments possessing nuclear or biological weapons—that borders can't stop. Meeting these challenges will take massive, sustained international cooperation.

Barnett still sees greater commingling among nations as necessary and eventually inevitable. His 2003 map was a snapshot of globalization at what turned out to be a peak moment. But he thinks that rising temperatures, and the population shifts they trigger, will spur a new surge of "vertical integration" around the globe. "The lower latitudes are just getting fried, literally. There's your crisis," says Barnett. "We are done with East-West integration, horizontal on a world map hung on a wall. And we now are finally forced to pursue North-South integration, vertical on a wall map." Indeed, the cover of his 2023 book *America's New Map* isn't a map at all—it's an American flag with 150 stars, signaling the United States' absorption of much of the Western Hemisphere.

Divisions among societies are never quite as clean as political maps suggest. If Barnett's forecast turns out to be at all accurate, the Core and Gap themselves are on the move—toward the poles. And what then?

"As our species niche drifts rapidly across the hemispheres, what will our artificial borders do?" the writer James Crawford asked in a 2023 essay. "Flex or open? Harden? Or break apart completely under the strain?"

These are questions the political maps of tomorrow must answer.

Antarctica: Research Stations and Territorial Claims

Note: Nine of the 16 Antarctic Treaty consultative nations have made no claims to Antarctic territory (although the Soviet Union and the United States have reserved the right to do so) and do not recognize the claims of the other nations. Brazil, however, has designated a zone of interest.

The Falkland Islands, South Georgia, and the South Sandwich Islands are administered by the U.K. and claimed by Argentina.

Summer Stations peak population		Year-Round Stations average population
none	300 and above	◉
none	75–135	◉
△	30–74	●
△	15–29	●
△	7–14	•
△	1–6	•

0 500 1000 Kilometers
0 500 1000 Miles

South Atlantic Ocean
Scotia Sea
Weddell Sea
Bellingshausen Sea
Ross Sea
Indian Ocean
South Pacific Ocean

Bouvetøya (Norway)
South Sandwich Islands (Falkland Is.)
South Georgia (Falkland Is.)
Falkland Islands (Islas Malvinas)
Argentina
Chile
Îles Crozet (France)
Îles Kerguelen (France)
McDonald Islands (Australia)
Heard Island (Australia)
Peter I Island (Norway)
Scott Island
Balleny Islands
Macquarie Island (Australia)
Campbell Island (New Zealand)
Auckland Islands (New Zealand)
Antipodes Islands (New Zealand)
Bounty Islands (New Zealand)
New Zealand
Tasmania
Australia

BRITISH CLAIM
NORWEGIAN CLAIM
undefined limit
ARGENTINE CLAIM
BRAZILIAN ZONE OF INTEREST
CHILEAN CLAIM
AUSTRALIAN CLAIM
FRENCH CLAIM
NEW ZEALAND CLAIM
20°W
25°W
53°W
74°W
90°W
45°E
136°E
142°E
160°E
150°W
area of inset
Antarctic Peninsula
Ranne Ice Shelf
Ross Ice Shelf
Antarctic Circle
South Pole

South Orkney Islands
Orcadas (Argentina)
Signy (U.K.)
SANAE III (South Africa)
Georg von Neumayer (Fed. Rep. of Germany)
Grunehogna (South Africa)
Dakshin Gangotri (India)
Novolazarevskaya (Soviet Union)
Syowa (Japan)
Molodezhnaya (Soviet Union)
Mizuho (Japan)
Halley (U.K.)
New Halley (U.K.)
Druzhnaya I (Soviet Union)
General Belgrano II (Argentina)
Filchner (F.R.G.)
General Belgrano III (Argentina)
Fossil Bluff (U.K.)
Druzhnaya II (Soviet Union)
Siple (U.S.)
Amundsen-Scott (U.S.)
Mawson (Australia)
Soyuz (Soviet Union)
Davis (Australia)
Komsomol'skaya (Soviet Union)
Mirnyy (Soviet Union)
Vostok (Soviet Union)
Oazis (Soviet Union)
Casey (Australia)
Byrd (U.S.)
Russkaya (Soviet Union)
McMurdo (U.S.)
Scott (New Zealand)
Vanda (New Zealand)
Cape Bird (New Zealand)
Gondwana (Fed. Rep. of Germany)
Lillie Marleen Hütte (Fed. Rep. of Germany)
Dumont d'Urville (France)
Leningradskaya (Soviet Union)

Antarctic Peninsula

Esperanza (Argentina)
Vicecomodoro Marambio (Argentina)
General Bernardo O'Higgins (Chile)
Capitán Arturo Prat (Chile)
Primavera (Argentina)
Teniente Matienzo (Argentina)
Larsen Ice Shelf
Palmer (U.S.)
Yelcho (Chile)
Faraday (U.K.)
Pres. Videla (Chile)
South Pacific Ocean
General San Martín (Argentina)
Rothera (U.K.)
Teniente Carvajal (Chile)
Antarctic Circle

1. Comandante Ferraz (Brazil)
2. Arctowski (Poland)
3. Jubany (Argentina)
4. Bellingshausen (Soviet Union)
5. Marsh/Frei (Chile)
6. Great Wall (China)
7. Artigas (Uruguay)

800773 (543391) 8-86

AFTERWORD:
THE MAP OF THE MOST SUCCESSFUL TREATY EVER

In the late nineteenth and early twentieth centuries, explorers racing to reach the South Pole touched off the question: Who owned the lands of Antarctica?

Roald Amundsen, a Norwegian voyager, led an expedition that got to the pole first, in December 1911. And even though Norway is about as far as you can get from Antarctica on planet Earth,[1] it made a claim on the continent. Robert Falcon Scott and a crew from Great Britain arrived at the South Pole just a little more than a month after Amundsen, and England proclaimed ownership of Antarctic territory too.

These declarations weren't just about bragging rights. Norway, the United Kingdom, and France were seafaring nations vying for routes and resources (such as whale oil and fish) in southern ocean waters. So were Australia and New Zealand, two of the southernmost countries in the world. So too were Argentina and Chile, both former Spanish colonies, each of which believed rights to the Western Hemisphere passed through Spain to it because of agreements stretching all the way back to our old friend the Treaty of Tordesillas in 1494 (see page 72). Germany staked out a chunk of land it called New Swabia when the Nazis sent an expedition to Antarctica in the late 1930s.

On political maps, most of these claims were necessarily pie-shaped. After all, if you choose any two points on Antarctica and draw lines southward from each one, the tracks will meet at the South Pole, creating a triangular wedge between them. Several of the slices overlapped, with no clear way to resolve their disputed borders. The onset of the Atomic Age and the Cold War raised the possibility that countries might station submarines or test nuclear weapons in Antarctica, or even come to blows there.

In 1959, in one of the great success stories in the history of international relations, a dozen nations—including seven with territorial

Antarctica: Research Stations and Territorial Claims shows the myriad and sometimes contradictory claims to the continent that were ratified in the Antarctic Treaty of 1961 (and have remained the same ever since—this version of the map was created by the CIA in 1986).

1 It's 10,358 miles from Oslo, Norway, to the South Pole—just about equal to the distances between New York and Los Angeles, Washington, DC, and Beijing, and Berlin and Moscow combined.

claims, the United States, and the USSR—came together to negotiate and sign the Antarctic Treaty. The agreement set aside the continent as a scientific preserve, guaranteeing freedom of research and prohibiting economic exploitation and military activity there. Today, there are more than fifty research stations across Antarctica, including bases established by India, Japan, Russia, South Africa, and the US.[2]

Most ingeniously, the Antarctic Treaty didn't force any countries to renounce the positions they had already taken. It didn't recognize or validate any particular claims at all. It simply let them be, even where they contradicted one another. It's as though you and your neighbor each asserted ownership of a tree standing between your properties, and rather than trying to settle your differences, you simply agreed never to let any harm come to the tree.

As a result, the map of Antarctica has looked exactly and ambiguously the same since 1961, when the treaty was ratified. Argentina, Chile, and Great Britain are still contesting various wedges between the longitudes of 25° and 80° West. The US and Russia still technically reserve the right to make territorial claims in the future, though they haven't yet.

So while Antarctica may have great mineral resources and geopolitical value, it also has peace. Glass half full or half empty, you make the call: A political map like this can prevent war, as long as when it comes to the place it portrays, hardly anybody lives there.

---

2 The United States built Amundsen-Scott Station directly over the South Pole in 1957.

ACKNOWLEDGMENTS

Power Lines is a book, rather than a dust-gathering pile of graph-paper pads and propaganda clippings, thanks to unstinting support from many sets of navigators who helped keep my compass true.

The team at Workman Publishing, with my editor, Bridget Monroe Itkin, leading the way, believed in the concept of making political maps interesting and even fun, and stuck with me long past the point of all reasonableness to get it done. The result is a book that I hope fulfills their mission of publishing objects that are both informative and beautiful. Bridget began working with me so long ago that this project had an entirely different subject. And through stretches when I faced significant personal and professional challenges, I can't say how many times she kept it alive, because I don't even know. It's been easy to enjoy collaborating with Bridget because she has improved the substance, tone, and structure of my work with every suggestion she has made.

Lia Ronnen, publisher and editorial director of the Workman Running Press Group, took a chance on me, for which I will always be grateful. Copy editor Chalcey Wilding went far beyond the typical bounds of her assignment: She checked difficult-to-confirm facts, asked important substantive questions, and, on her own initiative, unearthed material ranging from show-tune lyrics to an old Polish-language manuscript. Designer Katie Benezra created a template for presenting maps and a style for matching them with text that unified and elevated our whole book. Assistant editor Julia Perry was always attentive to detail, friendly, and patient, and helped track down last-minute permissions to reproduce maps. Moira Kerrigan, executive director of marketing and publicity, and Allison McGeehon, senior director of marketing and publicity, have promoted this book enthusiastically and creatively.

Many thanks also to Becky Koh, publishing director of Black Dog & Leventhal; senior production editor Brenna Franzitta; photo researcher Ken Yu; managing editor Claire McKean; creative director Suet Chong; typesetter Annie O'Donnell; production director Lillian Sun; associate group publisher Zach Greenwald; and editor Shoshana Gutmajer, who worked with me on an earlier idea.

These efforts would have been for naught without the encouragement of my family, whose members have endured countless dinner conversations about subjects like the results of the Thirty Years' War and the borders of

Imperial Japan. To my wife, Karen Keating, and our daughters Ellie and Samantha: You make it all possible and all worthwhile.

Thank you to Emily Greenberg for photography; Charmaine Chan, Matthew Goodrich, and Lucy Yang for help with translations; and Sara Krolewski for early-stage research assistance.

Special thanks also to geostrategist Thomas P. M. Barnett, Hereford Cathedral librarian Jennifer Dumbelton, and researcher Jim Siebold for being so generous with their time and insightful in key interviews.

I am hugely fortunate to have family, friends, and colleagues whose ideas, thoughts, and research helped shape *Power Lines*, including Shaun Assael, Gary Belsky, Rob Donlon, Neil Fine, Sini Gandhi, Gary Hoenig, Shane Kadidal, Pat and Fred Keating, Pam Keating, John McElhone, Richard Reeves, and Leo Ross.

Finally, I am grateful to everyone whose support literally kept me going over the past couple of years, including Jordan Brenner; the Colleran, Doten, Keating, Manning, and McElhone families; Sara, Andy, and Izabella Ross; Sarah McCrory; the Montclair High School carpool; and the staffs of the Apex Heart and Vascular Center in Nutley, New Jersey (particularly Dr. Sarina Sachdev and Dr. Anuj Shah), Mountainside Hospital in Montclair, New Jersey, and Summit Health in Clifton, New Jersey.

A NOTE ON SOURCES

I first began researching political maps systematically in the autumn of 2020, after I noticed just how the emotional lives of so many Americans (myself included) were bound up in the day-to-day shifts in red-and-blue presidential election maps, even though those illustrations are widely understood to be flawed representations of public opinion. Most of the world was still locked down because of COVID restrictions, and I had to pursue my initial inquiries online. Fortunately, I quickly found an array of amazing digital resources, foremost among them the Library of Congress, especially its Geography and Map Division. The library warehouses more than six million maps—the world's largest collection—and, just as important, it's dedicated to putting images of those holdings online and making them free and easy to find. I have particularly enjoyed, and learned from, its *Worlds Revealed* blog, where individual librarians present research on a wide range of subjects, often tying together information about disparate items from the library's archives. It's a site where you can lose yourself for hours and be the better for it.

Other archives that make for great spelunking include the Harvard College Library Map Collection, the Lionel Pincus and Princess Firyal Map Division of the New York Public Library, and the Osher Map Library and Smith Center for Cartographic Education at the University of Southern Maine.

I have done in-depth reporting on baseball card collectors and JFK assassination conspiracy theorists, and I can tell you, there are few buffs like map buffs. Cartography is a field where passions for geography, history, and art not only collide but augment one another, and when it comes to political maps, you can add ideology to the mix, too. Happily, enthusiasm for maps often translates to eagerness to share information. I have mentioned PJ Mode's fantastic, extensively annotated collection of persuasive cartography (page ix), which is now at Cornell University. David Rumsey, one of the world's leading collectors for decades, has donated a far huger (though not specifically political) trove to Stanford University, which has digitized more than 140,000 of his items for online access. Jim Siebold, an independent researcher, has written a series of monographs about maps made before 1800—again, not all political, but including many fascinating works—and placed 1,700 images on his website (www.myoldmaps.com).

In the same spirit of passionate generosity, Jonathan Crowe, a Canadian writer, started blogging about maps in 2003 and has since built the internet's best resource for keeping up to date about cartography. Political controversies, scientific developments, book reviews—you'll find them all, with helpful links, at The Map Room (maproomblog.com).

Two large-sized, beautifully illustrated books, both published by the University of Chicago Press, are well worth delving into for deeper looks at their particular subjects: *Picturing America: The Golden Age of Pictorial Maps* by Stephen J. Hornsby (2017), and *A History of America in 100 Maps* by Susan Schulten (2018).

A History of the World in 12 Maps by Jerry Brotton (Penguin Books, 2012) takes maps seriously as cultural documents that reflect the beliefs and power structures of their times. And it's a terrific read.

Two of the many books written by Mark Monmonier are particularly valuable if you're interested in political subjects: *How to Lie with Maps* (University of Chicago Press, 1991), now a classic, details the various ways maps can mislead, but never succumbs to nihilism. And *Rhumb Lines and Map Wars: A Social History of the Mercator Projection* (University of Chicago Press, 2004) delivers what its subtitle promises.

Finally, in a handful of cases in this book, I have included quotes where fuller passages would be additionally instructive: Verses of the *Iliad* are from the 1715–1720 translation by Alexander Pope (who put the whole epic into iambic pentameter). Daniel Boorstin's quotes about cartography retreating from science are from *The Discoverers* (Random House, 1983), his erudite, engaging history of humankind's scientific quests. W. E. B. DuBois wrote about World War I in "The African Roots of the War," in the May 1915 issue of *The Atlantic*. W. H. Auden's full poem *Partition* was first published in *City Without Walls* (Faber & Faber, 1969) and can be found online. Francis Bicknell Carpenter's recollections are from *Six Months in the White House with Abraham Lincoln*, an 1866 book. Christopher Hitchens's comments about Leon Trotsky are from an appearance Hitchens made on the television program *Uncommon Knowledge* on August 3, 2009.

ART CREDITS

Pages ii–iii, 182: Shawshots/Alamy Stock Photo; Page viii: Courtesy of the author; artist unknown; Page x: Courtesy of Geographicus Rare Antique Maps; Page xi: Courtesy of the Hoover Institution Library & Archives; Page xiii: Chronicle/Alamy Stock Photo; Pages xvi–1, 22: Geography and Map Division of the Library of Congress, Washington, DC; Page 2: Florilegius/Alamy Stock Photo; Pages 6–7: Album/Alamy Stock Photo; Page 10: Geography and Map Division of the Library of Congress, Washington, DC; Pages 14, 21: Courtesy of the Hereford Cathedral; Page 17: British Library/Alamy Stock Photo; Page 19: NPL/DeA Picture Library/Bridgeman Images; Pages 26–27: Gibson Green/Alamy Stock Photo; Pages 30–31, 46–47: Geography and Map Division of the Library of Congress, Washington, DC; Pages 32–33: Art Collection 3/Alamy Stock Photo; Pages 36–37: Courtesy of the Office of the US Department of State; Pages 38–39: David Rumsey Map Collection, David Rumsey Map Center, Stanford Libraries; Pages 42, 44–45: Heritage Images/Getty Images; Page 49: Geography and Map Division of the Library of Congress, Washington, DC; Page 51: Courtesy of Barry Lawrence Ruderman Antique Maps (raremaps.com); Pages 52–53, 55: Geography and Map Division of the Library of Congress, Washington, DC; Page 56: Science History Images/Alamy Stock Photo; Page 58: Created by the US Census Bureau; Pages 60–61: Geography and Map Division of the Library of Congress, Washington, DC; Page 64: Correo Oficial de la República Argentina; Pages 66–67, 96–97, 98: Geography and Map Division of the Library of Congress, Washington, DC; Pages 68–71: Heritage Image Partnership Ltd./Alamy Stock Photo; Pages 74–75: World History Archive/Alamy Stock Photo; Page 77: Geography and Map Division of the Library of Congress, Washington, DC; Pages 80, 83: Geography and Map Division of the Library of Congress, Washington, DC; Page 84: National Archives, Reference Number MPK 1/426; Page 88: Courtesy of the American Geographical Society Library, University of Wisconsin-Milwaukee Libraries; Pages 92–93: Courtesy of the Digital South Asia Library, University of Chicago; Page 97 (top): Courtesy of the US Department of State and Florida State University; Page 100: David Rumsey Map Collection, David Rumsey Map Center, Stanford Libraries; Page 103: Chronicle/Alamy Stock Photo; Page 104: Geography and Map Division of the Library of Congress, Washington, DC; Page 106: Courtesy of Wikimedia Commons; Page 108: Geography and Map Division of the Library of Congress, Washington, DC; Pages 112–113, 136–137: Courtesy of Mapping Inequality; Pages 114–115: Courtesy of Cornell University, PJ Mode Collection of Persuasive Cartography; Page 116: David Rumsey Map Collection, David Rumsey Map Center, Stanford Libraries; Pages 122–123: Geography and Map Division of the Library of Congress, Washington, DC; Page 125: MPI/Getty Images; Pages 126–127: Geography and Map Division of the Library of Congress, Washington, DC; Pages 128–129: Prints and Photographs Division of the Library of Congress, Washington, DC; Page 131: Courtesy of the Smithsonian; Pages 132–133, 135: Geography and Map Division of the Library of Congress, Washington, DC; Pages 140–141: Courtesy of Cameron Booth (transitmap.net); Page 144: Courtesy of the Special Collections

Research Center, Syracuse University Libraries; Page 147: Central Intelligence Agency and the United Nations; Page 148: Fotoarena/Alamy Stock Photo; Page 150: Ana Vizcarra Rankin, Global Optimization Diagram, 2012. Courtesy of the Pennsylvania Academy of the Fine Arts, Philadelphia; Pages 152–153: Nasa Image Collection/Alamy Stock Photo; Page 155: The Independent Commission on International Development Issues and Willy Brandt, North-South: A Program for Survival, © 1980 The Independent Commission on International Development Issues, by permission of The MIT Press; Pages 162–163, 194–195: From *Fortune* © 1941 Fortune Media IP Limited. All rights reserved. Used under license; Pages 164–165: Courtesy of Cornell University, PJ Mode Collection of Persuasive Cartography; Page 168: Prismatic Pictures/Bridgeman Images; Page 169: Courtesy of Cornell University, PJ Mode Collection of Persuasive Cartography; Page 171: Album/Alamy Stock Photo; Pages 172–173: Courtesy of Boston Public Library Norman B. Leventhal Map & Education Center; Pages 176–177: Courtesy of Cornell University, PJ Mode Collection of Persuasive Cartography; Page 179: *LIFE* magazine; Page 180: Courtesy of Cornell University, PJ Mode Collection of Persuasive Cartography; Page 185: Shawshots/Alamy Stock Photo; Page 186: Pictorial Press Ltd./Alamy Stock Photo; Pages 190–191: Courtesy of Cornell University, PJ Mode Collection of Persuasive Cartography; Page 193: The History Collection/Alamy Stock Photo; Page 198: From *Fortune* © 1940 Fortune Media IP Limited. All rights reserved. Used under license; Page 201: Hum Images/Alamy Stock Photo; Page 202: American Stock/Camerique/Superstock; Pages 204–205, 209: CPA Media Pte/Ltd/Alamy Stock Photo; Page 206: Japan-Manchoukuo Year Book Company; Page 207: From *Fortune* © 1935 Fortune Media IP Limited. All rights reserved. Used under license; Pages 210–211, 213: Bill Waterson/Alamy Stock Photo; Page 214: Shawshots/Alamy Stock Photo; Page 217: Prints and Photographs Division of the Library of Congress, Washington, DC; Pages 218–219: Courtesy of Cornell University, PJ Mode Collection of Persuasive Cartography; Pages 222–223: Courtesy of Cornell University, PJ Mode Collection of Persuasive Cartography; Page 226: From TIME. © 1952 TIME USA LLC. All rights reserved. Under use license; Page 228: From TIME. © 1944 TIME USA LLC. All rights reserved. Under use license; Pages 230–231: From TIME. © 1959 TIME USA LLC. All rights reserved. Under use license; Pages 232–233: Shawshots/Alamy Stock Photo; Pages 238–239: Geography and Map Division of the Library of Congress, Washington, DC; Page 242: Created by the Central Intelligence Agency and the National Security Archive; Pages 246–247, 248: Imaginechina Limited/Alamy Stock Photo; Page 250: Courtesy of the United Nations, Division of Ocean Affairs and the Law of the Sea; Page 254: Dimitrios Karamitros/Getty Images; Page 255: Australia Broadcast Company; Page 257: Map data © Google, INEGI; Page 258: Posted by J. D. Vance; Pages 260–261: Courtesy of Thomas Barnett; Page 263: Anadolu/Getty Images; Page 266: Geography and Map Division of the Library of Congress, Washington, DC.

INDEX

Page numbers followed by "n" refer to notes.